ST. JAMES'S PLACE

TAX GUIDE

2005–2006

ST. JAMES'S PLACE

TAX GUIDE

2005–2006

WALTER SINCLAIR, FCA

palgrave
macmillan

First published 2005 by
PALGRAVE MACMILLAN
Houndmills, Basingstoke, Hampshire RG21 6XS and
175 Fifth Avenue, New York, N.Y. 10010
Companies and representatives throughout the world

PALGRAVE MACMILLAN is the global academic imprint of the Palgrave Macmillan division of St. Martin's Press, LLC and of Palgrave Macmillan Ltd. Macmillan® is a registered trademark in the United States, United Kingdom and other countries. Palgrave is a registered trademark in the European Union and other countries.

ISBN 13: 978–1–4039–1340–1
ISBN 10: 1–4039–1340–4

This book is printed on paper suitable for recycling and made from fully managed and sustained forest sources.

A catalogue record for this book is available from the British Library.

10 9 8 7 6 5 4 3 2 1
14 13 12 11 10 09 08 07 06 05

Printed and bound in Great Britain by
Antony Rowe Ltd, Chippenham and Eastbourne

CONTENTS

PREFACE

Sir Mark Weinberg *President, St. James's Place Capital*

Thirty-four years ago, when Ted Heath was Prime Minister, Bobby Moore was captain of England's football team and people were still struggling to deal with the strange new decimal currency they found in their pockets, a young taxation expert by the name of Walter Sinclair believed that there was a gap in the market for an authoritative guide to the UK's labyrinthine tax system.

The world today is a very different place indeed. But the UK's tax system is still labyrinthine, and Walter Sinclair's book is still by far your most useful, accessible and comprehensive guide to it.

I am very pleased to continue the long association between this book and St. James's Place, and to commend this new edition to you with undiminished enthusiasm.

Indeed, many more people would benefit from reading it as I am quite sure that it could help millions throughout the country to identify new opportunities for more effective tax planning.

No matter how much money you have, and no matter how complicated your financial affairs, I could never claim that a source of expert financial advice is essential to you. You have an obvious alternative: you could do it yourself. But a quick flick through the pages of this *Guide* is enough to bring home the sheer scale of the task. Even benefiting from the technical knowledge and communication skills of a Walter Sinclair, you will recognise that getting to grips with the implications of taxation on your personal circumstances is a mighty challenge. And, important though it is, taxation is of course only one aspect of financial planning: it represents, in a sense, the visible tip of a much larger iceberg.

Dealing with that iceberg as a whole, so to speak, is the job of the members of the St. James's Place Partnership. They are very good indeed at what they do – as expert in their fields as Walter Sinclair is in his. Whatever your financial goals, however complex your financial affairs, you can expect from us the expert and personal advice you need to build and implement the right plan for your future.

With this in mind, I hope you find this new edition of Walter Sinclair's *Tax Guide* useful and interesting. I am sure that the more closely you look at it, the more you will appreciate the need for advice of the quality that St. James's Place provides.

ABBREVIATIONS USED IN THE *GUIDE*

ACT	advance corporation tax
AEI	average earnings index
AVC	additional voluntary contribution
BES	business expansion scheme
CAA	Capital Allowances Act 2001
CGT	capital gains tax
CGTA	Capital Gains Tax Act 1979
CIC	close investment holding company
COMP	contracted out money purchase
CPA	Civil Partnership Act 2004
CRCA	Commissioners for Revenue and Customs Act 2005
CTC	child tax credit
DLTA	Development Land Tax Act 1976
DPTC	disabled person's tax credit
EEIG	European economic interest grouping
EIS	enterprise investment scheme
ESOP	employee share option plan
FA	Finance Act
F2A	Finance (No 2) Act
FIFO	first in, first out
FPCS	fixed profit car scheme
FSAVC	free standing additional voluntary contribution
HMSO	Her Majesty's Stationery Office
ISA	Individual Savings Account
ITA	Inheritance Tax Act 1984
ITEPA	Income Tax (Earnings and Pensions) Act 2003
ITTOIA	Income Tax (Trading and other Income) Act 2005
LAPR	life assurance premium relief
LEL	lower earnings limit
MIRAS	mortgage interest relief at source
NRE	net relevant earnings
PAYE	pay as you earn
PEP	personal equity plan
PET	potentially exempt transfer
PHI	permanent health insurance
PIBS	permanent interest bearing share
PPP (PRO)	personal pension plan (protected rights only)
PRAS	pension relief at source
PRP	profit related pay
PSO	Pension Schemes Office
QCB	Qualifying corporate bond
RPI	retail prices index
S (Ss)	section (sections) of an Act
SAYE	save as you earn
Sch (Schs)	schedule (schedules) of an Act
SDLT	stamp duty land tax
SERPS	state earnings related pension scheme
SFO	Superannuation Funds Office
TA	Income and Corporation Taxes Act
TCGA	Taxation of Chargeable Gains Act 1992
TESSA	tax exempt special savings account
TMA	Taxes Management Act 1970
UEL	upper earnings limit
USM	Unlisted Securities Market
VAT	value added tax
VATA	Value Added Tax Act 1994
WFTC	working families tax credit
WTC	working tax credit

INTRODUCTION

Originally establishing itself as the *Hambro Tax Guide* 33 years ago, this book has appeared annually ever since, more recently being called the *J. Rothschild Assurance Tax Guide*. The book has been designed to be used both by the professional and non-professional. Solicitors, accountants and company secretaries will find it especially useful as a concise ready reference. Many others, company directors and executives, partners and sole-traders, employers and employees, will find in it much helpful information and advice when dealing with problems of personal and company taxation.

It illustrates the working of income tax, capital gains tax, corporation tax, inheritance tax and VAT in the UK. It is intended to continue revising the book annually in order to keep it up to date in accordance with the annual changes to the law.

This, the 34th edition, deals with the tax system at the time of writing for the 2005–06 fiscal year, including Finance Act 2005. Every chapter has been amended to reflect the many tax changes which have been made since the previous edition, including those relating to income tax and personal reliefs, investments, pensions, National Insurance, capital gains tax, corporation tax, inheritance tax, VAT, stamp duty and many, many others. To help keep track of the changes, this edition includes a recently introduced Chapter 1 which summarises this year's tax changes and is referenced to the relevant paragraphs in the *Guide*. As a new feature this year, tax planning pointers relative to this year's tax changes are included in this chapter.

This book has been appearing since 1972–73 and it is very interesting to consider some of the tax changes over its life, comparing that year with 2005–06.

		1972–73	2005–06
Income tax	Starting rate	–	10%
	Standard/Basic rate	38.75%	22%
	Top rate – at taxable income		
	£15,000 including surtax	88.75%	
	£32,400		40%
	Single personal relief	£460	£4,895
Capital gains tax rates (individuals)		30%	10/20/40%
Estate duty/inheritance tax threshold		£15,000	£275,000
	Top rate at £500,001	75%	
	Only rate in most cases		40%
VAT from 1 April 1973		10%	17.5%

Thus successive editions of the book have recorded falling rates for most taxes, apart from VAT and National Insurance contributions. What is more, many reliefs and taxes, have come and/or gone, such as:

- Capital transfer tax
- Development gains tax and development land tax
- Surtax
- Earned income relief
- Investment income surcharge
- Stock relief
- Life assurance relief on new policies
- Mortgage interest relief
- Married couples allowance (unless born before 6 April 1935)
- Stakeholder pensions
- Advance corporation tax and the imputation system
- Working tax credits and child tax credits

But what of the future? Of one thing we can be sure, there will be very many tax changes to include in the pages of subsequent editions.

Due to the volume of changes, it is not possible to retain in each new edition full information for previous years. Thus for the tax rules for previous years, reference to past editions is occasionally necessary.

Because the book concisely covers a very wide field, it has been necessary to omit some of the exemptions and qualifications with which tax law abounds: to adopt a familiar saying, 'When I say never, I mean hardly ever and when I say always, I mean almost always'. The book is intended to be only a general tax guide. If it cannot solve a problem, the time has come to look at one of the multi-volume tax textbooks or to consult a tax specialist.

Ideas on tax saving appear throughout the book. However, Chapter 26 deals with *tax-saving hints* and has many references to the other chapters for easy location of topics. Furthermore, this chapter contains particular reference to future tax planning in a section entitled 'Tax planning after the General Election' (26.8).

A particular feature to note is that all indexing and cross-referencing uses chapter and topic numbers. Thus 7.6 means the sixth-numbered topic in Chapter 7. Similarly 7.6.3 would mean the third subsidiary topic within that main heading. Cross-references to related chapter and topic numbers appear throughout the *Guide* in brackets and you will also find references to tax legislation where relevant under the appropriate topic title. Also, a glossary to help with the meanings of certain terms appears at the end of this book.

Since its inception, the *Guide* has included references to the tax legislation. Over the years, this has been consolidated into a number of Acts such as the Inheritance Tax Act 1984 (ITA), Value Added Tax Act 1994 (VATA), Capital

Allowances Act 2001 (CAA), Income and Corporation Taxes Act 1988 (TA) and Income Tax (Trading and other Income) Act 2005 (ITTOIA). The book is now referenced mainly to the consolidating Acts, using the abbreviations shown above and following the Preface.

The 2005–2006 *St. James's Place Tax Guide* brings together in a single volume all of the main taxes which are operating at present, enabling their total effect to be borne in mind. In planning for the future, however, account should be taken of the various avenues for short-term reform, as well as the longer term possibilities for capital gains tax, inheritance tax, income tax, etc. As new developments are crystallised, they will be covered in the future annual editions of this book.

I am most grateful to all those who have written to me with kind and helpful comments concerning the previous editions, some of which have been taken into account in the preparation of this volume.

I gratefully acknowledge the help given to me on this edition by E Barry Lipkin, LLB, FCA, ATII, TEP, Malcolm Cooper-Smith of St. James's Place, Rob Gaines LLB and P D Silke, BPhil, MSocSc, Solicitor.

WALTER SINCLAIR

Chapter 1

THIS YEAR'S TAX CHANGES

1.1 Introduction

This chapter summarises many of the changes to the tax rules and rates which take effect for 2005–06. Some were introduced by this year's Budget and Finance Bill, whilst others were announced and enacted previously. Tax planning pointers have been included in italics and these are amplified in Chapter 26. At the end of this chapter you will find a table of key rates and allowances for 2005–06.

You should note that not all of the changes included in the 2005 Budget have been enacted yet. Apart from changes announced for future years, the dissolution of Parliament in preparation for the General Election on 5 May, resulted in many Budget measures being omitted from the original Finance Bill 2005, when it was replaced by Finance (no. 2) Bill 2005.

1.2 Income tax

The rate bands have been widened and some of the personal allowances have increased.

1.2.1 Income tax rates (5.0.1)

- The basic rate remains at 22 per cent.
- The 10 per cent starting rate band has broadened by £70 to £2,090.
- The basic rate band has increased with inflation (5.1).

1.2.2 Allowances and reliefs

- Allowances such as personal allowance and age allowance have been indexed upwards (3.3).
- The pensions relief earnings cap goes up to £105,600 (14.3.1 & 14.6.2).
- Children's tax credit (3.4.3) increases for 2005–06.
- Working Tax Credit (WTC) increases for 2005–06 (3.4.4).

1.2.3 Income Tax (Trading and Other Income) Act 2005

This Act received Royal Assent on 24 March 2005 and operates from 6 April 2005. It restates with certain minor amendments, enactments regarding business, property, investment and miscellaneous income. One effect is that the 'Schedules' system (2.3) no longer applies to the relevant areas in the future.

1.3 Tax on employments

There are a number of minor changes relating to employments. Benefits in kind, regarding cars, are hit harder but there are relaxations regarding computers and cycles etc.

- Improved exemptions regarding employer-provided childcare benefits apply from 6 April 2005 (10.6.15).
- The emissions thresholds for company car tax reductions are lower (10.6.5).
- The legislation has been changed regarding profit-related securities such as shares in spin-out companies exploiting intellectual property.

1.4 Business taxation

Included in the provisions relating to businesses are capital allowances, film relief, alternative finance taxation and legislation consolidation.

- 100 per cent capital allowances is introduced on renovating or converting business property unused for at least a year in designated disadvantaged areas of the UK.
- Provisions are introduced to ensure that the taxation of finance arrangements with no interest is no more or less favourable than where interest is involved.
- The tax relief for limited budget films is extended to completions before 1 January 2007. At the same time, certain anti-avoidance measures are introduced.
- A consolidating Act, ITTOIA is introduced with effect from 2005–06, covering income from trades and other sources.

1.4.1 Corporation tax rates (13.2 & 13.7)

The main and small companies rates remain as before at 30 per cent and 19 per cent. For companies with low profits, a nil rate applies (13.2).

1.5 Capital gains tax

1.5.1 Rates and exemptions

- The capital gains tax rates for individuals remain in line with the income tax rates on savings income, being 10, 20 and 40 per cent (20.1).
- Annual exemption increases to £8,500 for individuals and £4,250 for certain trusts.

1.5.2 Civil partners

From 5 December 2005, single-sex partners registered under the CPA will broadly enjoy the same tax advantages as married couples. These include many relating to capital gains tax, such as being able to transfer assets from one partner to another free of that tax.

Partners within the CPA should consider tax saving opportunities which have been opened. For example, assets can be transferred from a wealthier partner to a less wealthy one, in order to make full use of available exemptions and lower rate bands.

1.6 Tax-efficient investments

The current ISA limits are being extended until 5 April 2010.

ISAs remain of interest, particularly if you are a higher rate taxpayer. However, you must pay particular attention to sound investment factors.

1.7 Trusts

1.7.1 Lower rate

From 2005–06, the first £500 of trust income is chargeable at the appropriate lower rate instead of the special trust tax rate.

1.7.2 Trusts with vulnerable beneficiaries

From 2004–05, certain trusts and beneficiaries can elect into a new scheme under which the tax is limited to that payable had income and gains gone direct to 'vulnerable beneficiaries'. Vulnerable beneficiaries include certain disabled persons and orphaned minors.

1.8 Pensions taxation

- The earnings cap for 2005–06 is £105,000 (14.3.4).
- The planned radical reforms will now take effect from 6 April 2006. There will be a single lifetime allowance and an annual allowance, initially set at £1.5m and £215,000 respectively (14.8).

Although the new pension rules will not take effect until 6 April 2006, it is wise to plan now. As a general rule, it will be safe to maximise your contributions prior to that date, within the revised cap of £105,600. Even if this brings you above the new £1.5m lifetime cap, transitional protection is likely to apply to prevent any charge on you. At all events, the new scheme encourages one to take a long-term view of pensions.

1.9 Inheritance tax

1.9.1 Rates

The nil rate band has increased to £275,000 for 2005–06 (22.5), £285,000 for 2006–07 and £300,000 for 2007–08.

The extra amounts of nil rate band provide scope for additional tax free gifts by will and during your lifetime.

1.9.2 Civil partners

The tax exemptions covering civil partners in accordance with the CPA (from 5 December 2005) are particularly valuable in the field of inheritance tax. In the same way that married couples normally are free from inheritance tax on assets passing between them, so are single-sex partners under the new rules.

Partners within the CPA should take full advantage of the scope for passing on assets free of inheritance tax to the surviving partner. However, as with married couples, the nil rate band should not be wasted.

1.10 Anti-avoidance etc.

Calling the General Election soon after the Budget resulted in certain of the original anti-avoidance measures being omitted from FA 2005. Those remaining include avoidance related to partnerships, films, double tax relief and employment-related securities.

Artificial tax avoidance schemes should always be approached with the utmost caution, but if you effect one, remember your responsibility to report it to the Revenue. If you are considering such a scheme, require the promoters to provide you with full information about the results of previous reports by them to the Revenue relevant to that scheme.

1.11 International matters

- Double tax relief is modified to ensure that foreign tax credit is limited to the UK tax on the trading profits that suffered foreign tax.
- New rules are aimed at companies distorting the controlled foreign companies provisions by using certain subsidiaries.
- Further provisions are introduced regarding international accounting standards.

1.12 Landfill tax (7.14)

The standard rate of landfill tax has gone up to £18 per tonne.

1.13 Value added tax

Changes include the following:

- The registration threshold increases to £60,000 (23.5).
- From 7 April 2005, air source heat pumps and micro combined heat and power units are added to the items subject to VAT at only 5 per cent.

1.14 Stamp duty

There are various new provisions including:

- The threshold for stamp duty land tax on residential property has been raised from £60,000 to £120,000.
- Relief regarding non-residential property in disadvantaged areas is removed.

1.15 National Insurance contributions

The burden is higher and details include the following:

- Class 1 – the weekly earnings level below which you pay no contributions as an employee becomes £94.
- Class 2 (self-employed flat rate) – the weekly rate increases to £2.10.
- Class 3 (voluntary) – the weekly rate becomes £7.35.
- Class 4 contributions start at an annual earnings level of £4,895 and the charge at 8% applies up to £32,760.
- From 2003–04 Class 1 employee and employer and Class 4 contributions each increased by 1 per cent. The 1 per cent charge extends above the respective main rate limits.

1.16 Key rates and allowances 2005–06

See table below.

Reference

INCOME TAX 5.0

Taxable income £	Slice £	Rate %	Total tax £
2,090	0–2,090	10	209.00
30,310	2,090–32,400	22	6,877.20
Remainder		40	

Note: Savings income in your £2,090–32,400 band is taxed at 20 per cent. Dividends within that band carry a 10 per cent tax credit (non-refundable) and attract no further tax.

Income tax allowances	£	3.0.1
Personal allowance	4,895	
Age allowance	7,090	
Age 75 or over	7,220	
income limit	19,500	
Married couple's allowance*		
Age 66–74	5,905	
75 and over	5,975	
Minimum amount	2,280	
Life assurance premium relief – only on pre-14 March 1984 policies	12.5%	

* relief restricted to 10 per cent.

COMPANIES (Year to 31 March 2006)	%	
Corporation tax – starting rate	Nil	13.2
small companies rate	19	13.7
full rate	30	13.7.1

CAPITAL GAINS TAX

Rate (individuals)	10%/20%/40%	20.1
Annual exemption (individuals etc.)	8,500	20.6

INHERITANCE TAX

Band £	Death rate %		22.5
0–275,000	Nil		
275,000 upwards	40		
Annual exemption		3,000	22.17

VAT

Main rate	17.5%	23.1
Registration threshold from 1 April 2005	60,000	23.5

Chapter 2

THE BASIS OF YOUR TAX LIABILITY

2.1 Who is taxable?

Individuals, partnerships, estates, trusts, companies, and certain other organisations that are resident in the UK are taxable on their income arising here. They are also liable on income arising abroad subject to the rules outlined later in this book. The taxation of the income of individuals is covered first; partnerships, estates, trusts and companies being dealt with in later chapters.

The UK income of non-resident individuals, companies and other entities may also be subject to tax here (19.1).

Similarly capital gains tax is payable on certain capital profits made by UK residents anywhere in the world (20.3). Non-residents, however, are not always liable to UK capital gains tax.

2.2 The taxes payable (TA 1988 Ss1, 1A & 1B)

A unified system of personal taxation operates under which there is, for 2005–06, a starting rate of 10 per cent, a basic rate of 22 per cent and a higher rate of 40 per cent (5.0.1). Your savings income falling within your basic rate band generally attracts 20 per cent (8.1–7). Certain different rates apply for previous years (26.2).

The capital gains tax rates for individuals are 10, 20 and 40 per cent. However, the first £8,500 of your net capital gains is not taxed (20.1).

Special rules apply to companies which are taxed on both income and capital gains at corporation tax rates (13.2).

Inheritance tax applies to wealth passing on death and in some other circumstances (Chapter 22).

2.3 What income is taxable? (TA 1988 Ss1 & 15–20)

The table below summarises the classes of income that are subject to income tax, or corporation tax for companies. The table also shows the 'Schedules' and 'Cases' under which the income was classified and taxed under the law. From 6 April 2005, with the introduction of ITTOIA (2.10), this classification no longer applies although the basic tax rules remain.

2.3.1 Classes of income (pre-6 April 2005)

Schedule A Income from land and buildings including rents and certain premiums from leases (7.1).

Schedule D This is divided into the following separate 'Cases':

Case I	Trades (11.1).
Case II	Professions or vocations (11.1).
Case III	Interest received, annuities and other annual payments (8.4).
Cases IV and V	Overseas income from certain investments, possessions and businesses (18.1).
Case VI	Miscellaneous profits not falling within any of the other Cases of Schedule D (15.1).

Schedule E Wages and salaries from employments (including directorships).

There are the following 'Cases':

Case I	This normally applies where the employee is resident in the UK and the work is done here (10.1).
Case II	Work done here by a non-resident, etc (10.2).
Case III	Work done wholly abroad by a UK resident whose salary is sent here during the course of the overseas employment excluding, however, income taxed under Case I or Case II (10.3).

Schedule F Dividends paid by companies and certain other distributions that they make (8.1).

2.4 Deduction of tax at source and tax credits

Under Schedule D Case III (and previously Schedule C) tax at now 20 per cent is frequently deducted at source by the payers and the recipients get the net amount. The former pay the tax over to the Revenue. Company dividend payments, however, are made without any tax deductions although the recipients are 'imputed' with a credit of ⅑ of the dividend.

Thus suppose that for 2005–06 you receive a dividend of £90: you will get a tax credit of £10 (£90 × ⅑) which is not reclaimable even if your income is low (16.7). If your income is high enough, however, you may be taxed at higher rates (5.0.1 + 5.6.1) on £100 (90 + 10).

Tax is also deducted at source in the case of certain annual payments (4.1) and income from wages and salaries under Schedule E (see 2.3.1). In the former case the payer of the income is entitled in certain circumstances to retain the tax deducted and need not pay it over to the Revenue.

2.5 The distinction between capital and revenue profits

Most of your income is subjected to income tax at the basic and perhaps higher rate, whereas, normally, capital profits are liable to capital gains tax or are tax free. The tax rates borne by income and capital gains are now broadly similar. However, the rules and reliefs are very different. The question is then: What is a capital profit?

Generally speaking, a capital profit is a profit which you realise on the sale of an asset where it is clear that you are not making it your business to buy and sell assets of that type. On the other hand, if you conduct a business in such assets your profits will be income.

2.5.1 Examples of capital transactions

- The sale of the house in which you live (also normally free of capital gains tax unless used for business) (20.23).
- The sale of your private motor car (also free of capital gains tax).
- The sale of shares you held as investments.
- The sale of a plot of land you inherited.
- The sale of the goodwill of your business.
- The receipt of an inheritance (also free of capital gains tax).
- The sale of a property which you had bought for investment purposes.
- The sale of a picture unless you are the artist or a picture dealer.
- The receipt of the proceeds of a 'qualifying' life assurance policy (9.3). (This is also normally free of capital gains tax.)

2.5.2 Examples of revenue transactions

- The sale of houses and land if you are a property dealer.
- The sale of motor cars if you are a car dealer.
- The sale of shares if you are a share dealer.
- The sale of pictures if you created them or are a picture dealer.
- The receipt of salaries, commissions, interest, dividends, rent, royalties, etc.

2.6 Revenue and capital expenses

In the same way that income and capital profits must be distinguished, you must separate revenue and capital expenses for tax purposes. The latter can only be charged against capital profits and the former against income. For example, the commission on the sale of shares acquired for investment is deducted in calculating your capital gains but if you are a share dealer then it is a revenue expense.

Also, in determining the assessable profits of a business, only revenue expenses may be deducted and capital expenses are prohibited as a deduction (11.3.2).

2.6.1 Tax-free income

Certain items in your income may be entirely free of tax. These are listed below.

(1) Casual gambling profits (for example pools, horse racing, etc.).
(2) Premium Bond winnings.
(3) Lottery prizes.
(4) Interest on authorised holdings of National Savings Certificates (TA 1988 S46).
(5) Bonuses paid at the end of 'save as you earn' contracts.

(6) Maturity bonuses payable on Defence Bonds, British Savings Bonds and National Development Bonds.
(7) Interest on Post-war Credits.
(8) Wedding and certain other presents from your employer that are in truth not given in return for your services as an employee.
(9) Certain retirement gratuities and redundancy monies paid by your employer (10.12).
(10) Any scholarship or other educational grant that you receive if you are a full-time student at school, college, etc.
(11) War widows' pensions; also comparable payments overseas (TA 1988 S318).
(12) Certain social security benefits (25.3.1) including:
  (a) earnings-related supplement of unemployment benefit (but not unemployment benefit itself)
  (b) sickness benefit (but not statutory sick pay)
  (c) maternity allowance and grant (but not maternity pay)
  (d) attendance allowance
  (e) child benefit
  (f) family income supplement (but retirement pensions under the National Insurance Scheme and family allowances are assessable)
  (g) mobility allowance
  (h) certain payments of income support, family credit or housing benefit; but taxable up to given limits if related to trade disputes or conditional upon availability for employment (TA 1988 S617)
  (i) short-term incapacity benefit paid during the first 28 weeks of incapacity (FA 1995 S141).
(13) Housing grants paid by local authorities, etc.
(14) German compensation payments to victims of National-Socialist persecution. Also Austrian and German state pensions paid to such victims from 6 April 1986.
(15) Wound and disability pensions.
(16) Allowances, bounties and gratuities paid for additional service in the armed forces.
(17) The capital part of a purchased life annuity (but not the interest portion).
(18) Your first £70 of interest each year from National Savings Bank Ordinary Deposits. This exemption from tax applies separately to husband and wife (TA 1988 S325).
(19) Certain allowances paid under job release schemes, as described in the Job Release Act 1977, within a year of pensionable age.
(20) Additional pensions and annuities paid to the holders of certain gallantry awards by virtue of those awards (TA 1988 S317).
(21) Part of your Profit Related Pay under an approved scheme (10.15).
(22) Income from 1 January 1991 on a TESSA (8.11).
(23) Compensation for mis-sold personal pensions (FA 1996 s.148).
(24) Jobfinder's grant, generally before 2003–04 (FA 1996 S152).
(25) Income from PEPs (8–10) and ISAs (8–12).
(26) Financial support to adopters by local authorities and adoption agencies (TA S327A).

2.7 Bank and building society interest

Any bank or building society interest which you receive normally has 20 per cent income tax deducted from it at source (8.6). If your income is sufficiently high, however, you will be charged an additional tax on the grossed up equivalent of the interest as if you had suffered tax on it at 20 per cent. The additional tax payable consists of higher rate income tax on the grossed up equivalent of the income, less tax on it at 20 per cent. Thus if you receive building society interest of £80 in the year then £100 (the grossed up equivalent) will be included in your total taxable income. The grossed up equivalent is determined by the formula:

$$\text{Interest received} \times \frac{100}{80} \text{ (that is, 100 less 20 per cent).}$$

2.8 Year of assessment

Income tax is an annual tax; thus it is your total income over each 12-month period that is assessed to tax. The year of assessment runs from 6 April to the following 5 April and so the tax year 2005–06 means the year ending 5 April 2006.

The income chargeable to tax for each year of assessment is computed according to the rules relevant to the various Schedules (see 2.3.1) as described later in this book. In general, an 'actual' basis is now required in which the income received during a particular year is assessable for that year.

For tax years prior to 1997–98, it was sometimes the income of the preceding year of assessment or of the accounting year ending in the preceding year of assessment, that was assessed. This 'preceding year basis' was normally used for the profits from trades and vocations, as well as interest assessed under Schedule D. For details please see later chapters (11.7 etc.).

The year to 5 April also forms the year of assessment for capital gains tax.

2.9 Period of assessment less than full year

It is possible for a taxpayer to have a period of assessment of less than 12 months. For example, a baby born during any year has a period of assessment running from the date of its birth until the next 5 April. If a taxpayer dies, his period of assessment runs from 6 April to the date of his death.

Notwithstanding that the period of assessment may be less than a year, the taxpayer receives the personal reliefs applicable to a whole year of assessment.

2.10 Where to find the law

Tax law is to be found in certain Acts of Parliament, case decisions, regulations and statutory instruments. The former are the normally annual Finance Acts and so called Taxes Acts, such as the Inheritance Tax Act 1984, the Taxation of Chargeable Gains Act 1982 and the Income and Corporation Taxes Act 1988 (ICTA).

Originally, ICTA consolidated the existing legislation regarding income tax and tax on companies, including that from trading, investment, land and employments. However, starting with the Capital Allowances Act 2001, areas of the legislation have been removed from ICTA and transferred to new legislation, where it is rewritten in a clearer style, generally without changing the meaning.

A major step in this process took place wth the Income Tax (Earnings and Pensions) Act 2003 (10.0) which is described in Chapter 10. An even more sweeping consolidation and rewriting of ICTA takes place from 6 April 2005. Its scope includes trading, property, savings and miscellaneous income, hence its lengthy title – the Income Tax (Trading and Other Income) Act 2005 (ITTOIA).

A summary of ITTOIA follows, so as to provide a broad outline of its contents. Since the old references are likely to prove helpful for the present, they are retained in this edition, together with some references to ITTOIA. Note that the classification of income into Schedules no longer applies.

2.10.1 Income Tax (Trading and Other Income) Act 2005 (ITTOIA)

Part		Sections	Schedules
1	Overview	1–2	1
2	Trading overview	3–4	2 (Parts 1–2)
	Income taxed as trading profits	5–23	2 (Part 3)
	Trading profits – basic rules	24–31	
	rules restricting deductions	32–55	
	rules allowing deductions	56–94	
	receipts	95–106	
	gifts to charities	107–110	
	herd basis	111–129	
	films and recordings etc.	130–148	
	other specific trades	149–172	
	Valuation of stock and work in progress	173–186	
	Unremittable amounts	187–191	
	Disposals and acquisitions of know-how	192–195	
	Basis periods	196–220	
	Averaging and adjustment income	221–240	
	Post-cessation receipts	241–257	
	Supplementary (trustees and insolvency)	258–259	
3	Property income	260–364	2 (Part 4)
4	Savings and investment income	365–573	2 (Parts 5–7)
5	Miscellaneous income	574–689	2 (Part 8)
6	Exempt income	690–783	2 (Part 9)
7	Rent-a-room and foster care reliefs	784–828	2 (Part 10)
8	Foreign income – special rules	829–845	2 (Part 11)
9	Partnerships	846–863	
10	Supplementary and general	864–886	3 and 4

Chapter 3

PERSONAL RELIEFS

According to your circumstances you can claim certain personal tax reliefs which are deducted from your total income in arriving at the amount on which you pay income tax.

3.0 Personal reliefs at a glance 2005–06

Type	Circumstances	Relief
Personal allowance		£4,895*
Life assurance relief (3.2.5)	Policy effected before 14 March 1984 on your own or wife's life – deduction from premium	12½% of premiums
Blind person's allowance (3.2.9)		£1,610*
Age allowance (3.2.10)	Age 65–74 – Single Age 75 or over – Single	£7,090* £7,220*
	Reduced by £1 for every £2 of excess income over £19,500 down to personal reliefs level	
† Married couple's allowance (3.2.1)	Age under 66 Age 66–74 Age 75 and over Minimum amount	NIL £5,905* £5,975* £2,280

* These allowances will be increased for future years in line with the retail price index (unless the Treasury otherwise orders).

† These allowances are restricted to 10% and only apply to those born before 6 April 1935.

3.1 Earned and unearned income

For tax purposes income is classified as being either 'earned' or 'unearned'. Earned income includes the following:

(1) The salary or wages from your job including any taxable benefits.
(2) Certain pensions or retirement annuities paid to you, including those under a Revenue approved scheme (10.11.1).
(3) Any income from a trade or profession in which you engage.
(4) Any income from a partnership provided that you work in it and are not merely a sleeping partner.
(5) Old age pensions and widow's pensions received under the National Insurance Act.

(6) Income from a patent or copyright if you actually created the subject matter.
(7) After leaving your employment, trade or profession, any taxable amounts that you receive from that source.
(8) Income from holiday lettings as defined (7.7).

The rest of your income is 'unearned' and includes:

(1) Dividends.
(2) Bank deposit interest.
(3) Building society interest received.
(4) Rents from property investments.
(5) Income from trusts.
(6) Interest from government or local authority stock.

3.2 Personal allowances (TA 1988 S257)

For 2005–06 there is a personal allowance of £4,895 (previously £4,745). This is available to individuals generally. However, a higher allowance may apply to those who have attained their 65th birthdays (3.2.10).

3.2.1 **Married couple's allowance** (TA 1988 S257A & FA 1998 S27 & FA 1999 Ss31–32)

From 6 April 1990, according to the rules, each married couple obtained a married couple's allowance, depending on their ages attained during the tax year. The following apply from 2001–02 to 2005–06:

	2001–02 £	**2002–03 £**	**2003–04 £**	**2004–05 £**	**2005–06 £**
husband and wife both aged under 65	Nil	Nil	Nil	Nil	Nil
husband or wife aged 65–74	5,365	5,465	5,565	5,725	5,905
husband or wife aged 75 and over	5,435	5,535	5,635	5,795	5,975
income limit	17,600	17,900	18,300	18,900	19,500

For 1994–95 relief for married couple's allowance was restricted to the lower rate (20 per cent) and to 15 per cent subsequently. From 1999–2000, the rate is 10 per cent.

The higher allowances for older people are reduced if the husband's annual income exceeds a set limit, currently £19,500. For every £2 of income received in excess of £19,500, the higher allowances are reduced by £1 until the minimum allowance (£2,280) is reached.

After 5 April 2000, married couple's allowance is only available where at least one of you was born on or before 5 April 1935. It has been withdrawn for younger couples.

Married couple's allowance automatically goes to the husband. However, any unused balance may be transferred to the wife. To do this, an election must be made to your Inspector of Taxes within six years of the end of the tax year. For example, for 1999–2000 Mr A had an income of £5,335. His personal allowance of £4,335 reduced this to £1,000 and this left £970, unused, from the married couple's allowance. Provided an election is made by 31 January 2006, £970 will be transferred to Mrs A to set against her income for 1999–2000.

From 6 April 1993, you can elect for the married couple's allowance to be split equally between you or go entirely to the wife. Otherwise, it goes to the husband. The election is needed before the start of the first tax year to which it applies. The wife may elect for the equal split but both must elect for her to receive it all.

In the year of marriage, the allowance is reduced by half for each complete month from 6 April until your marriage date.

Transitional relief applies for 1990–91 and subsequent years where the husband's income is not sufficient to cover his personal allowance. Prior to 6 April 1990, the unused allowance would be used against any income of the wife. The transitional relief is designed to ensure that the position is no worse than previously.

3.2.2 **Child relief**

Income tax child relief no longer operates but prior to 1979–80 was generally available at different rates depending on the age of the child. Child relief was replaced by child benefit (see below). A new children's tax credit operates from 6 April 2001 (3.4).

3.2.3 **Child benefit**

Tax-free child benefit has applied since 4 April 1977. It applies in respect of your children under age 16 and those under 19 receiving full-time education, satisfying the necessary rules. From 6 April 2005, the weekly rate is £17.00 (£17.55 for lone parents) for the first child and £11.40 for each other child.

3.2.4 **Life assurance relief** (TA 1988 Ss266–274)

Tax relief in respect of pre-14 March 1984 life assurance policies is given based on the premiums paid in the tax year. You now normally deduct the relief from your premium payments (see table below). The relief only applies to policies taken out *prior to 14 March 1984*. Premiums in respect of policies effected after that date attract no relief. Similarly, relief is not due on existing policies for which the benefits are enhanced after that date, for example, by exercising an option to increase the policy term.

3.2.5 **Rules for life assurance relief – pre-14 March 1984 policies**

(1) The policy benefits must include a sum payable on death or in certain circumstances provide for a deferred annuity.
(2) The policy must be effected with a UK, Dominion or Irish insurance company or one carrying on business here; or a Lloyd's Underwriter; or a registered friendly society.
(3) The policy must be on your own or your wife's life and either of you may pay the premiums.
(4) Special relief is given for sums paid under an Act of Parliament or under the rules of your employment to secure a deferred annuity for your widow or children after your death. The relief is given according to your income level by deducting the following percentages of the premiums from your tax bill:

Total income	% relief
Not over £1,000	half of basic rate of income tax
£1,001–£2,000	three-quarters of basic rate
over £2,000	basic rate of income tax

(5) Policies taken out after 19 March 1968 or changed after that date have to be 'qualifying policies' (9.3).
(6) A fixed percentage of each premium is deducted by you on payment and you keep this relief. The premium limit is the larger of ⅙ of your total income (after charges) and £1,500. Any over-deduction by you will be adjusted in your assessment at the end of the tax year or you may be directed by the Revenue to pay premiums without the deduction of tax relief.
(7) From 6 April 1989 the relief percentage is 12½ per cent.

3.2.6 **Example: Life assurance relief restrictions for 2005–06**

	£	Date effected	2005–06 premium £
Policy A – Sum assured	10,000	1.1.80	1,000
Policy B – "	20,000	5.4.82	1,500
Policy C – "	25,000	1.5.84*	2,000

* Policy C was effected after 13 March 1984 and thus does not qualify for relief. If total income for year = £12,000
Premiums eligible for relief restricted to ⅙ × £12,000 = £2,000
Life assurance relief for year = £250 (12½% × £2,000)

3.2.7 **Blind person's relief** (TA 1988 S265)

(1) The relief is given to registered blind persons.
(2) For 2005–06, the relief is £1,610.

(3) For 2004–05, the relief was £1,560.
(4) If a spouse cannot use all his or her allowance, it can be transferred to the other spouse even if he or she is not blind.

3.2.8 **Age allowance** (TA 1988 Ss257 & 257E)

(1) This applies for 2005–06 if you are over 65 by 5 April 2006.
(2) The personal allowance is increased to £7,090 if your age on 5 April 2006 is between 65 and 74 and to £7,220 if you have reached your 75th birthday. For the extra age allowance for married people, only one of you needs to be 75 by that time.
(3) The above allowance figures are restricted if your income exceeds £19,500. The restriction is one-half of the excess of your income over £19,500. Thus if your income is £20,500 your allowance is restricted to £7,090 – £500 = £6,590. Note that the £19,500 restriction is based on your 'total income' (5.2), which is before tax but after certain deductions. If you have any life policy gains, these must be included without top slicing relief (9.7).
(4) If your income is sufficiently high your personal relief is restricted to the normal rate (£4,895); but not below this.
(5) Transitional relief is available from 1990–91 where a man married to an older wife might have his allowances reduced due to the change that took place in the system. If the transitional relief is claimed, the husband's personal allowance is replaced by the single age allowance frozen at the 1989–90 level of £3,400, etc. He also obtains the higher married couple's allowance appropriate to his wife's age.

3.2.9 **Widow's bereavement allowance** (TA 1988 S262 & FA 1999 S34)

(1) This allowance applied to certain widows whose husbands died after 5 April 1980 and before 6 April 2000.
(2) The relief for 1999–2000 was £1,970 (previously £1,900) which was given if the husband died in the two years to 5 April 2000. The relief for 2000–01 was £2,000, which was available if the husband died in 1999–2000.
(3) The relief was equal to the married couple's allowance (for those under 65). Like that allowance, it was restricted to 20 per cent for 1994–95 and 15 per cent subsequently, becoming 10 per cent from 1999–2000.
(4) For relief to apply, the couple must have been living together.
(5) The allowance applied to the tax year of death, and to the following year also, unless the widow remarried before it began.

3.2.10 **Vocational training**

If you paid for your own vocational training, tax relief was available from 6 April 1992 to 5 April 2000, subject to the rules. Relief was given for training leading to National Vocational Qualifications and Scottish Vocational Qualifications. The relief is not available for 2000–01 and subsequently, when an Individual Learning Accounts scheme takes over.

From 6 May 1996, wider relief extended to individuals over 30 who paid fees for full time vocational courses lasting between 4 weeks and a year. Such courses did not need to lead towards a National Vocational Qualification or its Scottish equivalent.

Under Inland Revenue regulations basic rate tax relief was given by deduction at source, even if you paid no income tax. Otherwise, a claim was needed.

3.3 Indexation of personal reliefs (TA 1988 S257C)

For 1981–82 and subsequent years, certain personal reliefs were to be increased from their previous levels by not less than the proportionate increase in the retail prices index for the last calendar year. Starting with 1993, the year for comparison runs to September. With Parliamentary approval, however, a lower increase (or none at all as for 1993–94, 1994–95 and 2003–04 personal allowance) may be ordered by the Treasury.

The reliefs concerned are personal allowance, married couple's allowance (3.2.1), additional personal allowance for children (3.2.8), age allowance (3.2.10) and widow's bereavement allowance (3.2.11). Also, blind person's allowance (3.2.9) is indexed for 1998–99 and subsequently. Of course, indexation ceased to be relevant from 2000–01 for the reliefs which have been removed such as married couple's allowance for those under 65.

3.3.1 Example: Personal reliefs – general illustration

Mr A lives with his family at 1 Bridge Street. Their income consists of:

	Income assessable for 2005–06	
Name	**Earned £**	**Savings £**
Mr A	13,550.00	4,105.00
Mrs A	4,150.00	995.00

Mrs A pays an annual premium of £200 on a qualifying life assurance policy on Mr A's life taken out before 14 March 1984. How much income tax is payable by Mr A and Mrs A for 2005–06?

Earned income	13,550.00	4,150.00
Savings income	4,105.00	995.00
Total Income	17,655.00	5,145.00
Less:		
Personal allowance	4,895.00	4,895.00
	12,760.00	250.00
Income tax payable: at 10% (on £2,090)	209.00	25.00
on savings income (£4,105) at 20%	821.00	–
at 22% (on £6,565)	1,444.30	
	2,474.30	

Notes:

(a) On the levels of income shown above Mr A is not liable to higher rate (5.0.1).
(b) Life assurance relief of 12½% × £200 = £25 will be obtained by deduction from the premium payments.
(c) Mr A only pays 20% income tax on his investment income, since it lies within his basic rate band.
(d) The savings income normally will have been subject to 20% tax at source, which is set against the liabilities shown. It is assumed that no dividends are included since these are differently treated (8.1.7).

3.4 Working tax credit and child tax credit etc.

As you have seen, there are reliefs and allowances which reduce your taxable income. There are also tax credits which are offset against your income tax, so that you pay less and may even receive a net repayment. However, these tax credits are effectively social security benefits which are in general only available to those with lower incomes. An outline follows of the detailed rules. In particular, note that a revised system operates from 2003–04 (3.4.4).

3.4.1 Working families tax credit (WFTC)

Operating from October 1999, WFTC replaced social security family credit. If you were employed, from 6 April 2000, the tax credit was put through the PAYE system and went into your pay packet.

For 2001–02, your WFTC was reduced by 55% of the excess of your weekly net family income (after tax and excluding WFTC and child benefits) over £92.90 (previously £91.45).

Each week, your WFTC comprised various component parts shown below up to 5 April 2003:

	Pre 6.4.01 £	From 6.4.01 £	From June 2001 £	From 6.4.02 £	From June 2002 to April 2003 £
Basic tax credit	53.15	54.00	59.00	60.00	62.50
Each child under 16	25.60	26.00		26.45	
16–18	26.35	26.75		27.20	
Extra tax credit for working at least 30 hours	11.25	11.45		11.65	
Disabled child tax credit	22.25	30.00		35.50	
70 per cent of childcare costs up to £100 for one child and £150 for two or more children – £135 and £200 from June 2001					
Enhanced disability tax credit					
Lone parent/couple		16.00		16.25	
Child		41.05		46.75	

3.4.2 **Disabled person's tax credit (DPTC)**

DPTC replaced social security disability working allowance for 2001–03. There was a weekly basic tax credit for 2001–02 of £56.05 for a single person and £86.25 for a lone parent or a couple. These went up to £61.05 and £91.25 respectively in June 2001 and then £62.10 and £95.30 for 2002–03. Also, there were child tax credits as for WFTC as shown above, with that for a disabled child (£30.00) applying throughout 2001–02 and £35.50 for 2002–03.

As for WFTC, there were net income thresholds, above which tax credit was lost at 55p per £. These thresholds were £72.25 for a single person and £92.90 for lone parents or couples for 2001–02, and £73.50 and £94.50 for 2002–03.

3.4.3 **Children's tax credit (CTC)** (TA 1998 S257AA & Sch 13B, FA 1999 S30 & Sch 3, FA 2000 S34 & FA 2001 Ss52 & 53 & Sch 11)

This tax credit commenced on 6 April 2001. It replaced married couple's and other related allowances now phased out, including additional personal allowance and widow's bereavement allowance.

You qualified for the allowance if you had one or more children under 16 living with you. Relief was given at 10 per cent on £5,290 for 2002–03 (on £5,200 for 2001–02).

However, if you were a higher rate tax payer, your CTC could be reduced or removed altogether. You lost £1 of tax credit for every £15 that your taxable income exceeded the threshold (£29,900 for 2002–03).

For 2002–03 CTC increased to £10,490 for the year of a child's birth. Thus you receive this increased amount where a baby was born in the year.

3.4.4 **Revised system**

From 2003–04, WFTC, DPTC and CTC have been absorbed into a new system comprising two new tax credits. These are Child Tax Credit (CTC) and Working Tax Credit (WTC).

The new tax credits carry various advantages compared with the old ones such as higher levels. The annual details for 2004–05 and 2005–06 are shown opposite.

The various WTC and CTC elements to which you are entitled are aggregated and your total credits are reduced if your income is too high. The family element of CTC is reduced by 1/15 of the excess of your income above £50,000 while your other credits are reduced by 37 per cent of your excess income over £5,060.

		2004–05 £	2005–06 £
CTC:	Family element	545	545
	Baby addition	545	545
	Child element	1,625	1,690
	Disabled child element	2,215	2,285
	Severely disabled child element	890	920
WTC:	Basic element	1,570	1,620
	Couples and lone parent element	1,545	1,595
	30 hour element (for couples – both must work 30 hours jointly with one working at least 16 hours each week)	640	660
	Disabled worker element	2,100	2,165
	Severe disability worker element	890	920
	Childcare element – 70 per cent of childcare costs of up to:		
	For 1 child	7,020	9,100
	For 2 or more children	10,400	15,600

Chapter 4

ANNUAL PAYMENTS AND INTEREST

4.1 Annual payments apart from interest (TA 1988 Ss348–350 & FA 1988 Ss36–40)

If you make an annual payment it is normally considered for tax purposes as being the income of the recipient and is usually subject to income tax at the basic rate (22 per cent) by deduction at source. You should therefore deduct this tax in making each payment (different rules apply to payments between companies – 13.9.1). You will be allowed to retain all of the tax deducted provided that your income taxed at the basic or higher rate is sufficient to cover the amount of the payment.

For example, if you have suffered basic rate income tax of £200 in the tax year and you made an annual payment of £100 you deduct tax from the latter amounting to £22. You thus pay only £78 when making your annual payment. Your effective income tax bill is £200 – £22 = £178. If, however, your taxed income is less than your annual payments you will have to pay to the Revenue income tax at 22 per cent on the difference. So if your taxed income is nil in any tax year, you will have to account to the Revenue for basic rate income tax on your entire annual payments for that year.

The result of this procedure is to give you basic rate income tax relief on your annual payments provided your income taxable at the basic rate exceeds those payments. From 15 March 1988, new deeds of covenant and maintenance payments, although annual payments, are covered by different rules. Broadly, no tax relief applies to the payer and the recipient is not taxed on the payments.

Under certain circumstances relief is available against tax at the higher rates as well as the basic rate.

Examples are as follows:

(1) Annual payments under court orders entered into before 15 March 1988 for maintenance or alimony (6.8.3). (Relief also applies if the court order was applied for on or before 15 March 1988 and made by 30 June 1988.)
(2) Annual payments under deeds of covenant to individuals that were entered into before 7 April 1965 (now very rare).
(3) Certain annual payments under partnership agreements to retiring partners or their widows.
(4) Certain annual payments which you make in connection with the purchase of a business where the payments are made to the former owner of the business or his widow or dependants.
(5) Unlimited donations under deeds of covenant to charities (15.2.1).

4.2 What are annual payments?

(1) Examples of annual payments are annuities, alimony payments, maintenance payments to your divorced or separated wife, payments under *deeds of covenant* (6.5) and certain interest payments which are subject to special tax rules (4.3).

(2) They are normally paid under a binding legal obligation such as a contract or deed of covenant.

(3) The payments must be recurrent although repeated gifts (unless under covenant) are not annual payments.

(4) In the hands of the recipient an annual payment must neither form part of his trading profits nor consist of a payment for services rendered.

(5) Payments consisting of instalments of capital are not annual payments for tax purposes. In the case of life annuities, however, each payment is split between an income element (which is treated as an annual payment) and a capital element which is tax free.

4.3 Interest payments (TA 1988 Ss353–379)

Subject to the following, you must not deduct income tax from any payments of interest that you make. This means that most types of interest payments made by you personally will be gross without any tax deduction. An important exception concerned mortgage interest before 6 April 2000 (4.7).

If you pay 'annual interest' to anyone who lives outside the UK (unless you get permission to pay gross under a double tax agreement) you must deduct income tax at the basic rate (22 per cent) in making the payment.

If, however, you pay 'annual interest' in this country on an advance from an overseas bank carrying on business in the UK, you should not deduct income tax.

'Annual interest' is interest paid on a loan which is capable of continuing for a period exceeding one year. If, at the start of a loan, you agree that it should last for a stated period of less than one year then any interest arising will not be 'annual interest'.

Companies and local authorities must normally deduct income tax in making 'annual interest' payments and this applies to a partnership of which a company is a member. However, new rules apply from 1 April 2001 permitting gross payments between companies (13.9.1). Interest paid by a bank in the normal course of its business is normally paid subject to the deduction of income tax (8.7).

Subject to the rules which are outlined in the following pages, certain interest payments are allowed as deductions in computing your total income for income tax at the various rates.

4.4 Interest paid for business purposes

Note that interest paid for business purposes is allowable against your taxable business profits provided the loan is used wholly and exclusively for the purposes of your business, profession or vocation. This basic rule includes interest on bank overdrafts as well as that on other loans.

4.5 Tax relief for interest payments (TA 1988 Ss353–379)

In order to obtain relief for interest paid you must show that it is 'eligible for relief'. This term specifically excludes bank overdraft or credit card interest.

4.5.1 Tax relief for interest payments

Your interest is 'eligible for relief' if it is paid on loans raised for the following purposes:

(1) Subject to various restrictions, the purchase and improvement of buildings and land in the UK or Eire (4.6).

(2) Buying plant and machinery for use in a partnership which gets capital allowances on it where you are one of the partners.

(3) Buying plant and machinery (eg, a motor car) which is used in connection with an office or employment that you hold and for which you personally get capital allowances.

(4) Acquiring ordinary shares in a close company (13.17) or lending it money for use in its business. (This does not apply to a close investment company, or for shares bought after 13 March 1989 on which BES or EIS relief is claimed – 11.25 and 11.26.) To qualify for relief you must either own more than 5 per cent of its shares, or own some shares and work for the greater part of your time for the company. Shares owned by 'associates' (13.17) are included in the 5 per cent but not, after July 1989, if owned by an employee trust of which you are a beneficiary.

(5) Purchases by employees of shares in their company as part of an employee buy-out. (Employees and their spouses must together own more than 50 per cent of the company, ignoring excesses over 10 per cent holdings.)

(6) Purchasing a share in a partnership, or lending it money for use in its business if you are a partner. This applies whether or not you work in the partnership and also extends to investing in a co-operative.

(7) Paying inheritance tax arising on death. The personal representatives of the deceased obtain relief for interest paid within a year of raising the loan. If the interest cannot be relieved wholly in the year of payment it can be spread forward or backwards.

Note: Relief for interest on loans to purchase plant and machinery (see (2) and (3) above) is given for three years after the year of assessment in which the loan is taken out.

4.6 Loans for purchase and improvement of buildings and land (TA 1988 Ss354–358 & FA 1999 Ss37–41 & Sch 4)

Within the limits mentioned below, any interest which you pay on a loan raised to buy land or buildings, or to improve them, is 'eligible for relief'. This does not include overdraft interest but covers fixed bank loans and building society mortgages, etc. (Improvement loans only qualify for relief if applied for this purpose before 6 April 1988.) Interest on a loan to buy your home was generally withdrawn from 6 April 2000.

When you pay the interest you must normally own the property. However, from 16 March 1993, you continued to obtain relief when you bought a new home which became the security for a loan taken to buy and originally secured on the previous one.

The interest on any loan that you raise to pay off another loan previously obtained to buy property is also 'eligible for relief'. However, no relief is available on a loan obtained after 5 April 1988 to replace money borrowed to improve property. If, however, you merely carry out repairs to existing property without improving it then any loan interest incurred will not normally be treated as 'eligible for relief'.

The Revenue gave sympathetic consideration to cases where, for example, the husband bought the property and the wife paid the interest – the couple would usually get tax relief.

From April 1983 until 5 April 2000, mortgage interest up to certain limits was normally paid net of tax at the basic rate or less (see below).

Concerning a property loan raised after 26 March 1974, you only obtain tax relief if either (a) it is to purchase or improve your only or main residence and in general the interest pre-dates 6 April 2000 or (b) you let the property at a commercial rent for at least 26 weeks in the year and it is available for letting at other times. However, from 6 April 1995, interest is treated as a deduction from Schedule A income in the same way as other expenses are allowed. At the same time, the old rules cease to have effect. (The old rules continue to apply for corporation tax purposes.)

Under (a) your interest was restricted to that on a loan of £30,000 and if your borrowing exceeded this figure your interest relief was proportionately restricted. (In considering the £30,000 limit, no account was taken of interest which had been added to capital up to £1,000.) Before 6 April 1991, relief was available at the basic and higher rates of income tax. However, from that date, higher rate relief was withdrawn and relief was only granted at the basic rate.

From 6 April 1994, relief was restricted to 20 per cent on existing and new loans. An exception is for people over 65 who take loans on their homes to buy life annuities and will continue to obtain relief at the basic rate for the duration of existing loans. However, no relief is available for interest on loans taken out after 9 March 1999.

Regarding general home mortgages, from 6 April 1995 relief was further restricted to 15 per cent with 10 per cent applying from 6 April 1998 until 5 April 2000, after which the relief has been withdrawn.

Under (b) (see previous page) you are only allowed interest relief against your income from letting property. You continue to obtain higher rate relief under this category after 5 April 1991.

You also obtained relief up to 5 April 2000 for interest on a loan which you obtained before 6 April 1988 (but not subsequently) to buy a house for a former or separated spouse, or a dependent relative of your wife or yourself. A dependent relative is broadly defined as an elderly or infirm relative; also your widowed, divorced or separated mother. This interest counted, however, towards the £30,000 limit. Loans obtained for these purposes after 5 April 1988 did not qualify for relief.

Your interest relief was not restricted because you did not reside in your property, if you lived in job-related accommodation (10.6.13) and intended to make your property your main residence in due course (TA 1988 S356). A similar rule applied to interest paid on a loan to buy job-related accommodation where you were self-employed.

4.6.1 **Temporary relief**

You obtained relief for interest on a bridging loan of up to £30,000 for normally up to one year (or longer at the discretion of the Revenue) when you changed houses. Higher rate relief continued after 5 April 1991 on your existing but not your new bridging loan, if both were in place by that date. This included where there had been a formal offer and binding contract. This higher rate relief would normally only continue for up to one year, but could be extended at the discretion of the Revenue.

The position was improved from 16 March 1993, provided your old property was up for sale. It was no longer necessary to take a mortgage to buy a new home in order to obtain relief on your existing loan. This continued for 12 months from when the old property ceased to be your main residence (FA 1993 S57).

Similar rules apply if you are over 65 and have a life annuity 'home income plan'. You may now leave your home without losing relief on the loan to buy your annuity. Again, you need to have the property up for sale and relief continues for 12 months from when you move out. In both cases, the Revenue have a discretion to extend this period. For such loans existing on 9 March 1999 (and certain remortgages) that still qualify for relief, the relief rate was fixed at 23 per cent and the limit at £30,000 from 6 April 2000.

4.7 Deduction of tax from mortgage interest payments (TA 1988 Ss369–370)

Up to 5 April 2000, you were able to deduct tax from mortgage interest payments, provided the loan qualified for relief. Income tax was deducted at the basic rate from interest paid up to 5 April 1994. Subsequently, lower deduction rates apply. From 6 April 1994, the MIRAS (mortgage interest relief at source) rules applied using the 20 per cent lower rate instead of the basic rate of tax. Similarly, from 6 April 1995, the deduction rate was 15 per cent and from 6 April 1998 it was 10 per cent with no deduction being made after 5 April 2000.

Chapter 5

COMPUTING YOUR INCOME TAX BILL

Your 'total income' (see below) less your allowances for the tax year (3.0.1) will be subjected to income tax at the lower, basic and higher rates according to the following table:

5.0 Income tax rates for 2005–06

Slice of income £	Rate %	Total income (after allowances) £	Total tax £
2,090 (0–2,090)	10	2,090	209
30,310 (2,090–32,400)	22	32,400	6,877.20
Remainder	40		

Note: The 10 per cent rate only applies to earned income, pensions and savings income. Savings income excluding dividends (5.2(4)) in your £2,090–£32,400 band is taxed at 20 per cent. Dividends within that band carry a 10 per cent tax credit (non-reclaimable) and attract no further tax (5.6.1).

5.1 Indexation of income tax bands (TA 1988 S1)

Prior to 6 April 1988 there was a basic rate band followed by five higher rate bands. Each of those bands was to be increased in line with the retail price index. The index comparison was made for the previous December each year and the figures rounded up to the next £100. However, from 1993 onwards, September is used.

As with the indexation of personal reliefs (3.3), Parliament has the power to modify the effects of indexing the income tax bands. In fact no indexation increases were made at all for some years, whilst increases above the index were made for others. Starting with 1988–89, one higher rate of 40 per cent replaced the previous five. From 6 April 1992 a lower rate band applies. The starting levels for the income bands continue to be indexed, although no indexation increases were made for 1993–94 and 1994–95. The indexed changes must be reflected in your PAYE deductions on the first pay day after 14 June for 2005–06.

5.2 What is total income? (TA 1988 S835)

Your total income comprises your income for the tax year less specified deductions (5.3). The following classes of income will be included for each tax year:

(1) Income as assessed for the tax year under the following schedules*:

Schedule		Details	Para.
A		Land and buildings	7.1
D	Cases I & II	Trades and professions	11.1
	Case III	Interest, etc.	8.4
	Cases IV & V	Overseas securities and possessions	18.2
	Case VI	Miscellaneous	15.1
E		Earnings from employment (see also below)	10.1
F		Dividends	8.1

* *For post 2004–05 income, the classification into schedules no longer applies (2.10).*

(2) *The gross income actually paid to you in the tax year under the deduction of income tax at the source.* This will include Schedule D Case III. You will receive the net amount after suffering income tax but you will pay the higher rate of tax if appropriate on the gross amount. You will obtain a tax credit for the income tax suffered at source which will be deducted from your tax bill. The following would come within this category:

- The income portion of annuities.
- Interest on certain investments.
- Any annual payments which you receive (4.2).

Prior to 1996–97, tax was deducted at the basic rate, but a special 20 per cent rate now applies regarding deductions from savings income. However, annual payments are likely to have tax deducted at the basic rate (22 per cent).

(3) *Income distributions from discretionary and accumulation settlements* (21.4). Net payments made to you must be grossed up at 40 per cent and carry with them a tax credit of this amount which represents income tax effectively suffered by the settlement. (Before 6 April 2004 the rate was 34 per cent.) Thus if you receive £60 this is included in your total income together with a tax credit of £40. If you have an interest in possession (22.30), then your income only carries 22 per cent tax in the settlement. To the extent that the income from 6 April 1993 consists of dividends, your tax credit was 20 per cent and from 6 April 1999 it is 10 per cent.

(4) *Dividends received together with the relevant tax credits.* From 6 April 1999, the tax credit on dividends is 10 per cent of the gross, but you pay no more tax unless you are a higher rate (40 per cent) payer (5.6). After 5 April 1993 and before 6 April 1999, your dividends from UK companies carried with them tax credits of $^{20}/_{80}$ of the actual payments. This is equivalent to 20 per cent of the gross.

(5) *Your gross income taxed at source under PAYE* (10.14). This consists of your salary, etc. derived from your employment; it is subjected to lower,

basic and higher rate income tax at source. The tax suffered at source is naturally deducted from the tax bill on your total income.

(6) *The grossed up equivalent of any building society interest received.* This income is subject to 20 per cent income tax deducted at source but must be included in your total income gross. You gross it up by multiplying the income received by

$\frac{100}{100-20}$ (that is, $\frac{100}{80}$). You obtain a credit for the tax. For example, if

you receive £80 building society interest, your total income will

include £80 $\times \frac{100}{80}$ = £100 and you obtain a tax credit of £20. For

1995–96 and earlier years, basic rate tax (25 per cent) was deducted.

(7) *The grossed up equivalent of any bank interest, etc. paid to you* (8.7).

5.3 Total income – deductions

As well as normal business expenses, etc, which are deducted in arriving at the various income tax assessments, the following are deductible:

(1) Loan interest subject to the relevant rules (4.3). Regarding mortgage interest paid after 6 April 1991 in connection with your home, no deduction is allowable for relieving the excess of your higher rate over your basic rate liability (FA 1991 S27). For 1994–95, mortgage interest relief was restricted to 20 per cent with only 15 per cent relief applying from 1995–96 and 10 per cent for 1998–99 and 1999–2000, after which it generally ceased.

(2) Business losses and capital allowances.

(3) Annual payments under court orders for maintenance or alimony provided they are made before 16 March 1988 or applied for before that date and made by 30 June 1988. (For 1994–95, the relief was restricted to 20 per cent and to 15 per cent from 1995–96. For 1999–2000 it is 10 per cent, after which it is abolished.) Payments under new arrangements must be gross and are not deductible (6.8.3).

(4) Annual payments under deeds of covenant to individuals (excluding your infant children) that you entered into before 7 April 1965.

(5) Certain annual payments under partnership agreements to retiring partners or their widows.

(6) Annual payments to individuals under deeds of covenant entered into after 6 April 1965 and before 15 March 1988. In general these are not deductible from your income for higher rate income tax purposes. However, they reduce your total income for the purposes of the life assurance relief one-sixth rule (3.2.6).

(7) Certain annual payments which you make in connection with the purchase of a business where the payments are made to the former owner of the business or his widow or dependants.
(8) Covenanted donations to charities without limit. Also charitable donations under the 'gift aid' scheme and the 'millennium gift aid' scheme (15.2.1).
(9) Allowable personal pension contributions, retirement annuity premiums (14.6) and additional voluntary contributions (AVCs) (14.4).
(10) A proportion of certain transfers to reserves made by underwriters at Lloyd's or other approved underwriters.
(11) Personal reliefs and allowances (see Chapter 3). (These are, strictly speaking, deductions which are made from your total income rather than in its computation.)

5.4 Charges on income (TA 1988 S276)

The annual payments mentioned above (3)–(8) as well as various other charges on income (4.1) are paid under the deduction of basic rate income tax (22 per cent) (as was your allowable mortgage interest for 1993–94 (4.7)). From 1995–96 to 1999–2000, mortgage interest was generally payable under the deduction of lower tax rates, being 10 per cent for 1999–2000. To the extent that your income less allowances is not sufficient to cover your annual charges payments, your personal allowances, etc. must be restricted. (This restriction does not apply regarding mortgage interest.)

Thus, if your income for 2005–06 is £6,500 and your personal allowances and reliefs total £5,500, you can pay up to £1,000 annual charges without restriction. The £1,000 is paid by you under deduction of basic rate income tax. Thus you actually pay only £1,000 – 22 per cent × £1,000 = £780. You also pay to the Revenue tax at 22 per cent on £1,000 = £220. If your annual charges were £1,500, your total reliefs would be reduced to £5,000 so that your taxable income after allowances (£1,500) would be sufficient to cover your charges.

The income tax which you deduct from your annual payments must effectively be paid over to the Revenue. This is done by paying tax on that part of your income which is equal to such annual payments. Where, however, the payments in question are allowed as deductions in computing your total income (for example, (3)–(8) in 5.3) you get relief for the excess of your higher rate tax over basic rate tax or tax credit on income covered by those charges.

5.5 Deductions from tax payable

When your total tax liability is computed certain deductions from the tax payable must be made, either because you have already paid part of it or because of special reliefs. These deductions include the following:

(1) Life assurance relief on policies effected before 14 March 1984 only (3.2.5). Normally 12½ per cent of your qualifying premiums (9.3) (sub-

ject to the various rules) is deductible from your tax payable. You normally obtain this relief by deducting it from each premium payment.

(2) $^{20}/_{80}$ of your building society interest received; similarly $^{20}/_{80}$ of bank deposit interest, etc. (8.7). (This fraction was $^{25}/_{75}$ for 1995–96 and earlier.) From 6 April 1991 (but not previously), this tax is capable of being repaid.

(3) Tax credits on dividends received (8.1). The tax credit is $^{1}/_{9}$ of each dividend received, which is 10 per cent of the gross. This applies from 6 April 1999 (8.1.7) and covers tax on dividends within your £32,400 band. Above that, your gross dividends are taxed at 32.5 per cent and the 10 per cent tax credit offset.

(4) Tax paid under PAYE (10.14).

(5) Income tax deducted at the source at 20 per cent (25 per cent for 1995–96) on certain investment interest paid to you (such as on company debentures).

(6) Basic rate tax deducted from annual payments made to you during the year which are included in your total income.

(7) Tax at 40 per cent (34 per cent before 6 April 2004) on income distributions made to you during the tax year by discretionary settlements (21.5). The tax is computed on the gross equivalent of the distributions.

5.6 Investment income (TA 1988 S686)

For 1983–84 you were liable to an additional rate of 15 per cent on so much of your investment income as exceeded £7,100. Subsequently, the additional rate no longer applies to individuals.

Certain discretionary and accumulation settlements (21.5) are subjected to additional tax. In this case, the charge is made on all the income including that from both investments and otherwise. The general effect is that a combined 40 per cent rate is paid. (32.5 per cent is charged on gross dividends.) Higher rate tax is not normally charged on the trust income, however, unless it is distributed to beneficiaries who are themselves liable to the higher rate of tax. (See Chapter 21, 21.5, for fuller details.)

Effectively, as a higher rate tax payer, you suffer extra tax on your dividend income from 6 April 1993, because of the reduction in the tax credit from 25 to 20 per cent. However, if you are a basic rate payer you are not adversely affected since your tax on such investment income is limited to 20 per cent. (A similar position applies regarding the 10 per cent tax credit from 6 April 1999.)

For individuals, the tax rates on investment income follow exact rules. In general, property rents, etc., are taxed at the same rates as earned income (5.0.1). Your savings income (including building society, bank interest and dividends) is taken as the top slice of your income and the appropriate tax rates applied (5.6.1). Tax deducted at source and tax credits are offset, but for 1999–2000 and subsequently, the 10 per cent tax credit on dividends cannot be reclaimed. (Tax deducted from interest is still reclaimable.)

5.6.1 Income tax rates on investment income (before tax credits)

Within income band –	2003–04 up to £30,500 %	2003–04 over £30,500 %	2004–05 up to £31,400 %	2004–05 over £31,400 %	2005–06 up to £32,400 %	2005–06 over £32,400 %
Dividend tax credit on gross	10	10	10	10	10	10
Dividends	10	32.5	10	32.5	10	32.5
Other savings income	20	40	20	40	20	40

5.7 The assessment and payment of your income tax (TA 1988 Ss2–5 & TMA S59B)

This matter is considered in detail in Chapter 16. A uniform set of dates for the payment of income tax and capital gains tax was introduced as a part of the new self-assessment system. These dates apply for 1996–97 and subsequent years of assessment. The earliest payments under the new rules were due on 31 January 1997. Further payments on account of your 1996–97 liability were due on 31 July 1997, the final balance being payable on 31 January 1998, based on your income tax return. A similar scheme applies for subsequent years.

Long-standing rules normally apply for assessments raised for years up to and including 1995–96. In general, you needed to pay income tax at the lower, basic and higher rate by 1 January in the year for which the income was assessed, if the income had not already been taxed. If, however, your assessment was not agreed in time, then the tax was normally payable 30 days after the assessment was issued. Special rules applied where you appealed (16.4).

An exception to the above rule concerns your tax on business profits (11.1) which was payable in two equal instalments on 1 January in the year of assessment and the following 1 July. (For 1996–97 you made equal payments on account on 31 January 1997 and 31 July 1997, with the balance on 31 January 1998 and similarly for future years.)

Income tax at higher rates was due for payment by 1 December (31 January from 1996–97) following the year of assessment on any income from which basic rate tax had been deducted at source. This included income like building society and bank deposit interest as well as dividends, etc. If the assessment was not issued by 1 November following the year of assessment, the tax was normally payable no earlier than 30 days after the date of issue, special rules applying if you appealed (16.4).

5.7.1 **Example: Income tax computation**

Mr B has his own business from which his assessable profit for 2005–06 is £40,000. His other income for 2005–06 consists of £1,200 building society interest and £9,000 dividends received (notional tax credits £1,000). (Mr B is married, and for 2005–06 his wife's income will be taxed separately.) From the above, compute Mr B's income tax liability.

Mr B – Income tax computation for 2005–06		**£**	**£**
Earned income – business assessment			40,000.00
Investment income – building society interest:		1,200.00	
Add: 20% income tax			
	£1,200 × 20/80	300.00	
		1,500.00	
Dividends		9,000.00	
Add: Tax credit		1,000.00	
			11,500.00
Total income before personal reliefs and allowances			51,500.00
Less: Personal allowance			4,895.00
Taxable balance			46,605.00
Tax payable:			
Earned income	£2,090 at 10%		209.00
	£30,310 at 22%		6,668.20
	£2,705 at 40%		1,082.00
Building Society	£1,500 at 40%		600.00
Dividends	£10,000 at 32.5%		3,250.00
	£46,605		
Total tax			11,809.20
Less: Tax credit on dividends		1,000.00	
Tax credit on building society interest		300.00	
			1,300.00
Net further tax payable			10,509.20

5.8 Interest on overdue tax (TMA S86, etc.)

If you are late in paying your income tax you may be charged interest at 7½ per cent from 6 September 2004. Previous recent rates have been:

From	**Rate %**
6 February 1996	6.25
6 February 1997	8.5
6 August 1997	9.5
6 January 1999	8.5
6 March 1999	7.5

From	Rate %
6 February 2000	8.5
6 May 2001	7.5
6 November 2001	6.5
6 August 2003	5.5
6 December 2003	6.5

This interest is not deductible for income tax purposes. The exact rules are given later (16.8.2).

5.9 Fluctuating income

Because of the graduated nature of income tax rates, if your income fluctuates greatly from year to year you may find that your tax liability is high in some years and low in others. The result is that your total income tax over the years is more than it would have been had your income been spread evenly over those years. Certain special rules exist which have the effect of spreading lump sums of income over the period during which they have been earned.

So-called 'top slicing' relief is obtained when you receive certain large taxable sums in one year. You may effectively spread these sums over a stated period and recompute your tax liability on the basis that the income had been paid in this way. (The tax is payable for the year when you receive the income but the rate is normally lower.) What you do is to divide the lump sum (L) by the stated period (P) and calculate the tax payable (T) for the year on your other income plus (L/P). You then calculate the tax payable on your other income by itself and deduct it from (T). This gives the total tax payable on (L/P) and this tax is multiplied by P to give the total tax payable on (L).

A particular example where 'top slicing' applies is regarding the profit element in the proceeds of non-qualifying life assurance policies (9.7). Such policy proceeds are taxed at the excess of higher rate income tax over income tax at the basic rate, subject to the relief outlined above.

Chapter 6

HUSBAND, WIFE AND CHILDREN

This chapter deals, in particular, with the taxation of husband and wife. The independent taxation system operating from 6 April 1990 is covered. Regarding the rules which applied for 1989–90 and earlier years, reference should be made to previous editions of this book. (Some of the rules for independent taxation have been mentioned in Chapter 3.)

6.1 Independent taxation of husband and wife (TA Ss257–257F & Ss282–282B etc.)

From 6 April 1990, you and your spouse are each taxed separately on all of your income and capital gains. Each has a single person's relief and income tax rates (5.0.1). Similarly you each have a full capital gains tax annual exemption (£8,500).

Up to 5 April 2000, married couple's allowance (3.2.1) amounting to £1,970 for 1999–2000 was available for those under 65. A higher married couple's allowance was generally given to those entitled to age allowance (3.2.10). The relief became 10 per cent for 1999–2000. After that, the relief was generally withdrawn, an exception being where at least one party to the marriage was born before 6 April 1935.

Normally, married couple's allowance goes to the husband. However, if his income is insufficient to use it, part or all can be transferred to the wife. In the year of marriage, the married couple's allowance is reduced by 1/12 for each month between 6 April and the marriage date.

A special rule applies from 6 April 1993. You are able to elect for the married couple's allowance to be split equally between you or go entirely to the spouse (3.2.1). Otherwise it will be used as before.

Income from jointly owned property is taken as split equally between husband and wife, subject to the right to make a joint declaration to the contrary. The effect of the election is to split the income in the ratio of the respective shares of husband and wife in the asset. Interest on mortgages in your joint names was split equally between you. However, you could elect for any different split to apply, which could well save tax. From 6 April 2004, distributions from jointly owned shares in close companies (13.18) are no longer automatically split equally between husband and wife but according to the actual ownership.

The previous wife's earnings election (6.4) has no validity for 1990–91 and subsequent tax years. However, as mentioned above, all income is taxed separately, as are capital gains. As a result, your spouse and yourself will each have the annual capital gains tax exemption (20.6) for 1990–91 and subsequently. Thus each has £8,500 exemption for 2005–06.

An election for transitional relief (3.2.1) is available where a couple might have been worse off in 1990–91, because most of the income belongs to the wife and the husband's personal allowance exceeds his own income. The relief is limited for 1990–91 and future years to the husband's excess personal allowance.

6.2 When you marry

When you marry, various rules apply to both of you (6.1). Essentially you will be taxed separately on your income and capital gains, remaining responsible for your own tax returns. Thus at the end of the year in which you marry both you and your wife have to complete income tax returns.

Regarding the married couple's allowance (3.2.1) for the tax year of marriage (if available), this is restricted pro rata for every completed month during that year prior to your date of marriage.

6.3 Separate assessment (TA 1988 Ss283–285)

Prior to 6 April 1990, despite the fact that it was the husband who was taxed on both his own and his wife's income, it was nevertheless possible for a married couple to be assessed separately and to pay their respective shares of tax separately. However, from 6 April 1990, husband and wife are both taxed and assessed on their own income (6.2). Separate assessment was not the same as the separate taxation of your wife's earned income (6.4). Full details are given in earlier editions of this book.

6.4 Separate taxation of wife's earnings (TA 1988 Ss287 & 288)

Before the introduction of independent taxation from 6 April 1990, it was still possible to elect for the wife to be separately taxed on her earnings up to 5 April 1990 as if she were a single person. The husband was then taxed on the balance of their joint incomes (including the wife's unearned income) as if he also were single. Fuller details appear in previous editions of this book.

6.5 Deeds of covenant (FA 1988 S36)

Payments under deeds of covenant to charities (15.2.1) have provided a most tax-efficient means of passing money regularly to them. Such payments are a class of annual payments (4.1). The deed must be properly drawn up (most charities have prepared forms for covenanted donations) otherwise seek professional advice. From 6 April 2000, charitable covenants have become far less important because of the introduction of unrestricted gift aid (15.2.1).

Beneficial treatment also applies to payments under deeds of covenant to individuals, provided the deeds were entered into before 15 March 1988. A further condition is that an Inspector of Taxes must have received the deed by 30 June 1988, otherwise payments under such deeds are disregarded for tax purposes. The previous beneficial tax treatment which made deeds of covenant so popular for student children and also grandchildren was withdrawn for new covenants.

The deed needs to provide for payments at annual or more frequent intervals for a period capable of exceeding six years or until your death if earlier. (Note that this also applies to any supplementary deeds.) However, deeds of covenant in favour of charities (15.2.1) need only be capable of exceeding three years.

You are required to deduct income tax at the basic rate (22 per cent) from each payment according to the rules for annual payments (4.1). This does not apply to payments made by you under deed of covenant to any of your children who are less than 18 years of age and unmarried. These payments are disregarded for tax purposes as are payments under a reciprocal arrangement.

Deed of covenant payments to charities (15.2.1) are normally deductible from your total income for higher tax rate purposes without limit (FA 1986 S30).

Subject to the above, recipients of payments under deeds of covenant with low incomes can reclaim basic rate tax on them up to the amount of their unused income tax personal relief (£4,895). Thus suppose your grandson has no other income and you pay him £1,560 net under deed of covenant each year, tax of £440 will be reclaimable for him for 2005–06. (This assumes that you entered into the deed of covenant before 15 March 1988.)

6.6 The income of your children

No matter how young they are, there is nothing to prevent your children earning income in their own right and being taxed on that earned income. This also applies to investment income unless the investments were given by your wife or yourself and the child is neither married nor over the age of 18 at the time that the income is paid.

Settlements and arrangements made by you through which your child gets investment income normally result in your being taxed on that income if the child is neither married nor over 18. If the child's investment income which would otherwise be treated as your own is less than £100, however, you will not pay tax on that income (TA 1988 S660B). (This limit applies for each parent.)

You should obtain a tax return each year for each of your minor children who has any income (including trust income). Completing a return will often prove beneficial since if the child has suffered tax at source on any income (apart from dividends) this may be reclaimable in whole or part depending on its nature and on how much other income there is to set against the child's tax allowances. In such circumstances a repayment claim form can be submitted instead of a normal tax return (16.7).

If the child had little or no other income, then it was of benefit for it to be paid an annual amount under deed of covenant (6.5) by a friend or relative (not its parents, unless the child is over 18 or married). From 15 March 1988 the rules were changed (6.5) but existing deeds of covenant attract relief as before. The covenant payments are made under the deduction of income tax at the basic rate (22 per cent). If the child's income is small enough then the tax can be reclaimed on its behalf because he or she has the benefit of the full personal allowance (£4,895).

6.6.1 Example: Income of child

Mr A has one child, B, aged fourteen years, whose income for 2005–06 is as follows:

		Gross £
(1)	Dividends, including tax credits, on shares given to B by Mr A	200
(2)	Dividends, including tax credits (10% of gross), on shares given to B by his grandfather	1,000
(3)	Annual payment under deed of covenant from B's uncle effected before 15 March 1988	2,000
(4)	Interest on bank deposit (capital gifted by grandmother)	2,000

How much income tax is reclaimable on behalf of B for 2005–06?

Item (1) is not treated as B's income for tax purposes because it is regarded as the income of Mr A who gifted the shares to his child B.

The income tax payable by B for 2005–06 is calculated as follows:

	Gross £	Income tax deducted or tax credits £
(2) Dividends including tax credits on shares from grandfather	1,000	100.00
(3) Annual payment from B's uncle	2,000	440.00
(4) Deposit interest	2,000	400.00
Total income	5,000	940.00
Less: Personal allowance of	4,895	
Taxable amount	105	
Income tax due £105 at 10% (dividend income)		10.50
Add: restriction on repayment £895 at 10%		89.50
		100.00
Less: Income tax suffered by deduction at source and tax credits		940.00
Net income tax reclaimable		840.00

6.6.2 Child trust fund (CTF)

Children born from September 2002 will qualify for the new tax-efficient CTF and will have £250 allocated to the fund at birth. This is increased to £500 for children from low-income families qualifying for full child tax credit. Parents and others will be able to add up to a total of £1,000 to the child's CTF each year and at age 18 the full fund will be available, without restriction on the assets. The CTF scheme operates from April 2005.

6.7 Death of husband or wife

If you are a widower or widow you are regarded as a single person for tax purposes. This means that the personal reliefs for single persons will apply to your income. However, prior to 6 April 2000, you may have qualified for the £1,970 additional personal relief for children (3.2.8).

6.7.1 If husband dies

If a husband dies during the tax year his income for the period from 6 April to the date of his death will be subject to tax. A return of this income must be made by his executors who must arrange for payment of tax out of the estate funds.

For the tax year in which the husband dies, he will have the full personal allowance (£4,895 for 2005–06) and married couple's allowance (if applicable). However if his income is not sufficiently large to absorb the full married couple's allowance, the balance will go to his widow.

6.7.2 If wife dies

Where a wife dies, she is entitled to the entire personal relief (£4,895 for 2005–06). (Age allowance would alternatively be available in full if she is so entitled.)

6.8 Divorce or separation

If you are divorced or permanently separated you are regarded as a single person for tax purposes. This means that the personal reliefs for single persons will apply to your income. If, however, you were separated but maintained your wife by voluntary maintenance payments for which you got no tax relief, prior to 6 April 1990, you obtained the married man's personal allowance. Subsequent to that date, married couple's allowance (£1,970 for 1999–2000) applied in the tax year of separation only, subject to transitional relief (6.8.3).

You are treated as being permanently separated from your wife if you are separated under a court order or deed of separation; also if you are separated in such circumstances that the separation is likely to be permanent.

6.8.1 Divorce or separation during the tax year

On her divorce or permanent separation prior to 6 April 1990, a woman became a taxpayer in her own right and needed to submit a return from the date of divorce or separation to 5 April. She was then taxed as a single person getting the full 1989–90 personal allowance. Naturally, the independent taxation rules mean that after 5 April 1990, a woman is a taxpayer in her own right in any event.

Where a man is divorced or permanently separated during 1990–91 or later, he obtains the full personal relief for the year and married couple's allowance if appropriate.

6.8.2 **Claiming additional personal relief** (TA 1988 S260)

This relief ceased after 5 April 2000. For any tax year only one payment of additional personal relief (£1,970 for 1999–2000) was normally allowable for your children. If you were separated or divorced from your wife you needed to agree jointly who should claim the tax relief for your mutual children otherwise the relief was split in proportion to the respective contributions made by you and your ex-wife (or separated wife) towards the children's maintenance and education for the tax year.

As an exception to the general rule, if each parent looked after one or more children of a broken marriage, each could claim full additional personal relief. However, in the year of separation, only the wife (or ex-wife) was able to claim the relief.

6.8.3 **Alimony and maintenance payments** (TA 1988 Ss347A & 347B)

The rules regarding alimony and maintenance payments were changed in 1988. Where payments are made under agreements dated after 14 March 1988, they are to be made without the deduction of tax. At the same time, the recipients are not taxed on the payments. The payer obtained a limited amount of relief, equal to the annual amount paid or, if less, £1,970 (for 1999–2000). Subsequently, relief is only available if at least one party was born before 6 April 1935. This applies where one divorced or separated spouse makes payments to the other. For 1994–95, the relief was restricted to 20 per cent and to 15 per cent subsequently, with 10 per cent applying from 1999–2000.

If you are separated or divorced and you make any payments under a court order or a binding agreement entered into before 15 March 1988, for the maintenance of your children or your separated or ex-wife, then you should not deduct income tax at the basic rate from the gross payments. (Such deduction was normally required before 6 April 1989.) This extended to court orders applied for before 16 March 1988 and made by 30 June 1988; also maintenance agreements made before 15 March 1988 and variations of such orders or agreements.

After 5 April 1989, special rules apply to payments under these agreements. The payer gets tax relief on payments up to the level for which he obtained relief for 1988–89 and the recipient is taxable on no more than was taxable in 1988–89 (taking account of the exemption for a divorced or separated spouse of £1,720, etc.). All payments of maintenance due after 5 April 1989 should be made gross. Relief on up to £1,970 of the payments is limited to 10 per cent for 1999–2000. For 2000–01 relief on up to £2,000 is only available where at least one party was born before 6 April 1935. This figure increases as follows:

	£
2001–02	2,070
2002–03	2,110
2003–04	2,150

2004–05	2,210
2005–06	2,280

Payments to the adult children from 1996–97 are no longer to be treated as charges on the income of the payer nor as taxable income of the recipient (FA 1996 S149).

In general, tax relief for maintenance payments was withdrawn for 2000–01 and subsequent years. However, it is being retained as above where at least one of the parties was over 65 at 5 April 2000. (The special transitional relief where arrangements were set up before 15 March 1988 is being ended.)

Purely voluntary payments of maintenance should be paid without any tax deductions and these are not allowable as annual charges against your income; nor are they taxed on the recipient. As indicated, however (6.8), if you maintained your separated wife by voluntary payments only, then prior to 6 April 1990, you obtained the married man's personal allowance. If you are eligible (6.1) married couple's allowance normally applies in the tax year of separation only. However, if you separated before 6 April 1990 and the foregoing circumstances apply, you will normally continue to obtain this relief. This does not apply if you are divorced.

6.8.4 Foreign divorces

If the divorce is effected by a foreign court then different rules relate to the receipt or payment of alimony by residents of this country. Normally no tax will be deductible from the payments by a United Kingdom resident and a recipient resident in this country will be assessed to tax on the amount arising.

However, for 1992–93 and subsequent years, tax relief extends to payments under court orders of countries which are members of the EC; also written agreements enforceable under the law of those countries. Payments must be to a divorced or separated wife or husband for their maintenance, or for the maintenance of a child of the marriage. The relief was limited to £1,970 for 1999–2000. For 2000–01, relief (limited to £2,000) is only available where at least one of the parties was over 65 at 5 April 2000. From 2001–02, the relief is limited as shown in the table in 6.8.3 above.

6.9 Civil partners (FA 2005 S103)

Civil partners in accordance with the Civil Partnership Act 2004 (CPA) will be treated as married couples for tax purposes. The new rules will take effect from 5 December 2005, when CPA commences.

CPA will allow single-sex partners the opportunity of obtaining the new legal status of civil partners. This will entitle them to similar tax treatment to married couples. This will be particularly useful regarding freedom from capital gains tax and inheritance tax on asset transfers between two CPA partners.

Chapter 7

INCOME FROM LAND AND PROPERTY

The amount of income that you derive during the tax year from letting property such as a house, flat, factory or shop, less the deductions you may claim represent your net income from letting property and must be shown separately on your tax return. You must return your gross property income including certain lease premiums and also give full particulars of your expenses. If up to 5 April 1995 the income was derived from furnished lettings then the assessment was under Schedule D Case VI (15.1); otherwise it was generally under Schedule A. From that date, Case VI on furnished lettings only continues for corporation tax purposes.

From 6 April 1995, all property income is pooled and was assessed under Schedule A (7.1). This includes income from furnished lettings. The rules only relate to income tax and not corporation tax. However, broadly similar rules applying to corporation tax operate from 1 April 1998. (FA 1998 Ss38–41 & Sch 5). From 6 April 2005, the legislation has been consolidated into ITTOIA (2.10.1), mainly in Ss260–364. At the same time the classification as Schedule A income has been dropped (2.10).

7.1 The current property income tax system (TA Ss15 & 21–43G)

New, simplified rules apply to the taxation of the property income of individuals, partnerships, trusts and non-resident companies from 6 April 1995. However, the old rules continued to apply for companies until 1 April 1998. Thus, if you have appropriate property income, your assessments for 1995–96 and subsequent years will be covered by the new system (the references to Schedules A and D only apply before 2005–06). Points to note include the following:

(1) All of your property income normally is put into a 'pool' and taxed together under Schedule A, but on trading principles. Thus expenses are deducted on this basis (11.3), although the net is treated as investment rather than trading income. In general, an accruals basis is to be used for income and expenditure.
(2) Your furnished lettings income is no longer taxed under Schedule D Case VI, but pooled with the other Schedule A income.
(3) Any property losses which you are carrying forward from 1994–95 are offsettable against the combined profits of your property business for 1995–96. Similarly, any unused losses are carried forward to set off against future property business profits.
(4) The capital allowance rules (11.9) broadly continue for Schedule A purposes. However, from 6 April 1997 (1 April for companies), a 'pooling' basis applies (11.9.2). So far as furnished lettings are concerned, you are still able to make the 10 per cent wear and tear claim based on rents (7.5).

(5) Relief for interest payable in respect of a Schedule A business is obtained by deducting it like any other expense. Thus any excess of interest over your other net property income produces a loss. Furthermore, the old requirement is removed under which the property must be let or available for letting for at least 26 weeks in a year (4.6).
(6) Remember that under normal trading principles, any proportion of expenses attributable to personal use is not deductible but accrued expenses often would be.
(7) Overseas property income remains (before 2005–06) taxable under Schedule D Case V. However, the rules have been aligned more closely with the system for UK property income. For example, interest payable on a loan to purchase the property is deductible.
(8) Similar rules operate for companies from 1 April 1998. These effectively preserve the flexibility of reliefs currently available for corporate interest and management expenses (13.9).

7.2 Income from land and property (TA 1988 S15)

Annual profits or gains (that is, after deducting expenses) follow the previous Schedule A rules in respect of:

(1) Rents under leases of land (and buildings) in the UK.
(2) Income after 5 April 1995 from furnished lettings.
(3) Rent-charges, ground annual and feu duties, and any other annual payments arising out of land in the UK. This includes some way leaves and easements such as for cables and telephone lines (FA 1997 S60), etc.
(4) Other receipts arising to a person from the ownership of land in the UK or from rights or interests in such land.

7.2.1 Exceptions

(1) Yearly interest.
(2) Income including royalties from mines, quarries, etc. which were charged under Schedule D.
(3) Income from various other sources charged previously under Schedule D such as ironworks, gasworks, canals, docks, fishing rights, railways, bridges, etc.
(4) Income up to 5 April 1995 (and up to 31 March 1998 for corporation tax) from furnished lettings (that is, tenant entitled to use of furniture). This was assessed under Schedule D Case VI unless you elected within two years of the end of the relevant tax year that it should be taxed under Schedule A.

7.2.2 Expenses allowed against land and property income (TA 1988 Ss25–33)

(1) Repairs and maintenance including redecorating the premises during the lease.
(2) Insurance premiums against fire and water damage, etc. to the building.

(3) Management costs including costs of rent collection, salaries, advertising for new tenants, legal and accountancy charges, etc. If your wife takes part in the management, consider paying her a salary (1.2.9).
(4) Services that you are obliged to provide for the tenants but for which you get no specific payment.
(5) Any payments that you make for general, business and water rates, and council tax, but not in general community charge.
(6) Any payments that you make for any rent, rent-charge, ground annual, feu duty or other periodical payment in respect of the land.
(7) The cost of lighting any common parts of office blocks or flats and otherwise maintaining them.
(8) The upkeep of gardens of flats, etc. where the lease requires you to be responsible for this expense.
(9) Architects' and surveyors' fees in connection with maintenance but not improvements.
(10) Capital allowances (11.9) on any plant or machinery that you might use in the upkeep of your property (unless a dwelling-house).
(11) The upkeep of any private roads, drains and ditches, etc. on your land if part or all of the property is let and the expenditure is for the benefit of your tenants.
(12) In the case of an industrial building which is used by the tenant for industrial purposes (for example, manufacturing) you may get capital allowances on the building (11.11). This also applies to some hotels (11.15).
(13) When you live in a part of the premises you let to others you may not deduct the full amount of your expenditure from your income. Instead you must subtract from your expenditure some reasonable proportion because the premises were not wholly used to produce the income. You may calculate this proportion as being, for example:

$$\frac{\text{Area (or rooms) used by you}}{\text{Total area (or rooms)}} \times \text{Expenses}$$

(14) From 6 April 2004, capital expenditure on loft and cavity wall insulation in rented accommodation up to £1,500.

7.2.3 Special rules concerning expenses – old rules relating to years up to 1994–95 for income tax and to 31 March 1998 for corporation tax

Your expenditure in respect of maintenance and repairs is deductible if incurred by reason of dilapidation attributable to a period falling within the duration of the lease. All other expenditure must be incurred in respect of that period. If, however, you bought the premises subject to a lease, you normally get no relief for your expenses relating to the period prior to the purchase.

Special rules relate to a 'lease at full rent' which is one that produces sufficient income for you to pay for the maintenance, repairs, insurance and management of the premises in accordance with the undertakings in the lease. In that case you can charge expenses relating to a period after your purchase when the premises were empty immediately before they were let at full rent. You can also deduct expenses relating to a previous full rent letting that you made of the premises or a void period between lettings.

If you have a number of 'leases at full rent' that are not 'tenant's repairing leases', then you can set off expenses attributable to one such lease against the rents derived from another (a tenant's repairing lease is one where the lessee (tenant) is under an obligation to maintain the premises).

7.3 Losses

If in any tax year before 1995–96 your expenses for any property exceeded the rent and you did not get relief as above then the resultant loss was carried forward to be set off against future Schedule A income from the same property, or against income from other properties (provided let on 'leases at full rent' that were not 'tenant's repairing leases' (see above)). A loss from a property cannot be set off against income derived from a trade or business carried on.

From 6 April 1995 (7.1), any property losses carried forward are offsetable against your combined property business profits for 1995–96. Unused losses are available to carry forward to be relieved against future property business profits.

7.4 Assessment of land and property income (TA 1988 S22 & TMA S59A)

Tax under this Schedule is charged by reference to the income to which you become entitled in the tax year. This applies whether or not you actually receive the rents, etc. unless:

(1) you did not receive an amount to which you were entitled because of the default of the person who owed you the money and you took reasonable steps to enforce payment; or
(2) you actually waived payment of the rent, etc. (without receiving any other benefit) for the purpose of avoiding hardship.

Thus your 2005–06 assessment is based on the rents, etc. to which you are entitled in the year to 5 April 2006 less your allowable deductions for that year.

Prior to 1996–97, Schedule A income tax was payable on 1 January in the tax year. Thus your 1994–95 demand was payable on 1 January 1995. Since your income less expenses for that year would not have been known until after 5 April 1995 you were first assessed on the basis of the previous year (that is, 1993–94). When your rents, etc. and expenses were computed for the year 1994–95 and agreed with the Revenue, the assessment was adjusted and the required payment or refund made.

For 1996–97 and subsequent years of assessment, the new self-assessment rules apply. Payments on account of your total liability are required on 31 January in the year of assessment and the following 31 July, with any balance being due on the next 31 January. However, for 1996–97 itself, only one payment on account was normally required, on 31 January 1997. Each payment on account is generally based on half of the assessment for the previous year.

Income assessable (prior to 2005–06) under Schedule A is normally treated as investment income and prior to 6 April 1984 was subjected to the 15 per cent additional rate (5.6), if your investment income was sufficiently high. Schedule A income is not treated as 'savings income' and is thus not taxed at the 20 per cent rate. For 2005–06 the 10, 22 and 40 per cent rates apply to individuals (40 per cent for trusts).

7.4.1 Example: Assessment of property income

Mr A bought an old house some years ago and divided it into three flats each of which he lets unfurnished. Taking the rents and expenses shown in the example, assuming that Mr A has already used his personal reliefs and starting rate tax band and that he is not liable for the higher rate of tax, his assessments are as follows:

Year ended 5 April:	**2005**		**2006**	
	£	**£**	**£**	**£**
Rents receivable		6,000		6,500
Less:				
Expenses				
Business rates	900		1,000	
Water rates	120		130	
Garden upkeep	520		520	
Maintenance, light and heat of hall and stairs	330		350	
Exterior repairs and decorating	400		200	
Fire insurance of structure of building	220		220	
Accountancy	200		220	
Agents' rent collection charges	450		450	
		3,140		3,090
Net Schedule A assessments		2,860		3,410
Income tax payable		**2004–05**		**2005–06**
	(22%)	629.20	(22%)	750.20

Note: Income tax will be payable for 2005–06 (together with the tax on any other income) as follows:

Provisionally on 2004–05 basis		
31 January 2006 ½ × £629.20	314.60	
31 July 2006 ½ × £629.20	314.60	
		629.20
Balance on 31 January 2007		121.00
Total income tax liability for 2005–06		750.20

7.5 Furnished lettings

Under the old rules, unless you elected for Schedule A to apply (7.2), your income from furnished lettings was normally taxed under Schedule D Case VI on the actual income less expenditure for the tax year. However, from 6 April 1995, (1 April 1998 for companies) furnished lettings income was automatically assessed under Schedule A (7.1). From 2005–06, the Schedule A classification has been removed.

As well as expenses normally allowable for land and property purposes (7.2.2), you are also entitled to a deduction to cover depreciation on furniture and furnishings. This may be given to you as a deduction of the entire replacement cost from year to year.

More likely you will obtain a yearly deduction of 10 per cent of your rents less any rates, etc. and service costs which you pay. Thus, if your annual rents are £1,000 and you pay £200 in council tax, you can deduct £80 yearly to cover the depreciation and replacement of furniture and furnishings.

If, under the terms of a letting, you provide services such as laundry, meals, domestic help, etc. then you can charge the cost of these items against your taxable profit. If you provide such services, then your lettings income might possibly be treated as earned income. However, case law has made this less likely. Otherwise it would be unearned income, subject to special rules for holiday lettings (7.7).

As from 6 April 1992, the existing practice of including within the furnished lettings rules payments under licences was confirmed (F2A 1992 S58).

7.6 'Rent a room' (F2A 1992 Sch 10)

If you let a room in your house, valuable relief may be available to you for 1992–93 and subsequent years. The relief applies if you are an owner occupier, or a tenant and let furnished accommodation in your only or main home.

The relief covers gross rents of up to £4,250 for 1997–98 and subsequently (previously £3,250). If the gross rent is higher, you have the option of paying tax on the excess over £4,250, without any relief for expenses, or according to the normal furnished lettings rules (7.5). (Where any others share the rents, your exemption is limited to £2,125.)

For example, suppose that you let a room in your house and your gross rent for 2005–06 is £5,250, with allowable expenses of £1,250. If you are a basic rate tax payer, on the conventional basis, your income tax (ignoring any other allowances) is (£5,250 – £1,250) × 22% = £880. However, if you elect for the 'alternative basis', you only pay (£5,250 – £4,250) × 22% = £220.

You will need to elect for the 'alternative' basis to apply within one year of the end of the tax year to which it applies. After that, it remains in force until you withdraw it. Note that whilst the election is in force, no capital allowances are available, losses from previous years are carried forward to subsequent ones and balancing charges are added to your gross rental income.

7.7 Holiday lettings (TA 1988 Ss503–504)

Furnished holiday letting businesses which satisfy certain requirements qualify for reliefs only normally available where the activity is a trade for tax purposes. The accommodation must be available for holiday letting for at least 140 days during the year and actually let for at least 70 days (no let to normally exceed 31 days).

The income is treated as earned income; also capital gains tax roll-over relief (20.25) and retirement relief (20.29) apply. In general, although the income is normally assessed under Schedule A the letting activity is treated as a trade for the purposes of many tax provisions. These include payments by instalments, loss relief (11.22), capital allowances (11.8), personal pension contracts, etc.

The rules have changed since 6 April 1995, regarding holiday lettings income. Previously Schedule D Case VI applied (instead of Schedule A).

7.8 The taxation of lease premiums (TA 1988 Ss34–39 & Sch 2)

If you obtain a premium in connection with the granting of a lease of not more than 50 years' duration on any property that you own, then you will be assessed to income tax on part of such premium. The amount to be included in your income tax assessment is the premium, reduced by $\frac{1}{50}$ of its amount for each complete period of 12 months (other than the first) comprised in the duration of the lease. The balance of the premium which is not so charged normally attracts capital gains tax (20.1).

If you sell a lease rather than grant one you will normally be assessed to capital gains tax on any profit unless you are a dealer (7.10) or it is an 'artificial transaction' (7.11).

The following are also included with your taxable premiums:

(1) The value of any work that the tenant agreed to carry out to your premises to the extent that the present value of your property is enhanced.

(2) Any premiums paid to you in instalments. You include the aggregate of the instalments in the year that you grant the lease; but you can claim on grounds of hardship to pay the tax by instalments over a period not exceeding eight years, or ending with your last premium instalment if earlier.

(3) If you are granted a lease at a premium (£P) that is less than its market value (£M) and you then assign the lease at a profit, the amount of your profit is charged to income tax to the extent that it does not exceed (£M – £P).

7.8.1 **Reverse premiums** (FA 1999 S54 & Sch 6)

A reverse premium is a payment made by a landlord to induce you to take out a lease. The tax treatment previously has been disputed, but from 9 March 1999, reverse premiums are taxable as income. If you will be carrying on a trade or profession from the premises, your reverse premium will be taxed as part of your business profits. Otherwise, it will be taxed as investment income.

7.9 Woodlands

Prior to 6 April 1988, you were assessed to income tax under Schedule B in respect of woodlands if you occupied them with a view to obtaining a profit and managed them on a commercial basis. Subject to certain transitional provisions, income from woodlands has now been removed from the tax regime. Special treatment for inheritance tax (22.22) and capital gains tax (20.8.1) still applies.

7.10 Dealing in property

Normally when you sell a property which you acquired as an investment you will be liable to capital gains tax on any profit that you make (20.1). The maximum tax rate would then be 40 per cent.

If, however, you carry out a number of purchases and sales of land and/ or buildings you are likely to be treated as dealing in property and you will be taxed accordingly. This means that your profits must be computed as if you were conducting a trade (11.1) and you will be taxed on your adjusted profits as trading income. This income will be treated as being earned and you will be charged to income tax at the lower, basic and higher rate where applicable.

7.11 Artificial transactions in land

This is the heading of Section 776 of the 1988 Taxes Act. It may operate wherever you make a capital profit from selling land (or buildings) that you had purchased with a view to selling later at a profit. The Section also applies to sales of land indirectly held as trading stock and the sale of land (and buildings) that had been developed with the intention of selling them at a profit. However, it does not apply to trading profits from land already taxed as income.

Any capital profit arising in the above circumstances can be treated by the Revenue as being income on which you will be liable to pay income tax instead of capital gains tax. However, this has become less significant now that the top income tax and capital gains tax rates are both 40 per cent.

This Section does not apply to any purchase or sale by you of the house or flat in which you reside provided that it is your principal private residence (20.23).

If you believe that Section 776 might apply to any property sale that you have made or are planning, then you can apply for a clearance to the Inspector of Taxes to whom you submit your annual tax return. You should give the Inspector full written particulars of how the gain has arisen or how it will arise. He must then let you know within 30 days whether or not he is satisfied that your gain is outside the ambit of Section 776. If the Inspector does give you a clearance then provided your transaction proceeds exactly as you have described it to him, you will not be taxed under Section 776 in respect of your gain.

7.12 Agricultural land etc. (TA 1988 S33)

Basically farmers are chargeable to income tax in the same way as persons who carry on a trade or business (11.1). Certain special rules apply, however (15.6).

If you own any sand or gravel quarries, any rents and royalties to which you are entitled will be payable to you under the deduction at the source of basic rate income tax at 22 per cent. See also aggregates levy (7.15).

7.13 Land sold and leased back (TA 1988 S780)

Special provisions may apply when you sell a lease with less than 50 years to run and take a fresh lease on the same premises. If you had been obtaining tax relief for your rent payments under the old lease and your new lease is for a term of less than 15 years, you will be charged to income tax on a proportion of the capital sum that you receive for your old lease.

The proportion is given by the formula $\frac{16-n}{15}$ where n is the term in years of your new lease. Thus if you have, say, a 40-year lease, which you sell for £15,000 and take back a ten-year lease you will be charged to income tax on

$$£15{,}000 \times \frac{16-10}{15} = £6{,}000.$$

The balance of £15,000 – £6,000 = £9,000 will be treated as capital on which you may be liable to pay capital gains tax.

The income tax charge is raised under Schedule D Case VI unless the premises are used in your business, in which case your taxable trading profits are correspondingly increased.

The above rules are applicable to trusts and partnerships. They also apply to companies in which case the corporation tax charge (13.2, 13.2.1) may be adjusted.

There are certain rules for treating leases for longer periods than 15 years as being periods shorter than that time. This applies if you sell a lease and take a new one under which the rent for the earlier years of the lease is greater than that for the later years. For example, suppose you sell a 45-year lease for £30,000 and take back one for 20 years at £3,000 annual rent for the first ten years and £1,000 per annum for the remainder. Your new lease will then be treated as being for ten years and you will be charged to income tax on

$$\pounds 30{,}000 \times \frac{16 - 10}{15} = \pounds 12{,}000$$

7.14 Landfill tax (FA 1996 Ss39–71 & Sch 4 & FA 2003 S187)

A tax on waste disposals in and on landfill sites in the UK was introduced on 1 October 1996. Details are included in the 1996 Finance Act and these are supplemented by legislation in the summer of 1996 and subsequently. (New rules tax controllers of sites even if they are not the operators.)

There are two rates of tax. Inactive waste (which does not decay, pollute groundwater or contaminate land) is taxed at £2 per tonne, whilst £7 per tonne applied otherwise up to 31 March 1999. Subsequently, the higher rate became £10 per tonne, with £1 additions each year, for at least five years. Thus the rate from 1 April 2000 is £11 per tonne, becoming £12 per tonne from 1 April 2001, £13 per tonne from 1 April 2002 and £14 per tonne from 1 April 2003. From 1 April 2004, the rate is £15 per tonne and from 1 April 2005 it is £18 per tonne. HM Customs and Excise administer landfill tax and the operators of relevant sites should have notified their liability to be registered by 31 August 1996.

7.15 Aggregates levy (FA2001 Ss16–49 & Schs 4–10)

A new aggregates levy came into effect on 1 April 2002 which is run by Customs and Excise. There is a flat rate of £1.6 per tonne, applying to sand, gravel or crushed rock extracted in the UK (including its territorial waters) or imported. The aggregate becomes liable when it is commercially exploited. Exclusions include metal, coal, gemstones and industrial minerals.

Chapter 8

INCOME FROM DIVIDENDS AND INTEREST

8.0 Introduction

This chapter broadly covers savings income and dividends, including certain tax efficient investments. The legislation has been contained in ICTA and subsequent Finance Acts. However, from 6 April 2005, this broadly has been consolidated into ITTOIA, where the relevant areas are Ss365–573 and Parts 5–7 of Sch 2. Note that for years from 2005–06 onwards, references to schedules no longer apply although the basic rules remain.

8.1 How dividends are taxed (TA 1988 Ss1A & 20)

Any dividend paid to you by a United Kingdom company does not have tax deducted. The amount paid to you carries with it a tax credit of currently $\frac{1}{9}$ (13.6). Before 6 April 1999, the tax credit was $\frac{20}{80}$ and prior to 6 April 1993, it was $\frac{25}{75}$. These amounts respectively correspond to 10, 20 and 25 per cent of the grossed up dividends. Important changes apply from 6 April 1999 (8.1.7). Special rules may apply to any shareholders who live abroad (19.1.5).

Before 6 April 1999, United Kingdom companies in turn paid to the Revenue advance corporation tax (ACT) of normally $\frac{1}{4}$ of the dividends paid (13.6). From that date, ACT has been abolished. The following are examples of payments by companies to their shareholders (distributions) that are treated in this way:

(1) Dividends on ordinary shares.
(2) Dividends on shares with special rights such as preference and deferred shares.
(3) Capital distributions made in cash, such as dividends, paid out of the capital profits of a company.
(4) Scrip dividend options (8.9).

The gross amounts of your dividends including tax credits (and taxed interest) receivable in the tax year are included with your investment income for total income purposes (5.2).

8.1.1 Special rules after 5 April 1993

If you received a dividend of £60, instead of reclaiming £20 (£60 × $\frac{25}{75}$) before 6 April 1993, you could only reclaim £15 (£60 × $\frac{20}{80}$). If your top rate was 20 per cent, then so far as your dividends fell within this, there was no more tax to pay or be reclaimed. Previously your 25 per cent tax credit would have exceeded the 20 per cent lower rate and a repayment was available.

8.1.2 **Rules applying after 5 April 1999**

Where your dividends, taken to be the top slice of your income, fall within your starting or basic rate (22 per cent) bands, although the tax credit is only 10 per cent, you pay no more tax. To achieve this effect, the income tax rate on your dividends is taken to be 10 per cent. (Prior to 6 April 1999, dividends in your basic rate band were subjected to a 20 per cent rate.) Any dividends in the higher rate band (40 per cent) effectively bear the same tax as before. This is done by charging 32.5 per cent on the grossed dividend and offsetting the 10 per cent tax credit (8.1.7).

Charities are no longer able to reclaim dividend tax credits, but transitional relief applied up to 5 April 2004 (15.2.1). The tax credits reclaimable by pension funds are less and the position of trusts is also affected (21.5).

8.1.3 **Example: Income tax on dividends**

Mr A has a taxable income for 2005–06 of £33,000 after allowances. This comprises dividends of £9,000 together with tax credits of £1,000 and £23,000 salary.

Mr A will be liable to tax as follows for 2005–06:

	£		£
Salary	2,090	at 10%	209.00
	20,910*	at 22%	4,600.20
Dividends	9,400*	at 10%	940.00
	600	at 32.5%	195.00
			5,944.20
Less: Tax credits			1,000.00
Net tax payable			4,944.20

* Basic rate band £30,310.

8.1.4 **Dividends etc. and your return**

You must enter the amounts of your dividends in your income tax return (16.2). Previously, you were required to show, in the separate section provided, details of your dividends from each of your shareholdings with a full description of each holding, as well as the actual payments and relevant tax credits. However, from 1996–97, only the totals of dividends and tax credits should be entered.

As well as dividends, etc. from companies, you must include in your return the totals of the gross amounts of any payments due to you for taxed interest on government securities, trust income, and the income proportion of annuities, etc. All of these will have been taxed by deduction at the source before you receive them. Also include in this section any loan interest that has been taxed before you receive it and all unit trust dividends including those converted into new units instead of being paid direct to you.

8.1.5 **Income tax deduction vouchers**

Dividend vouchers show the actual dividend payment made to you together with the tax credit. Prior to 6 April 1999, the vouchers certified that advance corporation tax of an amount equal to the tax credit was to be accounted for to the Collector of Taxes. They may be sent to you even though the dividends are credited to your bank account (F2A 1992 S32).

Different certificates are provided for interest payments under deduction of income tax. These show the gross interest and the tax which is certified to have been deducted on the payment of the net interest to you. In the case of income distributions from trusts, tax deduction certificates are provided by the trustees (form R185E). All of these tax deduction certificates are accepted by the Revenue in connection with income tax repayment claims (16.7).

8.1.6 **Dividends from overseas companies** (TA S4)

Any dividends that you receive from overseas companies are normally net of both overseas tax deducted at source and United Kingdom income tax at 10 per cent. Prior to 6 April 1999, UK income tax was deducted at 20 per cent.

Before 6 April 1999, the United Kingdom income tax was sometimes at a lower rate than 20 per cent. This was because you may have been given some measure of relief from double taxation by the paying agents and collecting agents who are concerned with transmitting to you your overseas dividends. (For a fuller treatment of double tax relief see 18.6.)

You should enter on your tax return the total of the gross amounts of your overseas dividends and also show the amounts of foreign and UK tax deducted at source.

The gross amounts of your overseas dividends are included in your total income (5.2) but you may get some double tax relief in respect of the overseas taxes against your tax liability.

8.1.7 **Authorised unit trusts** (TA Ss468–468Q)

Dividends which you receive from an authorised unit trust carry a tax credit of currently ⅑th (¼ before 6 April 1999). As with other dividends, if you are a basic rate tax payer you pay no further tax. (Previously the trust paid a special corporation tax rate of 25 per cent, but from 1 April 1996, this has become 20 per cent.)

For distribution periods beginning after 31 March 1994, special interest distributions may be made. These were originally net of income tax at the basic rate (25 per cent) for which you obtained a tax credit. The tax deduction and credit from 6 April 1996 is 20 per cent. The trust obtains relief for the interest payments against its corporation tax on its interest income.

The tax treatment of foreign investors in authorised unit trusts has improved. Payments to them from certain underlying income, such as from Eurobonds, is now free of UK tax. Otherwise relief is often availa-ble under the interest article of the relevant UK tax treaty.

8.1.8 **Tax credits on dividends after 5 April 1999** (TA S231 & F2A 1997 S30)

As seen, radical reforms have taken place regarding the repayment of tax credits on dividends. This was stopped from 2 July 1997 regarding dividends on shares held by pension funds, including occupational (14.3) and personal pension (14.6) schemes.

Regarding individuals (8.1), nothing changed until 5 April 1999. After that date, if you have no tax liability, you are no longer able to reclaim tax credits on dividends. From the same date, ACT was abolished.

If you pay income tax, the intention is that the change results in your paying no more tax. From 6 April 1999, the tax credit has been halved to 10 per cent. If you are a lower or basic rate payer, your tax on the dividend plus tax credit is 10 per cent, leaving nothing to pay after setting off the 10 per cent tax credit. As a higher rate payer, you are taxed at 32.5 per cent on your gross dividends, leaving 22.5 per cent to pay net of the tax credit.

From 6 April 2004, a special tax rate of 32.5 per cent (previously 25 per cent) applies to the dividend income of those trusts which are at present liable to the 40 per cent rate (21.2.1). This particularly applies to discretionary and accumulation and maintenance trusts.

8.2 Interest paid on government securities etc. (TA 1988 Ss17 & 44–52, FA 1996 Ss73 & 79 & Schs 6 & 7 & F2A 1997, S37)

From 6 April 1998, interest on 'gilts' is normally paid gross, subject to the right to elect for payment less tax. Normally, Schedule D Case III applies (up to 2004–05).

Prior to 1996–97, the normal basis of charge to income tax was by deduction at source under Schedule C. This applied to interest payable on certain 'gilt edged securities' of the United Kingdom and overseas governments where the interest was paid here. However, from 1996–97, Schedule C has been abolished. (For companies, this applies for accounting periods ending after 31 March 1996.) Instead, Schedule D Case III (up to 2004–05) is generally applicable (8.4). From 6 April 1996 normally income tax was deducted at the lower rate (20 per cent). Previously, basic rate income tax was deducted.

The tax was assessed on the Bank of England or other paying authority concerned who deducted it from the interest paid to you resulting in your receiving only the net amount. The gross amounts, however, must be entered in your income tax return. (No tax deduction was required where paying agents paid foreign dividends into recognised clearing systems.)

Certain UK government securities held for you on the National Savings Stock Register or Trustee Savings Bank Register carried gross interest without any tax deduction. Interest was also paid gross on 3½ per cent War Loan and on holdings of UK government securities which produce less than £2.50 gross interest for you half-yearly. Income tax was then assessed under Case III of Schedule D (8.4).

Provided that a claim was made to the Revenue on behalf of the individual concerned, the interest on certain specified United Kingdom government securities was paid gross to any owner who is not ordinarily resident in this country (17.3.1). However, from 6 April 1998, interest on 'gilts' is normally paid gross in any event.

8.3 Bond washing – accrued income (TA 1988 Ss710–728)

(1) Rules were introduced to prevent tax saving by selling *securities* with accrued interest and thereby receiving extra capital instead of income. Previously, this would have at most only borne capital gains tax.
(2) The accrued income scheme covers transfers after 27 February 1986. In addition, anti-avoidance rules cover the previous year. A special new regime regarding companies was included in the 1996 Finance Act, mainly affecting corporation tax for accounting periods ending after 31 March 1996 (13.27).
(3) *Securities* excludes shares in a company but covers loan stocks, etc. whether issued by the UK or other governments or companies. Thus 'Gilts' are included and 'Corporate Bonds' (20.19). National Savings Certificates and War Savings Certificates are excluded, as are certain securities redeemable at a premium. Certificates of Deposit are also excluded but profits on disposal are assessable under Case VI (15.1).
(4) If you transfer *securities* with accrued interest, so that the purchaser receives the next interest payment, you are taxed under Schedule D, Case VI (15.1) on a portion of that interest. The proportion is A/B. 'B' is the total days in the period for which the interest is paid and 'A' is the part of the period during which you held the *securities*. When the purchaser receives his first interest payment, his taxable amount is reduced by the proportion A/B.
(5) If you transfer *securities* but receive the next interest payment, your taxable amount is reduced by the proportion (B – A)/B. The purchaser is taxed on the same proportion, which actually corresponds to his ownership.
(6) The above rules do not apply if you trade in securities, nor if you are neither UK resident nor ordinarily resident (17.3.1). You are also excluded if the nominal value of your securities does not exceed £5,000 at any time in the year of assessment or previous year. A similar rule applies to the estates of deceased persons and trusts for the disabled.
(7) If you sell foreign securities but are not permitted to have the proceeds remitted to you, your tax charge is delayed until they can be sent.
(8) Transactions taxed under these rules are normally excluded from other anti-avoidance provisions.

(9) Special rules apply to the issue of securities in tranches after 18 March 1991. Accrued interest included in the issue price qualifies for relief and tax relief for the interest deemed to be paid by the issuer is restricted to the amount taxable in the hands of the subscriber.

(10) The accrued income scheme no longer normally applies to transfers under sale and repurchase agreements (FA 1995 S77 & FA 1997 S76).

(11) For deaths after 5 April 1996, the accrued income scheme no longer applies to the transfer of a person's securities to his or her personal representatives, or normally to legatees.

8.4 Interest not taxed at source (Schedule D Case III) (TA 1988 S18)

Subject to the deduction of tax at source (8.6 and 8.7), tax is charged under Schedule D Case III for years up to 2004–05 on the following:

(1) Any interest whether receivable yearly or otherwise.
(2) Any annuity or other annual payment received without the deduction of tax.
(3) Discounts.
(4) Income from securities payable out of the public revenue unless already charged under Schedule C (8.2). From 1996–97 (accounting periods ending after 31 March 1996 for companies) all income previously assessed under Schedule C comes within Schedule D Case III.
(5) Various kinds of investment income as specifically directed.
(6) The discount portion of the proceeds of 'deep discount securities' (8.8).
(7) For years after 2004–05, the rules apply without the Schedule D Case III classification.

8.4.1 Examples of Schedule D Case III income

- Bank deposit interest generally up to 5 April 1985. (Composite rate rules then applied up to 5 April 1991 followed by tax deduction at source – 8.7.)
- Discount on treasury bills.
- National or Trustee Savings Bank interest (TA S349) apart from the £70 tax free portion from National Savings Bank Ordinary Deposits (2.6.1).
- Income from government securities in general following abolition of Schedule C (8.2).
- Gross payment of share and loan interest by a registered industrial and provident society.

8.5 Basis of charge under Schedule D Case III (TA 1988 S61 & FA 1994 S206 & Sch 20)

For years prior to 1996–97 you were normally assessed to income tax on your Case III income arising during the previous tax year. However, *an actual basis of assessment applies from 1997–98*, 1996–97 normally being based on half the income for the two years to 5 April 1997 (the transitional basis). Special rules must be followed for fresh income and sources that have come to an end (see below). No deductions are allowed in computing the assessable income.

Note that after 2004–05, the Schedule D Case III classification is dropped but the rules still apply.

A company is assessed to corporation tax on its actual Case III income for each of its accounting periods (13.6.2).

Your income is normally included when it is due to be paid to you whether or not it is actually paid. For example, if Case III interest is payable for each year ended 31 December in June and December, your assessment for 1996–97 would normally be based on the income for the year to 31 December 1996.

Your 1995–96 assessment would have been payable on 1 January 1996. However, under the new system (16.1), you pay on account on the basis of the previous year's assessment including other income. This was normally in one sum on 31 January 1997 for 1996–97, and two instalments on 31 January and 31 July 1998 for 1997–98 and correspondingly for subsequent years. Any balance is then payable on the next 31 January. (In general, your payments cover your entire income tax liability.)

8.5.1 **Special rules for fresh income** (TA 1988 S66)

If you acquire a new source of Case III income your assessments will be as follows:

(1) If your new source of income is acquired after 5 April 1994, you will be assessed on an actual basis for 1994–95 and all subsequent years.
(2) For the tax year when the income first arose, provided this was before 1994–95, you were assessed on the income actually arising in that year. The following rules also applied.
(3) Where the income first arose on 6 April in the preceding tax year your assessment for the second year was based on the income of the first tax year (subject to (5) below).
(4) Where the income first arose on any day other than 6 April in the preceding tax year your assessment for the second tax year was based on the income actually arising in that year.
(5) Your assessment for the third tax year was based on the income arising in the previous tax year (subject to (6) below).
(6) You have the right to elect that your first assessment to be made on the basis of the income for the previous tax year, should be adjusted to the actual income arising in the year of assessment. This would normally apply to the third year of assessment except in (2) above. The election should be made to your Inspector of Taxes within six years of the end of the year of assessment concerned.

(7) Where you elect for the year 1995–96 to be on actual (see above) the transitional basis for 1996–97 does not apply. Instead, 1996–97 is on actual.

8.5.2 **Special rules where source of income ceases** (TA 1988 S67 & FA 1994 Sch 20)

(1) Under the new system operating for new sources from 1994–95 and otherwise from 1998–99, cessation does not affect the assessment basis. Otherwise, the rules were as follows.
(2) Under the old system, if a source of Case III income ceased during a tax year you were assessed for that year on the actual income arising from 6 April in that tax year until the closure or disposal of the source.
(3) Your assessment under Schedule D Case III for the tax year preceding that in which the source ceased was adjusted if the actual income for that year was greater than the assessment already made.
(4) Any adjustment required for the preceding year (see (2)) was separately assessed on you.
(5) Strictly speaking the cessation rules should be applied to each source but in practice the Revenue did not apply them to the closure of one bank deposit account if you had others that continued.

8.6 Building society interest (TA 1988 Ss477A–482)

Building society interest is normally paid to you less the deduction of 20 per cent income tax at source (25 per cent prior to 1996–97). The system is similar to that which applies for bank interest (8.7). If your income is sufficiently low (8.7) you can request that the interest is paid to you gross.

There was a composite rate arrangement for building societies and banks (8.7) which was abolished as from 6 April 1991. Basic rate income tax was then deducted from the interest until 5 April 1996, subject to a self-certification arrangement, for those not liable to tax (8.7). From 6 April 1996, income tax is deducted from the interest at 20 per cent and unless you are a higher rate (40 per cent) tax payer, you pay no further tax.

As an exception, certain certificates of deposit for at least £50,000 issued by building societies after 5 April 1983 carry gross interest. Interest payable on 'qualifying time deposits' (broadly time deposits for at least £50,000 and for less than a year) is paid gross. Building societies are able to pay interest gross to non-resident individuals and quoted Eurobond holders; also to charities and registered Friendly Societies.

In 1991, rules were introduced to deal with permanent interest bearing shares (PIBS). You are taxed as if they are 'debt' rather than 'equity'. Thus income tax is deducted from your interest. No capital gains tax arises but the bond washing and accrued income scheme (8.3) apply.

8.7 Bank interest (TA 1988 Ss479–485)

From 6 April 1991, bank deposit interest is normally paid subject to the deduction of income tax at source. From 6 April 1996, tax is deducted at 20 per cent (previously 25 per cent) and you pay no more tax on the interest unless your top rate reaches 40 per cent. In contrast to the previous composite rate scheme (next page), where appropriate, you are able to reclaim the tax. If your income is sufficiently large, higher rate tax will apply, any assessments being on an actual basis.

There are arrangements under which if you are not liable to tax you may receive the interest gross. You need to complete a certificate enabling each financial institution to pay you gross. You must certify that to the best of your knowledge, you do not expect to be liable to tax and the information which you have given in the form is correct. If you knowingly make a false declaration, you may be subject to penalties. This also applies where you deliberately fail to inform your bank or building society that you have become liable to tax.

Until 5 April 1991, the same composite rate as for building societies applied to interest paid by banks and certain other financial institutions. Foreign currency deposits and local authority deposits were also within the scheme. Individuals receiving interest were treated as having suffered basic rate tax, giving rise to a notional tax credit as with building society interest (above).

If you are not ordinarily resident in the UK (17.3.1), you can be excluded from the tax deduction arrangements, so that deposit interest is paid to you gross. However, you need to supply the bank, etc. with a declaration regarding your residence status and you must tell them if this changes. Note also that under Extra Statutory Concession B13, if you are not resident in the UK and receive bank interest, etc. without the deduction of income tax, in certain circumstances, the Inland Revenue will take no steps to pursue your liability to income tax.

Normally excluded from the tax deduction rules are debentures, loans by a deposit taker in the course of business, certain quoted loan stocks, also 'qualifying certificates of deposit' and 'qualifying time deposits', both of which needed to exceed £50,000 when issued and had a life of at least seven days. The income on such deposits is normally payable gross, even if now in 'paperless' form. Lloyd's premium trust funds and solicitors' and estate agents' undesignated client accounts were also excluded.

8.8 Deep discount and deep gain securities (TA 1988 Sch 4 & FA 1996 S102)

Special rules apply to deep discount securities issued after 13 March 1984. These are securities issued at a discount of more than half of one per cent for each year of their life or more than 15 per cent overall. Effectively the discount is treated as income accruing over the life of the security and when you dispose of your investment, you are normally taxed on the accruals under Schedule D Case III (before 2005–06).

Exceptionally, you are taxed on the 'income element' arising on certain securities issued after 19 March 1985 from 'coupon stripping operations'. These are where a company acquires securities and issues its own related stocks – normally deep discounted with varying maturity dates.

The company issuing the security gets *annual* relief for the accruing discount. The rules do not apply to certain securities exchanged for others issued before that date, not of the deep discount type, provided the new redemption date and price do not exceed the original ones.

For disposals after 13 March 1989, the deep discount rules apply to a wider range of investments. Certain variable deep discount securities are now included, but not index-linked bonds satisfying various conditions. These conditions include a limit on capital profits on redemption equal to the rise in the retail price index. Also, the interest rate must be reasonable and commercial; payments being at least annual. The securities must be issued for a period of at least five years.

A security issued after 31 July 1990 is not a 'deep discount security' if under the terms of issue there is more than one date when the holder can require it to be redeemed. Where securities are issued in tranches after 18 March 1991, any accrued interest included in the issue price is excluded from the price used to compute the 'deep discount' or 'deep gain'.

'Deep gain securities' issued after 13 March 1989 are treated in a similar way to deep discount securities. A 'deep gain' means that the redemption price exceeds the issue price by more than 15 per cent or half of one per cent for each completed year.

A security is not to be classed as a 'deep gain security' solely because it may be redeemed early if the issuer fails to comply with the issue terms, is taken over or is unable to pay its debts. Also, 'qualifying convertible securities' are excluded. These are, in general, bonds issued from 9 June 1989 which are convertible into ordinary shares of the issuing company and give the investor an option to 'put' the bond back to the issuer. Bonds issued from 12 November 1991 are not caught simply through the potential operation of default or event risk clauses.

From 1996–97, one set of new rules broadly covers the above ground, relating to securities which have effectively been issued at a discount and are held by private investors. (Unstripped gilts are not covered.) In general, you are assessed under income tax (not capital gains tax) on any profits on the disposal or redemption of such securities.

8.9 Scrip dividend options (TA 1988 Ss249–251)

Your taxable dividend income (8.1) includes any shares in UK resident companies (17.3.3) which you obtain by exercising an option to take a dividend in such a form. In this case, you are treated for tax purposes as if you had received the dividend in cash. If, however, the cash equivalent is substantially less than the market value of the shares, on the day when market dealings commence, the Revenue may substitute that market value for the cash value.

8.10 Personal Equity Plan (PEP) (TA 1988 Ss151 & 333 & FA 1998 S6)

A scheme to encourage the purchase of shares in UK incorporated companies commenced on 1 January 1987. It is called the Personal Equity Plan (PEP). After 5 April 1999, you can make no further investment in PEPs. However, you are allowed to keep those which you have and continue to enjoy their tax advantages, as indicated below.

(1) Provided you were aged over 18, resident and ordinarily resident in the UK (17.3.1) you were eligible.
(2) A maximum of £6,000 could be invested each tax year. In addition, you were able to invest £3,000 in a 'single-company PEP' each tax year.
(3) From 6 April 1989 there has been no minimum holding period in order to obtain tax relief.
(4) The funds must be substantially invested in the ordinary shares of public companies quoted on a UK (or EC) stock exchange or dealt in on the Unlisted Securities Market. However, a unit trust and investment trust element is allowed. The limit is £6,000 each tax year in qualifying unit and investment trusts. (This includes investment trusts investing exclusively in qualifying unit trusts.) .
(5) From 6 April 1995 the PEP scheme includes investment in specified corporate bonds and convertibles in UK non-financial quoted companies. Also included are preference shares in UK and EC quoted companies.
(6) A manager must look after your PEP investments but they will belong to you and you are able to choose which you buy.
(7) Re-investment of dividends and proceeds is allowed in excess of the limits.
(8) There is now no limit on the amount of cash that can be held tax-free in a PEP, provided the cash is eventually invested in shares, etc.
(9) You were allowed to buy shares through new issue offers and transfer all or part of your allocation into a PEP. This included privatisation issues and also issues of shares in building societies converting to plc status.
(10) Subject to the above, re-invested dividends (and accompanying tax credits) are free of income tax. (Also, tax can be recovered on dividends distributed.) Similarly re-invested capital profits are not subjected to capital gains tax.
(11) No further investment was allowed into PEPs after 5 April 1999, when the new Individual Savings Account (ISA) took over. However, you will be able to keep your existing PEPS without prejudicing your ISA investment potential. Furthermore, until 5 April 2004, but not thereafter, your PEPs reclaimed the 10 per cent tax credit on dividends received.

(12) As from 6 April 2001, the rules regarding remaining PEPs have been aligned with the ISA rules. Single company and general PEPs can now be merged. PEPs may now invest in the less restricted range available for ISAs, for example listed shares worldwide. Written withdrawal requests are no longer required. Notification by telephone, fax or Internet will suffice. Part of a PEP can now be transfered to a new fund manager, rather than just the whole PEP.

8.11 Tax exempt special savings accounts (TESSAs) (TA Ss326A–326C)

Investment into a TESSA was allowed up to 5 April 1999, subject to the following rules:

(1) You were able to invest in one TESSA only.
(2) Only individuals aged at least 18 were eligible.
(3) Your TESSA could be with a bank or a building society.
(4) The account must run for a five year period and maximum total deposits of £9,000 were allowed. Of this, up to £3,000 could be invested in the first year and no more than £1,800 in subsequent years, up to the £9,000 maximum.
(5) No capital must be withdrawn before the five year period expires, otherwise all tax advantages are lost.
(6) Income may be withdrawn subject to a notional basic rate deduction (22 per cent). Thus if there is £400 of gross income in your TESSA for the year, you will be allowed to withdraw £312.
(7) When your TESSA matured, you could open a new one in accordance with the above rules. Alternatively, if you had held your TESSA for the full five year term, you could open up a new one within 6 months, with a maximum first-year deposit of the capital from your first TESSA. However, the accumulated income was not available for reinvestment in this way.
(8) No new TESSAs can be taken out after 5 April 1999, but those taken out by that date are allowed to run their full course. When your TESSA matures, you are able to transfer the capital (not interest) into an ISA without affecting the amount you can subscribe.

8.12 Individual Savings Account (ISA) (FA 1998 Ss75–77)

The ISA scheme operates from 6 April 1999. Significant changes were made from 6 April 2001 which are reflected below.

If you are resident, ordinarily resident and now 16 or over, you are able to invest through a new ISA from 6 April 1999. The scheme also applies to Crown servants and their spouses. For each of the first seven years, you can put in up to £7,000. Up to £3,000 each year can go into cash (including National Savings) and £1,000 into life assurance of a single premium nature. The balance will normally be invested in shares. These limits are now being retained until 5 April 2010.

The government guarantees that the scheme will continue for at least ten years. Everything in your ISA is tax free. There is no capital gains tax and the 10 per cent tax credit on dividends accrues to ISAs until 5 April 2004. After that date, ISAs are not able to reclaim this tax credit. Another advantage is that you are able to make withdrawals as you please.

ISAs are administered by managers in accordance with detailed government regulations. These include for example, rules for determining the recovery of tax relief wrongly given. Furthermore a penalty might be levied instead of recovering the relief. Sometimes interest might be charged on the ISA investments rather than taxing an individual investor directly.

8.13 Venture Capital Trusts (VCTs) (TA S842AA & Schs 15B & 28B, FA 1995 Ss70–73 & Schs 14–16 & FA 2002 S109 & Sch 33)

A new form of highly tax efficient investment was introduced in 1995–96. The actual shares in VCTs must be quoted, but because they invest mainly in smaller non-quoted companies, there is a tangible degree of risk. However, the tax benefits are substantial.

(1) VCTs need Inland Revenue approval, which can be provisional for up to three years.

(2) The conditions for approval include the VCT's income being mainly from shares or securities, at least 70 per cent of its investment being in 'qualified holdings' of which at least 30 per cent is in ordinary shares. The holding in any one company may not exceed 15 per cent of the VCT's investments, nor must it retain more than 15 per cent of its income from shares and securities. At least 10 per cent of a VCT's total investment in any company must be held in ordinary non-preferential shares. In general, VCTs may not provide majority funding for companies, ignoring all fixed rate preference shares and loans.

(3) 'Qualified holdings' are in unquoted companies which exist wholly for the purpose of carrying on one or more qualifying trades. This is broadly defined as for EIS purposes (11.26). From 27 November 1996, investment in the parent of a group may qualify where non-qualifying activities do not form a major part of the group's activities as a whole.

(4) Investments of no more than £1 million in any one company count towards the 70 per cent requirement mentioned above, but not if its gross assets (or those of its group) broadly exceeded £10 million before 6 April 1998. For investments made in qualifying companies after 5 April 1998 the gross asset limit per company is increased to £15 million before the investment and £16 million afterwards. If any of the companies become quoted after holdings are acquired by a VCT, their shares are treated as qualifying for a further five years.

(5) For funds raised after 16 March 1998, various property backed activities are excluded (also for EIS purposes). These include farming, market

gardening, forestry, property development and running hotels, guest houses and nursing/residential care homes.

(6) The following tax benefits are available to you provided you are at least 18 years of age, invest no more than £200,000 from 2004–05 (previously £100,000) in VCTs each tax year (to 5 April) and hold your VCT shares for at least five years. Regarding VCT shares issued after 5 April 2000, you only need hold them for three years.

(7) You obtain 40 per cent relief on your investments in new VCT shares, which you deduct from your income tax liability. This applies for 2004–05 and 2005–06 (previously the rate was 20 per cent).

(8) Any dividends which you receive from a VCT will be free of income tax.

(9) Your disposals of VCT shares will be free of capital gains tax.

(10) If you subscribed for new VCT shares up to 5 April 2004, you were able to defer paying tax on a corresponding amount of capital gains on any asset disposals after 5 April 1995. The gains must arise during the year before and the year after the VCT shares were issued. This reinvestment relief (maximum 40 per cent) was available in addition to the 20 per cent relief (7). However, the relief will in general be recalled if you dispose of your VCT shares without replacing them by others.

(11) If a VCT makes an issue of shares, it will have had 12 months in which to invest the money in companies which qualify for the scheme. From 7 March 2001, only 80% needs to be so invested in the first 12 months with the remainder being invested in the following year.

(12) From 16 June 1999 VCTs are allowed to retain shares received in exchange for an existing holding in preparation for a stock market flotation and also shares from exercising conversion rights in qualifying shares or securities held as investments.

(13) From 17 April 2002 relief will not be lost on account of VCTs being wound up or merging.

Chapter 9

LIFE ASSURANCE

9.1 Introduction

Earlier in this book, certain tax aspects of life assurance are touched on. This chapter deals with them in more detail, together with related subjects such as permanent health insurance and purchased life annuities.

Life assurance used to enjoy a highly favoured status for tax purposes. Since 1984, this has been reduced but some benefits still remain and these are examined below.

Remember, you should not enter into life assurance arrangements merely to save tax, but for the primary benefits they confer. However, the tax benefits certainly make them more attractive.

9.2 Types of life assurance

There are three main kinds of assurance policy which you can take out on your life:

(1) Term assurance: the sum assured is only payable if the event insured occurs during the term of the policy.
(2) Whole of life: the sum assured is payable if the event insured occurs at any time in your life.
(3) Endowment: the amount insured is payable on your death within the term of the policy or otherwise at its end.

However, the tax treatment of your life assurance premiums and policy proceeds mainly depends upon whether the policies are 'qualifying' or 'non-qualifying'. (*Single premium bonds* are probably the most important type of non-qualifying policy.) But for both categories, whilst the policy is in force, the income and gains are the responsibility of the insurance company.

In recent years *critical illness policies* have become popular. These pay the benefits when the life assured suffers from and survives a serious illness from a range which typically includes heart attack, cancer and stroke.

9.3 Qualifying policies (TA 1988 Sch 15)

Qualifying policies have various tax advantages. For example, if you took out the policy before 14 March 1984, subject to the rules (3.2.6) tax relief will be available on the premiums at the rate of 12.5 per cent.

If you realise any gains under your policy, you are not liable to basic rate tax. Furthermore, the proceeds are generally completely tax-free provided you have been paying the premiums for at least ten years (9.5). In the case of an endowment policy, this period is three-quarters of the policy term, if less than ten years.

The main rules which must be satisfied for a life policy to be treated as 'qualifying' are as follows:

(1) The premiums must be payable at annual or more frequent intervals. The total term must be at least ten years although term assurance policies may be shorter.
(2) The premiums payable in any 12 month period should not exceed twice those in any other 12 month period, nor for whole life policies one-eighth of the total premiums payable in the first ten years and in the case of an endowment policy the full term.
(3) For an endowment policy, the sum assured must represent at least 75 per cent of the total premiums for its term. However, this percentage becomes 2 per cent less for each year that your age at the start of the policy is more than 55.
(4) The sum assured under a whole of life policy must be at least 75 per cent of the total premiums assuming death occurs at 75. But for a term policy on your life, expiring before your 75th birthday, there are no restrictions on the sum assured.
(5) Benefits under a policy can include participating in profits and those arising through disability.
(6) Different rules may relate to certain categories of policy, such as industrial assurance, mortgage protection and family income.
(7) A policy may contain certain options. If so, they must all be considered together at the start of the policy to make sure that the policy remains a qualifying one no matter which options are exercised.
(8) Certain policies which are connected to each other are non-qualifying. This applies where one policy has to lapse if the other one does and both would be non-qualifying if taken together. Another instance is where either policy carries benefits which are beyond normal and reasonable expectations.

9.4 Life assurance relief (TA 1988 Ss266–274)

Tax relief is only available in respect of premiums which you pay on qualifying policies which were effected before 14 March 1984. The detailed rules are described earlier (3.2.6).

Subject to these rules, you deduct the relief from your premium payments at the rate of 12.5 per cent of the eligible premiums.

Where a qualifying policy was made paid-up or surrendered during its first four years, the life assurance premium relief could be clawed-back in whole or part. These rules are now outdated, but partial surrenders from policies effected after 26 March 1974 and before 14 March 1984 may give rise to a 'claw-back'.

The rules only apply if there is a surrender of part of the policy rights later than its fourth year and this has happened at least once previously. The claw-back is limited to relief on the premiums for the year of the surrender, etc. and the insurance company will pay it over to the Revenue.

9.5 The taxation of life assurance policy proceeds (TA 1988 Ss539–552 & TCGA 1992 S210)

Whether your policy is qualifying or not, there is an assumption that tax at 20 per cent has been paid. In addition, you would pay no basic rate income tax (22 per cent) on the proceeds. However, you may be liable to the excess of higher rate tax over the 20 per cent assumed rate. This applies particularly for non-qualifying policies, as described over the page. Thus, for the tax year 2005–06 an individual could have a tax liability of 40 per cent minus 20 per cent = 20 per cent on any gain made on a UK non-qualifying policy.

The position with qualifying policies is that you will normally incur no income tax on the proceeds in any event, provided you pay premiums for a required period. This is at least ten years (or until death, if earlier). For an endowment policy, the required period is limited to three-quarters of the term of the policy.

In the normal course of events, you will have no capital gains tax liability on the proceeds of a life assurance policy (22.8.1). However, if you are not the original beneficial owner and purchased the policy for money or money's worth, the exemption does not apply.

Income tax on your policy proceeds may arise, if a *chargeable event* occurs. As mentioned earlier, no basic rate income tax is payable. However, if your income, together with the appropriate proportion of your policy gain is large enough, higher rate tax will arise (9.6) and the excess over the basic rate is payable.

Chargeable events in the case of a non-qualifying policy include its maturity or total surrender, where you assign it for money or money's worth and the death of the person whose life was assured. Also included are 'excesses' on partial surrenders. However, if you assign a policy to your husband or wife, this is not a chargeable event.

The above chargeable event rules are modified for qualifying policies. Maturity or death is only included where the policy had been made paid up within its first ten years (limited to three-quarters of its term for an endowment policy).

Similar modified rules apply for an assignment for money or money's worth, a surrender, making the policy paid up within the policy period, or an 'excess' on a partial surrender. These will only be chargeable events if they take place within that period (ten years, etc.).

If you borrow money against a non-qualifying policy at an uncommercial rate of interest, this could be treated as a chargeable event if the policy dates from after 26 March 1974.

9.5.1 Assignment of joint policies

There are special rules that apply when a policy is currently held by two or more people and the ownership is transferred to one of them, or the policy is owned by one person and is to be subsequently owned by two or more people. Typically, this can often happen on divorce.

The assignment of a part of the policy from one joint owner to the other can result in a chargeable gain arising and tax being charged on the person assigning their interest. Similarly, assignments from a sole owner into joint names of the assignor and another will be affected.

These rules will only apply to assignments that are treated as assignments for money or money's worth. Assignments that are gifts are not affected by these rules.

9.6 How the gains on chargeable events are computed and taxed (TA 1988 S541)

(1) The gain on a chargeable event must be ascertained and in general the details will be supplied by the life assurance company. It is their duty to send a certificate to the Revenue giving detailed information about your policy and the gain made (TA 1988 S552).
(2) In general, the gain is the investment profit on the policy, taking account of earlier capital benefits (other than any related to disability).
(3) Any benefit from death included in the proceeds is not treated as part of the taxable gain.
(4) No basic rate income tax, nor normally capital gains tax will be payable (9.5).
(5) 'Top slicing relief' is often available on your gain. This is described below (9.7) and effectively adjusts the tax taking account of the number of complete years for which you have held the policy. However, since no basic rate income tax is payable, you only pay the excess over the 20 per cent tax assumed already paid.
(6) A gain is regarded as the top part of your income for tax purposes and higher rate income tax is calculated, taking account of any top slicing relief. A credit of 20 per cent of the gain is allowed, resulting in you only paying tax at 20 per cent at the most.
(7) Normally it is the policyholder who will be liable for any tax on a gain. However, if a policy is held on trust, it is normally the settlor who is taxed but he can recover the tax from the trustees (TA 1988 Ss587 & 551).
(8) Life insurance companies will tell the policyholder the amount of any gain he or she has made in the previous tax year. This will help taxpayers complete their self-assessment tax return.

9.7 Top slicing relief (TA 1988 S550)

This relief is available to individuals but not companies. The rules include the following:

(1) The tax on your gain is payable for the fiscal year when it arises, but you obtain spreading relief on the basis of the number of complete years (Y) for which you have held the policy.
(2) What you do is to divide your investment gain (G) by (Y). This gives the 'slice'.
(3) Next, calculate the tax (T) payable for the year on your other income plus the 'slice' (G ÷ Y).
(4) You then calculate the tax payable on your other income by itself and deduct it from (T). This gives the total tax on the 'slice' (G ÷ Y).
(5) The total tax on the 'slice' is then divided by the 'slice' to give the tax rate on it and the special rate (20 per cent) is deducted, since this is not payable on your gain. The remaining percentage is applied to your gain (G) to give the tax payable.
(6) Certain categories of income and relief are ignored for the purposes of the above. Examples are lease premiums charged as rent (7.8.1) and compensation for loss of office (10.12) EIS relief is not ignored.

9.8 Example: Top slicing

Mr A purchased a single premium bond for £15,000 in February 2000 and realises it in March 2006 for £27,000, his gain being £12,000. His other taxable income for 2005–06 is £31,400. The tax on the gain is as follows:

	£	£
'Slice' = gain £12,000 ÷ 6 (complete years held)		2,000
Other taxable income + 'slice'		33,400
	£	£
Tax rate on 'slice'		
£31,400–£32,400 at 22%	220	
£32,400–£33,400 at 40%	400	
Total tax on 'slice'	620	
Average tax rate on 'slice'		
$\frac{620}{2000} \times 100\%$	31%	
Less: assumed rate of 20%	20%	
Rate applicable to gain	11%	
The tax payable on the gain is thus 11% × £12,000 =		1,320

9.9 Partial surrenders and excesses (TA 1988 S546)

If you make a partial surrender of a life policy (often by cashing in part of a single premium bond) it may give rise to tax, subject to the following rules:

(1) You have an allowance of 5 per cent for each 'policy year' (which starts with the day you took it out and each subsequent anniversary). This is calculated on the premium(s) (normally a single premium on a bond) and is set against your partial surrenders.
(2) Your total allowances are limited to 100 per cent of your premium(s).
(3) Unused allowances and partial surrenders are carried forward from previous years. When a partial surrender is made, you only pay tax on any excess.
(4) When your policy ends, you may have an overall gain on it which is less than the excesses which have previously been added to your income. If so, you can normally obtain higher rate relief (the excess over the 20 per cent rate) on the difference. This is called 'deficiency relief'. (However, deficiency relief will only be allowed where the previous gains formed a part of your income and not someone else's. If they did not, for example where the policy was owned be someone else previously when the earlier gains arose, then those earlier gains will not be taken into account, restricting the deficiency relief available to you).
(5) When there is an excess in a policy year, you obtain top slicing relief (9.7). As usual, you pay tax for the fiscal year in which the policy year ends based on your highest rate, less the special rate (20 per cent).
(6) For the first partial surrender or on final termination, the period which you use for the purposes of top slicing is the number of policy years since your policy started. Otherwise, you take the number of complete policy years since the last 'excess'.
(7) If any of your policies were issued before 14 March 1975, special rules apply. Broadly, withdrawals used to be fully taxed with no 5 per cent allowance each year. Such policies only obtain the benefit of this allowance for partial surrenders in policy years beginning after 13 March 1975.

9.10 Example: Partial surrenders – excesses

Mr A takes out a £20,000 single premium bond and withdraws £2,000 after each of policy years 3, 4, 5 and 7. He then surrenders the remainder for £20,000 after the end of policy year 8. His gains will be as follows:

Years	Allowances available £	Cumulative withdrawals £	Gain £
1	1,000 (5% × £20,000)	0	0
2	2,000	0	0
3	3,000	2,000	0
4	4,000	4,000	0

Years	Allowances available £	Cumulative withdrawals £	Gain £
5	5,000	6,000	1,000
6	1,000	0	0
7	2,000	2,000	0
8		*surrender*	*see below*

When the bond is surrendered after eight policy years, Mr A will have a further gain of £7,000. This is the excess of the bond proceeds (£28,000) over the original cost (£20,000), less the earlier gain (£1,000).

The earlier gain of £1,000 will be top-sliced (9.7) over five years and the £7,000 gain over eight years. The excess of higher rate tax over the 20 per cent rate will then be charged as appropriate.

9.11 Inheritance tax

There are two aspects of inheritance tax in relation to life assurance. There is the incidence of the tax on life assurance policies, particularly the proceeds on death. There is also the important use that can be made of life policies in inheritance tax planning. These subjects are dealt with in Chapter 22 (22.27).

9.12 'Key man' policies

These are policies taken out by a company on the lives of its directors or executives. The following points should be noted:

(1) The normal purpose is to protect the company against the death of the 'key man', although in certain cases where the employee and company are unconnected the proceeds can be paid out free of inheritance tax to the next of kin.
(2) Provided the 'key man' is not 'connected' with the company and a term policy is used for not more than about five years, the premiums are allowable for tax but the company will be taxed on any proceeds.
(3) Where the 'key man' has a substantial holding of the company's shares so that he is 'connected' with it, the premiums will not be deductible. Any proceeds will normally only be taxable if there is a chargeable event (9.5).
(4) This treatment (in (3) above) is also likely where the policy has one or more of the following attributes: a term of more than about five years; is for a capital purpose; has a surrender value.
(5) The treatment of the proceeds of pre-14 March 1989 policies held by companies is broadly similar to those owned by individuals.
(6) Where a company-owned policy has been effected after 13 March 1989, it is treated as non-qualifying, for the chargeable event provisions. Any chargeable gains are in general taxable on the company under Schedule D Case VI. The charge is limited where the policy is taken out to secure a company debt, and the debt was incurred to buy land or construct property that is used in the trade.

9.13 Permanent health insurance

This is intended to provide you with an income, should illness or disability prevent you from working. Contracts frequently take the form of non-qualifying life assurance policies. For taxation purposes, disability benefit payments are not regarded as rights surrendered (9.5).

If your employers pay the premiums on your policy, they would normally obtain a tax allowance on the basis that it is part of your own taxable remuneration package. Where you pay the premiums, you will not usually obtain any tax relief.

Any permanent health benefits paid to you from personally owned policies are tax free.

9.14 Purchased life annuities (TA 1988 Ss656–658)

When you buy an annuity from a life assurance company, the effect is the reverse of a life assurance policy. Instead of paying periodic premiums and getting back a lump sum, you pay a lump sum to receive an annuity periodically. This is based on your age when you purchase it. However, you may have a joint annuity together with your spouse and then the younger of your respective ages would be used.

Annuities are of great importance to pension arrangements (Chapter 14). When you retire, one or more annuities are often purchased for you by the pension fund(s) and special tax rules apply.

The normal tax rule for a purchased life annuity is that it is treated as comprising a non-taxable capital element and the rest is taxable income. The capital part is regarded as a return of the premium and is fixed from the start of the annuity. The life company will normally inform you of the split and deduct basic rate income tax from the income part of each payment.

For example, suppose you pay £10,000 for an annuity of £1,000 for the rest of your life. The company tell you that the capital part of each instalment is £400 and the income part is £600 from which they will deduct basic rate tax of £132. You will thus be paid £868. If you are a higher rate payer, you will pay further income tax of £600 × (40% – 22%) = £108.

Because of the tax-free element, annuities are useful tax-planning tools. This is particularly true as you become older, since the rates improve. But remember that you will be parting permanently with the capital. Some annuities compensate for this by guaranteeing a minimum span, even if you should die meanwhile. One point to watch is that you will not be able to save tax through the independent taxation rules by assigning an annuity to your spouse (TA1988 S685 (4A)).

9.15 Guaranteed income bonds

Guaranteed income bonds normally provide you with a fixed income for a stated period. After that, your original investment is returned to you, or you might be able to take an annuity for life. These bonds resemble annuities but have various structures.

For example, there could be a combination of a temporary immediate annuity and a deferred lifetime one. Another common arrangement is to have a series of term or endowment life policies.

Considering an annuity combination, you would receive a temporary annuity for, say, ten years. The income element would be subject to income tax, but not the capital portion of each instalment. You would then either take an annuity for life under the deferred contract or receive your original outlay.

If you choose the money-back option, you will be charged basic rate income tax (and higher rate if your income is sufficiently high) on the excess of the proceeds over the original cost of your deferred contract. This applies for contracts effected from 26 March 1974. Profits on earlier contracts are not subject to the basic rate.

9.16 European insurance policies

If you take out a policy with a European insurance company, rules will ensure that you only pay the difference between the higher rate and the basic rate of tax (currently 18 per cent) provided tax of at least 20 per cent has been paid within the company's funds. This puts European policies on a broadly similar tax basis to UK policies.

9.17 Miscellaneous aspects

(1) Policies owned by trusts

There are differences to the way any gain made from non-qualifying policies are taxed, when owned by trustees.

Normally any gains will be added to the income of the person who created the trust, and he or she will have an excess tax liability (that is, 40% – 20% = 20%) if they are a higher rate tax payer at the time. (If the policy is with a non-UK insurer there will be a liability to the 20 per cent tax rate as well. This allows for the fact that most non-UK policies grow free of all UK taxes within their funds.)

However, when the person who created the trust died before 17 March 1998 and the policy started before that date, the gain will usually be free of all taxes, provided the policy is not increased. This is known as the 'Dead Settlor Rule'.

For trusts where the person who created the trust dies on 17 March 1998 or later, the gain will usually be treated as income of the trust and taxed at 40 per cent. The trustees are liable in this situation.

If the trustees are non-resident, the gain will be treated as income of the trust and taxed on any UK beneficiaries entitled to benefit under the trust, to the extent that they receive benefit from the trust.

Normally any gain made on a policy held by trustees is taxed on the person creating the trust. In some cases, for example where the person creating the trust is dead, the gain will be taxed on the trustees.

Loans taken by trustees will be treated as part surrenders and taxed in the same way.

(2) Personal Portfolio Bonds

Personal Portfolio Bonds are usually single premium insurance bonds, often arranged with offshore life assurance companies, which allow the owner to choose the underlying investments, rather than investing in a fund available to other investors as well. Thus the fund is unique to the policyholder.

There is an annual tax charge on a 'deemed gain' of 15 per cent of the premium paid. Thus if the original investment is £100,000, the deemed gain at the end of the first year will be £15,000. If the owner is a UK taxpayer and pays tax at 40 per cent, the tax charge will be £6,000 (£15,000 × 40 per cent) assuming the investment is with a non-UK insurance company. At the end of each subsequent year the gain – and thus the tax – is increased by 15 per cent.

The object of the tax charge is to discourage UK residents from investing in these very specialised investments. These rules do not apply to other investments with insurance companies, where the investor chooses one or more funds which are available to other investors.

These rules apply to Personal Portfolio Bonds taken out before 17 March 1999.

9.18 Policies held by charities

Occasionally, life assurance policies are held by charities. With effect from 9 April 2003, a charity will usually have no tax liability on any gain made on a UK policy.

9.19 Policies effected by non-residents with UK companies

Policies effected by non-residents with UK life assurance companies benefit from the fact that there is no tax payable within the funds. On return to the UK, they are only taxed at the higher rate, with a credit equal to the basic rate of tax.

For policies taken out or enhanced from 17 March 1998, there will be a tax charge at all rates, including basic rate.

Chapter 10

INCOME FROM EMPLOYMENTS AND PAYE

10.0 Income Tax (Earnings and Pensions) Act 2003 (ITEPA)

The taxation of your income from employments had fallen mainly within TA 1988 and subsequent finance acts. However, that legislation has been consolidated into ITEPA, which takes effect from 2003–04. This aims at increased clarity and includes rules previously existing as concessions and practice.

A summary of ITEPA follows, so as to give a broad outline of its contents.

Part			Sections	Schedules
1	Overview – abbreviations etc.		1–2	1
2	Charge to tax on employment income		3–61	
3	Earnings and benefits treated as earnings		62–226	
4	Employment income –	exemptions	227–326	
5		deductions from earnings	327–385	
6		not-earnings or share related	386–416	
7		share-related income and exemptions	417–554	2–5
8	Former employees – deductions for liabilities		555–564	
9	Tax on pension income		565–654	
10	Social security income		655–681	
11	PAYE		682–712	
12	Payroll giving		713–715	
13	Supplementary, definitions, etc.		716–725	6–8

Your income from employments or from any office that you hold is normally taxed under Schedule E. From 6 April 1989, a receipts basis broadly applies (10.13). Before 6 April 2003, Schedule E was divided into *three cases* as follows (TA 1988 S19). From 6 April 2003 there is no classification into *cases*, but the rules have broadly similar effect (ITEPA Ss14–26).

10.1 Schedule E Case I

This applied if you were both resident and ordinarily resident (17.3.1) in the UK. Your income tax assessment under this case was usually based on the actual UK income during the tax year.

This case also applied to any work which you did wholly abroad (unless you worked for a non-resident employer and were yourself not UK domiciled).

Tax was due on all earnings, even when the employment was not held at the time they were received. This also applied for Cases II and III (below).

10.2 Schedule E Case II

This applied if you were either not resident in the UK or resident but not ordinarily resident here. Then you were normally assessed to tax under this case on your earnings for duties performed here.

10.3 Schedule E Case III

This applied if you were UK resident and did work wholly abroad but remitted salary here during the course of your overseas employment. The assessment was based on the actual amounts remitted to this country in the tax year (18.1) but if one of the other cases (see above) applied to the income, then Case III did not operate. This case normally only applied to non-UK domiciled people.

10.4 The distinction between Schedule D Case I or II and Schedule E

This distinction is sometimes very fine – for instance in the case where you have a number of part-time employments and do some of the work at home. If you can show that you are in fact working on your own account and are self-employed (not an employee) then you will be assessed under Schedule D which normally results in your being able to deduct more of your expenses from your taxable income than if you were assessed under Schedule E. Divers and diving instructors are normally assessable under Schedule D (TA 1988 S314). The Inland Revenue are becoming increasingly insistent that entertainers and journalists should be assessed under Schedule E. When this happens, agents' fees will still be allowable as expenses (ITEPA S352), subject to a cumulative limit of 17.5 per cent of the taxable earnings.

10.5 Employment outside the UK

If your UK employment involves you in work abroad this is normally treated as being derived from your employment in this country and is included in your taxable income. However, in respect of any work that you do abroad, special rules apply which may result in your paying less tax (18.3).

10.6 Amounts included in your income

Any amount that you derive from your office or employment is normally included in your taxable income. This applies to the value of any payments in kind as well as cash.

10.6.1 **Typical items**

- Normal salary or wage.
- Overtime pay.
- Salary in lieu of notice (often tax free – see 10.12).
- Holiday pay.
- Sick pay from your employer, including statutory sick pay.
- Sickness insurance benefits paid to you (all sickness benefits are taxable immediately except to the extent that you have paid for these yourself).
- The value of luncheon vouchers in excess of 15 pence per day.
- Cost-of-living allowance.
- Christmas or other gifts in cash excluding personal gifts such as wedding presents.
- Annual or occasional bonus.
- Commission.
- Director's fees.
- Director's other remuneration.
- Remuneration for any part-time employment.
- Salary paid in advance.
- Payment for entering into a contract of employment.
- Tips from employer or from customers or clients of employer.
- Settlement by employer of debts incurred by employee.
- Payment by employer of employee's National Insurance contributions.
- Value of goods supplied free of cost to employee by employer.
- Value of shares or other assets received from employer for no charge, or amount by which their market value exceeds any payment made for them.
- Fringe benefits (see below).
- Unapproved pension scheme contributions.
- Travelling allowances in excess of expenditure incurred for business use (10.6.4).
- Share options (10.9.2).
- Job release allowances capable of beginning earlier than a year before pensionable age.
- Maternity pay.
- Statutory paternity and adoption pay, from April 2003 (FA 2002 S35).
- Payments under *restrictive covenants* including (after 9 June 1988) where separate from the contract of employment.
- Various non-cash benefits such as tradable assets and readily convertible assets (ITEPA S19).

10.6.2 **Fringe benefits** (ITEPA Ss62–289 & Schs 2–5)

This is a wide term used to describe any tangible benefit which you obtain from your employment that is not actually included in your salary cheque. Fringe benefits are taxable according to the rules outlined below.

If you are an employee earning less than £8,500 each year, including the value of any benefits, then the taxation of your fringe benefits is on a comparatively favourable basis. If, however, you earn over £8,500 or are a director, then you are normally taxed more strictly on the actual value of the benefits obtained. If you fall into this latter class then your employers must submit to the Revenue a form P11D for you every year. This form covers your expenses and benefits (10.7).

You are not caught by the rules as being a *director*, if you own no more than 5 per cent of the company's shares and work full time for it. Any shares owned by relatives and associates count towards your 5 per cent. (In the case of charities, etc. you do not need to work full time.) If you work for several companies which are connected, your earnings including benefits must be taken together for the purposes of the rules.

The taxation of certain fringe benefits is summarised in the following table according to whether or not you are a P11D employee (that is, a director or earning over £8,500).

10.6.3 **Fringe benefits – taxation 2005–06**

	Details	Non-P11D employee	P11D employee or director
(1)	Free private use of motor car supplied by your employers. Car mileage allowance	Tax free (provided some business use is made)	Taxable (10.6.5)
(2)	Provision of motor van	Tax free (provided some business use)	Taxable (10.6.7)
(3)	Company house occupied rent free	Taxed on annual value of benefit (that is, open market rental and expenses paid) unless you need to occupy house to do your job properly	Taxed on annual value unless you must live there to perform your duties (10.6.13)
(4)	Board and lodging	If you receive cash you are taxed on it Otherwise tax free	Taxed on cost to employer of board and lodging subject to a limit (10.6.13)
(5)	Working clothing, for example, overalls	Tax free	Tax free
(6)	Suits and coats, etc.	Taxed on estimated second-hand value	Taxed on full cost to employer
(7)	Private sickness insurance cover	Tax free	Taxed on premiums paid by your employer (10.6.11)

Details	Non-P11D employee	P11D employee or director
(8) Interest-free loan	Tax free	Taxable subject to certain exemptions (10.6.9) – to participator, etc. of close company (13.17.3) – employee shareholdings (10.9.4)
(9) Share options	Taxable with certain exceptions (10.9)	Taxable with certain exceptions (10.9)
(10) Employee's outings	Tax free	Normally tax free
(11) Luncheon vouchers	Tax free up to 15p per day – excess taxable	Tax free up to 15p per day – excess taxable
(12) Subsidised staff canteen	Tax free	Tax free provided facilities available to all staff
(13) Pension and death in service cover	Normally tax-free (10.11)	Normally tax-free (10.11)
(14) Cash vouchers	Taxable (10.6.12)	Taxable (10.6.12)
(15) Season tickets and credit cards	Generally taxable (10.6.12)	Generally taxable (10.6.12)
(16) Assets at employee's disposal	Normally tax free	Taxable (10.6.8)
(17) Scholarships from employer for children of employee	Normally tax free	Taxable with some exceptions (10.6.14)
(18) Long service awards of articles or employer company shares; after 20 years' service and each further 10 years; maximum £50 for each year	Tax free	Tax free
(19) Security assets and services provided after 5 April 1989 (10.6.8)	Tax free	Tax free
(20) Childcare	Tax free	Tax free subject to conditions (10.6.15)
(21) Mobile telephones, if privately used	Tax free	Tax free (10.6.16)
(22) In-house sports and recreational facilities	Tax free	Tax free (10.6.17)

	Details	Non-P11D employee	P11D employee or director
(23)	Removal expenses and benefits	Tax free up to limit (10.6.18)	Tax free up to limit (10.6.18)
(24)	Employee liabilities and indemnity insurance	Tax free (10.6.19)	Tax free (10.6.19)
(25)	Work-related employer-funded training	Tax free	Tax free
(26)	Corporate loan	Tax free	Tax free up to limit (10.6.8)
(27)	Works buses	Tax free	Tax free (10.6.21)
(28)	Bicycles	Tax free	Tax free subject to rules (10.6.21)
(29)	Education and training	Tax free	Tax free subject to conditions (10.6.23)
(30)	Payments by employers towards incidental homeworking costs	Tax free	Tax free subject to rules (10.6.24)

10.6.4 Travelling and entertainment allowances (ITEPA Ss337–342, 356–358 & 369–376)

An allowance or advance that you derive from your employer to meet the costs of travelling, entertaining or other services you perform on his behalf is not taxable provided that you actually incur expenditure for these purposes. (Your employer is able to deduct the payments from his taxable profits. Entertaining expenses, however, are not normally deductible.) Should you incur expenditure of less than the full allowance or advance and are not required to pay back the unexpended portion to your employer, this excess must be included in your taxable income.

If you are a P11D employee (10.6.2) any allowance made to you by your employers for travelling, etc. is normally included in your taxable income in full. If you incur travelling expenses, etc. in the course of your employment you must make a claim to that effect and you will be allowed to deduct from your taxable income the amount of your expenses. If you are not a P11D employee (or director) any expense allowances or payments on your behalf are not normally included in your taxable income.

Your employer can pay you free of tax up to 20p for each mile for which you use your own cycle for business travel. If you use your own bicycle for business travel you can claim capital allowances on a proportion of the cost (11.9).

Payments made to you by your employer to cover your personal incidental expenses when you stay away from home overnight on business are now tax-free up to certain limits. The expenses covered include newspapers, personal telephone calls and laundry. The exemption runs from 6 April 1995 and the limits are £5 each night in the UK and £10 overseas.

You are not in general allowed any deduction for your travelling expenses between your home and your employer's place of business. Thus if your employer makes you any allowance for this expense it is wholly taxable in your hands. However, certain benefits are tax-free (10.6.21). No tax is payable on travel facilities provided for *servicemen* and *servicewomen* going on and returning from *leave* (ITEPA S296).

From 6 April 1998, site based employees get relief for the cost of travelling to and from a site and for subsistence when staying there, provided no more than 24 months is spent at that location. Also, from that date, the position is improved regarding travel and subsistence between home and a temporary place of work. You now obtain relief for your full costs without having to offset any saving through not doing your normal commuting. (ITEPA S338).

If you *travel abroad* in connection with your employer's business, the cost is allowable. If you also have a holiday abroad during the same trip you will be taxed on an appropriate proportion of the cost of your trip as a personal benefit. If your employers pay for your wife to accompany you (and she is not an employee herself) her own trip would normally be taxed as a personal benefit although some allowance could be obtained if, for example, she acted as your secretary during the trip or it was necessary for her to go for reasons of your health.

No benefit is assessed on you if your employer pays for the actual journeys of your family in visiting you, provided you *work abroad* for at least 60 continuous days. This applies to your wife (or husband) and any of your children who are under 18 on the outward journey. Also covered are journeys by your family in accompanying you at the beginning of your overseas period or by you back to the UK at the end. Two return trips for each person are covered by the rule, in any tax year (ITEPA Ss369–375).

Any travel expenses paid by your employer covering journeys to and from the UK will be tax free where you are UK resident and working abroad.

Members of Parliament are allowed no deduction for expenditure incurred to cover staying away from home in London or the constituency. However, the Additional Costs Allowance paid to meet these expenses is not taxable (ITEPA S292). Exemption now extends to payments for travelling and related expenses when MPs visit an EU institution or agency or the National Parliament of another EU state, on Parliamentary duties. Candidate or applicant countries are also included. From April 1999 members of the Scottish Parliament, Welsh and Northern Ireland Assemblies are treated in the same way for tax purposes as MPs.

Certain payments by employers to their employees for travel between work and home are tax free. Exemption is given by an Inland Revenue concession (A66) which covers working until at least 9 pm on no more than 60 occasions in a tax year. Furthermore, there must be no regular pattern. Subject to these points, the cost of a taxi or hired car will not give rise to tax on the employee. This now extends to where your car sharing arrangements for commuting fail through unforeseen circumstances (breakdown or late working, etc.) and your employer pays for your journey home.

Another concession concerns non-cash gifts from third parties (that is, not the employer). These are tax free in an employee's hands providing the cost is no more than £250 in the tax year from any one source (previously £150). There is a similar exemption regarding entertainment provided by third parties. Credit tokens and non-cash vouchers are included. There is no limit but the person providing the benefit must not be the employer or anyone connected with him, nor must it be provided in recognition of particular services regarding the employment.

Employees are not taxed on annual staff parties such as for Christmas if the total expenditure per head is no more than £150 (previously £75).

10.6.5 **Motor cars** (ITEPA Ss114–153, 167 & 169–172)

The following rules apply to you if yours is a director's or *higher paid* employment (10.6.2):

New system

(1) From 2002–03, a new method of calculating car benefits applies. This is based on 15–35 per cent of the car's price, depending on its level of carbon dioxide emissions. The 15 per cent rate applied for 2003–04 up to 155 grams per kilometre of CO2. There was a 3 per cent supplement for diesel cars, but the 35 per cent maximum still applied. The business mileage discounts go and older cars are differently treated. Full details from 2003–04 to 2006–07 are shown in the following table.

	2003–04 g/km	**2004–05 g/km**	**2005–06 g/km**	**2006–07 g/km**	**Percentage of list price**
Cars registered from 1.1.98					
CO_2 emissions up to:	155	145	140	140	15
each additional 5 g/km					extra 1
maximum from:	255	245	235	235	35
Cars registered before 1.1.98 with no CO_2 emission figures:					
Engine size up to 1400cc					15
1401–2000cc					22
over 2000cc					32

(2) From 2003–04 a new car fuel basis applies, directly linked to CO2 emissions. A percentage applies, based on the emissions on the above scales (1) from 15 per cent to 35 per cent, with a 3 per cent supplement for diesels. These are applied to a fixed price, which is £14,400 for 2003–04, 2004–05 and 2005–06.
(3) Special rules apply if you own your car but are paid a mileage allowance (10.6.6).
(4) Changes in motor vehicles provided for staff must be notified to the Revenue quarterly
(5) If you would otherwise be within the car benefit scheme and you are offered an alternative to the car of say cash, the offer of an alternative will not, of itself, alter your tax. You will be taxed on what you actually get, car benefit or cash.
(6) Provided you do not have the use of a particular car but simply take one from a car pool and do not garage it at home overnight, you will not normally be assessed to any benefit; subject, however, to the further condition that any private use of the car is merely incidental to your business use thereof.

Old system

(1) From 6 April 1994, company car benefits are based on their list prices. (Previously, scales of benefits applied.) A classic car over 15 years old is taxed on its market value provided this is over both £15,000 and list price. The price of your car is taken as its list price when first registered plus the price of any extras provided with the car. Also included is the cost of accessories added after 31 July 1993 if over £100 including delivery and fitting. However, from 1995–96 accessories designed solely for the disabled are not included.
(2) For each of the 5 years to 5 April 1999 you were taxed on 35 per cent of this value, with discounts of one-third if you drove over 2,500 business miles in a year and two-thirds if more than 18,000. (The full 35 per cent normally applied to a second business car.) This adjusted figure was reduced by one-third, if the car was more than four years old at the end of the tax year. Where the list price plus accessories, etc. exceeds £80,000, the benefit was calculated on this figure.
(3) For 1999–2000, 2000–01 and 2001–02, the basic taxable value of your car remained at 35 per cent. However, this became 25% if you drove over 2,500 business miles and 15% if more than 18,000 (the full 35 per cent normally applying to a second business car). These respective figures were reduced by 25 per cent if the car was more than 4 years old at the end of the tax year.
(4) The provision of petrol for a higher paid employee was taxed by applying an additional scale charge. This only applies if your employer bears any of the cost. If your scale benefit was halved because your business mileage reached 18,000 (see (2) above), your

fuel benefit was also halved. However, this relief does not apply to the fuel benefit for 1993–94 and subsequent years. From 1998–99, the petrol scales were:

Engine size			Scale charges		
	1998–99	1999–2000	2000–01	2001–02	2002–03
	£	£	£	£	£
0–1400cc	1,010	1,210	1,700	1,930	2,240
1401–2000cc	1,280	1,540	2,170	2,460	2,850
Over 2000cc	1,890	2,270	3,200	3,620	4,200

(5) A different fuel scale applied for diesel vehicles as follows:

Engine size			Scale charges		
	1998–99	1999–2000	2000–01	2001–02	2002–03
	£	£	£	£	£
0–2000cc	1,280	1,540	2,170	2,460	2,850
Over 2000cc	1,890	2,270	3,200	3,620	4,200

10.6.6 **Car mileage allowances** (ITEPA Ss229–236)

(1) You are entitled to relief for travelling expenses concerning your employment. Mileage allowances paid to you where you use your own car for work are taxable to the extent that they exceed your allowable expenses, including capital allowances.

(2) To reduce the administrative work involved there is the *fixed profit car scheme* (FPCS). Under this, your taxable mileage 'profit' may be calculated using the excess of the mileage rate paid to you over the appropriate FPCS 'tax free' rate. The authorised mileage rates for 2001–02 were:

	Cars up to 1500cc	Cars 1501–2000cc	Cars over 2000cc
First 4,000 miles	40p	45p	63p
Over 4,000 miles	25p	25p	36p

(3) The authorised mileage rates from 2002–03 are:

Cars and vans:	On the first 10,000 miles in the tax year	40p
	On each additional mile over 10,000 miles	25p
Motor cycles:		24p
Bicycles:		20p
Each business passenger: (that is, fellow employee) per mile		5p

(4) Capital allowances were available to you if you use your car for work, but this does not apply for 2002–03 and subsequently. The allowances were based on the proportion relating to business use.
(5) If you borrowed money to buy a car to use for work, interest relief was available on a more general basis since 6 April 1990. This does not apply after 2001–02.

10.6.7 **Vans etc.** (ITEPA Ss154–166 & 168)

From 6 April 1993, you are taxed on any benefit that you obtain from having the use of a company van, using a standard amount of £500. This is reduced to £350 for vans which are at least four years old at the end of the tax year. The charge is apportioned if several employees share a van. However, you can elect to be taxed on £5 for each day that you have the use of a van.

No extra charge is made for any fuel provided by your employers. Furthermore, vans over 3.5 tonnes are usually outside the benefit charge, as in general are other commercial vehicles above that weight.

From 6 April 2004, you are no longer taxed on any benefit where you are required to take an emergency vehicle home, when you are on call. This might apply if you work for the fire, police or ambulance services.

A similar exemption applies from 6 April 2005, provided you are not allowed other private use. Radical changes are to follow from 6 April 2007, when the charge will increase to £3,000, with an extra £500 for private fuel.

10.6.8 **Use of assets** (ITEPA Ss201–210)

If your employer places an asset at your disposal for your personal use (for example, a television set) your annual taxable benefit is 20 per cent of its market value when you first began to use it. (For assets placed at your disposal prior to 6 April 1980, the benefit is 10 per cent.) This rule does not apply to cars (see above) nor to land for which 'annual value' is used (S531) and only relates to those in director's or *higher paid* employment (10.6.2).

For assets provided after 5 April 1980 by your employer, a special rule applies if you subsequently become the owner. You will then have a taxable benefit of the excess over what you pay for the asset, of the original market value less the previous annual benefit assessments. This is increased to the excess of market value over price paid when you obtain the asset from your employers.

From 6 April 1989, employees (and self-employed people) who face a special threat to their *personal physical security* obtain special relief. However, the threat must arise directly out of their particular job or business. The relief extends to services and assets provided by the employer, such as alarm systems, security guards, bullet-resistant windows, etc. In appropriate circumstances, no benefit charge will be made.

If your employer loans you computer equipment, it is likely that no tax charge will result for 1999–2000 or subsequently. The first £500 of annual benefit is exempt. If the loaned computer is sold to you at market value after 5 April 2005, there will be no taxable benefit in kind.

10.6.9 **Beneficial loan arrangements** (ITEPA Ss173–191)

(1) If you or a 'relative' have a loan by reason of your director's or *higher paid* employment at no interest or at a lower rate than the 'official' one then you will be taxed on the benefit of your interest saving compared with the official rate, subject to the following rules.
(2) The 'official rate' varies periodically. Recent rates are:

From	%
6 October 1995	7.75
6 February 1996	7.25
6 June 1996	7
6 November 1996	6.75
6 August 1997	7.25
6 March 1999	6.25
6 January 2002	5

(3) 'Relative' means parent, grandparent, child, grandchild, etc., brother, sister or spouse of yourself or any of the relatives aforementioned.
(4) For 1994–95 and subsequent years, the benefits from loans totalling up to £5,000 are exempted. No charge to tax was made for 1991–92, 1992–93 or 1993–94 if the annual cash value of the benefit did not exceed £300.
(5) From 6 April 1994, you are taxed as if you had been given the equivalent in cash of a cheap or interest-free loan. Where appropriate you are then given tax relief as if you had paid interest on the loan at the 'official rate'.
(6) Up to 1994–95, any loan which replaced a beneficial loan was treated as the original one and was thus potentially taxable. From 1995–96, this no longer applies for arms-length replacement loans.
(7) From 2000–01, if your beneficial loan qualifies for full tax relief, it no longer needs to be reported. Also, the exemption for loans made on normal commercial terms is extended where their terms are varied.

10.6.10 **Director's PAYE** (ITEPA S223)

Where a company accounts for PAYE (10.14) to the Inland Revenue in respect of certain directors and this exceeds the amounts which they suffer, the excess is treated as their income. This does not apply to directors owning less than 5 per cent of the company's shares who work full time for it, nor to directors of charities, etc.

10.6.11 **Medical insurance** (FA 1989 Ss54–57, FA 1994 S83 & Sch 10 & F2A 1997 S17)

Non-directors earning less than £8,500 annually are not taxed on medical insurance premiums borne by their employer. Otherwise, employees and directors are taxed on such premiums (an exception being regarding overseas service).

From 1990–91 relief for private medical insurance was available for those aged 60 and over. From 6 April 1994, relief was limited to the basic rate. Where a contract covered a married couple and one died, the other could claim relief for its remainder.

Relief was withdrawn for private medical insurance premiums paid on policies taken out or renewed after 1 July 1997. An exception was made for contracts arranged before 2 July 1997 but not executed until later.

10.6.12 **Vouchers and credit tokens** (ITEPA Ss73–96)

All employees (and directors) are normally taxed on the value of cash vouchers received as a result of their employment. That value is the money for which the vouchers are capable of being exchanged. The rules include cheque vouchers and credit tokens such as credit and charge cards. However, lower paid employees of transport undertakings are not taxed on transport vouchers provided under arrangements existing at 25 March 1982.

Rules in the 1994 Finance Act aim to ensure that vouchers and credit tokens are properly valued for tax purposes. This must be according to the expense to those paying for the vouchers, etc. From 6 April 2002, vouchers evidencing entitlement to minor benefits which are exempted under these regulations are free of tax.

10.6.13 **Living accommodation provided for employees** (ITEPA Ss97–113)

In general, living accommodation provided to you because of your employment results in a taxable benefit. You are taxed on the open market rental value of the property, or the actual rent paid by your employer, if this is more. Amounts which you pay towards the cost are deducted.

You are exempted from the charge, however, if any of the following circumstances apply:

(1) You have to live in the accommodation in order to perform your duties properly.
(2) It is customary in your type of employment to have accommodation provided and it helps you to do your job better.
(3) Your employment involves you in a security risk and special accommodation is provided with a view to your safety.
(4) From 6 April 2000, minor amounts of private use of assets and services which you mainly use for work purposes are exempted.

The above exemption also covers rates paid for you, but does not apply in circumstances (1) and (2) if you are a director, unless you have broadly no more than a 5 per cent shareholding and work full time or work for a charity, etc.

If your employment is 'director's or *higher paid*' (10.6.2), you will still be assessed on payments by your employer for your heating, lighting, cleaning, repairs, maintenance and decoration, etc. as well as on the value (20 per cent – 10.6.8) of domestic furniture and equipment provided. A limit applies, however, which is 10 per cent of your net emoluments from your job which is after deducting capital allowances, pension contributions and expenses claims, and excludes the expenditure for your benefit.

An additional charge applies to houses costing the employer more than £75,000 or, if purchased more than six years previously, worth more than that figure when first occupied by the employee after 30 March 1983. The additional benefit is broadly based on the excess of the cost, etc. over £75,000. This is subjected to the rate of interest in force in relation to beneficial loans (now 5 per cent) at the start of the year of assessment (10.6.9). (From 6 April 1996, the above special rules take precedence and only the balance is charged as basic Schedule E income, if that is in point.)

10.6.14 **Scholarships** (ITEPA Ss211–215)

You will be assessed on the value of any scholarships awarded by your employer to your children, provided you are a director or *higher paid* employee (10.6.2), subject to certain exceptions. However, the scholarships will remain tax free in the hands of your children.

An exception is where a scholarship comes from a fund or scheme from which at least 75 per cent by value goes to scholars otherwise than by reason of their parents' employment. (Overseas employees who are the parents of scholars are not included in the 75 per cent.)

10.6.15 **Childcare** (ITEPA Ss270A & 318)

From 6 April 1990, subject to certain rules, childcare facilities provided by your employer will not give rise to any benefit charge on you. You must either be a parent or foster parent of the child and the care may not be provided on domestic premises. Other conditions include your employer running the nursery at your workplace or elsewhere; or jointly with other employers. Childcare benefits also remain free from any charge to National Insurance contributions.

From 6 April 2005, your employer is able to contract direct with a nursery, child-minder or after-school club thereby providing you with tax-free benefits or childcare vouchers up to £50 weekly plus associated administrative costs.

10.6.16 **Mobile telephones** (ITEPA S319)

From 6 April 1991 to 5 April 1999 you were taxed on a standard amount of £200 yearly, on each mobile phone provided by your employers. (This included car phones – 10.6.5.) However, if you had no private use, or were required to make good the full cost of such use and did so, there was no tax charge. As from 6 April 1999, the charge was removed.

10.6.17 **Sporting and recreational facilities** (ITEPA Ss261–263)

From 6 April 1993, benefits in kind are not taxable in connection with workplace sports and recreational facilities provided by your employer for use by staff generally. The exemption covers in-house facilities and those provided by outside firms for the staff in general. However, the exemption does not extend to yachts, cars and aircraft, or overnight stays.

10.6.18 **Removal expenses and benefits** (ITEPA Ss271–289)

If you start a new job or move with your present employer after 5 April 1993, statutory relief is available for relocation expenses and benefits. (Previously there was certain extra-statutory relief.) The relief covers such items as disposal and acquisition expenses, transporting belongings, travelling and subsistence and bridging loans. However, there is an overall limit of £8,000 and this also applies to freedom from benefit charge where your employer bears the costs. The £8,000 limit does not cover existing reliefs for expenses concerning work overseas (18.5.3).

If your employer provides you with a bridging loan, any unused part of your £8,000 expense allowance will result in reducing the beneficial loan charge (10.6.9). There is a formula that converts unused allowance into a number of days which reduces the period for which the charge is made.

10.6.19 **Employee liabilities and indemnity insurance** (ITEPA Ss346–350)

From 1995–96, if you incur expenditure on indemnity insurance or legal costs etc. relating to your employment, you obtain tax relief. Similarly you are not taxed if your employer meets these costs. Relief extends six years after you leave the employment, for any years when you incur such expenses relating to your former employment.

10.6.20 **PAYE settlement agreements** (ITEPA Ss703–707)

Under 'annual voluntary settlements', employers may meet their employees' tax liabilities on a range of minor benefits in kind and expense payments. From 1996–97, these are known as 'PAYE settlement agreements' and new regulations apply.

10.6.21 **Commuting benefits** (ITEPA Ss237 & 242–249)

From 6 April 1999 you are not liable to tax on the following benefits provided by your employer:

(1) Works buses with at least 12 seats used to bring you and other employees to and from work. From 2002–03 minibuses taking 9 to 11 passengers are included.
(2) General subsidies to public bus services used by you and other employees provided you pay no less than the general public, unless it is a local stopping service.
(3) Bicycles and cycling safety equipment provided for your commuting.
(4) Parking facilities for cycles and motorcycles at work. Meals and refreshments can now be provided tax free on official cycle to work days.
(5) From 6 April 2005, where you sell at market value a cycle loaned to you by your employer.

10.6.22 **Income from employment and your return**

You must enter in your return your occupation and your employer's name and address. Show your total gross earnings before any deductions and the tax deducted. Normally separate 'supplementary pages' should be used for each of your employments including directorships. If your duties are performed wholly abroad, this must be indicated.

Include separate details of any director's fees voted by each company before deductions. Also show any part-time or casual earnings. If your spouse has any income of this kind, it must be shown separately in his or her own return. (Prior to 6 April 1990, it was normally all included in the husband's return.)

You must give details of your benefits-in-kind including goods and vouchers received as well as living accommodation. Also show details of any share options granted by your employer (10.9), when these are exercised.

If you are a P11D employee (10.6.2) you must enter the total amount of any expenses payments made to you and the total cost to your employer of any benefits provided for you. If the Inspector has granted a dispensation to your employer, however, you may leave the relevant expenses payments out of your return. (A dispensation will be granted if the Inspector is satisfied that all of the expenses payments are covered by allowable expenses.)

Any leaving payments and compensation must be separately shown (10.12). A separate section in your return is provided for details of your expenses in employment (10.8) including fees or subscriptions to professional bodies and superannuation contributions.

10.6.23 **Education and training** (ITEPA Ss250–260)

From 6 April 2000, new training relief operates where your employer contributes to your education or training and you are an individual learning account holder. The contributions are exempt from tax and National Insurance contributions provided the training or education qualifies for a grant or discount from the Department for Education and Employment, etc. Your employer must also make similar contributions available to all employees on similar terms.

10.6.24 **Incidental homeworking costs** (ITEPA S316A)

From 6 April 2003, if you work all or part of your time at home and your employer contributes to any additional household costs, subject to the rules, this is tax free, up to £2 per week, no supporting evidence is needed and beyond this, evidence must be provided to the effect that the payments are wholly in respect of your additional household expenses incurred in carrying out your duties at home.

10.7 Expense payments for directors and others (form P11D)

If you have a director's or higher paid employment (10.6.2), your employers must complete a form P11D for each tax year in respect of all benefits in kind and expense payments made to you or on your behalf.

For 2004–05, particulars to be entered by your employer on your form P11D regarding any expenses payments made and benefits, etc. provided by him would include the following, unless covered by a dispensation. (Inland Revenue Pamphlet IR69 explains the procedure under which your employer can request a dispensation from the Inspector of Taxes regarding various business expenses such as scale rate payments for travelling and subsistence.) The amounts entered must include VAT even though this is recovered by the employer.

(1) Cars owned or hired by employer:
 - (i) Make, model and date of registration.
 - (ii) Price of car and optional extras provided originally and those added later.
 - (iii) Period for which car available to you in year.
 - (iv) Payment by you towards running costs.
 - (v) Approved CO_2 emissions if registered after 31 December 1997.
 - (vi) Capital contributions towards cost (maximum £5,000).
 - (vii) Cash equivalent of each car and of fuel.

(2) Cars owned by you:
 - (i) Allowances from employer towards your running expenses.
 - (ii) Contribution from employer towards purchase price, depreciation or hire.

(3) Entertainment – all payments made exclusively for entertaining including the amount of any round sum allowance, specific allowances, sums reimbursed and sums paid to third persons (entertaining disallowable to your employer must still be included).

(4) General round sum expense allowances not exclusively for entertaining.
(5) Travelling and subsistence – fares, hotels, meals, etc. and payments from your employer for travel between your home and work from which no PAYE has been deducted – expenses regarding overseas employments.
(6) Subscriptions.
(7) Private medical and dental attention, treatment and insurance.
(8) Educational assistance for self or family including scholarships awarded to you or your family.
(9) Goods and services supplied free or below market value – equivalent cash benefit.
(10) Work done to your own home or other assets by your employer.
(11) Wages and upkeep of personal or domestic staff provided by your employer.
(12) Cost of vouchers and credit cards given to you by your employer.
(13) House, flat, etc. provided by employer – address of property.
(14) The market value of any cars or other assets given to you by your employer (other than personal gifts outside the business).
(15) Home telephone – cost of rental – calls.
(16) Nursery places provided for your children.
(17) Other expenses and benefits including your own National Insurance contributions (if paid by your employer), holidays, home telephone, etc., payments towards cost of your own car.
(18) Beneficial loans – particulars of loans giving rise to benefit assessment including the maximum amount during the year (10.6.9).
(19) Should you have any share related benefits, a box is provided to be ticked.
(20) Vans available for private use (10.6.7) – enter the standard charge (£500 or £350 for older vans) and reduce this for shared vehicles etc.
(21) Tax paid on behalf of the employee.
(22) Qualifying and non-qualifying relocation expenses.

Optional working sheets are available regarding cars and fuel, vans and relocation expenses.

The above items are entered on your P11D and then your employer deducts the following:

(1) The amounts of any of the above expenses that you have repaid to your employer (unless already deducted from the items shown).
(2) Amounts included above from which tax has been deducted under PAYE.

Forms P11D must be sent to the Inland Revenue so as to arrive by 6 July 2005. Employees should receive copies by the same date.

It is also necessary for employers to complete a simple confirmation that all necessary forms P11D have been completed and returned to the Revenue.

10.8 Deductions you may claim (ITEPA Ss327–385)

You may claim any expenses which you have to incur wholly, exclusively and necessarily in performing the duties of your employment. These do not include:

(1) The cost of travel between home and work (but see 10.6.4 and 10.6.21).
(2) The cost of business entertainment except where the expense is disallowed in computing your employer's tax assessment or is reasonable entertainment of an overseas trading customer.

If you are a director or a P11D employee (10.6.2) you should make a claim to the Revenue in respect of any allowable expenses that have been included by your employer in your form P11D. The claim should certify that the expenses covered were incurred 'wholly, exclusively and necessarily' in performing the duties of your employment. You will not then be taxed on payments for such expenses made by your employer whether made to you or third parties.

Any expenses that you personally incur in connection with your employment should be included on your return and these include:

- Overalls, clothing and tools.
- Travelling.
- Business use of your own car including capital allowances (11.9.11).
- Home telephone and other expenses (1.2.9).
- Professional fees and subscriptions relating to your work.
- Your own contributions to any approved superannuation (pension) scheme operated by your employers (10.12).
- In certain employments (for example, entertainment industry) such expenses as hairdressing, make-up, clothes cleaning, etc.
- Certain relocation expenses (10.6.18).

10.9 Share option and share incentive schemes (ITEPA Ss417–554 & Schs 2–5)

Over the years, there have been a variety of relieving provisions relating to tax on share option and share incentive schemes. The following pages describe some of these and reflect important changes brought about by the Finance Act 2000, including a new all-employee share plan (10.9.7) and an enterprise management incentives scheme (10.9.9). From 2003–04, ITEPA has regrouped the legislation and used certain new abbreviations such as SIPs (share incentive plans), CSOPs (company share option plans) and EMIs (enterprise management incentives). Note that where income tax remains payable, there may also be National Insurance contributions, although the employer's position is being improved.

10.9.1 Unapproved share option schemes

As a director or an employee of a company, you may be granted an option to take up shares in the company. When you exercise your option, the notional 'gain' will be included in your Schedule E assessment for the tax year in which you exercise the option. (This does not apply if you exercise your option under an approved scheme – see below.) You thus pay income tax on the 'gain' (as earned income) calculated thus:

Market value of shares on day you exercise option (that is, when you take up the shares)		£A
Less: Price paid by you for the shares	£B	
Price paid by you for the option (if any)	C	D
Assessable 'gain'		£E

If you subsequently sell the shares themselves at a profit, subject to the share incentive scheme rules (10.9.3), this will be liable to capital gains tax (20.1) calculated as follows:

Net proceeds obtained on the sale of the shares		£F
Less: Price paid by you for the shares	£B	
Price paid by you for the option (if any)	C	
Gain already assessed under Schedule E	E	A
Capital gain		£G

10.9.2 Approved company share option schemes (CSOPs) (ITEPA Ss521–526 & Sch 4)

Special rules apply to options granted under an approved scheme, which can extend to groups. In particular, the gain will only be taxable when the shares are sold and capital gains tax (not income tax) will apply. On the grant of an option to an employee, the company's capital gain is the amount (if any) paid. Important changes apply for options granted after 16 July 1995, otherwise they continue to be within the old rules. The conditions for Inland Revenue approval include the following:

(1) Each participant may hold options over shares with a maximum value at the time of grant of £30,000. (Under the old rules, the limit applying to options granted before 17 July 1995 was £100,000 or four times the current or previous year's emoluments if greater.)
(2) The options may not now be granted at an exercise price which is 'manifestly' less than the market value of the shares at the date of the grant.
(3) You cannot exercise your option earlier than three years or later than ten years after its grant.

(4) You must be a full-time director or employee when the option is granted to you but may leave before its exercise. Part-timers may be included in schemes approved from May 1995.
(5) Before 9 April 2003, you could only exercise approved options once every three years (FA 2003 Sch 21).
(6) No participant can have a 'material interest' (broadly 10 per cent of the shares) in the company or group if close (13.17).
(7) The options must be non-transferable and the shares fully paid ordinary shares. These shares must form part of the capital of the company (G) granting the option, or its parent, or a consortium company owning at least 5 per cent of the ordinary shares of G.
(8) Shares subject to special restrictions may not be used, although employees may be required to sell their shares when their employment ends.
(9) Where a company has two classes of issued ordinary shares, most of the class of shares used in the scheme needed to be held by outsiders. However, a class of shares can now be used of which the majority is held by directors or employees and gives them control of the company.
(10) Redeemable shares cannot be used, except in the case of registered worker co-operatives.
(11) If a company with an approved share scheme is taken over by another company, it is possible for the options to be exchanged for options over shares in that other company. Certain conditions must be satisfied, including having the replacement options governed by the rules of the original scheme.
(12) Where loans are obtained by employees to exercise their options, conditions regarding security and repayment are not regarded as 'restrictions'. Thus the shares are not debarred on this account.

10.9.3 **Savings related share option schemes** (ITEPA Ss516–520 & Sch 3)

Any notional or real gains from an approved savings related share option scheme will be free of income tax. However, some capital gains tax may be payable. Under such a scheme you are given an option to buy shares in the company which employs you or its controlling company. (You would not be eligible if you controlled more than 25 per cent of the shares and it is a close company – 13.17.)

You must save the money to buy the shares through a special SAYE contract set to produce the required cost of the shares on its maturity. (The proceeds from SAYE linked schemes set up under earlier legislation may also be used.) SAYE contracts may now be arranged by banks, and building societies.

Early exercise of the option is normally only allowed in special circumstances, such as death, disability, retirement or redundancy. Early exercise is also allowed if the company or part of its business in which you work leaves the group operating the scheme. You may exercise an option at the due time, even though you then work for a company which is only associated with the company granting the option, providing it is under its control.

The maximum permitted monthly contribution is £250 and no minimum monthly contribution below £5 can be stipulated. Also, the future purchase price of the shares must not be manifestly less than 80 per cent of the market value of the shares when the option is granted. You must normally exercise the option within six months of reaching pensionable age. However, this becomes an age between 60 and 75 specified for the scheme. where it is approved after 25 July 1991.

10.9.4 **Share incentive schemes** (ITEPA Ss723–4 & Schs 7–8)

These are schemes under which you are allowed to purchase shares in the company where you work because of your employment or directorship and not simply because of a general offer to the public. If you obtain shares under certain incentive schemes, you are broadly assessed to income tax under Schedule E on the increase in the market value of your shares between their acquisition date and the earliest of the following:

(1) seven years from when you bought the shares;
(2) the time when you cease to be a director or an employee of the company;
(3) the time when you sell the shares; and
(4) the time when your shares cease to be subject to any special restrictions.

The above rules apply to shares from incentive schemes acquired before 26 October 1987. Certain *profit sharing schemes* (10.9.6) were excluded provided various conditions were satisfied. For acquisitions of shares or interests in shares after 25 October 1987, the previous rules apply in essence with some changes. However, those not charged under Schedule E Case I in respect of the employment are excluded. Also excluded are acquisitions arising from public offers.

Income tax may be chargeable in certain circumstances, such as the removal or variation of restrictions over the shares; or the creation or variation of rights in the shares owned or other shares in the company. However, this does not apply if the company is employee-controlled because of holdings of shares of the same class, nor if it is a subsidiary (but not a 'dependent subsidiary' – see below); nor if a majority of the shares of the same class are held other than by directors and employees, associated companies, etc. The tax is levied on the value increase resulting from the removal of restrictions, etc.

Special benefits, such as a capital distribution, or the sale of rights in a rights issue may be taxable. However, unless the company is a 'dependent subsidiary' wider exemption applies. Broadly, employee shareholders are not taxed on their special benefits where they are available to at least 90 per cent of shareholders and a majority of the shares are held by non-employees.

A 'dependent subsidiary' is one whose business is mainly carried on with group members. Furthermore, any increase in the value of the company during its accounts period must be limited to 5 per cent. The directors must give the Inland Revenue a certificate within two years of the end of the accounts period. You are liable on shares in a 'dependent subsidiary' in the same way as other shares (see above).

10.9.5 **Employee shareholdings** (ITEPA Ss417–446)

Special rules apply if you are a director or *higher paid* employee (10.6.2) and you acquire shares at an undervalue by reason of your employment. The shares need not be in the company which employs you.

You are treated as obtaining shares at an undervalue if you pay less than the market value of fully paid shares of the same class at that time. This applies whether or not you are under any obligation to pay more at a future time. Subject to certain relaxations (see below) you are taxed on the shortfall of what you pay for the shares compared with market value when you bought them. This shortfall is treated as an interest free loan (10.6.9) and you are treated as if your taxable earnings were increased by the benefit of such a loan. This continues until the shortfall is ended or the shares are sold, even if you cease your employment.

In general, relief is not completely withdrawn if the price is too low; it simply does not apply to the benefit represented by the difference in price. Also, if there are several offers to the public of shares of the same class, a 10 per cent overall limit applies but up to 40 per cent of the shares comprised in one offer may go to employees. Furthermore, different directors or employees can obtain a different mix of shares offered to the public at the same time, provided the aggregate benefit is similar. This exemption extends to a public offer comprising a package of shares in more than one company and also 'special benefits' such as bonus shares.

If you obtain shares through a priority allocation to the employees of your company, when it offers shares to the public, special rules apply. You will not be assessed on any benefit provided no more than 10 per cent of the offer goes to employees, all entitlements are on similar terms and the arrangement is not exclusively for directors or highly paid employees. In the case of a fixed price issue the employees must subscribe at that price, whilst for a tender issue the lowest price successfully tendered applies.

From 17 March 1998, certain shares subject to forfeiture are taxable on issue to employees (the rules are modified for acquisitions after July 1999 to prevent a double charge). Similarly, convertible shares issued to employees from that date are taxed on conversion. This differs from the previous practice.

10.9.6 **Profit sharing schemes** (TA 1988 Ss186–187 & Sch 9)

Tax relief is available for employees participating in a company share scheme which has been approved by the Revenue. Under such a scheme, trustees are allowed to acquire shares in the company to the value of up to £3,000 or 10 per cent of salary, subject to a ceiling of £8,000. For this purpose you take your salary for the current or previous year, whichever is the higher. If the trustees receive qualifying corporate bonds as the result of a takeover or reconstruction, they can keep these. Alternatively they can distribute them in due course to the participants.

A participant must agree to his shares remaining with the trustees for at least two years unless he dies, becomes redundant or reaches normal retirement age. However, for schemes approved after 25 July 1991 an age must be specified between 60 and 75 for all members.

The scheme must be open fairly to all employees within the company or group with five years' service or more. The employers may allow those with shorter service to join, however. Any dividends on the shares are paid over to the participants.

When the trustees sell any of a participant's shares after two years, a percentage will be charged to income tax. The percentage is calculated on the original value (less any capital receipts already charged to income tax as below), or the proceeds of the shares if less, as follows:

Period held – years	% taxable post 7.85	% taxable post 4.96
2–3	100	100
4–5	75	Nil
5 or more	Nil	Nil

The appropriate percentage (see above) of capital receipts less an allowance is charged to income tax. The allowance is £20 for each year until disposal plus £20 in addition, with a maximum of £60 (£100 before 1997–98). There is a special 50 per cent abatement of the charge for employees leaving due to injury, disability, redundancy or reaching pensionable age.

No new schemes will be approved after 5 April 2001, unless a full application was submitted by that date. Furthermore, approval of a scheme may be withdrawn where appropriations from both a scheme and an all-employee share plan are made in the same year. Appropriations to you of shares after 31 December 2002 no longer command income tax relief and by that date, corporation tax relief on payments to the scheme are being phased out. From 21 March 2000, anti-avoidance rules bite regarding the approval of certain schemes involving controlled service companies and loans to employees.

10.9.7 **All-employee share ownership plans (SIPs)** (ITEPA Ss488–508 & Sch 2)

The scheme operates from 28 July 2000, but free shares can be awarded for performance periods beginning earlier. The rules are lengthy, and the following are some of the main details:

(1) Your employer can put into a plan for you up to £3,000 of shares each year, free of income tax and National Insurance. (The shares could be awarded for reaching performance targets.)

(2) The plan must be open to all staff on a fair basis, according to the rules.
(3) Instead of providing free shares, a plan can be set up to supply partnership shares. You will then be able to buy partnership shares out of your pre-tax salary. The maximum amount is £1,500 each year and this is free of tax and National Insurance.
(4) Your employee can give you up to two free shares for each of your partnership shares.
(5) The company obtains corporation tax relief on the cost it bears in providing you with shares.
(6) Dividends held by a plan on your behalf may be reinvested up to a limit of £1,500 in any tax year.
(7) If you keep your shares within the plan for five years, you pay no income tax or National Insurance on them. Keeping them for at least three years means that you only pay tax and National Insurance on the initial value and not on any increase.
(8) Where you keep the shares in the plan until you sell, you pay no capital gains tax. Otherwise, this arises on any increase in value outside the plan.
(9) If you leave your job, your shares must come out of the plan. Where you leave within three years, your employers can decide whether you lose your free shares.
(10) You obtain capital gains tax roll-over relief (20.25.2) where you sell company shares to a plan.
(11) Approved profit sharing schemes are being phased out (10.9.6), subject to transitional measures such as where a new plan provides partnership shares.
(12) From 6 April 2000, business assets taper relief extends to shares owned by employees in certain non-trading companies where they work.
(13) From 2003–04, with the introduction of ITEPA, the schemes have become known as approved share incentive plans (SIPs).

10.9.8 **Enterprise management incentives (EMIs)** (ITEPA Ss527–541 & Sch 5)

(1) These are share option incentive schemes operating from 28 July 2000.
(2) Subject to the rules, options on up to £100,000 worth of shares each can be granted to originally no more than 15 key employees. FA 2001 removed the limit on the number of employees and allows up to £3m of shares in total. If your own limit is reached, no more options can be granted to you under the scheme for three years.
(3) Normally no income tax or National Insurance is payable when you exercise an option under the scheme.
(4) When you sell the shares you obtain capital gains tax taper relief generally going back to the date of grant of the option.
(5) A simple notification process applies instead of a formal approvals system. This entails notice of the option being given to the Revenue within now 92 days of its grant.
(6) To be eligible for the scheme, you need to work at least 25 hours weekly (or if less, 75 per cent of your working time) for the company (or its

subsidiary). Also, together with your 'associates' including family, you must not have a 'material interest' in the company or any group company (broadly 30 per cent).

(7) The scheme is available only for small higher risk companies. They must be independent trading companies with gross assets of no more than £15 million. There are detailed rules for qualification, similar to those for VCT and EIS companies (11.26).

10.9.9 **Shares in research institution spin-out companies** (ITEPA Ss451–460 & TCGA S119A)

New measures concern research institution employees who acquire employment-related shares in spin-out companies into which the employer transfers intellectual property. Starting from 2 December 2004, the value of the intellectual property will be ignored on transfer to the spin-out company, PAYE and National Insurance only being charged on benefit later flowing to the employee. (Transitional relief is available on election before 16 October 2005).

10.9.10 **Setting-up costs of employee share schemes** (TA 1988 S84A & 85A)

The costs of setting up various types of employee share schemes are allowable for tax purposes. These include all-employee profit sharing schemes (10.9.6), all-employee share ownership plans (10.9.7), all-employee savings-related share option schemes (10.9.3) and discretionary share option schemes (10.9.2). If Revenue approval is obtained more than 9 months after the end of the period of account when the expenditure was incurred, allowance is given for the period when approval is given.

10.10 Employee share ownership trusts (ESOTs) (ITEPA Ss549–554, TA 1988 S85A, FA 1989 Ss67–74 & Sch 5, TCGA 1992 Ss227–235 & FA 2000 S54)

Tax relief for ESOTs (employee benefit trusts) applies to contributions made to qualifying trusts from 27 July 1989. The main features are:

(1) ESOTs may borrow to acquire their shares rather than relying on funds provided by the employer company.
(2) ESOTs may provide a market in unquoted shares and may distribute larger amounts of shares than under Profit Sharing Schemes (10.9.6).
(3) All employees of the company and its subsidiaries, who work 20 or more hours weekly and have been employed for at least five years must be beneficiaries of the ESOT.
(4) Beneficiaries may also include ex-employees and ex-directors within 18 months of leaving; and employees and directors who work at least 20 hours weekly. (Part-timers may be included in trusts established from May 1995.) However, those with a 'material interest' in the company (broadly 5 per cent) must be excluded.

(5) Funds from the company must be used within nine months after the end of the company's accounting period in which they were received. The funds must be used in buying ordinary shares in the company, servicing and repaying borrowings, paying benefits and paying expenses.
(6) The shares must be distributed within seven years of their acquisition to all accepting beneficiaries on similar terms. This period is twenty years for ESOTs set up after April 1994.
(7) Payments to an ESOT by the company or a subsidiary are allowed for corporation tax. However, the trust itself is taxable on its income and capital gains. Also, employees receiving shares at less than market value will be liable to income tax.
(8) Capital gains tax roll-over relief (20.25) is available, subject to certain conditions, for disposals of your company shares to an ESOT before 6 April 2001. Replacement assets must be purchased within six months of the sale. (Broadly, your dwelling house and BES shares are not allowed as replacement assets qualifying for relief.) If the replacement assets are disposed of without other assets being acquired, the deferred gain will be brought into charge.
(9) An ESOT may transfer shares to a new employee share ownership plan, provided the ESOT owned the shares on 21 March 2000 or bought them with funds held on that date. There is no claw-back of earlier corporation tax relief.
(10) The costs of setting up an ESOT are an allowable deduction for tax purposes.
(11) Prior to 1 January 1992, a tax charge could arise from a share-for-share exchange. Subsequently, there is no tax charge provided the new holding stands in place of the old for capital gains tax purposes (20.18.6).
(12) Broadly from May 1996, it is possible to operate savings related share option schemes in conjunction with qualifying ESOTs.

10.11 Retirement pension schemes (ITEPA Ss386–400 & 565–654, TA 1988 Ss590–617 & 630–655; FA 1989 Ss75–77 & Schs 6 & 7 & FA 1993 S112)

Any National Insurance contributions that you pay as an employee are not deductible from your taxable income. Your employer, however, deducts his share of such contributions from his taxable profits. On your retirement your state pension is taxable as earned income, on the basis of the actual amount for the tax year, and any widow's pension payable to your wife is also taxable in this way. There is an Earnings Related component in the State Scheme, out of which you may be contracted (14.2.1). 'Contracting-out' using an occupational scheme relieves you and your employer of the obligation to pay higher rate National Insurance contributions (25.2).

Any pension paid to you out of your employer's own staff super-annuation scheme is taxable as earned income. The same applies to any retirement pension paid by your employer that has not been provided for under any scheme. Reference should be made to Chapter 14 for a fuller treatment of pensions.

Retirement schemes are either 'contributory' or 'non-contributory'. In the latter case the employer bears the entire cost and in the former case the employee makes his own regular contributions to the scheme. If you work for a big company it may run its own exempt approved pension scheme which will put aside funds to provide pensions for its employees. A separate pension trust is set up and investments are made on which generally no UK tax is payable either on income or capital gains. The employees' contributions (if any) are deductible from their taxable earnings, subject to certain limits, and amounts paid by the company are deductible from its taxable profits. Furthermore no 'benefit in kind' assessments are made on the employees. To qualify for this taxation treatment Revenue approval must be obtained (14.3.2).

Instead of managing their own exempt approved pension scheme many employers arrange for it to be operated by an insurance company. In return for annual premiums paid to it based on the salaries of the employees covered, the insurance company provides retirement pensions and also sometimes lump sum payments in the event of the death in service of any employee. Subject to Revenue approval (see below) the company deducts the contributions that it pays from its taxable profits and the employees deduct their contributions (if any) from their taxable earnings.

From 1 July 1988, *personal pension schemes* (14.5) have been available for those not in staff superannuation schemes (or for the purposes of 'contracting-out'). Contributions may be paid by the employer or employee. From October 1987, 'free standing' AVC contracts operate (14.4).

If a new scheme is to obtain Revenue approval it must satisfy various conditions (14.3.2). Separate rules apply to personal pension schemes. For further details please refer to Chapter 14 (14.5 and 14.6).

Important changes to the rules for the approval of pension schemes and regarding tax relief on contributions operate from 6 April 2001. The object is to create an integrated tax regime for personal pensions and stakeholder pensions. Radical reforms of the pension system will take effect from April 2006.

10.12 Compensation for loss of office (ITEPA Ss401–416)

If a 'golden handshake' payment is made to you on your retirement, resignation, redundancy or removal from that office, etc. at least the first £30,000 will normally be tax free. However, this exemption depends on the payments being not otherwise taxable.

From 1 November 1991, Inland Revenue practice changed regarding *ex gratia* payments made on retirement or death. These may now be taxed under the rules relating to pension schemes (Chapter 14). However, Revenue (PSO) approval will be available if the normal retirement benefits scheme requirements are satisfied and the lump sum *ex gratia* payment is the only lump sum relevant benefit potentially payable from your employment. The tax treatment of *ex gratia* termination payments other than on retirement or death is generally unchanged and the excess (if any) over £30,000 will be taxed as your earned income.

Benefits are now taxable only to the extent that they actually arise. Furthermore both payments and benefits now are taxable for the year in which they are enjoyed or received, rather than for the year of termination.

The employer is usually able to deduct 'golden handshake' payments from his taxable profits unless for example they are abnormally high payments to controlling directors or are made in connection with a sale of the actual business or made just before its cessation.

If you have a service contract that provides for a lump sum payment to be made to you when you leave your employer this payment will not be tax free because it is treated as arising out of your employment. This point should be borne in mind when service contracts are drawn up.

Any payments received by a former employee in the following circumstances are normally tax free:

(1) *Ex gratia* payments on the death or permanent disability of the employee.
(2) Terminal grants to members of HM Forces.
(3) *Ex gratia* payments on the termination of a job where the employee worked abroad either:
    (a) for three-quarters of his entire term of service; or
    (b) for the whole of the last ten years; or
    (c) where the total service is more than 20 years, for half the total service period including any ten of the last 20 years.

From 16 March 1993, *counselling services* provided by your employer on your redundancy are tax free. (Previously, they would normally have counted towards the £30,000 exemption.) The services include advice on adjusting to job loss, writing CVs, interview skills, job searches and providing office equipment (ITEPA Ss310 & 311). The arrangements have now been extended to part-time employees and courses of two years' duration.

10.13 The assessment basis (ITEPA Ss3–37)

Up to 5 April 1989, many directors and certain others were assessed to income tax on their emoluments on what was known as the 'accounts basis'. This involved paying tax for a tax year based on your director's remuneration, etc, for the accounts year ending therein. Thus, if your remuneration for the year to 31 December 1987 was £25,000, this was assessed for 1987–1988.

From 6 April 1989, the earnings of *all* directors and employees are assessed for the year in which they are received and not for the year for which they were earned. (Certain pensions are to be assessed under Schedule E on an accruals basis.) However, transitional provisions dealt with situations where income was either taxed twice or not at all. In general, the earnings were taken out of assessment for the year when earned and taxed only in the year received, provided relief is claimed.

Where emoluments for an accounting period ending after 5 April 1989 are paid more than nine months after the end of that period, they must be added back in the employer's tax computations and only allowed as a deduction when paid. This applies where the remuneration relates to any period after 5 April 1989.

10.14 The PAYE system (ITEPA Ss682–712)

Most of the Schedule E income tax payable on earnings from employments in this country is collected under the 'pay as you earn' system (PAYE), which covers starting, basic and higher rate income tax. Your employer is responsible for administering the PAYE on your own wages and that of your fellow employees. From each wages payment that you receive, whether it be weekly or monthly, your employer must deduct the relevant income tax and National Insurance contributions, paying to you the net amount. (If income tax has been previously over-deducted by your employer or if you suddenly become entitled to higher relief you may be due to receive a repayment which your employer will make to you.)

10.14.1 Payment

Your employer has to pay over to the Collector of Taxes the total PAYE income tax deductions (less refunds) and National Insurance contributions in respect of the previous month. The time limit is by the nineteenth day of the following month. If payment is not made, it is now open to the Collector to send an estimated demand which must be paid within seven days unless:

(1) The correct PAYE is paid.
(2) The Collector is satisfied that nothing further is due.
(3) The Collector is invited to inspect the PAYE records.

For 1992–93 and subsequent years, interest is due on any amounts outstanding after the following 19 April (that is, 19 April 1993, etc.).

After 5 April 1992, employers whose monthly payments of PAYE and National Insurance contributions are less than a fixed amount are allowed to pay quarterly. From 6 April 2000 the figure is £1,500 (previously £1,000). Payments are then made to the Inland Revenue for the quarters ending 5 July, 5 October, 5 January and 5 April, and each is due within 14 days.

10.14.2 Records

Your employer is required to keep separate tax details for each of his employees (including directors but not partners). However, he is allowed to use his own records which may be computerised. Otherwise he may use the official Deductions Working Sheet (form P11). This can be used for weekly or monthly paid employees. For a weekly paid person the following particulars are entered and calculated:

(1) National Insurance contributions.
(2) Statutory sick pay and statutory maternity pay.
(3) Student loan deductions.
(4) Gross pay for the week.
(5) Cumulative pay for the tax year to date.
(6) Total 'free pay' to date (see below).
(7) Total taxable pay to date (3–4).
(8) Total tax due to date (see below).
(9) Tax to be paid or repaid for the week (see below).
(10) Tax credits.

(Similar details for each month are entered for monthly paid employees.) The total 'free pay' to date is obtained from 'Table A' in the tax tables provided by the Revenue. This table shows for each week the 'free pay' applicable to each code number (see below). If your total pay is less than your 'free pay' to date then you pay no more tax for that week and would normally get a refund.

From 6 April 1993, 'Tables A' are known as 'Pay Adjustment Tables' and also give the amounts to add to your pay where you have a K code (10.14.3). From 6 April 2001, student loan deductions and tax credits (3.4) are included.

The tax to be paid or repaid for the week (see (7) above) is calculated by subtracting the total tax due to date for the previous week from that for the current week (see (6) above). The total tax due to date is found each week from the tax deduction tables. These show the tax attributable to the relevant total taxable pay to date.

The tax deduction tables in use are designated tables SR, B, C and D. Table SR shows the amount of tax due at the starting rate of 10 per cent. (Table LR applied before 6 April 1999, showing the tax due at the lower rate of 20 per cent.) Table B shows tax due at the basic rate. Table C shows for each week or month (see below) the amounts to be taxed at the higher rate.

If you have only one employment your tax is calculated from table B if your earnings are below the higher rates level, unless only the starting rate applies. (Before 6 April 1999, lower rate applied instead of starting rate.) Should your earnings make you liable for higher rate income tax, however, your PAYE tax payable is calculated from table C which is in fact supplementary to table B.

Where your earnings are substantial and you have more than one employment the Revenue will normally direct that tables B and C are used for your main employment. For your other employments, however, they might issue you with code D0. This means that tax at 40 per cent is applicable to those employments. The 'D' codings merely provide the Revenue with a very approximate method of taxing at source your salaries from employments other than your main one.

The Revenue provide monthly tax deduction tables for use where salary payments are made on a monthly basis. The Deductions Working Sheet has a column in which to enter the amount deductible for earnings-related National Insurance contributions, which are collected through the PAYE system.

10.14.3 Your code number

Your code number is calculated from your income tax allowances and reliefs. It is allocated to you by the Inspector of Taxes and takes into account all the reliefs to which you are entitled against which some of your other income may be set off. Account may also be taken of any Schedule E income tax underpaid or overpaid for the previous year.

Coding notices are only sent to cover changes. Otherwise the code for the previous year must be used. The notice itemises the various allowances and reliefs to which you are entitled (3.0.1). Any other necessary adjustments are also shown on your coding notice which shows at the bottom the adjusted balance of your allowances and also the code number which corresponds to that figure. The Inspector will probably obtain the details for your coding notice from your last income tax return.

In order to convert your total allowances and adjustments into your code number, you simply divide by ten and round down to the nearest whole number. Thus if your allowances, etc. for 2005–06 total £4,895, your code number is 489. For administrative purposes, your code number will normally end in A, H, L, P, T, V or Y depending on your main personal reliefs (single, married couple's, age, etc.). There are also K codes (see below). When these reliefs increase instructions are issued by the Revenue to employers to augment the relevant codes accordingly. In these cases revised coding notices are not needed.

The above remarks normally apply to your coding in respect of your main employment. If you have other employments and the Revenue consider that your taxable earnings after deductions for the year 2005–06 will not exceed £32,400, you will be coded 'BR' in respect of each of your other employments. This means that table B (10.14.2) is applied to your total earnings from each employment except your main one. No deductions are normally made for your allowances, etc. because these are included in your coding for your main employment. If, however, your earnings are likely to exceed £32,400 then the Inspector of Taxes is likely to allocate you with 'D' codings (10.14.2) in respect of your supplementary employments.

From 6 April 1993, a system of K codes operates. These cover car and other benefits etc., which increase your taxable pay. Another application is where your state retirement pension exceeds your personal allowances. It is hoped that this arrangement will facilitate the collection of tax on benefits. If you have a K code instead of a normal one, your employer simply adds the appropriate amount to your taxable pay rather than deducting it.

As from 6 April 2004, unless you object, the Inland Revenue are empowered to take account of any of your non-PAYE income in determining your code number. This may result in a higher percentage of your earnings provisionally being paid in tax, but this is subject to an overriding limit of 50 per cent.

10.14.4 Employers' PAYE returns

At the end of each tax year your employer must complete a form P35 and send this to the Revenue. End of year returns P14 must be completed for each employee and sent with the P35. The P14s are completed from the Deductions Working Sheets (P11) or other records and include National Insurance number, date of birth, final tax code, total pay, tax and National Insurance contributions, as well as any Statutory Sick Pay and Statutory Maternity Pay. Also any forms P11D required for the year (10.7) should be sent to the Revenue.

The form P35 is a summary of the total tax due to be deducted for the tax year in respect of all of the employees. The earnings-related National Insurance contributions are also entered for each employee. The total Statutory Sick Pay and Statutory Maternity Pay details are also included. The details are obtained from the tax deduction cards. The total income tax due to be paid over for the year by the employer is then found by adding up all of the tax entries on the form P35 and from this is deducted the total of the actual payments made. A similar procedure is followed regarding the earnings-related National Insurance contributions except that the amount to be paid over also includes the employer's contributions.

The balances shown by the form P35 represent underpayments or overpayments of PAYE income tax and earnings-related contributions: if the employer has underpaid he should send a cheque with the form and if he has overpaid a repayment will subsequently be received.

There are time limits for submitting the forms which must be carefully watched. Penalties (16.9.3) may arise on forms P14 and P35 not submitted by 19 May following the tax year. Thus the 2004–05 forms should have been submitted by 19 May 2005. (By concession, the Revenue allow the forms to be received on the last business day within seven extra days.)

At the end of each tax year the employer should issue to each of his employees a form P60 which is a certificate of gross earnings for the year and of income tax deducted under PAYE and now forms part of the P14 pack (P14/P60). This must be done by 31 May.

10.14.5 Change of employer

If you leave your employment your old employer should complete for you a form P45 showing your name, district reference, code number, week or month number of the last entries on your tax deduction card, total gross pay to date and total tax due to date. Your old employer sends part 1 of the form P45 to his Inspector of Taxes and hands to you parts 2 and 3 which you must give to your new employer and part 4 for you to keep. The latter enters your address and date of starting on part 3 and sends it to his Inspector.

Your new employer should prepare for you a tax deduction card in accordance with your form P45 and deduct PAYE tax from your wages in the normal way.

If you are not able to give a form P45 to your new employer, he will normally deduct tax under the 'emergency' system which assumes you are single and gives you no other allowances. If this happens you should make an income tax return to the Inspector of Taxes or supply the necessary details to him, so that he can issue you with your correct code number which your employer will then use, making any necessary tax repayment to you.

Form P46 is available for you to complete if you do not have a P45 when you start a new job. It covers whether you are a school leaver or whether it is your main job or an additional one which you are starting. The P46 enables you to indicate your circumstances so that your employer will know whether to deduct basic rate tax from your salary or use an emergency code. (There is also a coding claim form P15 for use in establishing your coding.)

10.14.6 **Extension of scope of PAYE** (ITEPA Ss696–702)

Rules were introduced operative from May 1994 to prevent employers avoiding PAYE by paying staff in assets. Payments through third parties such as offshore trusts are also targeted. Similar rules operate in relation to National Insurance contributions from 1 December 1993.

If you are paid income by an intermediary, this is treated as paid by your employer for PAYE purposes. Also, if you are given part of your income as 'tradable assets', this is now caught by the PAYE net. Examples of 'tradable assets' are gold and commodities. The rules extend to vouchers and credit tokens used to provide these assets. From 3 July 1997, the assignment by employers of trade debts to employees is also caught.

10.15 Profit Related Pay (TA 1988 Ss169–184 & Sch 29, FA 1995 Ss123 & 137, FA 1997 S63, FA 1998 S62 & Sch 11 & FA 1999 S16)

Valuable tax relief operated from 6 April 1987 in respect of Profit Related Pay (PRP), but has been phased out, not applying for periods beginning after 31 December 1999. Fuller details appear in previous editions.

For profit periods beginning after 31 March 1991 and before 1 January 1998, all of your PRP was free of income tax up to the lower of £4,000 or 20 per cent of your PAYE pay for the year. Subsequently, the relief was phased out, as follows:

Profit period beginning	Ceiling for relief £
1 January 1998–31 December 1998	2,000
1 January 1999–31 December 1999	1,000
From 1 January 2000	NIL

10.16 Service companies etc. providing personal services (ITEPA Ss48–61)

Rules operate from 6 April 2000 to counter the avoidance of tax and National Insurance contributions by supplying personal services through service companies, partnerships and other intermediaries. Broadly, the intermediary is responsible for deducting any extra tax and National Insurance as well as that on salary already paid to you as follows:

(1) The rules apply where your services are contracted to a client by an intermediary, without whom you would have been treated as being an employee of the client.
(2) Existing case law is used to define 'employee'.
(3) Engagements are excluded where your client is an individual who is not in business or your only income from the intermediary is fully taxed under Schedule E and you are entitled to no further income or capital (with minor exceptions).
(4) Intermediaries are responsible for operating the legislation. If you work through a service company, it will deduct PAYE and National Insurance from your salary in the normal way. At the end of each tax year, you will be charged Schedule E tax and National Insurance on any balance of the income for your services received by the intermediary and not paid to you as salary and benefits in kind. You are allowed to deduct certain expenses (5).
(5) As well as all expenses otherwise deductible under the normal Schedule E expenses rules, the intermediary can deduct certain approved scheme employer pension contributions; also an extra 5 per cent on the relevant gross income and employer's National Insurance including that on the deemed payment to you. Also treated as expenses from 2002–03 are reimbursements and mileage allowances.
(6) Where the intermediary is a partnership, it might be caught by the rules if you have a close connection, like being entitled to at least 60 per cent of its profits or where partners share profits according to their relevant engagements. Where the rules apply, income received gross from all of your relevant engagements (net of expenses) are deemed paid to you at the end of the tax year and charged to tax and National Insurance contributions. Your taxable partnership share (if any) will then exclude the deemed amount already taxed.
(7) From 10 April 2003, certain domestic workers such as nannies and butlers are brought within the rules for income tax. This applies normally where personal service companies are being used. (New National Insurance rules will follow.)

Chapter 11

INCOME FROM BUSINESSES AND PROFESSIONS

11.1 Trades, professions and vocations

The profits from trades, professions and vocations were normally assessed for 2004–05 and previous years under Schedule D Case I (trades) and Schedule D Case II (professions and vocations). However, from 2005–06 onwards, with the introduction of ITTOIA (2.10), the income is no longer classified for income tax purposes into schedules, although the basic rules remain. (ITTOIA does not apply for corporation tax purposes.) There are certain special rules which apply to partnerships (Chapter 12) and companies (Chapter 13).

Trade includes manufacturing, retailing, wholesaling and all kinds of trading ventures.

A profession is defined as an occupation requiring special intellectual skills, sometimes coupled with manual skills (for example doctor of medicine, architect, accountant, barrister).

A vocation has been defined as the way that a person passes his life (for example composer, author, actor, singer).

11.2 What is trading?

Your regular business will normally be treated as a trade (previously assessed under Schedule D Case I). There are, however, certain other activities which might constitute trading depending on the circumstances. The following are some general guidelines:

(1) Regular buying and selling normally constitutes trading although this does not usually apply to purchases and sales of shares by an individual.
(2) An isolated transaction might be held to be trading if it is by its very nature commercial. For example, a single purchase and sale of a quantity of unmatured whisky is normally treated as a trading transaction. This is because the ownership of unmatured whisky is mainly for commercial purposes.
(3) Isolated transactions involving the purchase and sale of works of art are not normally trading. Here the works of art are owned to be admired and not exclusively (if at all) for commercial purposes. Capital gains tax, however, might be payable on sales of works of art for over £6,000 each (20.24).
(4) Isolated transactions in income producing assets are not usually treated as trading. Capital gains tax would normally apply (20.1).
(5) If you do something to your purchase before selling it the sale might be considered to be trading. For instance, if you buy a ship, convert it and then sell it you will be treated as trading.
(6) Repetition of the same transaction is evidence of trading.
(7) If you deal in property this is likely to be treated as trading (7.10).

(8) The possession of expert business knowledge in connection with a transaction that you carry out will increase your chances of being treated as trading.

11.3 What business expenses are allowed?

In computing the amount of your profits to be charged to tax, you are allowed to deduct any sums wholly and exclusively incurred for the purposes of the trade, profession or vocation, subject to various special rules (see below). Only expenses of a revenue nature are deductible, however, and these must be distinguished from capital expenditure (2.6).

11.3.1 Allowable business expenses

To the extent that they are incurred wholly and exclusively for business purposes the following are deductible (the list is not exhaustive):

(1) The cost of goods bought for resale and materials used in manufacturing.
(2) Wages and salaries paid to employees, together with National Insurance payments. This includes employees seconded on a temporary basis to charities (TA 1988 S86) and to certain educational bodies including local authorities FA 1999 S58.
(3) Pensions paid to past employees and their dependants.
(4) Redundancy payments to employees including certain voluntary payments on business cessation, up to three times the statutory amount (TA 1988 S90).
(5) The running costs of any premises used for the business including rent and rates, light and heat, repairs (not capital improvements), insurance, cleaning, etc.
(6) Discounts allowed on sales.
(7) Carriage, packing and delivery costs.
(8) Printing, postage, stationery and telephone.
(9) Repairs to your plant and machinery.
(10) Staff welfare expenses.
(11) Insurance regarding loss of profits, public liability, goods in transit, burglary, etc.
(12) Advertising.
(13) Trade subscriptions.
(14) Professional charges of a revenue nature – for example audit fees.
(15) Legal charges of a revenue nature, for example debt collection, preparing trading contracts and settling trading disputes.
(16) If you pay a premium for the lease of your business premises and the recipient is taxed under previously Schedule A you can claim the cost of the premium as a deduction from your business profits spread over the term of the lease.
(17) VAT on your purchases and expenses if you are not registered for VAT. (If you are registered you set this VAT against that on your sales and only charge your purchases, etc. excluding VAT.)
(18) Travelling expenses including hotel bills and fares on business trips but excluding the cost of travelling between your home and business (unless you also do business from home).
(19) The entertaining of your own staff but not entertaining UK or overseas customers.
(20) Gifts which incorporate an advertisement for your business provided that the value for each recipient each year did not exceed £10 (TA 1988 S577). From 2001–02 this limit increases to £50.
(21) Bad debts which arose in the course of trading. Also provisions made for specific debtors whom you anticipate may not pay. Also, any debt which you release after 29

November 1993 as part of a formal voluntary arrangement. Special rules limit the relief available for doubtful sovereign debt due from overseas governments, etc. normally to banks. Broadly, the allowable amount for 1990–91 is limited to the 1989–90 level and scaled up by 5 per cent annually thereafter.

(22) A trader's expenses of obtaining patents are normally allowable. The outright purchase of a patent is a capital expense, however, which normally qualifies for capital allowances.

(23) Running expenses of motor vehicles excluding such proportion as is attributable to private use.

(24) Interest payments including hire purchase interest. Relief for bank and other interest is normally given on the basis of payments rather than accruals.

(25) The incidental costs of obtaining loan finance which carries deductible interest (TA 1988 S77). Costs concerning repayment, providing security and abortive exercises are covered; but not stamp duty, foreign exchange losses, issue discounts or repayment premiums. This relief extends to certain convertible loan stocks.

(26) Pre-trading expenditure, of a revenue nature, incurred within seven years before starting to trade (TA 1988 S401). For companies it is treated as falling on the first day of trading; for individuals it was regarded as a separate loss (11.22). However, for businesses set up after 5 April 1995, individuals are treated like companies in this respect.

(27) Contributions before 1 April 2000 to local enterprise agencies approved by the Secretary of State. However, you obtained no relief if you (or those connected with you) were entitled to benefits from the agencies (TA 1988 S79).

(28) Similar rules applied to contributions to training and enterprise councils made from 1 April 1990 to 31 March 2000 (TA S79A).

(29) Work training provided by an employer for employees about to leave their current jobs, or who have just left. Training courses must provide improved skills or knowledge for use in new jobs or business and the employee is not taxed on the benefit. Courses must not exceed one year and must take place within the UK (TA 1988 S588).

(30) Security expenditure (FA 1989 Ss112 & 113). This is allowed for the self-employed (including partners) regarding assets or services to meet personal security threats arising from their businesses.

(31) Certain revenue expenditure incurred concerning waste disposal sites from 6 April 1989 (TA Ss91A–B). Expenditure on preparing a site is allowed according to the proportion of its capacity filled with waste in the accounts year. Expenditure on making good a site is given in the year of payment or on commencement of trade if later. However, no allowance is given for expenditure on which capital allowances (11.8) are given.

(32) Certain payments for football ground improvements made by pool promoters (FA 1990 S126).

(33) Gifts of equipment, manufactured, sold or used in the trade, to schools and other educational establishments. The relief has now been extended so as to cover all charitable causes (TA S83A).

(34) The setting-up costs of certain employee share schemes from 1 April 1991 (10.9.6).

(35) Contributions from 30 November 1993 to 31 March 2000 to a Business Links organisation (FA 1994 S145).

(36) Class 1A and (from 6 April 1999) Class 1B National Insurance contributions on car benefits for employees (TA 1988 S617).

(37) Contributions to the Individual Learning Accounts of employees, subject to the rules, after 5 April 2000 (10.6.23).

(38) Contributions to the running costs of Urban Regeneration Companies from 1 April 2003 (TA S79B).

11.3.2 **Expenses not deductible from business profits** (TA 1988 S74)

(1) Any payments or expenses not wholly and exclusively laid out for the purposes of the business.
(2) Expenses incurred for the private or domestic purposes of yourself or family.
(3) Where expenses contain some business and some private element the proportion attributable to the latter is not deductible. In the case of a private dwelling house used for business purposes the deductible proportion is not normally allowed to exceed two-thirds of the rent and other costs.
(4) Any capital used for improvements to your business premises.
(5) Any loss not connected with the business.
(6) Any reserves and provisions made for anticipated expenses such as repairs, retirement benefits, etc. including general bad debts reserves but not reserves for specific bad debts (nor contributions under approved pension plans).
(7) Any annuity or other annual payment (other than interest) payable out of the profits (4.2).
(8) Payments of income tax, capital gains tax and corporation tax, etc.
(9) Your own drawings as the owner or part owner of the business.
(10) Depreciation and amortisation of plant and machinery, motor vehicles, buildings, etc. Capital allowances are normally available however (11.9).
(11) Any royalty payment from which you deduct income tax.
(12) Entertaining expenses unless in connection with your own staff.
(13) Professional charges of a capital nature. For example legal fees in connection with a new lease, architects' fees for designing a new building, accountants' fees connected with the purchase of a new business. These expenses can often be added to the cost of the assets for capital gains tax purposes (20.10).
(14) Fines for illegal acts and connected legal expenses.
(15) Charitable donations, unless wholly for business purposes (TA 1988 S577). (Note special rules for non-close companies (15.2.1) and gift-aid.)
(16) Political donations.
(17) The cost of acquiring capital assets such as plant and machinery, motor vehicles, buildings, etc. Capital allowances are frequently available however (11.9).
(18) Expenditure after 10 June 1993 involved in payments which are criminal offences; payments after 29 November 1993 resulting from extortion by terrorist groups or other criminals and payments overseas, such as bribes, which would be criminal if made in the UK (TA S577A).

11.4 The computation of your assessable profits (TA 1988 Ss74–112)

If you conduct a business or profession you will normally have annual accounts prepared on a commercial basis including a profit and loss account or an income and expenditure account. Your annual accounts should normally be drawn up to the same date in each year but need not coincide with the tax year (which ends on 5 April).

From April 1990, simpler accounts are permitted from 'small businesses'. These were individuals and partnerships with a turnover less than £10,000 a year. This figure was increased to £15,000 for accounts submitted after 6 April 1992. A simple three line account is needed showing total turnover, purchases and expenses and net profit. Tax returns from April 1991 allow the three line account to be incorporated therein. However, accurate business records must still be kept.

The profit shown by your annual accounts will form the basis of your assessment, but it will normally require adjustment in some or all of the following ways:

(1) Add to your profit any non-deductible expenses that have been charged in your accounts (11.3.2).

(2) Deduct from your profit any items included in your accounts which are not taxed under previously Cases I and II of Schedule D either because they are non-taxable or because they are otherwise liable to tax. Examples are:
   - ▶ Capital profits liable to capital gains tax (20.1).
   - ▶ Interest receivable (8.4).
   - ▶ Rents receivable (7.1).
   - ▶ Interest received net, income tax having been deducted at source (8.2); also dividends (8.1).
   - ▶ Amounts originally set aside as reserves and now recredited in your accounts provided the original amounts were not allowed against your taxable profits.

(3) Deduct from your profit any allowable expenses not already charged in your accounts.

(4) Exclude from your profits government grants towards the cost of specified capital expenditure or compensation for loss of capital assets. Other grants under the Industries Act 1972, etc. are now generally taxable. However, regional development grants under the Industrial Development Act 1982 and certain grants to assist industry in Northern Ireland are normally exempt.

(5) If you have recently left the unemployment register to set up a business you may be receiving Enterprise Allowances. These are paid for one year at a weekly amount and are now taxable under previously Schedule D Case VI (15.1). They should therefore be eliminated from your assessable trading profits. (However, Enterprise Allowances are liable to Class 4 National Insurance.)

(6) Add to your profit any trading profits not already included.

(7) From your profits adjusted as above, deduct your capital allowances for the year (11.8).

(8) Under the current year basis (11.7.4 and 11.8.2) capital allowances are based on the accounting period and treated as deductible expenses. (This started from 1997–98 for businesses existing on 5 April 1994 and from commencement for newer ones.)

11.4.1 Example: Trading income computation

Mr A carries on a manufacturing business. His accounts for the year to 31 December 2005, which show a net profit of £39,000, include the following:

	£		£
Expenses		**Income**	
Depreciation of motor vehicles	4,300	Bank deposit interest	70
Depreciation of plant and machinery	6,700	Profit on sale of motor car	1,050
Bad debts provision (5% × sales debtors)	1,650	Bad debts provision no longer required (general)	200
Legal expenses re debt collection	200		
Legal expenses re new lease (not a renewal)	270		
Charitable donations (non business nor under gift-aid)	90		
Entertaining expenses	2,250		

Assuming capital allowances of £10,500 for the year ended 31 December 2005, compute Mr A's adjusted Case I profit.

Mr A – Trading income computation based on accounts for year ended 31 December 2005

	£	£
Net profit per accounts		39,000
Add: Disallowable expenses:		
Depreciation (£4,300 + £6,700)	11,000	
General bad debts provision	1,650	
Legal expenses re new lease	270	
Charitable donations	90	
Entertaining expenses	2,250	15,260
		54,260
Less:		
Bank deposit interest	70	
Profit on sale of motor car (capital)	1,050	
Bad debts provision no longer required	200	
Capital allowances	10,500	11,820
Adjusted profit		42,440

11.4.2 **Basis change – adjustment** (FA 2002 S64 & Sch 12)

New rules apply where a business has a change of accounting basis or in the way in which tax adjustments are made to accounting profits, whether through change in the law or practice. These rules apply to changes of basis in accounting periods ending after 31 July 2001.

The new rules are to ensure that on a change of basis, profits are only taxed once and trading expenses only relieved once. Also, spreading relief is given regarding tax payable on prior year adjustments.

11.5 Stock valuation

An important factor in the preparation of business accounts is the valuation of stock and work in progress. This is the amount of unsold raw materials, finished goods and work in progress that was owned at the end of the accounts period. The stock, etc. must be valued at each accounting date and the profits are augmented by the excess of the closing stock over the opening stock or decreased by the deficit. It is clear that if the closing stock is valued on a more generous basis than the opening stock then the profits shown will be higher than the true profits and vice versa.

The Revenue pay careful attention to the manner in which businesses value their stock and they normally insist that for tax purposes the opening and closing stocks are valued on the same basis. The usual basis adopted is that each item in stock is valued at the lower of its cost or net realisable value. The exact cost to be included may or may not contain an addition for expenses depending on the exact basis adopted. The general rule in ascertaining cost is that identical items should be identified on the basis that the earliest purchases were sold or used first (FIFO). In all cases the method chosen must be used consistently. 'Net realisable value' is what it is estimated will be obtained from disposing of the stock in the ordinary course of business at the balance sheet date, after allowing for all expenses in connection with the disposal.

Rules operate from 29 November 1994 to prevent the manipulation of stock values for discontinued businesses. These are to stop tax advantages being obtained from selling the stock to a connected party at an untrue valuation (TA S100 (1A–1G)).

11.6 Stock relief

Stock relief was brought into effect by the Finance Act 1975 and withdrawn for periods of account beginning after 12 March 1984. Relief was broadly based on average price increases as reflected in an 'All Stocks' index. Fuller details are given in earlier editions of this book.

11.7 Basis of assessment (TA 1988 Ss60–63A & ITTOIA Ss196–220)

The present system has operated since 1996–97 (11.7.4). The assessment for that year was based on the average profits for the two years ending in 1996–97. After that, the assessment for any year is based on the accounts for the year ending within the year of assessment. Thus, if your accounting date is 31 December, your 2004–05 assessment will be on your profits for the year to 31 December 2004.

The normal basis of assessment under Cases I and II of Schedule D was previously the profits of the accounts year ending in the preceding tax year. This applied for 1995–96 and earlier years of assessment.

Thus if a business made up its annual accounts to 30 September its 1995–96 Schedule D Case I assessment was based on the profits for the year to 30 September 1994 (that is, ending in the preceding tax year 1995–96). Special rules apply to the opening and closing years (see below) and also where you change your accounting date.

11.7.1 The current year basis (FA 1994 Sch 20, FA 1995 S122 & Schs 21 & 22, TA Ss60–63A)

(1) If your business commences *after 5 April 1994*, the new basis applies at once. Otherwise, it applied for 1997–98 and future years with special rules for 1996–97.

(2) The basic rule is that you are assessed on the adjusted profits for your accounts year which ends in the year of assessment. Thus if you make up your annual accounts to 30 September, your 2004–05 assessment is based on your profits for the year to 30 September 2004.

(3) For 1996–97, your assessment was normally based on the average of your profits for the two years ending in 1996–97. Thus if your taxable profits for the year to 30 September 1995 were £20,000 and for the year to 30 September 1996 they were £30,000, your 1996–97 assessment was £25,000. This was subject to certain anti-avoidance rules (11.7.6). Normally, you had the option of preparing one set of accounts for the 24 month period ending in 1996–97. Half of the profits for this period was then assessed for 1996–97.

(4) Exceptionally, your transitional base period may have covered more or less than 24 months, perhaps due to a change of accounting date. Your 1996–97 assessment was then based on the proportionate profits for one year. Thus if the period was 30 months for which your profits were £60,000, your 1996–97 assessment was $^{12}/_{30} \times$ £60,000 = £24,000.

(5) Under the new rules, the first year of assessment for a business is based on the profits to the next 5 April (apportioned in days). Say you *commenced trading* on 1 July 2004, your 2004–05 assessment is based on your profits from that date to 5 April 2005.

(6) The assessment for your second tax year of trading is normally based on the profits for the year ended on your accounting date falling within that

tax year. Thus, if 30 June is your accounting date, your 2005–06 assessment is usually based on your profits for the year to 30 June 2005. However, say your commencement date was 1 September 2004, the 2005–06 assessment will be based on the profits for the first complete year, to 31 August 2005.

(7) When your business ceases, the assessment for the final period will be on an actual basis from the end of your previous base period. Thus suppose you stop trading on 30 April 2005 and your accounting date is 30 June, your 2005–06 assessment will be on the profits from 1 July 2004 to 30 April 2005.

(8) Where a business changes its accounting date the aim will be to tax 12 months' profits for all years except the first and last. This may mean that some profits are taxed twice. However, the intention is that over the lifetime of a business, its profits are fully taxed, but only once. Hence 'overlap relief' will be given where the business ends or a basis period exceeds 12 months, in respect of profits taxed more than once.

(9) 'Overlap relief' often results where a business starts after 5 April 1994. For instance, if you started to trade on 1 July 1994 with a 30 June accounting date, the period 1 July 1994 to 5 April 1995 would be taxed twice. Supposing your proportionate profits for that period are £20,000, you will get relief of this amount when your business eventually ceases.

(10) Special rules cover such areas as losses (11.22.1), capital allowances (11.8.2) and partnerships (12.2).

11.7.2 **Transitional provisions – anti avoidance** (FA 1995 Sch 22)

Since your assessment for 1996–97 was normally based on the average of your profits for the two years ended in 1996–97, there was apparent scope for saving tax. By switching profits into those two years from the adjoining ones, only half would count. However, this was legislated against.

The basic rule is that where you artificially shifted income or profits into your transitional periods (2 years ending in 1996–97) you could be additionally taxed on 1¼ times the amount on which you tried to save tax. However, you were not taxed if you could show that the main benefit which you expected was not a tax one or that the sole purpose was a bona fide commercial one. A *de minimus* exemption also applied. This was £10,000 of profits shifted by an individual.

11.7.3 **Opening and closing years – old system** (TA 1988 Ss61–63)

(1) If your business commences after 5 April 1994, the new current year basis applies throughout (11.7.3). *The following applies where you commenced to trade on an earlier date.*

(2) In the first tax year of a business, profession or vocation the assessment was based on the profits from the starting date until the following 5 April. If accounts had been prepared for the first full year or other period to bridge that date, then the profits were apportioned on a time basis.

(3) The assessment for the second tax year of a business trade or vocation was normally based on the profits for the first complete 12 months of operations.
(4) The third year's assessment was normally on the preceding year basis subject to the election option mentioned under (5).
(5) The taxpayer had the option to elect that the assessment for both the second and third tax years (but not only one of them, nor subsequent years) should be based on the actual profits for those years. The election was required within seven years of the end of the second year of assessment.
(6) For the tax year in which a trade, profession or vocation *permanently stopped*, the assessment under Schedule D Case I or II was based on the actual profits from the previous 6 April until the date of cessation.
(7) Regarding the two years prior to the tax year in which the cessation took place, assessments normally were made on a preceding year basis. However, the Revenue could make additional assessments to cover any excess of the actual profits for those years.

11.8 Capital allowances (CAA etc.)

You are not normally allowed to deduct from your taxable profits the cost or depreciation of capital assets. You can, however, deduct capital allowances in respect of the cost of certain assets used in your business or profession including the following:

(1) Plant and machinery (11.9) – this category also includes furniture, fittings, office equipment and motor vehicles, together with the thermal insulation of industrial buildings and of making certain buildings comply with the fire regulations. Other categories of included expenditure relate to safety at sports grounds and stadia (11.9.9) security (11.9.10) and computer software and IT equipment (11.9.15).
(2) Industrial buildings (11.11) – this includes factories and some warehouses, etc.
(3) Agricultural and forestry buildings, etc. (11.14).
(4) Hotel buildings, etc. (11.15).
(5) Scientific research expenditure (11.17).
(6) Patents and know-how (11.18).
(7) Mines, oil wells, etc. (11.20) and dredging (11.19).

If you have expenditure which qualifies for allowances under more than one of the above heads, you will be able to make an irrevocable choice. This applies for accounting periods ending after 27 July 1989 (FA 1989 Sch 13).

11.8.1 Base period (CAA S6)

For a business, profession or vocation (including partnerships) the capital allowances are computed according to the assets purchased and those used in the annual accounts period (that is, the base period). For these purposes, you must take the date when the expenditure was incurred. This is now generally when the obligation to pay becomes unconditional, unless, for example, part of the capital expenditure is payable more than four months later. Under the old system, a deduction was made from the Schedule D Case I or Case II assessment in respect of the total capital allowances for that tax year.

For example, if a business made up its accounts to 31 December each year then its Schedule D Case I assessment for 1995–96 was based on its accounts for the year to 31 December 1994 (ending in the preceding tax year). Similarly its 1995–96 capital allowances were based on the year to 31 December 1994. (See 11.8.2 below for the new rules introduced with the current year basis.)

Under the old system, special rules applied where there were base periods of less than one year. Where one base period applied to two tax years, the additions during the base period were allocated to the earlier tax year for the purposes of calculating the allowances. If there was a gap between base periods, it was added to the second base period unless this marked a cessation of trading – in this case you added the gap to the first period.

11.8.2 **New current year assessment rules** (FA 1994 Ss211–212 & Sch 20)

New capital allowances rules were introduced in line with the current year basis (11.7.4). These took full effect for 1997–98 and future years, regarding businesses existing at 5 April 1994. Capital allowances are treated as trading expenses. Similarly, balancing charges are regarded as trading receipts. Capital allowances have to be claimed in the tax return.

Capital allowances are now related to the period for which accounts are drawn up, rather than the year of assessment. However, any unrelieved amounts from 1996–97 and earlier years are to be included with the allowances for the first accounts ending after 5 April 1997.

For the *transitional year of assessment*, 1996–97, capital allowances were normally based on a two year period ending therein. This corresponded with your assessment basis. Thus if your accounting date was 30 September, your 1996–97 capital allowances were based on the two years to 30 September 1996. You used the opening balances, additions and disposals attributable to that period, taking writing down allowance (11.9.2) for one year.

11.8.3 **VAT Capital Goods Scheme adjustments** (CAA Ss234–246 etc.)

Extra VAT paid under the VAT Capital Goods Scheme qualifies for capital allowances in the year of payment. Similarly, VAT repaid from that date reduces the appropriate expenditure pool for capital allowances purposes in the year of receipt. This particularly affects businesses which are partly exempt (23.3) from VAT such as those in banking, finance, insurance and property.

The items covered are limited to computers and computer equipment worth at least £50,000 and land and buildings worth at least £250,000. The VAT adjustments generally arise on changes of use.

11.9 Capital allowances on plant and machinery

In general, expenditure qualifies for 25 per cent writing down allowance each year, however, special rules apply to long-life assets (11.9.8), motor vehicles (11.9.11), plant which you lease out (11.9.14) and computer equipment, etc. (11.9.15). Expenditure in the year to 31 October 1993 may also have qualified for first-year allowance at 40 per cent for plant and 20 per cent initial allowance for industrial and agricultural buildings, etc. Expenditure after 1 July 1997 on plant and machinery may also attract first year allowance (11.9.1).

Balancing charges and allowances can arise when plant is sold (11.9.4). The main allowances available on plant purchased new or second-hand between 26 October 1970 and 1 April 1986 were normally a first-year allowance for the year of purchase and a writing down allowance for each subsequent year.

To claim relief, you needed to notify the Revenue within two years after the chargeable period when you incurred the expenditure. If you still own the asset, you can claim relief for a later period within two years of its end. The notification requirement does not apply as from 1 April 2000 (FA 2000 S73).

11.9.1 **First-year allowances** (CAA Ss39–51)

Expenditure on plant and machinery after 1 July 1997 obtains first year allowance subject to certain conditions. The rates are 50 per cent to 1 July 1998 and then 40 per cent on expenditure thereafter. A special 100 per cent rate applies for spending on machinery or plant for use in Northern Ireland in the four years starting 12 May 1998. The relief is limited to small- and medium-sized businesses, including companies and groups, broadly satisfying two of the following three conditions:

(1) turnover not more than £11.2m
(2) assets not more than £5.6m
(3) not more than 250 employees.

For 'small businesses' (11.9.15) the rate increases to 50 per cent for the year to 31 March 2005 for companies and to 5 April 2005 for other businesses. After that, it reverted to 40 per cent.

Exclusions include machinery and plant for leasing, cars, long-life assets (11.9.8), sea-going ships and railway assets. If you incurred expenditure on plant and machinery during the year to 31 October 1993, you obtained a first-year allowance of 40 per cent of the cost, with no restriction regarding the size of business. If you wish you can disclaim all or part of your first year allowance. If first-year allowance is taken, writing down allowance is not available until the second year.

From 1 April 2001, expenditure on designated energy-saving products and technologies attracts 100 per cent first year allowance. Such expenditure after 16 April 2002 also qualifies for 100 per cent first year allowance where the asset is for leasing, letting or hire.

Expenditure after 16 April 2002 and before 1 April 2008 on new low emission cars which are either electrically propelled or emit no more than 120 k/gm of carbon dioxide obtains 100 per cent first year allowance. Also included is plant and machinery to refuel cars with natural gas or hydrogen fuel. Furthermore, for expenditure after 16 April 2002, the capital allowance restrictions for cars costing over £12,000 and leased cars (11.9.1) are removed for low emission cars, qualifying for the 100 per cent allowance.

After 31 March 2003 100 per cent first year allowance is available on expenditure on designated environmentally beneficial technologies and products (CAA S45H).

Current and previous first year allowance rates are summarised below and further details are given in the 1989–90 and earlier editions of this book.

Expenditure date	Rate of allowance %
After 21.3.72 and before 14.3.84	100
After 13.3.84 and before 1.4.85	75
After 31.3.85 and before 1.4.86	50
After 31.3.86 and before 1.11.92	nil
After 31.10.92 and before 1.11.93	40
* After 1.7.97 and before 2.7.98	50
* After 1.7.98	40
# From April 2004 for one year	50
# From April 2005	40

* restricted to small and medium sized businesses – 100% applies where used in Northern Ireland and expenditure is after 11 May 1998 (also certain IT expenditure).

\# For 'small businesses' only.

11.9.2 **Writing down allowance** (CAA Ss11–20 & 55–70)

Each asset is put into a 'pool' at its cost price (less any first-year allowance obtained) and a writing down allowance of 25 per cent is given on the balance. You can take less than 25 per cent in any year and this also applies to companies (13.10). Writing down allowance was not normally given for the first year, if first-year allowance was obtained. Only 6 per cent may be available on long-life assets bought after 25 November 1996 (11.9.8).

The 'pooling' rules normally apply to Schedule D businesses. However, from 6 April 1997 (1 April for companies) capital allowances are also to be computed on a 'pooling' basis regarding machinery and plant used for a property letting business. This will normally relate to all your Schedule A income (7.1).

Where you obtain no first-year allowance, writing down allowance runs from the first year. Unlike first-year allowances, writing down allowances previously only applied when the assets concerned were brought into use. However, from 1 April 1985, they are available from when the expenditure is incurred.

If the base period is less than a year, the rate of writing down allowance is proportionately reduced. Thus, if the base period for a business is only six months for a given year of assessment, then any writing down allowances for that period would be at the rate of $25\% \times 6/12 = 12.5\%$. For 1996–97, there was normally a two year base period (11.8.2). However, only one year's writing down allowances were taken.

11.9.3 **Ships** (CAA Ss127–158)

Free depreciation by postponing first-year allowances was available with regard to new ships. This extended to expenditure on second-hand ships incurred after 31 March 1985. The same principle still applies regarding writing down allowances on expenditure on new ships after 13 March 1984 and second-hand ships after 31 March 1985. The allowances can be 'rolled-up' and used at will. These rules do not apply, however, to certain leasing situations where capital allowances are restricted (11.9.14).

You can claim to defer a balancing charge on a ship disposal. It is now necessary that you reinvest the proceeds in other shipping within six years and relief is available across groups of companies.

11.9.4 **Sales of plant and machinery – balancing allowances and charges** (CAA Ss55–70)

If you sell an item of plant from your 'pool' of purchases, you simply deduct the sale proceeds from the 'pool' balance. If the proceeds exceed the original cost of the plant, however, you only deduct the cost from the pool and the excess is a capital gain. Should the sale proceeds exceed your 'pool' balance, the excess is treated as a balancing charge and it is added to your assessment for the relevant year. By means of the balancing charge, the Revenue recoup the excess of capital allowances that would otherwise have been given to you. Note that your time of sale is taken as the earlier of completion or when possession is given. This rule is of general application for most capital allowance purposes.

Regarding plant, etc. (apart from some motor cars) purchased after 26 October 1970, balancing allowances normally only occur in the event of a cessation. If you cease permanently to trade during a period then you receive for that period a 'balancing allowance' equal to the remainder of your 'pool' (of expenditure on assets after 26 October 1970 less allowances already obtained) less its disposal value.

If assets are sold from one person (company, etc.) to another, both being under common control, both may elect within two years that the tax written down value is passed from one to the other. The effect is that there is no balancing allowance or charge. (These provisions must now be assumed always to have had effect regarding qualifying hotels, scientific research assets and commercial buildings in enterprise zones, providing both parties are entitled to capital allowances.) A similar election may be made within two years after the succession of a trade between connected persons (for example where a trade passes from one company to another under common control).

Balancing charges and other balancing adjustments are not applicable regarding certain transfers of UK trades from a company situated in one EC member state to a company situated in another. The consideration must consist of shares or securities and the transfer must be for commercial reasons and not with a main purpose of saving tax.

A new anti-avoidance measure prevents a balancing charge being obtained where the proceeds have been reduced by means of a tax avoidance scheme (CAA S570A).

11.9.5 Example: Capital allowances on plant and machinery

Mr A has been carrying on a small manufacturing business for many years and makes up his accounts to 31 December each year. At 31 December 2003 the capital allowances written down value of his plant, etc. was £8,100. Mr A purchased the following new plant:

Date	Description	Cost £
on 2 February 2004	Typewriters	1,000
on 1 May 2004	Machinery	5,000
on 30 November 2004	Machinery	2,000

Compute Mr A's capital allowances for 2003–04 and 2004–05.

		'Pool' £	Total allowances £
Balance forward		8,100	
2003–04 writing down allowance		2,025	2,025
Balance forward		6,075	
2004–05 (base period year to 31 December 2004)			
Additions:			
2 February 2004		1,000	
1 May 2004		5,000	
30 November 2004		2,000	
		14,075	
First year allowance			
£1,000 at 40%	400		
£7,000 at 50%	3,500		
Writing down allowance			
£6,075 at 25%	1,518	5,418	5,418
Balance forward		8,657	

11.9.6 **Short-life assets** (CAA Ss83–89)

A special rule applies to short-life plant and machinery which you buy for your trade. You can elect to have the writing down allowances on that plant calculated separately from your 'pool' (de-pooling). The election must be made within two years of the year of acquisition. De-pooling does not normally apply to assets leased to non-traders, or to cars or ships.

When you sell the assets, there will be a balancing allowance or charge, not normally otherwise arising. However, if the machinery or plant has not been sold within five years, it must be transferred to your 'pool' at its tax written-down value.

11.9.7 **Example: Short-life assets – de-pooling**

Mr B makes up his business accounts to 31 December and bought plant for £100 on 30 June 2000, for which he made a de-pooling election. The plant is sold for £10 on 15 May 2004. The capital allowances computations are as follows:

Year ended 31 December		£
2001	cost	100
	25% writing down allowance	25
		75
2002		19
		56
2003		14
		42
2004		10
		32
2005	Sale proceeds	10
	Balancing allowance	22

Note: If the plant had not been disposed of by 31 December 2005, the written down value would be transferred to the general plant pool.

11.9.8 **Long-life assets** (CAA Ss90–104)

On assets bought after 25 November 1996, your writing down allowance is only 6 per cent, subject to the following:

(1) The 6 per cent rate applies to plant and machinery with an expected life when new of at least 25 years.

(2) Expenditure during the year to 1 July 1998, by a small or medium sized business (11.9.1) attracts a first year allowance of 12 per cent.

(3) Your business will be outside the rules if it spends no more than £100,000 each year on such assets (reduced pro rata for associated companies).

(4) Other exclusions are motor cars and machinery and plant in a building used as a dwelling house, shop, showroom, hotel or office.

(5) Ships continue to attract 25 per cent as do railway assets bought before 2011.
(6) Expenditure before 2001 under contracts effected before 26 November 1996 continues to attract 25 per cent relief.
(7) If applicable, a separate pool is needed for your long-life assets.
(8) Where you sell a long-life asset for less than its tax written down value, in order to gain a tax advantage, it is treated as sold for that value.

11.9.9 **Safety at sports grounds** (CAA Ss27, 30–32 & 63)

If relief is not otherwise available, you can claim capital allowances at 25 per cent on the reducing balance on certain safety expenditure at sports grounds. You must be trading and the grounds designated under the Safety of Sports Grounds Act 1975. From 1 January 1989 this is extended to include 'regulated stands' (broadly providing covered accommodation for 500 or more spectators).

11.9.10 **Security assets** (CAA Ss27, 33 & 63)

Expenditure after 5 April 1989 on 'Security assets' may qualify for capital allowances (25 per cent on reducing balance). You must acquire the assets to meet a special threat to your personal security which arises by virtue of your trade or profession. Partnership and sole traders are covered by the rules.

11.9.11 **Motor vehicles** (CAA Ss74–82)

If you buy a car for use in your business you will obtain the 25 per cent writing down allowance for every year including the first. Special rules apply, however, to cars costing over £12,000 in which case your allowance for any year is restricted to 25 per cent × £12,000, that is, £3,000. Each car that costs over £12,000 must be treated as a separate 'pool' which, when sold, gives rise to its own balancing allowance or balancing charge. For cars purchased before 11 March 1992 the limit was £8,000.

Cars purchased for no more than £12,000 were all put into a separate pool (CAA S41). This pool also includes assets acquired before 1 April 1986, which you lease out and which did not qualify for first-year allowance (11.9.14). This rule has been abolished from the start of the chargeable period including 1 April 2000 for corporation tax and 6 April 2000 for income tax. The balance on the separate pool is then included in the main pool. However, you have the option of delaying this for one year.

First-year allowances are not given on motor vehicles unless they are designed to carry goods; or are of a type unsuitable for use as private vehicles; or are vehicles for hire to the public such as taxis or certain hire cars; or are provided for the use of the recipients of certain mobility allowances and supplements; otherwise, they are available for small and medium enterprises (11.9.1). From 17 April 2002 100 per cent first year allowance applies to low emission cars (11.9.1).

If your car is leased through your business (or company) and its equivalent retail cost price exceeds a given limit, the rental deduction from the taxable business profits is correspondingly restricted. The limit is £12,000 retail cost equivalent if the car was first rented after 10 March 1992 and £8,000 if earlier. This restriction is not to apply to hire purchase arrangements where there is an option to purchase for 1 per cent or less of the original retail cost.

The actual deductible rental is found by multiplying the true rental by $(12{,}000 + \frac{RP - 12{,}000}{2})$ and dividing it by the RP (retail price of the car when new).

11.9.12 Example: Higher priced motor cars

On 31 January 2001 and 21 June 2001 Mr C purchased for use in his business two cars costing respectively £8,000 and £14,000. The second of these is sold on 30 June 2003 for £7.000. The Revenue direct that 20 per cent of the use of each car should be treated as being for private purposes. Mr C prepares his annual accounts to 31 July each year. Compute the capital allowances available on the cars up to 2004–2005 on the basis that no cars are then purchased or sold up to 31 July 2004.

	(1) £	(2) £	Total allowances £	Allowances available to business (80%) £
2001–02				
Additions 31 January 2001	8,000			
21 June 2001		14,000		
Writing down allowance	2,000	3,000	5,000	4,000
	6,000	11,000		
2002–03				
Writing down allowance	1,500	2,750	4,250	3,400
	4,500	8,250		
2003–04				
Proceeds 30 June 2002		7,000		
Balancing allowance		1,250	1,250	
Writing down allowance	1,125		1,125	
	3,375		2,375	1,900
2004–05				
Writing down allowance	844		844	675
Carried forward	2,531			

Notes:

(1) Car (2) is subject to the £12,000 restriction.

(2) Because the business use is restricted to 80 per cent the balancing allowance is restricted in this way.

11.9.13 **Hire purchase** (CAA Ss67–69)

If you buy plant or machinery on hire purchase you are entitled to full capital allowances as soon as you bring it into use in your business. You receive allowances on the capital proportion of the total instalments – the interest proportion is allowed against your business profits in the year that the respective instalments are paid. Thus if you buy under hire purchase a machine whose cash cost would be £1,000 and you are paying a total of £1,600 over three years, you get capital allowances on £1,000 as soon as you start to use the machine. You would also deduct the interest of £600 from your profits for the three years during which you are paying off the instalments (that is about £200 each year).

11.9.14 **Machinery for leasing** (CAA Ss70 & 105–126)

You are normally able to obtain 25 per cent writing down allowance (11.9.2) on expenditure to buy assets which you lease out. However, subject to the rules, 40 per cent first-year allowance may have been available on expenditure during the year to 31 October 1993 (but not after 1 July 1997). A separate pool is used for all such assets purchased before 1 April 1986 and certain cars (11.9.11). Prior to 1 April 1986 plant purchased for leasing qualified for first-year allowance, subject to various rules noted in earlier editions of this book. One requirement was that the assets were used for 'qualifying purposes' for the 'requisite period' (four years of use or earlier disposal).

Where an asset ceased to be used for qualifying purposes during the *requisite period* (above), the capital allowances were recomputed as if no first-year allowance had been given. This normally gave rise to a balancing charge when use for *qualifying purposes* ceased.

Broadly for chargeable periods ending after 1 July 1998 expenditure on assets used in 'finance leasing' only qualify for 25 per cent writing down allowance in the year of purchase according to the time held in that year. However, no such restriction applies subsequently.

Where new plant or machinery is sold and leased back, the lessor can claim capital allowances, provided the lessee does not do so, the parties are not connected and the sale is within 4 months of the equipment being brought in to use. This new rule operates from 28 July 2000.

Anti-avoidance legislation operates concerning leasing partnerships from which a loss benefit otherwise would be obtained from first-year allowances (15.10.6). Wider provisions prevent your offsetting capital allowances from casual leasing activities against other income (15.10.6). For expenditure incurred after 10 March 1982 on assets leased outside the UK and ships or aircraft let on charter further restrictions apply (15.10.6). As from 19 December 2003, wider restrictions apply on leased ships (FA 2003 S169 & Sch 32). Special capital allowances rules also apply to film production costs (11.21).

11.9.15 **IT equipment and computer software** (CAA Ss71–73 & FA 2003 Ss165–166)

A 25 per cent writing down allowance is available for capital expenditure on the outright acquisition of computer software. From 10 March 1992, this extends to capital expenditure on software licences and access to electronic transmission. The expenditure is treated as if on plant and may rank for first year allowances in the case of a small or medium sized business (11.9.1).

'Small businesses' can claim 100 per cent first year allowances on their investment in the three years to 31 March 2004 in information and communication technology (IT). This broadly comprises computers, equipment and peripherals such as printers and keyboards, high-tech communications technologies (third generation mobile phones etc.) and related software (unless acquired after 25 March 2003 with a view to sub-licensing).

The relief is limited to 'small businesses', including companies and groups, broadly satisfying two of the following conditions:

(1) turnover not more than £2.8 million
(2) assets not more than £1.4 million
(3) not more than 50 employees.

11.9.16 **Definition of plant and machinery** (CAA Ss21–25)

Special rules were introduced which provide that buildings and structures do not qualify as plant for capital allowances purposes, nor does land. These rules cover expenditure incurred from 30 November 1993, unless under a contract made before that date and incurred before 5 April 1996. Earlier expenditure is not affected and established exceptions under case law are preserved.

The expression 'building' includes such items as walls, gates, main services, waste disposal and fire safety systems, sewerage, drainage and lift shafts. Items not affected include electrical and water systems provided for the trade, manufacturing equipment, furniture and fittings, cookers, dishwashers etc., other machinery, movable partition walls, decorative assets for hotels, etc. and advertising displays.

'Structures' include tunnels, bridges, pavements, roads, inland navigations, dams, sea walls and weirs. Items not affected include altering land to install machinery, dry docks, jetties, etc. to carry plant, pipelines, indoor and outdoor swimming pools, fish tanks and railway lines. The rules only mention what is not plant; otherwise, existing law must be followed.

11.10 Fixtures – entitlement to capital allowances (CAA Ss172–204)

Detailed rules apply to clarify who is entitled to capital allowances where machinery or plant is installed in a building or on land and becomes a fixture.

The rules may treat the plant as belonging to you for capital allowances purposes even though you are not the owner. This includes boilers and radiators installed in a building as part of a central heating system. These rules prevail where they conflict with the hire purchase ones.

If you lease a piece of equipment and it becomes a fixture at a building, you will obtain capital allowances if you jointly elect with the lessee. Where you pay to be granted a lease including a fixture on which the lessor would obtain capital allowances, you can jointly elect that you receive the allowances.

Lessors can now claim capital allowances on heating equipment installed under the Government's affordable wealth programme where the expenditure is after 27 July 2000 and before 2008.

Modifications to the rules took effect from 24 July 1996 with a view to:

(1) Provide for a joint election of purchaser and vendor as to the amount of the sale price to be apportioned to fixtures
(2) Prevent the acceleration of allowances on fixtures
(3) Stop allowances exceeding the original cost of a fixture, and
(4) Bar allowances on fixtures leased to non-taxpayers if the lessor has no relevant interest in the land.

Expenditure on designated energy-saving equipment which a business is contracted to provide and operate under an energy services agreement comes within the above rules from April 2001. Normally the equipment would be attached to land in which the business holds no interest.

11.11 Industrial buildings (CAA Ss271–360)

The cost of new industrial buildings that are used in your business (that is, factories, warehouses, etc. and some repair shops) qualify for industrial buildings allowances. Qualifying expenditure also includes additions and improvements to industrial buildings. From 6 April 1991, industrial buildings allowance extends to the construction of toll roads.

Now also included are import warehouses which store goods or materials imported into the UK. From 6 April 1995, the relief covers privately financed public roads under the Design Build Finance and Operate initiative.

Each year (including the first) a writing down allowance of 4 per cent of the original cost is obtained. (The allowance is 2 per cent if the expenditure was incurred before 6 November 1962.) Up to 25 per cent of the capital cost of an industrial building may relate to a non-qualifying use without restricting the allowances.

Prior to 1 April 1986 and for the year to 31 October 1993, expenditure qualified for initial allowance as follows:

Date of expenditure After	and before	Rate %
12 November 1974	11 March 1981	50
10 March 1981	14 March 1984	75
13 March 1984	1 April 1985	50
31 March 1985	1 April 1986	25
31 March 1986	1 November 1992	Nil
31 October 1992	1 November 1993	20

Building costs after 31 March 1986 normally do not attract initial allowances apart from in Enterprise Zones (11.12). However, 20 per cent initial allowance was available for qualifying buildings constructed under a contract entered into between 1 November 1992 and 31 October 1993. Also, the buildings must have been brought into use for the purposes of the trade by 31 December 1994. In cases where the expenditure was in the same year as the building was brought into use, both initial and writing down allowance were available.

If a building on which industrial buildings allowances have been obtained is sold then the sale proceeds must be compared with the balance of original cost less initial allowances and writing down allowances obtained. Any excess proceeds will be assessed as a balancing charge and any deficit will be allowed as a balancing allowance. This now applies even if you had ceased to use the building for industrial purposes. Any excess of the proceeds compared with the original cost must be disregarded for this purpose but may give rise to a capital gain (20.2).

11.11.1 **Space above shops etc.** (CAA Ss393A–W)

Subject to the rules, 100 per cent initial allowance is given on expenditure after 11 May 2001 on renovating or converting space above shops and other commercial buildings to flats for letting.

(1) The property must be pre-1980.
(2) There must be no more than 5 floors and those above ground level originally constructed for mainly residential purposes.
(3) At the time of the conversion the ground floor must be rated for broadly shops, offices, restaurants and medical use.
(4) The upper floors need to be empty or used as storage for at least a year before the conversion.
(5) Each new flat must be self-contained with its own access and have no more than four rooms apart from kitchen and bathroom.
(6) High-value flats are excluded. For example the rent limit for a four-room flat in Greater London is £480 per week.
(7) The rules resemble those for industrial buildings, but are simplified.

11.11.2 **Business premises renovation allowances** (CAA Ss360A–Z4)

An initial allowance of 100 per cent is to be available on renovating and converting business property in a 1997 designated disadvantaged area of the UK. A condition is that the property has been unused for at least a year.

11.12 Enterprise zones (CAA Ss281 & 298–304)

The Government have designated a number of Enterprise Zones. One of their attractions is that expenditure on industrial and commercial buildings including hotels qualifies for 100 per cent initial allowance. Unusually shops and offices are included. Less than the full initial allowance may be claimed in which case 25 per cent writing down allowance (straight line) is available on the original expenditure until used up.

Enterprise Zone allowances are now restricted to exclude expenditure incurred more than ten years after the expiry of the zone. Expenditure payable after 15 December 1991 on an unused building is no longer denied Enterprise Zone allowances because it is bought after the expiry of the zone's ten-year life. Also, allowances are to be available on used buildings sold, within two years of being brought into use after that date.

(The time limit is 31.8.94 if it would have expired from 13.1.94 to 31.8.94.) In this case, the purchaser obtains limited relief where part of the expenditure was incurred when the site was in an Enterprise Zone and part was not.

Where you own the freehold and sell a long lease in your property for a capital sum, this has not given rise to a balancing charge. However, buildings purchased by you in enterprise zones on or after 13 January 1994 may produce balancing charges if disposed of in this way. The new rules provide for balancing charges on sales of the long leases within seven years (25 years in cases with guaranteed exit arrangements).

11.13 Agricultural buildings allowance (CAA Ss361–393)

If you are the owner or tenant of any farm or forestry land, you will obtain allowance for your expenditure on certain constructions on that land. These include farmhouses, farm or (generally only up to 19 June 1989) forestry buildings, cottages, and fences, etc.

The allowance is given in the form of an annual writing down allowance of 4 per cent on your original expenditure. (Previously, an initial allowance of up to 20 per cent could also be claimed. The balance was eligible for writing down allowance of 10 per cent of the original cost for each year including the first.) With the exception of the year to 31 October 1993, for expenditure incurred from 1 April 1986, there is no initial allowance and the writing down allowance is reduced to 4 per cent. (The old rates applied if expenditure was incurred before 1 April 1987 under a contract effected before 14 March 1984.)

Expenditure after 31 March 1986, attracting 4 per cent writing down allowance is generally written off over a 25 year period. However, if you sell or demolish the building within that time, you can elect for a balancing adjustment (that is, balancing allowance or charge – 11.9.4). This also applies if the building is destroyed. The election must be made within two years after the end of the relevant year of assessment (accounting period for a company).

If your expenditure is on a farmhouse, then your allowance will normally be based on only one-third (maximum) of the total cost to take account of the personal benefit.

11.14 Hotel buildings (CAA Ss277, 279 & 317)

Expenditure incurred on the construction or improvement of certain hotel buildings qualifies for an annual writing down allowance of 4 per cent of the original cost. If the hotel is in an Enterprise Zone (11.12), expenditure qualifies for relief at special rates (100 per cent initial allowance, etc.). To qualify for the allowance, the hotel must have at least ten bedrooms for letting to the public and provide breakfast and an evening meal. Also, it must be open for at least four months in the season from April to October inclusive.

11.15 Assured tenancies (CAA Ss490–531)

A 75 per cent initial allowance followed by 4 per cent writing down allowance was available on qualifying expenditure incurred between 9 March 1982 and 14 March 1984. From 14 March 1984, the initial allowance was phased out, but the writing down allowance remains for expenditure incurred before 1 April 1992. The allowances are given on dwellings let on assured tenancies by bodies approved by the Secretary of State for the Environment under the Assured Tenancies Scheme. Assured tenancies allowances are treated as capital allowances, which enables them to be included in group relief claims (13.13).

The expenditure on each house or flat qualifying for allowance is limited to £40,000 (£60,000 in Greater London). Regarding expenditure after 4 May 1983 (unless under existing contracts) only landlords which are companies qualify for the allowance.

11.16 Research and development (R&D) relief (CAA Ss437–451 & FA 2003 S168 & Sch 31)

From 6 April 2000 (1 April 2000 for companies) a new definition is brought in for R&D as being activities that fall to be so treated in accordance with normal accounting practice in relation to UK companies. However, the Treasury are empowered to make altering and supplementary regulations.

From 1 April 2000, 'small and medium companies' (11.9.1) are entitled to R&D relief, subject to the rules:

(1) The qualifying R&D expenditure must be at least £10,000 (previously £25,000) in a 12-month accounting period (scaled down for shorter accounting periods). The £10,000 expenditure threshold also applies to 11.16.1 and 11.16.2 below.
(2) The expenditure must relate to a present or projected trade of the company and not be capital, nor subsidised and can include staffing costs (including certain externally provided workers), consumable stores and certain intellectual property.
(3) Relief against taxable profits is given at 150 per cent of the R&D expenditure.
(4) Companies which are not yet in profit may elect to take a non-taxable R&D tax credit of up to 16 per cent of the 150 per cent relief, that is, 24 per cent of the R&D cost. This may be encashed.
(5) The R&D credit is limited to PAYE and NIC liability for the period.
(6) From 1 April 2004, a wider definition of R&D applies and qualifying expenditure now also includes software, power, fuel and water.

11.16.1 **Larger companies' R&D relief** (FA 2002 S53 & Sch 12)

For expenditure from 1 April 2002, larger companies obtain R&D tax credit at 25 per cent, in addition to relief for their actual expenditure. Thus they obtain relief for 125 per cent of their expenditure, compared with 150 per cent for 'small and medium' companies (see above).

11.16.2 **Vaccines research relief** (FA 2002 S54 & Schs 13 & 14)

The 2002 Finance Act brought in 150 per cent relief for corporation tax on expenditure for certain vaccines and medicines in the fields of TB, malaria, HIV infection and AIDs.

11.17 Scientific research (R&D) allowance (CAA Ss437–451)

Capital expenditure incurred on scientific research for the purposes of your trade is wholly allowed in the year that the expenditure arises. Any revenue expenditure will be allowed as a charge against your taxable profits provided that it is related to your trade or it is medical research related to the welfare of your employees. From 6 April 2000 (1 April for companies) the term R&D (11.16) is defined and this replaces 'scientific research' for these purposes.

One hundred per cent allowance is given on capital expenditure excluding the cost of land and houses. However, scientific research allowance and industrial buildings allowance are not given on the same expenditure. Disposal proceeds of scientific research assets are normally treated as taxable trading receipts, to the extent that together with any allowances, they exceed the original cost. From 1 April 2000, 150 per cent allowance (or a corresponding tax credit) is given for small and medium companies (11.16).

11.18 Patent rights and 'know-how' (CAA Ss452–483)

The 1985 Finance Act changed the allowance basis for both patent rights and 'know-how', so that from 1 April 1986, only a 25 per cent writing down allowance applies.

Prior to 1 April 1986, if you purchased a patent to use in your business then you obtain a writing down allowance of 1/17 of the expenditure for each of the 17 years starting with that in which you made the purchase. If you sell the patent then the excess or deficit of the proceeds compared with the unexpired balance of cost (after writing down allowances) is treated as a balancing charge or allowance (11.9.4). If, however, the proceeds exceed the original cost, then you are assessed to income tax on this excess (normally spread over six years or the remainder of the patent if less). Note that costs in connection with creating and registering your own patents are treated as deductible revenue expenses (TA 1988 S83).

If you purchase patent rights from a connected person, your allowances may be limited, by reference to the vendor's disposal value for capital allowance purposes. Otherwise, it is necessary to use your capital expenditure, or if smaller, the market value of the rights on your acquiring them, or normally the original acquisition costs of the vendor.

Any payments that you made before 1 April 1986 to obtain 'know-how' for your business or profession entitled you to a writing down allowance of 1/6 of such expenditure for each of the first six years.

Regarding companies, the new intellectual property rules (13.29) apply to assets created or acquired by them after 31 March 2002 in place of the above.

11.19 Dredging (CAA Ss484–489)

For dredging expenditure after March 1986, an annual writing down allowance of 4 per cent on the original amount is due. Previously an initial allowance of 15 per cent applied, together with writing down allowance at 4 per cent each year on a straight line basis.

11.20 Mineral extraction (CAA Ss98–121)

Expenditure before 1 April 1986 attracted initial and writing down allowances related to output, etc. These have been replaced by writing down allowances at 25 per cent or 10 per cent, depending on the nature of the expenditure. Pre-1 April 1986 balances qualify for the new reliefs. Balancing allowances or charges arise under the present system where mineral deposits cease to be worked or the mine, etc. is sold.

11.21 Films etc. (F2A 1992 Ss40–42 & 69, F2A 1997 S48, FA 1999 S62, CAA Sch 2 & FA 2002 Ss99–101)

Films, tapes and discs with at least a two-year life normally qualified for capital allowances. However, this was withdrawn from 10 March 1982 for overseas films but continued for British made films (including those for television). Unless the film, etc. is trading stock, the rules provide for the production expenditure not qualifying for capital allowances to be written off over the film's income-producing life. Film investment is sometimes made by means of limited partnerships. However, relief for limited partners' losses after 19 March 1985 was severely restricted (12.4).

The production of qualifying films (those with sufficient EC content) obtains special relief from 11 March 1992. Pre-production costs incurred from that date attract relief at once, up to a limit of 20 per cent of total budgeted cost; production expenditure on films completed after 10 March 1992 is to be written off as to one-third each year starting with the completion of the film, as is the cost of acquiring qualifying films.

Special relief applies for British qualifying films costing no more than £15m. For production expenditure and certain acquisition costs incurred after 2 July 1997 and before 1 January 2007, 100 per cent write-off will be allowed when each film is completed. New rules of a clarifying nature operate generally from 6 April 2000 (FA 2000 S113). Generally from 17 April 2002, 'British qualifying films' must be intended for release in the commercial cinema and the production expenditure relievable must be paid no later than four months after the films' completion.

From 10 December 2003, rules take effect aimed at preventing tax avoidance through contrived exits from businesses where tax relief has resulted from trading losses generated from film tax reliefs.

Further anti-avoidance provisions operate from 2 December 2004 (FA 2005 Ss59–71 & Sch 3). These are designed to prevent relief being given for more than the entire cost of a film; also using film relief alongside tax deferral for more than 15 years.

11.22 Relief for losses (TA Ss380–391)

11.22.1 Losses under the new current year basis

The previous system under which relief was allowed for business losses is outlined on the next page (11.22.2). Broadly, this system still applies but with some alterations.

Among the changes relating to the move to the current year basis (11.7.4) are the following:

(1) Losses are computed on the basis of the periods for which the accounts of the business are prepared, instead of the fiscal year basis. However,

businesses etc. set up before 6 April 1994 could continue to set 1995–96 trading losses against other income for that year or 1996–97.

(2) Relief for trading and professional losses under S380 (11.22.2) is allocated differently. It is now to go against your income either of the year of loss or the preceding year and you can choose which has priority.
(3) Similarly, the rules regarding losses on certain unquoted shares (20.14) have changed, as have those for terminal losses (11.24) and losses in new businesses (11.23). (Losses on qualifying unquoted shares suffered in 1993–94 could be relieved against 1993–94 or 1994–95 income.)
(4) In general, the new rules took effect from 1997–98 for businesses existing at 5 April 1994 and otherwise from commencement.
(5) An election to the Revenue must be made within 12 months from 31 January following the year of assessment.

Various rules remain from the old system including:

(1) If you make a trading loss in the year and have insufficient other income for the year to offset it, you can claim relief against capital gains for that tax year. If there are still unused trading losses after absorbing other income for the following year, relief is available against the capital gains for that year (20.13).
(2) Note that you are not allowed to carry a loss forward from one trade to another. You should remember this if you change businesses. A move to a nearby shop in the same trade may be in order, however.
(3) Your loss in the first year of assessment of a new business includes *pre-trading expenditure* of a revenue nature (11.3.1). This applied to individuals and partnerships regarding such expenditure within seven years before trading commences (TA 1988 S401).
(4) Income tax relief is claimable for certain losses on disposals of *unquoted shares in trading companies* by original subscribers (20.14). These losses take precedence over claims under S380.
(5) Loss relief is given before personal reliefs and allowances (3.0.1, etc.) which cannot be carried forward. Thus these may be lost through your income being absorbed by losses. If possible, carry the losses forward in these circumstances so that your allowances are not wasted.

11.22.2 The previous system

If the adjusted results for your business, profession or vocation showed a deficit of income compared with expenditure for a particular year then your assessment under Case I or Case II of Schedule D was nil for the related tax year. The loss for the year was augmented by your capital allowances and the resultant total loss was available for relief. This was first given against (a) your other income for the tax year in which you suffered the loss and (b) that for the following tax year. ((a) includes your business assessment on the profits for the year prior to the loss.)

The above loss relief arose under TA 1988 S380 and you needed to claim it by making the required election to your Inspector of Taxes within two years of the end of the tax year to which it related. If your loss was not entirely relieved as above then you could and can still claim that the balance should be carried forward and set off against future profits from the *same* trade, profession or vocation (TA 1988 S385).

Note that for the transitional year, 1996–97, your assessment was normally based on your average profits for the two years ending with your accounting date within 1996–97 (11.7.2). If you made a loss for one of those years, this counted as nil and the loss was available for relief as above.

11.22.3 **Example: Relief for losses**

Dr D makes a loss of £20,000 in his practice for the year to 31 December 2004 having made a profit of £6,000 for 2003. For 2005 his profit is £22,000. His only other income is taxed dividends, which including tax credits amount to £5,000 for 2003–04 and £6,000 for 2004–05. What loss relief can Dr D obtain?

Dr D's loss of £20,000 for the year to 31 December 2004 will be allocated to the tax year 2004–05 (11.22.1).

	£
2003–04 loss relief (S380)	
Against 2003–04 Schedule D Case II assessment	6,000
Against 2003–04 dividends	5,000
2004–05 loss relief (S380)	
Against 2004–05 dividends	6,000
2005–06 loss relief (S385)	
Against 2005–06 assessment on trading income	3,000
	20,000

(The assessment for 2005–06 becomes £22,000 – £3,000 = £19,000)

11.23 Loss in new business (TA 1988 S381)

If you carry on a business or profession personally or in partnership, a special relief is available. This applies to any loss which you make in your first year of assessment, or in any of the next three years. A written claim is required within two years of the end of the year of assessment.

The losses include capital allowances, and certain pre-trading expenditure (see above). They are offset against your income for the three years of assessment prior to the year in which the losses are made, taking the earliest first.

11.24 Terminal losses (TA 1988 Ss388 & 389)

If you cease to carry on a trade, profession or vocation and make an adjusted loss in your last complete year of trading, you get relief for this so-called 'terminal loss'. The relief is augmented by your capital allowances apportionable to your last 12 months of trading. The terminal losses are allowed against your business assessments for the three years of assessment prior to that in which you cease to trade. Under the new rules (11.22.1) this is extended to include the tax year of cessation.

11.25 Business Expansion Scheme (BES)

Under the BES, subject to the rules, you obtained income tax relief in a year of assessment in respect of amounts subscribed for shares in a qualifying company during that year up to £40,000 in total. A qualifying company exists to carry on one or more *qualifying trades*. The BES operated regarding shares issued from 6 April 1983 up to 31 December 1993. From 1 January 1994, the Enterprise Investment Scheme (EIS) operates (11.26). This has many common features such as mainly similar rules for qualifying trades (11.26(5)).

Further details of the BES are given in previous editions of this book.

11.26 Enterprise Investment Scheme (TA Ss289–312)

Regarding new investment from 1 January 1994, the Enterprise Investment Scheme (EIS) replaced the Business Expansion Scheme. The EIS is available for purchases of ordinary shares in 'qualifying' unquoted trading companies. Important features are:

(1) You obtain income tax relief at 20 per cent on your investment.

(2) For 1994–95 and subsequent years, you were allowed to invest up to £100,000 in EIS companies. For 1998–99 and subsequently, the limit was £150,000 each tax year and from 2004–05 it is £200,000.

(3) Subject to a maximum of £25,000 (£15,000 before 1998–99), half of the amount that you invest between 6 April and 5 October in any year can be carried back to the previous tax year.

(4) There was previously a limit of £1,000,000 on the amount that a company could raise in a year on which EIS relief was given, but this limit has been removed from 6 April 1998. However, from that date, participation is limited to companies with gross assets of under £15m before an investment and £16m after it.

(5) 'Qualifying companies' are unquoted trading companies which carry on a qualifying activity for at least three years. The range of qualifying activities is broadly similar to that for BES (11.25), but does not include private rented housing. The following rules regarding qualifying trades and companies apply broadly both for BES and EIS:
   (a) A trade whose income is mainly from royalties and licence fees does not qualify but exceptions are film production and distribution and for shares issued after 5 April 2000, intangible assets created under the corporate venturing scheme (13.28) by a small company.
   (b) Companies whose business consists of certain research and development in general qualify.

(c) Ship chartering is a qualifying trade. Charters must not exceed one year and the ships must be UK registered and owned, managed and navigated by the company. (Pleasure craft are excluded.)
(d) Wholesaling or retailing goods normally collected or held as investments is not a qualifying trade, unless the company actively tries to sell them. Examples are fine wines and antiques.
(e) Certain parent companies are qualifying companies if all their subsidiaries are wholly owned. This extends to tiers of companies provided they are each at least 90 per cent owned. Subsidiaries can even be resident abroad if the group's trade is mainly within the UK.
(f) For funds raised after 16 March 1998, various property backed activities are excluded (also for VCT purposes). These include farming, market gardening, forestry, property development and running hotels, guest houses and nursing/residential care homes.

(6) You must hold your EIS shares for at least three years or else your relief will be withdrawn. Before 6 April 2000, the minimum holding period was five years.
(7) For EIS shares on which relief has not been withdrawn, there is capital gains tax exemption when they are first sold. Any loss you make in these circumstances is available against capital gains or on election against income.
(8) From 27 November 1996, investment in the parent of a group of companies may qualify where non-qualifying activities only form a minor part of the group activities as a whole. Previously, all group companies needed to qualify.
(9) To obtain relief, you need to be a 'qualifying investor'. That means that during the period you are not 'connected' with the company (holding over 30 per cent of the shares or an employee). This applies from incorporation (or if later, two years before issue) to five years after the issue of the shares.
(10) You can become a paid director and still qualify for EIS relief, provided you were not connected with the company or its trade before the shares were issued.
(11) The scheme extends to companies trading in the UK, whether or not incorporated and resident here. Furthermore, you will be entitled to relief on EIS shares, provided you pay UK income tax, even if you are not UK resident.
(12) If you subscribe for EIS shares you will be entitled to reinvestment relief where you realise capital gains on other assets after 28 November 1994, when you are UK resident and ordinarily resident. The EIS shares must be purchased within one year before and three years after the disposals and a claim to the Revenue is needed. Subject to the rules, your gains are deferred until you dispose of the EIS shares. After 5 April 1998 you obtain unlimited capital gains tax deferral relief where chargeable gains are invested in EIS shares. This also applies to trustees.

(13) If you defer a capital gain on one EIS investment by investing in another and so on, you will obtain taper relief (20.12) for the cumulative period. This applies provided your shares in the first EIS company were issued after 5 April 1998 and sold after 5 April 1999.
(14) EIS reliefs are not lost where its qualifying trade is affected by the company being liquidated. For shares issued after 20 March 2000, the same applies regarding going into receivership.
(15) From 7 March 2001, companies have 24 months (previously 12 months) to employ all of the money raised, provided that 80% of this has been applied during the first 12 months.
(16) Companies which float on a recognised stock exchange after an EIS share issue from 7 March 2001 no longer normally cease to qualify.

11.27 Earnings basis and cash basis (FA 1998 Ss42–46 & Sch 6)

If you are carrying on a trade, you will normally be taxed on an 'earnings basis'. This means that your sales for each accounts period are included as they arise and not when you receive the money. Sales normally arise when they are invoiced. In a retail shop the sales usually arise as the customers pay over the counter. Your expenses are also deductible on an arising basis and the actual date of payment is not relevant. Your profit or loss will also reflect any increase or reduction in your stock and work in progress.

If you are carrying on a profession or vocation, however, the Revenue may have taxed you on a 'cash basis', which means by reference to the actual cash received, taking no account of uncollected fees at the end of each accounts period. (Sometimes a mixed earnings and cash basis was allowed.)

The cash basis was usually used for barristers. Other professions prepared their opening accounts on an earnings basis but had the option of later switching to a cash basis. Often the expenses were calculated on an arising basis but in some small cases the actual expense payments were used ignoring accruals.

The cash basis has generally been withdrawn. This normally first applied to your accounts for the accounts year beginning after 6 April 1999. However, special rules apply for accounts for more or less than twelve months. In the case of new barristers (and advocates in Scotland), the cash basis can be used for their first seven years of practice.

Suppose that your accounts are prepared to 30 June each year. Your accounts to 30 June 2000 will be prepared on an 'earnings basis' and the excess of the taxable profits on that basis (reflecting any increase or decrease in work in progress) must be calculated as compared with on the 'cash basis'.

You will be normally taxed under Schedule D Case VI on the excess spread over 10 years starting with 2000–2001. This is restricted to 10 per cent of the profits for each particular year, if less, with the balance payable for the tenth year.

11.28 Post-cessation receipts (TA 1988 Ss103–110)

If, after you permanently cease your trade, profession or vocation, you receive amounts relating to those activities, they are known as 'post-cessation receipts'. An example is a late fee payment that had not been included in your accounts because they are prepared on a cash basis or the fee was not included in your outstandings.

Post-cessation receipts are usually taxed under Schedule D Case VI (15.1). They are normally treated as earned income and you can set off unrelieved losses and capital allowances from before the cessation. You can, however, elect that any post-cessation receipts for the first six years after cessation should be added to your income from the business, etc. on its last day of trading.

Relief is available for those born before 6 April 1917 and in business on 18 March 1968 who are taxed on a fraction of their post-cessation receipts varying between $\frac{19}{20}$ and $\frac{5}{20}$. The latter fraction applies if you were born before 6 April 1903; if you were born before 6 April 1904 the fraction is $\frac{6}{20}$ and so on.

11.29 Class 4 National Insurance contributions (TA 1988 S617 & FA 1996 S147)

You will be liable to pay the contributions if you are self-employed in accordance with the rules in Chapter 25 (25.5). For 1985–86 and subsequent years up to 1995–96, you could claim relief for half of your Class 4 contributions. Your total income (5.2) was reduced accordingly. However, this relief was withdrawn for 1996–97 and subsequent years, the Class 4 rate being reduced from 7.3 per cent to 6 per cent to compensate, although it has now gone up to 8 per cent.

11.30 Remediation of contaminated land (FA 2001 S70 & Schs 22 & 23)

Companies which acquire contaminated land for the purposes of their trade or schedule A business are now able to claim 150 per cent of their clean-up costs as follows:

(1) Expenditure after 11 May 2001 is covered and the land can be held as a capital asset or trading stock.
(2) Land is in a contaminated state if because of substances in on or under the land, harm is or might be caused or controlled waters polluted and nuclear sites are excluded.
(3) Only expenditure on remediation which is in addition to normal site preparation costs comes within the scheme.
(4) If any loss results, the normal loss and group relief provisions apply.
(5) Should a loss result, a cash payment can be opted for.

11.31 Foster carers (FA 2003 S176 & Sch 36)

If you provide foster care services, directly or through an agency, to local authorities, from 2003–04 you will be treated as having no profit and no loss for the tax year if your turnover is less than a given limit. This comprises a fixed amount of £10,000 per residence for a full tax year plus £200 per week for each child cared for under 11, increasing to £250 if 11 or over. If your turnover exceeds the limit, you have the option of being taxed on the excess, or according to the normal business profit and loss rules.

11.32 Alternative finance arrangements (FA 2005 Ss46–57 & Sch 2)

(1) New measures take effect regarding the taxation of post 5 April 2005 finance arrangements not involving the receipt or payment of interest.
(2) The rules apply to both individuals and companies investing or borrowing money under arrangements not using interest.
(3) One of the parties to a transaction must be a bank or other financial institution and the usual arrangements involve buying and selling assets.
(4) Alternative finance arrangements will be treated as giving rise to interest for taxation purposes.
(5) After 5 April 2005, banks and building societies offering alternative finance products will have to apply the rules for deduction of tax at source.
(6) The new provisions entail more favourable SDLT (24.4) treatment.

Chapter 12

PARTNERSHIPS

Special rules relate to the taxation of partnerships and these are covered in the following sections. Note that, a new system operates generally from 1997–98 and for partnerships *starting after 5 April 1994* (12.2). From 2005–06, rewritten legislation is applied by Ss846–863 in ITTOIA (2.10).

12.1 What is a partnership?

Partnership is the relationship which exists between two persons in business together with the object of making profits. There does not necessarily have to be a written partnership agreement but the partnership must exist in fact. If no partnership is in fact operating then, even though there may be a written agreement, it would not make the partnership exist.

Since the assessment of a partnership differs from that of an individual in certain respects, the Revenue will seek to establish whether a partnership in fact exists. Points to consider include:

(1) Is there a written partnership agreement?
(2) Can the partners close down the business and are they liable for its debts?
(3) Do the partners' names appear on business stationery?
(4) What arrangements exist for dividing the profits (and property on dissolution)?

12.2 Partnerships under the new current year system (TMA Ss12AA–AE, 93A & 95A & TA Ss111–118)

In line with the new current year basis, changed rules apply broadly from 1997–98 for partnerships carrying on business on 5 April 1994.

These apply at once for partnerships commencing after that date. Points to note under the new system include the following:

(1) You are assessed on your share of the profits individually, rather than the partnership being assessed on the total.
(2) All partnership expenses and capital allowances are deducted from its profits.
(3) The profits are allocated to the period of account of the partnership, rather than the year of assessment and split according to the profit sharing ratios for the former.
(4) Your assessment is computed as if your profit share were derived from a trade or profession carried on by you alone. This deemed trade or profession runs from when you joined the partnership until you leave it (or it ceases). If you had originally commenced trading by yourself, the deemed trade goes back to when you started.

(5) A change of partners after 5 April 1994 is not regarded as a cessation (12.5), provided there is at least one person who was a partner both in the old partnership and the new one. Consequently, the continuation basis election (12.6) is no longer needed and has been withdrawn.
(6) With effect from 1996–97, self-assessment rules took effect. These include new partnership returns from 1996–97 and enquiry procedures.
(7) Your partnership assessment for 1996–97 was on the *transitional basis*, provided it was carrying on business on 5 April 1994. For example:

	£
Adjusted profits for the year to: 30 June 1995	30,000
30 June 1996	40,000
	70,000
Average for 1996–97	35,000
Capital allowances for 1996–97 (say)	5,000
Divisible between partners in 1996–97 profit sharing ratios	£30,000

(8) One partner may be made responsible for partnership tax returns, etc. If he or she is not available, a 'successor' may so act.
(9) The 1996–97 partnership assessment was normally payable on 1 January and 1 July 1997. For 1997–98 (and subsequently), you make payments on account on 31 January and 31 July 1998 of normally half your liability for 1996–97, with a balancing payment by 31 January 1999. For example, suppose your 2003–04 liability is £20,000 and your 2004–05 liability is £25,000, you will pay for 2004–05:

	£
on 31 January 2004 (½ × £20,000)	10,000
31 July 2004 (½ × £20,000)	10,000
31 January 2005 (balance)	5,000
	25,000

(10) On the conversion to the 'earnings basis' (11.27) any 'catching-up charge' will be allocated to the partners by reference to their profit shares for each of the ten years over which it is spread.

12.3 How partnership income was taxed – old system (TA 1988 S111)

The following describes the system prior to the current year system (12.2) including some basic points which continue.

A joint assessment to income tax under Case I or Case II of Schedule D (11.1) was made on the partners in respect of the partnership profits. This included lower rate, basic rate and higher rate income tax (if any) on the profits. The rules for the opening (11.7.1) and closing years (11.7.2) were generally followed as for individuals, as were those for capital allowances (11.8).

However, there were special rules covering partnership changes (12.5). The 'precedent partner' (normally the senior partner), had to make a joint return of the partnership income each year.

Partnership investment income was and is split between the partners in their profit-sharing ratios and they personally pay any income tax arising.

When the partnership income had been determined for the purposes of Schedule D Case I or Case II, it was split between the partners according to the proportions in which they shared profits during the tax year. These proportions were not necessarily the same as the profit sharing ratios during the year when the profits were actually made.

Under both the old and the new system, where a partner is remunerated partly by way of a salary and partly by receiving a share of the profits, the salary is normally not assessed as such but is included in his assessable profit share. Interest paid to partners in respect of their capital is also treated as part of the assessable profit share of each partner. Such interest is not an annual payment (4.1), nor is it taxed as investment income (8.1).

12.4 Partnership losses (TA 1988 Ss380–381 & 387)

Where a partnership has an adjusted loss for any accounting period, that loss is apportioned between the partners in the same ratio as a profit would have been split. Thus the loss is split according to the profit sharing ratios applying to the year of assessment corresponding to the tax year in which the loss is made. For example, if a loss was made in the year to 5 April 1995 this was split between the partners according to their profit sharing ratios for the tax year 1995–96 (assuming that the preceding year basis of assessment applies). However, a loss made in the transitional year 1996–97 was split in the profit sharing ratios for that year and similarly for 1997–98 and future years.

Each partner can use his partnership losses as he chooses according to the various rules for obtaining loss relief (11.22). Thus he can claim for the loss to be relieved against his other income tax assessments for the tax year in which the loss is actually made or the previous year. (Under the old system, relief for the loss was available for the year of the loss and the following one.) Also he can carry forward any unused balance of the loss to be set off against future profit shares from the same partnership; this applies even if the partnership had been treated as discontinued because of a partnership change (see below).

If you are a limited partner, so that your risk is limited to the capital which you have invested, your loss is also restricted in the same way. This applies broadly to losses after 19 March 1985. This has been extended to general partners by FA 2004. All partners joining after 25 March 2004 may be affected and for existing partners, the rules may restrict trading losses incurred after 9 February 2004.

Provisions in FA 2005 Ss72–79 address the recovery of excess relief and tax avoidance involving films (15.10.22).

The new rules normally apply for the first four years of a partner's membership and only bite if he or she works within the partnership for less than a weekly average of ten hours. In that case, loss relief is restricted to the partner's 'contribution' by way of capital introduced, retained profits, etc. If a further contribution is made, restricted loss relief may be used in a later period (TA 1988 Ss118ZE–ZK).

12.5 Changes of partners (TA 1988 S861–63 & 113)

If there was any change in the make up of a partnership caused either by a partner leaving or dying or a fresh partner joining, the partnership was treated as ceasing for taxation purposes unless the continuation election described below was made. However, different treatment applies under the rules for changes after 5 April 1994 (12.2). A complete change in the ownership still triggers a deemed cessation. However, a partial change in the identity of the partners is treated as a continuation.

Previously, the effects of cessation caused by a change of partners were similar to any other Schedule D Case I or Case II cessation (11.7.2). Thus the assessment for the final tax year was based on the actual profits for that year and the Revenue have the option to increase the assessments for the two previous tax years to the actual profits for those years.

For changes after 19 March 1985, the first four years were assessed on an actual basis and then the previous year basis applied, unless you elected for years five and six to be on an actual profit basis. This was subject to a continuation election (12.6).

There are some special rules governing partnerships between individuals and a company (TA 1988 Ss114–115).

12.6 Election for continuation basis (TA 1988 Ss113 & 116)

Under the old system, within two years of the date of a change in the members of a partnership an election could be made to the Revenue that the partnership should be taxed on a continuation basis. The election applied for changes before 6 April 1994 (12.2). It could be made provided that at least one of the partners in the old partnership remained as a partner in the new partnership. All of the partners in both the old and the new partnership signed the election. Fuller details are included in previous editions of this book.

12.7 Partnership capital gains (TCGA S59)

When a partnership asset is sold in circumstances that if owned by an individual capital gains tax would have been payable, this tax is assessed on the partners according to their shares in the partnership asset. Thus if a capital gain of £1,000 is made from the sale of a partnership asset on 1 January 2006 and A, B, C and D share equally in the partnership assets, a capital gain of £250 each must be added to the capital gains tax assessments for 2005–06 of A, B, C and D respectively (20.1).

Where a share in a partnership changes hands, a share in all of the partnership assets is treated for capital gains tax purposes as changing ownership and this might give rise to capital gains or capital losses for the partner who is disposing of his share. Thus if A, B and C are equal partners and A sells his share to D, A is treated for capital gains tax purposes as disposing of a one third share in each of the partnership assets to D.

12.8 Overseas partnerships (TA 1988 S112)

If you are in partnership carrying on a trade or business and the control and management of the trade or business is outside the UK then the partnership is treated for tax purposes as being non-resident. This follows even if you or some of your other partners are resident here (17.3.4) and some of the business is conducted in this country.

Any profits arising from the partnership trade or business in this country are assessed here under Schedule D Case I. The firm is assessed in the name of any partner resident in the United Kingdom. Regarding the partnership profits earned abroad, these are assessable in respect of any profit shares of the partners resident here under Schedule D Case V according to the special rules outlined in Chapter 18. This now generally applies even if under a double tax agreement, the profits of the overseas partnership arising abroad are exempt from UK tax. From 1997–98 each partner is assessed separately (12.2).

12.9 European economic interest groupings (TMA Ss12A & 98B & TA S510A)

Tax rules regarding European Economic Interest Groupings (EEIGs) operate from 1 July 1989. Such 'groupings' are business entities set up by two or more European community member states with simpler rules than traditional company law bodies – they are more akin to partnerships in some respects. EEIGs may not be formed to make profits for themselves but rather benefit all of their members. Likely activities are packing, processing, marketing and research.

An EEIG is transparent, so far as tax on income and capital gains is concerned. Thus these will only be charged to tax in the hands of the members. However, this does not apply to the deduction of tax. Thus an EEIG based in the UK is responsible for operating PAYE.

12.10 Limited liability partnerships (LLPs) (TA Ss118ZA–118ZD & TCGA Ss59A & 169A)

Measures have been introduced to ensure that LLPs incorporated under the Limited Liability Act 2000 are treated as partnerships for tax purposes. Also, when an LLP goes into liquidation, chargeable gains held over on business gifts will fall into charge. Further provisions prevent tax loss where LLPs are used for investment and property investment.

Chapter 13

COMPANIES

13.1 Introduction

The following is a general outline of the taxation of companies that are resident in the UK or are trading here through a branch or agency. In the latter case it is normally only the profits arising in this country that are taxable here. It must be stressed that the actual provisions are lengthy and many details have been omitted in this summary. Note that ITTOIA (2.10) has no effect for corporation tax purposes.

13.2 Corporation tax on profits etc. (TA 1988 S6 & FA 2003 S133)

The tax on the profits, etc. of companies is called corporation tax which is charged at the present rate of 30 per cent, subject to special relief for companies with profits under £1,500,000 (13.7). Full corporation tax is now charged both on a company's profits and its capital gains (13.15).

Corporation tax applies not only to limited companies, but also to certain associations and unlimited companies. A company's income must be considered for each accounting period (13.4). It is charged to corporation tax on the basis of the actual income assessable for each accounting period according to the rules of the various cases of Schedule D (2.3.1) or other Schedules if applicable.

The rate of corporation tax is normally fixed by Parliament in the Finance Act each year for the preceding 'financial year'. A 'financial year' commences on 1 April and for example the financial year 2005 is the year to 31 March 2006. The Finance Act 1999 fixed the rate for financial year 2000 at 30 per cent and this rate has also been fixed for financial years up to 2006 by subsequent Finance Acts ending with that for 2005. The following table shows the rates of corporation tax over the years.

13.2.1 Full corporation tax rates

Financial year	Tax rate %	Taxable fraction of capital gains
1973–82	52	15/26
1983	50	3/5
1984	45	2/3
1985	40	3/4
1986	35	6/7*
1987–89	35	All
1990	34	All
1991–96	33	All

Financial year	Tax rate %	Taxable fraction of capital gains
1997–98	31	All
1999–2006	30	All

* All if gains after 16 March 1987.

13.3 Company dividend payments

If a company pays dividends, these are paid gross to the shareholders. However, prior to 6 April 1999, tax of 20/80 of the dividend was paid over to the Revenue as what was known as 'advance corporation tax' (13.17). ACT has been abolished for dividends etc. after 5 April 1999 (13.17). The ACT could be deducted from the company's corporation tax bill, so that effectively a lower rate was paid.

From 6 April 1993 to 5 April 1999, UK shareholders obtained a tax credit of 20/80 of their dividends but (if liable) paid the higher rate on their dividends plus tax credits. Thus a dividend of £80 carried a tax credit of £20 and you paid higher rate tax on £80 + £20 at 40 per cent making £40. But you deducted the credit of £20 and only paid £20. If your top tax rate was the basic rate you paid no extra tax on your dividends, under the rules (FA 1993 S77).

The imputation of income tax in the shareholders' hands on their dividends resulted in the system having been known as the '*imputation system*' of corporation tax. However, from 6 April 1999, the tax credit for individuals is 1/9 (10 per cent of the gross), the company no longer normally obtains any set-off against its corporation tax, nor must it pay the tax credit to the Inland Revenue.

13.4 Accounting periods for corporation tax (TA 1988 Ss8, 10 & 478 & Sch 30)

Corporation tax is charged in respect of accounting periods. These usually coincide with the periods for which the company prepares its annual accounts but cannot exceed 12 months in duration. Thus, if a company prepares accounts for a period of 18 months, the first 12 months will constitute one accounting period and the remaining six months are treated as another accounting period.

The actual tax is payable nine months after the end of each accounting period, in accordance with the 'pay and file' system (13.4.1). (Previously, the payment date was stretched to 30 days from the date of issue of the assessment, if this was later.)

Interest may arise on overdue corporation tax in accordance with the rules (16.8.2). Interest rates are as follows:

	Accounting periods ending after:	
	30 September 1993	30 June 1999 – on income tax on company payments
From	Rate %	Rate %*
6 September 2004	6	7.5
6 December 2003	5	6.5
6 August 2003	4.25	5.5
6 November 2001	5	6.5
6 May 2001	6	7.5
6 February 2000	6.75	8.5
6 March 1999	5.75	7.5
6 January 1999	6.5	8.5
6 August 1997	7.5	–
6 February 1996	6.25	–
6 March 1995	7	–
6 October 1994	6.25	–
6 January 1994	5.5	–
6 March 1993	6.25	–

* Tax-deductible

13.4.1 The pay and file system (TMA Ss59D & 87–87A, TA 1988 Ss8, 10, 419 & 826 & FA 1998 S117 & Schs 18 & 19)

The Keith Committee made various proposals on filing accounts' interest and penalties which were enacted in 1987. These took effect starting with the first accounting period of each company which ended after 30 September 1993. (The new filing arrangements only apply where notices to make corporation tax returns are issued after 31 December 1993.) The scheme is called the 'pay and file system'. Particular points are:

(1) Subject to (9) below, companies must pay corporation tax nine months after their accounting dates, whether or not assessments have been raised. For accounting periods ending after 30 June 1999, groups of companies are able to pay on a group-wide basis.
(2) Tax paid late or repaid by the Revenue carries interest from the required payment date.
(3) Accounts (and normally, subject to notice being issued, a return) are required to be submitted to the Revenue within 12 months from the accounting date.
(4) If accounts are filed late without excuse, penalties are as follows:

	Penalty		% of
	Basic £	Persistent failure £	unpaid tax
Return overdue by:			
Up to 3 months	100	500	
Over 3 months	200	1,000	
Delay from end of return period:			
Over 18 months			10
Over 24 months			20

(5) Companies should ensure that their accounting systems provide adequate information to comply with the new rules.
(6) If a company cannot supply actual figures, estimated ones will be accepted provided all reasonable steps have been taken to provide correct ones. These must then be supplied shortly.
(7) Losses are formally determined by assessment, in the same way as profits. Formal determinations also apply to capital allowances, management expenses and charges available for surrender as group relief.
(8) For accounting periods ending on or after 1 July 1999 corporation tax returns require companies to make self-assessments of their tax. Also there is a new scheme enabling the Revenue to make enquiries into returns, subject to giving notice.
(9) A new system of quarterly corporation tax payments for large companies took effect for accounting periods ending after 30 June 1999. The payments are based on the estimated liability, with a balancing amount. The payment dates for a large company with a 31 December 1999 year end are 14 July 1999, 14 October 1999, 14 January 2000 and 14 April 2000. A large company (without associated companies) is normally one with annual profits of at least £1.5m (FA 1998 S30). However, companies whose tax liability is no more than £10,000 (£5,000 for accounting periods ending before 1 July 2000) are excluded. Interest is payable at rates which change frequently and interest payable is now 1 per cent above the base rate, being 5.75 per cent from 16 August 2004. From the same date interest on overpaid instalments is 4.50 per cent.
(10) Instalment payments gradually increase over 4 years so that large companies pay the following percentages in instalments, with the balance 9 months after the end of the accounting period:

Year	%
1	60
2	72
3	88
4	100

13.4.2 Notice of coming within corporation tax

FA 2004 introduced for companies the obligation of informing the Inland Revenue when they come within corporation tax for the first time or come within it again, after having been dormant. Notice is required within three months of the start of the first relevant accounting period, together with other information which may be prescribed. Non-compliance could result in penalties of £300 for initial failure and then £50 per day, with up to £3,000 for fraudulently or negligently providing information.

13.5 Repayment supplement and interest on overpaid corporation tax (TA 1988 S825 & 826 & FA 1998 S35 & Sch 4)

This applies for a company if it receives a tax repayment more than a year after the date that corporation tax is due for the relevant accounting period. However, no repayment supplement is due for accounting periods ending after 30 September 1993, although interest is payable (see below). Any repayment supplement is tax free, and is calculated from the date one year after the due date for paying corporation tax until the end of the tax month (ending fifth day of next month) in which the repayment is made. If the original tax had not been paid, by the anniversary of the due date, the interest runs from the anniversary following the payment of the tax. Where loss relief was claimed (13.11), repayment supplement may arise with reference to the accounting period of the loss, rather than any earlier period when the original profits were made. The rates are as on overdue corporation tax payments (13.4).

For accounting periods *ending after 30 September 1993*, tax-free interest is paid on overpaid tax. For corporation tax, interest normally runs from the payment date (or due and payable date, if later) to the date of repayment. The rates are as follows:

	Accounting periods ending after:	
	30 September 1993	**30 June 1999**
From	**Rate %**	**Rate %**
1 October 1993	3.25	–
6 January 1994	2.5	–
6 October 1994	3.25	–
6 March 1995	4	–
6 February 1996	3.25	–
6 August 1997	4	–
6 January 1999	3.25	5
6 March 1999	2.75	4
6 February 2000	3.5	5
6 May 2001	2.75	4
6 November 2001	2	3
6 August 2003	1.25	2
6 December 2003	2	3
6 September 2004	2.75	4

For accounting periods ending after 30 June 1999, interest on underpaid corporation tax is tax deductible and interest received on overpaid corporation tax is taxable. (Interest rates have been correspondingly adjusted.) Furthermore, interest on income tax repayments is paid from the day after the end of the accounting period.

13.6 Small companies rate (TA 1988 S13, FA 1999 Ss27–29, FA 2000 S36 & FA 2005 S11)

This is the term used to describe the special reduced corporation tax rate which is charged on company profits which do not exceed certain limits for a given accounting period. The rate is 19 per cent from 1 April 2002. The profits in question comprise those on which corporation tax is paid together with 'franked investment income' (13.17.4) for the period. The rate was 21 per cent from 1 April 1998 and 20 per cent for the 3 years from 1 April 1999. However, small companies rate does not apply to close-investment holding companies for chargeable accounting periods beginning after 31 March 1989 (13.18).

The small companies rate applies to periods after 31 March 1973 and previous rates have been as follows:

	%
3 years to 31 March 1986	30
Year to 31 March 1987	29
Year to 31 March 1988	27
8 years to 31 March 1996	25
Year to 31 March 1997	24
2 years to 31 March 1999	21
3 years to 31 March 2002	20

From 1 April 2000 a 10 per cent starting rate was introduced alongside the full and small companies rates (13.7). For the years to 31 March 2003, 2004, 2005 and 2006 the starting rate is 0 per cent.

The small companies rate is to be charged on the profits of a company with no 'associated companies' (see 13.8) provided these do not exceed £300,000. If the profits are between £300,000 and £1,500,000, some marginal relief is given. These figures have been fixed for the year to 31 March 1995 and subsequently. Prior to this they were £250,000 and £1,250,000 for the 3 years to 31 March 1994 and £200,000 and £1,000,000 for the year to 31 March 1991.

The tax is then broadly the full corporation tax rate (13.2.1) on the profits less a fixed fraction (currently $^{11}/_{400}$) of the amount by which they fall short of £1,500,000, etc. Thus there is now a marginal rate of 32.75 per cent within the £300,000–£1,500,000 profit band. This assumes there are no 'associated companies' (see 13.8). For financial years 1991–1995, the fraction was $^{1}/_{50}$ with $^{9}/_{400}$ applying for 1996 and $^{1}/_{40}$ for 1997–2002.

If a company has 'associated companies', then the above-mentioned figures of £300,000 and £1,500,000 must be divided by one plus the number of 'associated companies' connected with the company under consideration. Thus, if five associated companies comprise a group, they will each pay 19 per cent on their profits for the year to 31 March 2005 if these are no more than £60,000 (£300,000/5) each. If any of the companies has profits between £60,000 and £300,000 (£1,500,000/5), some marginal relief is obtained.

13.7 Starting rate of corporation tax (TA S13AA, FA 1999 Ss28 & 29 & FA 2005 S12)

Beginning with Financial Year 2000, there is a starting rate of corporation tax which applies where a company's profits do not exceed £10,000 (proportionately less if there are associated companies). The rate for Financial Years 2000 and 2001 was 10 per cent with 0 per cent applying for 2002, 2003, 2004 and 2005.

If the profits are in the £10,000–£50,000 band, marginal relief is available. This is found by calculating tax at the small companies rate and deducting 19/400 of the difference between £50,000 and the profits. (For 2000 and 2001 this fraction was 1/40). Thus taking profits of £20,000 and assuming a 19 per cent small companies rate, the corporation tax is:

	£
£20,000 at 19 per cent	3,800
Less 19/400 of (£50,000 – £20,000)	1,425
	2,375

13.7.1 Non-Corporate Distribution Rate (NCDR) (TA 1988 S13AB & Sch A2)

FA 2004 has introduced legislation into TA 1988 which in certain cases applies NCDR to at least part of a company's profits where distributions are made after 31 March 2004 to persons other than companies.

(1) For NCDR to apply, the underlying rate of corporation tax must be lower than the NCDR.
(2) The rate for NCDR is 19 per cent for the financial years 2004 and 2005.
(3) Underlying corporation tax is the percentage of corporation tax chargeable on the basic profits for the accounting period ignoring NCDR.
(4) The basic profits are those on which corporation tax finally falls to be borne.
(5) Subject to (1) above, NCDR is charged on the amount of the company's basic profits that matches the amount of non-corporate distributions and the remaining profits at the underlying rate.
(6) Where an accounting period straddles 1 April 2004, the period before that date is separately treated and the profits apportioned accordingly.
(7) For example, if a company's profits are £9,000 and it pays dividends of £6,000 to individuals, the underlying rate is 0% and so NCDR applies on dividends of £6,000 at 19 per cent = £1,140. The remaining profits of £3,000 are at 0 per cent starting rate, thus the total tax is £1,140.

13.8 Associated companies (TA 1988 Ss416 & 417)

These are companies which are either under common control or one controls the other. Control broadly comprises voting power or entitlement to the greater part of either the profits, or the assets on liquidation.

In considering whether two companies are under common control, shares held by a husband and wife and their minor children are considered as one. If, however, one company is controlled by an individual and another company is controlled by a more distant relative, such as his brother, the two companies are not normally treated as being 'associated'.

Also 'associated' are the settlor of a trust and its trustees. Furthermore, if you are interested in any shares held by a trust, you are 'associated' with the trustees. Two companies can be associated if both are interested in the same shares.

13.9 The computation of assessable profits (TA 1988 Ss8–9 & 337–341)

It is strictly speaking necessary to compute the income assessable under each Schedule (and Case of Schedule D) and aggregate these to find the total amount chargeable to corporation tax. All corporation tax assessments are made on an 'actual' basis, however, instead of the preceding year basis that sometimes applied for income tax purposes; for example, Schedule D Case I.

The adjustments to the accounts profits that are required for corporation tax purposes follow with some modifications of the normal rules for income tax assessments described earlier in the book. The following are some of the necessary adjustments:

(1) Deduct any franked investment income (13.17.4).
(2) Add back payments made for non-business purposes (11.3.2).
(3) Add back capital losses and payments and deduct capital profits and capital receipts. The capital gain less capital losses of the company must be computed for the accounting period according to the capital gains tax rules (20.1).
(4) Add back legal and other professional charges relating to capital projects.
(5) Add back business entertaining unless in connection with the company's own staff (11.3.2). Gifts of advertising articles such as diaries, pens, etc. of less than £10 value to each customer are also allowable.
(6) Add back depreciation and amortisation charged in the accounts in respect of fixed assets.
(7) Adjust the interest payable and receivable to the actual gross payments and receipts during the accounting period (if this is different from the amount shown in the accounts).
(8) Deduct capital allowances for the accounting period (see below and 11.8).
(9) Add back any balancing charges and deduct any balancing allowances (11.9.4).

(10) Add income tax at 20 per cent to any building society interest received. This income tax is calculated by multiplying the actual interest received by 20/80 (2.7). The tax must then be deducted from the total corporation tax payable. (Prior to 6 April 1996 the rate was 25 per cent.)
(11) Add accruals of rent from members of the same group of companies who have already obtained tax relief (15.10.11).

13.9.1 **Withholding tax on interest and royalty payments** (TA Ss349A–D & TMA S98 (4A–C))

Under the old system, tax deduction at source was required where interest or certain royalty payments were made from one company to another. Exceptions included where both companies were in the same group and there was a group income election or interest was paid to a bank.

The following changes take effect from 1 April 2001:

(1) No tax is to be withheld on international bond interest, nor on most payments of interest or royalties between companies where the recipient is chargeable to corporation tax on that income.
(2) The paying company needs to be satisfied that the recipient is within the charge to corporation tax.
(3) If it later transpires that the recipient is outside the charge to corporation tax, the paying company is liable for the tax and interest.
(4) The administrative burden of deducting tax and accounting for it to the Revenue has been relieved.
(5) Payments of interest and royalties from companies to individuals continue to be paid under the deduction of tax.

From 1 October 2002:

(1) Companies do not need to deduct withholding tax from royalties, interest, annuities, etc. paid to specified tax-exempt bodies and certain partnerships which include tax-exempt bodies.
(2) UK companies are able to pay royalties without prior Inland Revenue clearance to non-residents whom they reasonably believe will be able to reclaim tax deducted under a double tax treaty. The royalties may be paid gross or less a reduced tax rate in line with the treaty rate.
(3) Yearly interest may be paid gross by a dealer in financial instruments as principal, who is authorised under the Financial Services and Markets Act.

From 1 January 2004, exemption from withholding tax applies for interest and royalties between associated companies in different member states of the European Union. FA 2004 incorporates the relevant EU Directive.

13.9.2 **Management expenses – investment business** (TA 1988 Ss75, 75A & 130)

From 1 April 2004, companies with investment business qualify for relief for their expenses of managing investments, regardless of whether they are investment companies under the legislation, which was a previous condition.

Relief is extended to non-resident companies which have a UK permanent establishment. The timing rules are changed so as to bring the relief in line with the accounting treatment.

13.10 Special capital allowances rules for companies

The normal capital allowances rules for businesses, etc. (11.8), apply to companies subject to a number of special rules including the following:

(1) An individual in business can claim that his writing down allowances should be at a lower rate than the normal rate of 25 per cent. Companies also have this right (CAA S24).
(2) Where there is a 'company reconstruction without change of ownership' as a result of which one company takes over all of the assets and business of another company, the former continues to receive exactly the same capital allowances on the assets transferred as the old company would have got. A reconstruction without change of ownership takes place if at any time during the two years following the reconstruction, no less than 75 per cent of the acquiring company belongs to the same people who owned no less than 75 per cent of the old company. (This is treated for all corporation tax purposes as a continuation of the trade (TA 1988 Ss343–344).)
(3) Special rules now apply where a UK trade is transferred in exchange for shares from one EC company to a company in another EC state. Balancing adjustments are not made, subject to certain conditions (11.9.4).
(4) Under the 'pay and file' system (13.4.1), a formal claim for capital allowances is needed. This is included in the new corporation tax return. You no longer need to disclaim allowances, since you simply claim the required amount.
(5) From 6 April 1995, companies starting further trades may have their capital allowances on plant etc. restricted for the first accounting year (FA 1995 S102).

13.11 Losses (TA 1988 Ss393–396, 768 & 768A–C & Sch 28A)

Company trading losses arising from 2 July 1997 can be carried back against profits for the preceding year. This compares with a previous three year carry back facility. This change also applies to losses on loan arrangements, financial instruments and foreign exchange transactions. However, the carry-back period remains three years for trading losses in the year before a trade ends (13.14).

Improved loss carry-back rules applied for accounting periods ending after 31 March 1991. Losses made in such accounting periods and arising before 3 July 1997 could be relieved against profits for the three previous years.

As an alternative to the above, a repayment of tax deducted at source from interest received and tax credits on dividends (where applicable) can be obtained. Otherwise the losses will be carried forward and relieved against future profits. (This is subject to possible restriction if the ownership of the company changes, similar to above.) Losses on shares in qualifying trading companies sold by investment companies can be set off against their surplus franked investment income. This follows the general relief against income now available for such losses made by investment companies (20.14).

Anti-avoidance rules may operate to bar relief where there is a change of trade. Furthermore, relief is denied where there is a change of ownership and a major change in the nature or conduct of the trade within a 3-year period.

The anti-avoidance provisions relate in modified form to capital losses and formerly ACT. Investment companies are normally covered, where there is a change in the ownership of such a company after 28 November 1994. Excess management charges and charges on income brought forward from before the change will not be allowed against subsequent income and gains if:

(1) During the three years afterwards, the capital (as defined) increases by at least £1m or more than doubles, compared with in the year before, or
(2) There is a major change in the nature or conduct of the business within 3 years before and 3 years after the change, or
(3) The business had become small or negligible before the change and subsequently revived.

Under the 'pay and file' system, a trading loss in an accounting period ended after 30 September 1993 is normally set off against future profits in the same trade. However, an exception is where claims already have been made to relieve the loss in other ways. The new corporation tax return form includes spaces to keep track of the losses. The company will be able to set aside the carry-forward, so as to use part or all of the losses as group relief.

13.12 Reconstructions (TA 1988 Ss343 & 344)

A 'company reconstruction without change of ownership' (13.10(2)) has other advantages apart from capital allowance continuity. In particular where a company takes over the trade and assets of another and they are under at least 75 per cent common ownership, any trading losses are carried over with the trade. However, the unused tax losses may be restricted if the original company is insolvent when its trade is transferred.

13.13 Group loss relief (TA 1988 Ss402–413 & Sch 18 & TCGA Ss170–192A)

In a group of companies (that is, parent and subsidiaries) the trading losses (including capital allowances, etc.) of respective group members can be offset by way of group relief against the profits of others provided that:

(1) The necessary claim is made within two years of the end of the accounting period.

(2) The group relationship exists throughout the respective accounting periods of the loss making and profit making companies. Otherwise the relief is only obtained for the period during which the group relationship exists; profits and losses being apportioned on a time basis if necessary.

(3) The parent and subsidiary companies are all resident in the UK up to 31 March 2000 and the parent has at least a 75 per cent interest in each of the subsidiaries. Also the parent company must be entitled to at least both 75 per cent of the distributable profits of each subsidiary and 75 per cent of the assets available on the liquidation of each subsidiary. Option arrangements, etc. made after 14 November 1991 are to be taken into account in calculating the percentages, as if they had been exercised.

(4) Subject to certain special rules group relief also applies to a consortium where UK companies own between them ordinary shares of a loss making company or of a holding company which owns 90 per cent of a loss making company. It is necessary for 75 per cent or more of the ordinary shares to be owned by the consortium with no less than 5 per cent held by each member (thus the maximum number is 20). Losses for accounting periods made by consortium companies can be surrendered down to a company which is jointly owned.

(5) Where a company joins or leaves a group during its accounting period the time apportionment basis (see above) may be set aside if it operates unfairly. A 'just and reasonable method' is then used. A similar rule applies in consortium situations.

(6) Subject to certain conditions, a loss can be claimed partly as group relief and partly as consortium relief. Also, consortium relief can flow through to other companies in a consortium member's group.

(7) It should be noted that no group relief is available for the losses of dual-resident investment companies (15.10.15).

(8) The scope of group relief was much widened from 1 April 2000, from when groups or consortia qualify even where established through overseas companies. Thus the UK subsidiaries can surrender group relief to one another. From the same date, group relief extends to UK branches of non-resident companies.

13.14 Terminal losses (TA 1988 S394)

These were available to a company in a similar way to an individual who ceases trading (11.24). Thus, a company was entitled to claim to set off a terminal loss incurred in its last 12 months of trading against its profits for the three preceding years.

The terminal loss rules only apply for companies incurring losses in an accounting period ending before 1 April 1991. Losses in subsequent periods may in any event be relieved against profits for the three previous years (13.11).

13.15 Companies' capital gains and capital losses (TCGA Ss8 & 170–192 & Schs 7A & 7AC, TA 1988 Ss345–347, 400 & 435 & Sch 29)

The capital gains of companies are now charged to corporation tax at the normal rates. Thus a gain made by a company with £1.25m profits bears 30 per cent tax. However, a gain of £20,000 made by a company with £50,000 other taxable profits pays the 20 per cent small companies rate on the gain (13.7).

The new tapering relief system for individuals, etc., does not yet apply to companies, whose gains continue to be computed by allowing indexation relief up to the time of sale (20.12). However, the Government are giving further consideration to the matter.

An exception concerns the capital gains which life assurance companies make for their policyholders. These remain taxed at 30 per cent. This only applies to the policyholders' funds; any shareholders' profits are now taxable under the new arrangements.

Capital losses in accounting periods may be set off against gains, so that the net gains are taxable. Chargeable gains can be relieved by means of capital losses in the same period or those brought forward from previous periods. Trading losses can be set off against capital profits of the same period or the previous period. Trading losses in accounting periods ending after 31 March 1991 and arising before 3 July 1997 can be set off against gains going back three years (13.11). Capital profits can also be set off by group loss relief claims (13.13). Trading losses brought forward from previous periods, however, can only be set off against future trading profits and not against future chargeable gains.

Capital losses (20.13) incurred by a company can only be set off against any capital gains of the company in the same accounting period or a future accounting period. Unused capital losses can be carried forward to future years even if the company has ceased trading whereas a cessation prevents trading losses from being carried forward. Companies are prevented from manufacturing capital losses by sales from large holdings (2 per cent upwards) of another company's shares and buying them back within a month if quoted and six months otherwise.

Under TCGA S13 UK resident and domiciled shareholders of an overseas company can have its capital gains apportioned to them if the company would have been close if UK resident. This rule also covers overseas trusts with shares in such companies. The effect is that UK beneficiaries of the trusts could then be taxed, if they receive any benefit (20.32). The apportionment of gains accruing after 27 November 1995 will depend on the extent of each UK shareholder's participation in the overseas company.

As from 15 March 1988, the exploitation of capital gains tax indexation allowance through inter-group financing was countered. From the same date, the rules were amended to ensure that share exchanges by companies in the same group do not result in capital gains or losses being charged or allowed more than once.

As from 1 January 1992, F2A 1992 introduced various rules concerning capital gains tax where a trade owned by one EC company is transferred to another in exchange for shares or securities. Of particular importance is where a UK trade is transferred in this way from a company resident in one EC country to one resident in another. Under these circumstances, the assets are treated as being transferred at values giving no capital gain or loss, provided certain anti-avoidance provisions are not infringed.

Previously, it was possible for a group of companies to buy a company with unused capital losses and then introduce their own assets prior to sale. Any gains on sale would then be offset against the losses. This was stopped for sales after 15 March 1993 regarding losses from a company which joined the group after 31 March 1987. Losses it subsequently realises on assets it held on joining the group after that date are also restricted. Post-11 March 1994 disposals of these assets are included, even if first transferred within the group.

Subject to certain conditions including the following, gains on disposals by companies of shares after 31 March 2002 are exempt from tax and losses are not allowable:

(1) During a continuous 12-month period beginning not more than 2 years before the disposal, broadly at least 10 per cent of the shares must be held.
(2) Subject to the above, disposals of options and convertible securities are also exempt.
(3) The company making the disposal must be a trading company or member of a trading group.
(4) The company whose shares are being sold must be a trading company or the holding company of a trading company or subgroup.

13.16 Groups of companies (TA 1988 Ss402–413, TCGA Ss170–181 & FA 2002 Ss42 & 43)

Various special provisions relate to groups of companies (broadly parent and subsidiaries). A subsidiary company is classified according to the percentage of its ordinary capital owned (directly or indirectly) by its parent. Thus a 51 per cent subsidiary is over 50 per cent owned by its parent; and a 75 per cent subsidiary is not less than 75 per cent so owned. For these purposes, loan financing may play a part in calculating the percentage owned, unless 'normal commercial loans' (TA 1988 Sch 18).

Some of the main rules relating to groups of companies are as follows:

(1) Group loss relief is available in respect of a parent company and its 75 per cent subsidiaries subject to various rules (13.13).

(2) Subject to an election to the Revenue, dividend payments from 51 per cent subsidiaries to the parent could be made without having to account for ACT. A similar rule relates to inter-group interest payments. These provisions only apply to companies resident in the UK. Also included are payments from a consortium-owned trading or holding company to the consortium members, where the consortium owns at least 75 per cent of the ordinary shares. Each consortium member must own at least 5 per cent.

There needs to be a group relationship in an economic sense between the companies. For example, one company needs not only more than 50 per cent of the other but also to be entitled to more than 50 per cent of the distributable profits and of the assets in a winding up.

(3) Transfers of assets within a group consisting of a parent and its 75 per cent subsidiaries do not generally give rise to capital gains tax. Before 1 April 2000, this only applied to UK resident companies, but now the requirement is that the assets remain within the UK tax net. (Certain dual resident companies are excluded.) The parent must be effectively entitled to over 50 per cent of the profits of the subsidiary and of its assets on winding up.) When the asset leaves the group, however, capital gains tax is paid on the entire chargeable gain on the asset whilst it was owned by any group company (TCGA S171). Also, rules restrict schemes to reduce tax on selling subsidiaries (15.10.17).

Assets are charged when a company leaves the group (TCGA Ss179 & 179A). Also, capital gains tax on an asset can be charged where two companies are degrouped together. For a company leaving a group after 31 March 2002 all or part of its gains or losses arising on that account may be reallocated to other members of that group. Furthermore the degrouping charge can be postponed by applying a modified form of business rollover relief.

(4) Capital gains tax 'rollover relief' (20.25) applies to a UK group consisting of a parent company and its 75 per cent subsidiaries. The gain on an asset sold by one trading company may be 'rolled over' against the purchase of an asset by another trading company (excluding certain dual resident companies) in the group (TCGA S175). (Property holding and non-trading companies which hold assets used for trade by trading companies in the group are also included.) Also, relief applies for disposals under compulsory purchase orders where another group company acquires replacement land.

(5) If a parent company holds more than 50 per cent of the ordinary shares of a subsidiary and is entitled to more than 50 per cent of its distributable profits and more than 50 per cent of its assets on liquidation, the parent could transfer to its subsidiary relief for ACT. If the subsidiary ceases to be owned by the parent, any unused ACT is lost unless the companies remain in the same overall group.

(6) A special rule applies to interest payments between companies under common control, including a parent and 51 per cent (or more) subsidiaries. To prevent relief for the payer occurring in one year and tax being paid the next, the interest is to be treated as received on the day when paid. This rule applies where the paying company obtains relief for the interest as a charge on income and the recipient is taxed under Case III (8.4).

(7) ACT surrendered from one group company to another, which remained unused was lost if there was a major change in the recipient company's business within three years.

(8) The 1998 Finance Act introduced various anti-avoidance measures which took effect from 17 March 1998. Where a company with capital gains joins a group from that date, the group losses which it can offset are restricted.

(9) For disposal from April 2000, group companies can elect to bring together gains and losses into a single company without transferring the asset within the group. Any payment of the gain or loss between the group companies concerned is tax neutral (FA 2000 S101).

13.16.1 **Group rules introduced with 'pay and file'** (FA 1989 S102, FA 1998 Sch 18)

With the introduction of 'pay and file' (13.4.1) for accounting periods ended after 30 September 1993, revised rules operate for groups, including the following:

(1) In a group of companies, a refund of tax in one company can be set off against liabilities in other companies by election. The object is to avoid companies being penalised by the differential between interest payable and receivable under the new system.
(2) Improved and more flexible procedures are introduced concerning group relief claims (which must be included in the claimant company's tax return).
(3) Claims may be made and be capable of being withdrawn within two years of the end of the accounting period. If later, this is to be extended to the date that the profits and losses for the period are determined, but no more than six years from the end of the period.
(4) Trading losses which have been relieved against the profits of a later period will be allowed to be reallocated and surrendered as group relief.
(5) New rules applying for accounting periods ending after self-assessment is introduced (on or after 1 July 1999) make it easier for companies to make and withdraw ACT surrenders (FA 1996 Sch 25). This is of only limited application, following the abolition of ACT.
(6) There are rules concerning reductions in group relief surrenders for accounting periods ending after 30 June 1999. If unpaid, the resultant extra tax can be recovered from group companies to the extent that they benefited from the surrender.

13.17 ACT on dividends, distributions etc. (TA 1988 Ss14, 209, 238 & 239, FA 1998 Ss31–32, Sch 3 & FA 1999 S91)

Companies had to pay 'advance corporation tax' (ACT) at 20⁄80 on their payments of dividends (13.3). This tax was also payable on other 'qualifying distributions'. (Prior to 6 April 1994, various other rates applied.) ACT was abolished for dividends and other qualifying distributions made after 5 April 1999.

13.17.1 Distributions

There are two different classes of distribution known as qualifying and non-qualifying distributions. Qualifying distributions are dividends and similar payments. Other examples are interest on certain securities and Equity Notes. Non-qualifying distributions are those which are really distributions of special sorts of shares, etc. which carry a potential future claim on the company's profits: for example, bonus debentures or bonus redeemable shares. Whereas qualifying distributions were subjected to ACT, in the case of non-qualifying distributions, no ACT was payable by the company. The shareholder got no tax credit (20 per cent) and was not liable to such tax on the non-qualifying distribution. He was, however, liable to the excess of his higher rate tax over the tax credit rate (20 per cent) on the actual value of the non-qualifying distribution.

From 8 October 1996 to April 1999, new treatment applied to certain distributions which were linked to transactions in securities. These included where companies purchased their own shares. (FA 1997 Sch 7.) The distributions were treated as foreign income dividends (13.17.7), so as to deny the recipients any repayment of the tax credits. (Share dealers took such distributions into their trading profits from 26 November 1996.) Broadly, from 6 April 1999, the foreign income dividends scheme no longer applies.

13.17.2 Accounting periods for ACT (TA 1988 Sch 13 & 16 & FA 1996 Schs 23 & 24)

Companies accounted to the Revenue for ACT on a three-monthly basis. Returns were made for each three months to 31 March and 30 June, 30 September and 31 December respectively – and so on. Also if the company's accounting period did not end on one of these dates, the period of three months during which it ended was divided into two separate periods for which returns were submitted.

13.17.3 Franked payment (TA 1988 S238 & FA 1998 Sch 3)

This was defined as being a qualifying distribution made by a company together with the relevant ACT. Thus, a qualifying distribution of £8,000 represented a franked payment of £10,000 (that is, £8,000 + £8,000 × 20⁄80). This has no relevance regarding distributions made after 5 April 1999, in view of the abolition of ACT.

13.17.4 **Franked investment income** (TA 1988 S238)

This consists of income from a UK resident company (17.3.3) being distributions in respect of which tax credits are obtained. A company's franked investment income is the amount including the relevant tax credits. Thus if a company receives a dividend of £900, this is treated as being franked investment income of £1,000 (that is, £900 + £900 × 1/9).

13.17.5 **Setting off ACT against 'mainstream' corporation tax** (TA 1988 Ss238–246)

As its name suggests, advance corporation tax was a pre-payment of the main or mainstream corporation tax bill of a company. The latter was only ascertained when accounts were submitted to the Revenue after the end of the accounting period.

There was a limit to the amount of ACT which could be off-set against a company's 'mainstream' corporation tax liability. This limit was the amount of ACT which would be paid on a full distribution of the company's income and capital gains but before the deduction of any tax. ACT could be set off against corporation tax on capital gains (13.15). In computing this full distribution, account was taken of the notional ACT payable.

A company obtains relief for overseas tax suffered by deducting it from the corporation tax falling on the same income. The rules ensured that the net corporation tax charge on foreign income, after double tax relief and ACT, was at least the latterly 11 per cent minimum.

13.17.6 **Carry-back and carry-forward of ACT** (TA 1988 Ss239 & 245 & FA 1998 S32)

Any ACT which was not relieved against corporation tax payable for the accounting period in which the relevant distribution was made, because of the restriction mentioned above, was known as 'surplus ACT'. This surplus ACT could be carried back and off-set against corporation tax payable for any accounting periods beginning in the six years preceding that in which the relevant distribution was made. A claim to this effect must be made within two years of the end of the period for which the surplus ACT arises.

Any surplus ACT which is not carried back as above may normally be carried forward without time limit to be set off against future corporation tax payable. Relief was restricted if within three years there was both a change in the ownership of the company and a major change in the nature or conduct of its trade (or this becomes negligible). ACT relating to an accounting period before the change in ownership cannot be carried forward to a period after that change. Furthermore, ACT arising after such a change cannot be carried back before the change, where this occurs after 15 March 1993.

Following the abolition of ACT for qualifying distributions made after 5 April 1999 (13.17), the benefits of surplus ACT carried forward are preserved by '*shadow ACT*'. As a result, subject to a limit of 20 per cent of its corporation tax profits, a company can obtain relief for surplus ACT from previous years, allowing for notional ACT on dividend payments. This is illustrated by the following example for a company accounting to 5 April 2000, with past surplus ACT of £80,000:

	£
Taxable profits	120,000
ACT set-off limit 20%	24,000
Dividends £40,000	
Shadow ACT 25%	10,000
Past ACT now set off	14,000
Surplus ACT forward	66,000

[The net corporation tax liability is £120,000 × 20% – £14,000 = £10,000]

13.17.7 **Foreign income dividend scheme** (FA 1994 S138, Sch 16 & FA 1996 Sch 27 & F2A 1997 S36 & Sch 6)

Under the foreign income dividend (FID) scheme, from 1 July 1994, a company could elect to pay an FID. ACT was payable, but FIDs carried no tax credit. If the dividend was paid out of foreign income profits, the company was able to recover surplus ACT. The FID scheme was aimed at the surplus ACT arising when UK corporation tax was reduced or eliminated by relief for foreign tax.

Broadly from 8 October 1996, certain distributions linked to transactions in securities and companies purchasing their own shares were treated as if they were FIDs (13.17.1). As a result, they earned no tax credit. However, shareholders subject to income tax were treated as though the FIDs had borne income tax at 20 per cent.

Broadly, the FID scheme does not apply for post-5 April 1999 dividends. Thus no election can be made for such a dividend to be an FID. Excess FIDs are not to be carried forward. However, FIDs could be matched with overseas profits of subsequent accounting periods but no later than the end of the first period which starts after 5 April 1999.

13.18 Close companies (TA 1988 Ss414–430 & Sch 19 & FA 1989 Ss103–107 & Sch 12)

Special provisions relate to 'close' companies, more particularly, for periods beginning before 1 April 1989 and are described in greater depth in previous editions of this book. Close companies are broadly those under the control of five or fewer persons and their 'associates'. The latter term includes close family such as husband, wife, child, father, mother, brother, sister, etc. A quoted company is not 'close', however, if not less than 35 per cent of its voting shares are owned by the general public.

There is also an alternative test by reference to whether five or fewer persons and their 'associates' would receive broadly the greater part of the company's assets on liquidation which would be available for distribution.

A UK subsidiary of an overseas parent company is 'close' if the latter would have itself been 'close' if resident here. It is thus seen that most small or medium companies are likely to be 'close' companies unless they are subsidiaries of non-close companies. The majority of 'family' companies are 'close'.

13.18.1 **Apportionment of income under the imputation system** (TA 1988 Ss423–430 & Sch 19 & FA 1989 S103 & Sch 12)

For periods beginning *before 1 April 1989*, the Revenue could apportion among the shareholders the excess of the 'relevant income' of a close company over its distributions. For property investment companies the threshold was £251. Subject to the rules, such as abatement, 'relevant income' consisted of not more than the company's 'distributable investment income' plus 50 per cent of its property income. (Special rules applied where a company ceased to trade.)

13.18.2 **Loans and distributions for close companies** (TA 1988 Ss418–422)

A special provision regarding close companies which remains operative is that if they make loans to their 'participators' (see below) or associates of the latter, the companies are charged tax at 25 per cent on the amounts. (If the loan is repaid to the company, the tax will be repaid.) Thus if a loan of £8,000 is made to a participator the company will be assessed to tax of 25 per cent × £8,000 = £2,000. Loans by companies controlled by or subsequently acquired by close companies are also covered by this rule.

Under rules which apply for loans made in accounting periods ending on or after 31 March 1996, the tax is due 9 months after the end of the accounting period. If the loan is repaid before the tax is due, it is not necessary to pay the tax. Previously, the due date was only 14 days after the end of the accounting period in which the loan was made and the Revenue could assess loans even if repaid.

Should a close company lend money to a participator or his associate and then release the debt, higher rate tax is assessed on the recipient in respect of the grossed up equivalent of the loan. Thus in the above example, if the company releases the participator from his debt he will pay higher rate tax on £10,000 (£8,000 + £2,000). A deduction of £2,000 will be made, however, from the total tax payable.

The meaning of the term 'distribution' (dividend, etc.) is extended in the case of close companies to include living expenses and accommodation, etc. provided for a 'participator' (or his associate). A 'participator' means broadly a person having a share or interest in the capital or income of a company, including, for example, a shareholder or loan creditor. The effect of treating a payment as a distribution is that it is not deductible from the taxable profit of the company.

13.19 Close investment holding companies (CICs) (TA S13A)

(1) Provisions having effect for accounting periods beginning after 31 March 1989 imposed harsher taxation on certain Close Investment Holding Companies (CICs).

(2) A CIC is a close company which is neither a 'trading company' nor a member of a trading group, nor a property investment company (which lets to non-connected persons).

(3) Broadly, a trading company is one which exists wholly or mainly for the purpose of trading on a commercial basis.

(4) Dealing in property or shares does not cause a company to be a CIC. Similarly, mixed property dealing and investment companies are not CICs.

(5) CICs are subject to 30 per cent corporation tax regardless of their level of profits. They do not obtain the benefit of the 19 per cent small companies rate or the start up rate.

(6) If a shareholder waives, or does not receive a dividend, the extent to which someone else is entitled to be repaid a tax credit may be restricted. The Revenue may request information and make 'just and reasonable' restrictions. This does not apply where, for example, there is only one class of shares.

(7) Where a CIC takes out a life assurance policy after 13 March 1989, profits subsequently realised will be taxed, subject to the rules.

13.20 Non-resident companies trading in the UK (TA 1988 S11 & FA 2003 Ss148–156 & Schs 25–27)

Where a non-resident company (17.3.3) carries on a trade in this country through a branch or agency here, corporation tax is charged in respect of the profits of the branch or agency. If those profits are also subject to tax in the country of residence of the company, double tax relief may be available (18.6). (Special rules apply where companies become non-resident (17.3.3).)

Regarding accounting periods of non-resident companies which begin after 31 December 2002, the rules for applying UK corporation tax on income and chargeable gains substitute 'permanent establishment' for 'branch or agency' (in this country). Subject to certain provisions and any relevant double tax treaty, a company has a permanent establishment in a territory if it has a fixed place of business there through which the business of the company is wholly or partly carried on; or an agent acting there on behalf of the company has and habitually exercises authority to do business on behalf of the company.

For accounting periods starting after 31 December 2002, UK branches of overseas companies are subjected to new rules which restrict the debt and effectively the interest deduction claimable for tax purposes.

13.21 UK companies with overseas income

Any overseas income of a company that is resident in this country is subject to corporation tax on the gross amount of such income. Double tax relief is frequently available in respect of overseas income that is taxed both in the UK and abroad.

If a UK company receives a dividend from an overseas company from which withholding tax has been deducted, the gross dividend is included in the taxable profits subject to corporation tax. Normally, double tax relief for the withholding tax suffered is given against the corporation tax payable. (Withholding tax is tax that is 'withheld' from the dividend when the latter is paid. It is thus a form of tax deducted at source.) In addition, if at least 10 per cent of the voting capital of the overseas company is owned by the UK company, relief is given for the 'underlying tax' (that is, the proportion of the total tax paid by the foreign company attributable to its dividends). Also in these circumstances, in certain cases no basic rate tax is to be charged on the paying and collecting agents (F2A 1992 S30). In no case, however, can the double tax relief rate exceed 45 per cent (18.6).

FA 2005 introduces further restrictions, limiting foreign tax credit to the UK tax on so much of the trade profit as is derived from the income suffering foreign tax. There are also new anti-avoidance rules.

13.22 Controlled foreign companies (CFCs) (TA 1988 Ss747–756 & Schs 24 26 & FA 2002 Ss89 & 90)

The Revenue are able to impose extra tax on UK companies with interests in CFCs, subject to certain rules including the following:

(1) The overseas company must be under overall UK control. This is now satisfied if two companies, etc., control it and only one is UK resident, each having at least 40 per cent.
(2) The overseas company must be subject to tax in its country of residence which is less than 75 per cent of that payable if it were UK resident.
(3) A UK company (together with associates, etc.) has at least a 10 per cent interest in the overseas company.
(4) Acceptable dividend payments which are made by a company not resident at the time of payment, will exclude the charge. For accounting periods beginning after 27 November 1995, the requirement for trading companies is 90 per cent (previously 50 per cent) of the profits, calculated as for UK tax purposes. For investment companies this figure has always been 90 per cent but capital profits and foreign tax are deducted from the profits. Also,

investment companies are now able to make distributions for such periods out of profits of earlier periods not yet taxed under the CFC rules.

(5) The charge is excluded if the controlled foreign company satisfies an 'exempt activities' test. For this, the company must have a business establishment where it is resident and be managed there. Also it must broadly be a trading or qualifying holding company rather than an investment company.

(6) Exclusion is also available through a motive test. The foreign company's transactions must be carried out for commercial reasons and not for the main purpose of saving UK tax nor diverting profits from the UK.

(7) Certain foreign companies quoted on foreign stock exchanges are also excluded.

(8) There is no charge if the foreign company's profits for the year are less than £50,000. (For accounting periods beginning before 17 March 1998 this figure was £20,000.)

(9) A list has been published of excluded countries which will not be regarded as low tax countries for the purposes of the above rules. In general, the list excludes tax havens and normally applies where at least 75 per cent is 'local source' income (90 per cent for accounting periods beginning before 17 March 1998).

(10) Where applicable, the profits of the overseas company are apportioned to any UK companies with at least a 10 per cent interest and corporation tax is charged at the appropriate rate for each. A deduction is then made for any 'creditable tax' (overseas tax, etc.) which is similarly apportioned. Appropriate relief is then given where dividends are paid by the overseas company.

(11) Various anti-avoidance provisions have been introduced (15.10). For example, CFCs can include dual resident companies.

(12) From 23 March 1995, where profits need to be calculated for the CFC rules, they are expressed in the currency used in the company's accounts.

(13) For accounting periods ending after 30 June 1999, CFC charges are brought into the corporation tax self-assessment system.

(14) From 9 March 1999, dividends paid by a CFC to the UK no longer count towards the acceptable level (90 per cent etc.) if they are paid out of UK dividends (or other distributions) not counting towards its chargeable profits.

(15) Further anti-avoidance provisions operate from 21 March 2000. These cover holding companies, intra-group service companies, control (see (1) above) and 'designer' tax rates.

(16) A loophole is closed by FA 2001 S82 regarding artificial schemes to exploit the acceptable dividend policy rules.

(17) The Treasury have reserve powers to specify countries for which the CFC exemptions will not apply. Also, UK resident companies from 1 April 2002 can be caught by the CFC rules, even if treated as non-resident under a double tax agreement.

(18) FA 2003 introduces further modifications. Eligible companies in Hong Kong and Macao will continue to claim CFC exemption through the 'exempt activities test'. Also, a loophole is closed which had been exploited by companies carrying on warranty or credit protection business.

(19) FA 2005 (Ss89 & 90) restricts relief involving certain related companies and regarding CFCs for which exemption is available under the acceptable distribution policy test.

13.23 Demergers (TA 1988 Ss213–218)

Special rules assist two or more trading businesses in 'demerging' where they are carried on by a single company or a group. In demergers, subject to the detailed provisions:

(1) Where a company distributes shares in a 75 per cent subsidiary (13.17.1) to its shareholders this is not treated as a distribution.

(2) Relief also applies where one company transfers a trade to a second company which in turn distributes its shares to the shareholders of the first.

(3) Capital gains tax relief applies to any distribution which you receive in the above circumstances until you sell the actual shares.

(4) There was also certain relief from development land tax and stamp duty in demergers.

(5) The provisions only apply to the genuine splitting off of trades or trading subsidiaries. There are anti-avoidance provisions to counter, for example the extraction of tax-free cash from companies subject to an advance clearance procedure.

13.24 Unquoted company purchasing its own shares (TA 1988 Ss219–229 & FA 1997 S69 & Sch 7)

The 1981 Companies Act enables companies to purchase their own shares and issue redeemable equity shares. If the proceeds exceeded the original cost, the excess would be treated as a distribution under existing law and taxed in the same way as a dividend. Thus the company would pay ACT on the excess and an individual receiving the payment would pay higher rate tax on the grossed up excess less a tax credit (13.17.5). However, with effect from 8 October 1996, these distributions were treated as foreign income dividends (13.17.7). As a result, recipients were not able to obtain any repayment of tax credit.

With the abolition of both FIDs and ACT from 6 April 1999, the system has broadly reverted to the original one for shareholders. Either capital gains tax treatment applies (see below) or the excess of the proceeds over the original cost is taxed as a company distribution (8.1.7).

Under the rules, in certain circumstances the company paid no ACT and the shareholder's liability was and is restricted to capital gains tax (unless he is a share-dealer, in which case the gain is treated as his income). Stamp duty relief applied up to 27 October 1986, but not subsequently. Broadly, the conditions for relief are as follows:

(1) The company must not be quoted nor be the subsidiary of a quoted company. (Shares dealt with on the Unlisted Securities Market are not treated as quoted.)
(2) The company must be a trading company or the holding company of a trading group.
(3) The purchase or redemption of the shares must be mainly to benefit a trade of the company or its 75 per cent subsidiary.
(4) The shareholder must be UK resident and ordinarily resident, having normally owned the shares for at least five years (three years in specified cases such as inherited shares, where ownership by the deceased is also counted).
(5) If the shareholder keeps part of his shareholding in the company (or its group) his shareholding must be substantially reduced. Broadly, this means reducing his interest by at least 25 per cent and not being 'connected' (that is, holding with 'associates' 30 per cent of the shares, etc.).
(6) If the payment is used for capital transfer tax or inheritance tax within two years after a death, (4) and (5) above do not apply and relief is due, provided that to pay the tax out of other funds would have caused undue hardship.
(7) Advance clearance application may be made to the Revenue.
(8) As indicated, the above rules do not apply where a company buys back its shares from a dealer, who is taxed under Schedule D Case I or II (11.4), receiving no tax credit.

New regulations allow listed companies which purchase their own shares to hold them and either sell them back into the market or cancel them. Such 'Treasury Shares' will be treated for tax purposes as cancelled when bought and newly issued when sold. When a venture capital trust (8.13) issues shares from 'Treasury', no income tax relief is due to individual investors.

13.25 Foreign exchange gains and losses (FA 1993 Ss92–96, 125–170 & Schs 15–18, FA 1995 Ss130 & 132 & Sch 24, FA 2000 Ss105 & 106 & FA 2002 Ss79–81 & Sch 23)

A special tax system for company foreign exchange transactions applies to companies for their first accounting periods starting after 22 March 1995 and is now substantially revised (10). This replaces the previous system which lacked certainty. Particular features in the new scheme include the following:

(1) Exchange gains and losses on monetary assets (cash bank deposits and debts, etc.) and liabilities are taxed or relieved as income as they accrue.
(2) Capital gains tax is no longer to be charged on any monetary assets in foreign currency.

(3) Exchange differences on monetary items are recognised as they accrue.
(4) Where certain conditions are met, the calculation of trading profits before capital allowances, in currencies other than sterling, is permitted and sometimes required (11).
(5) Unrealised exchange gains above certain limits may be deferred, where they arise on long-term capital items.
(6) Where a borrowing matches a monetary asset, exchange differences may be deferred until the asset is disposed of.
(7) For the purposes of the rules, the ECU is to be regarded as a foreign currency.
(8) Transfers of assets by way of security are ignored and the company continues to be regarded as holding them.
(9) Exchange differences on debts must be computed from when the obligation to pay arises rather than when payment is due (if later).
(10) Certain important changes generally apply for accounting periods beginning on or after 1 January 2000 and ending from 21 March 2000.
(11) When calculating their taxable profits, companies are to use the currency of their accounts (or branch financial statements), provided that this accords with normal accounting practice. This is also to apply to exchange gains and losses.
(12) New rules have effect for accounting periods beginning after 30 September 2002, except for certain anti-avoidance provisions. The above foreign exchange legislation is generally repealed and incorporated in the loan relationships provisions (13.27).

13.26 Interest rate and currency contracts and options (FA 1994 Ss147–177 & Sch 18)

The tax treatment of financial instruments to manage interest rates and currency risks for companies have been reformed. The rules apply for accounting periods beginning on or after 23 March 1995. Profits and losses on 'qualifying contracts' are normally to be taxed or relieved on an income basis when they accrue. These broadly include currency or interest rate contracts or options acquired under the new rules.

13.27 Loan relationships (FA 1996 Ss80–105 & Schs 8–15)

Detailed new rules apply for companies with effect from 1 April 1996, regarding 'loan relationships'. This applies to debts which are loans under general law and whether owed to or by the company. In general, the rules treat all profits and losses on loans made by companies as income, interest payments being taxed or relieved as they accrue rather than are paid. Assets covered are taken out of the capital gains tax regime. Certain revised transitional rules apply from 14 November 1996.

The new rules apply to corporate bonds, Permanent Interest Bearing Shares and other corporate debt. Gilts held by companies are also covered, apart from profits and losses on 3.5% Funding Stock 1999/2004 and 5.5% Treasury Stock 2008/12.

Finance Act 2002 introduced new and wider rules for derivative contracts, replacing the old financial instrument rules. As a result, favourable tax treatment is restricted for convertible, exchangeable and asset-linked securities. The loan relationship rules are revised as are those for connected party bad debts.

For accounting periods beginning after 30 September 2002, the provision preventing exchange gains and losses being taken into account under the loan relationships legislation is removed. At the same time detailed new rules regarding foreign exchange are assimilated into that legislation (FA 2002 Sch 24).

From 9 April 2003, a new rule aims at blocking a loan relationship avoidance scheme which attempted to create a tax deduction for interest or discount which is accrued but never paid.

Further changes have been introduced by FA 2004, including some relating to certain venture capital limited partnerships, companies with insolvency proceedings and those which emigrate. Certain assets which contain a derivative element will now be divided so that such part is subject to capital gains rules and the loan relationship balance taxed according to the loan rules. Exchange gains and losses on certain loans can now be matched, even though not taken to reserve.

13.28 Corporate venturing scheme (CVS) (FA 2000 S63 & Schs 15 & 16)

A new tax incentive scheme operates broadly from 1 April 2000 to encourage companies to invest in small higher risk trading companies and to form wider corporate venturing links.

(1) The focus is on the same types of company as for the EIS (11.26) and VCT (8.13) schemes.
(2) Investment relief, being a 20 per cent reduction in corporation tax, is given on the cost of new CVS ordinary shares held for 3 years or more.
(3) Gains on sales of CVS shares can be deferred if invested in other CVS shares.
(4) Relief for allowable capital losses net of investment relief can be claimed against gains or income (if gains are insufficient).
(5) A CVS company cannot be controlled by any corporate venturer.
(6) At least 20 per cent of its ordinary shares must be owned by individuals and not more than 30 per cent by a corporate venturer.
(7) CVS relief applies to shares issued from 1 April 2000 to 31 March 2010 provided that at issue, they are unquoted and there are no arrangements to be listed.
(8) Previously, all money raised needed to be used within 12 months but from 7 March 2001, only 80 per cent must be so used with the balance used in the next 12 months.

(9) From 17 March 2004, the rules are relaxed regarding subsidiaries. Companies will qualify under the scheme even if they have 51 per cent subsidiaries or 90 per cent subsidiaries which are property management companies or benefit from the CVS money raised.

13.29 Intangible fixed assets (FA 2002 S84 & Schs 29 & 30)

A new corporation tax regime covers intangible fixed assets, such as intellectual property and goodwill acquired or created from 1 April 2002 (including their preservation and maintenance). The provisions allow tax relief to be obtained normally at the rate at which the assets are depreciated in the same accounts, subject to a minimum annual amount of 4 per cent. Such assets will cease to be within the capital gains rules. However, gains on disposals from 1 April 2002 of assets created or acquired before that date may on election be rolled-over into new qualifying assets acquired before that date and within a year of the disposal.

New anti-avoidance rules aimed at inter-group transfers operate after 20 June 2003 (FA 2003 S184).

13.30 International Accounting Standards (IAS)

For periods beginning after 31 December 2004, companies adopting IAS to draw up their accounts can use these for tax purposes, which was not previously the case. However, companies in the same group are barred from obtaining a tax advantage through treating the same transaction as being under IAS rules in one group company and UK practice in another.

Among detailed changes made to the legislation is the introduction of relief for companies which add R&D expenditure (11.16) to the cost of intangible assets in accordance with IAS. FA 2005 contains various technical amendments, generally effective from 1 January 2005. Also, securitisation companies will be able to be taxed on the old basis. (Such companies are special purpose vehicles normally involved in issuing securities to the market.)

Chapter 14

PENSIONS

14.1 Introduction

With the increase in life expectancy and the decrease in the average age of retirement, pension planning grows in importance. You will need to plan for a longer retirement and should aim to receive an adequate pension during that period.

This chapter is mainly concerned with the tax aspects of pension arrangements as they will affect you. There are three main categories:

(1) The State scheme (14.2)
(2) Occupational pension schemes (14.3)
(3) Personal pension schemes (14.4) including stakeholder pension schemes from 6 April 2001 (14.8).

So far as you are concerned, these categories are not necessarily mutually exclusive. You can certainly expect some State pension. If you belong to an occupational scheme provided by your employers, then you may still be able to make contributions to personal pension schemes.

The main tax benefits of approved personal pension and occupational pension schemes are:

- Full tax relief at highest marginal rates on employer and member contributions.
- Contributions paid by an employer are not taxed as a benefit.
- The pension fund is free of UK tax on income and capital gains (although it is not possible to reclaim tax credits on dividends).
- Retirement benefits may include a substantial lump sum which is currently tax-free.
- A substantial tax-free lump sum is also payable in the event of death before taking the retirement benefits.
- The retirement pension (and any dependant's pension) is taxed as if it were earned income, but is not subject to a National Insurance liability.

Contributions are now able to be paid on someone else's behalf, including on behalf of a minor child.

A pension scheme member may also be provided with substantial life assurance cover. Its cost will be met by the employer or the member and will be relievable against tax.

14.2 The State scheme

The State pension scheme provides a basic pension subject to the claimant having an adequate National Insurance contribution record. Employees may also qualify for a graduated pension on contributions from April 1961 to April 1975, the State Earnings Related Pension Scheme (SERPS) on contributions between April 1978 and April 2002 and the State Second Pension (S2P) on contributions from April 2002. The Pension Credit is designed to ensure that all pensioners and pensioner couples receive a minimum level of income. Whilst the State pension will usually only increase with prices, the Pension Credit will increase with national average earnings. The Pension Credit resembles income support and comprises a guaranteed credit (in effect the amount needed to ensure a minimum income from all sources and available from age 60) and a savings credit. The savings credit allows a higher level of benefit where income before the Credit exceeds the savings credit threshold. However, it will be reduced (by 40 pence in the pound) where income exceeds the 'appropriate minimum guarantee'. The savings credit is available from age 65.

The basic pension is shown later (25.3.1). To obtain the maximum, you need to have paid or to have been credited with National Insurance contributions for roughly 90% of your working life.

SERPS and S2P derive from your National Insurance contributions (25.2.2), unless you are contracted-out (14.2.1). Your employer will account for their contributions and yours with PAYE remittances (10.14).

Contributions which count for State pension benefits are only payable on part of your earnings (25.2.2). Broadly, your SERPS pension was designed to provide between 20% and 25% of a band of earnings. The actual amount would depend on when you retired. The lowest percentage was planned to apply to people retiring in the late 2030s onwards.

From 6 April 2002, employees and some disabled people and carers will be able to qualify for the State Second Pension. It is earnings related initially, but will move to a flat rate when the government is assured of the success of Stakeholder pensions. Those individuals who pay National Insurance, but whose earnings are low, disabled people and carers are assumed to have earnings of £12,100 (2005–06) for these purposes. As a broad rule, earnings between the National Insurance threshold and £12,100 qualify for a State Second Pension of 40%. The next £15,700 (2005–06) qualifies for a 10% pension and the £4,950 (2005–06) above that (to the Upper Earnings Limit of £32,760 in 2005–06) qualifies for a pension on that band of 20%. The averaging effect means that an indivdual who has consistently had earnings above a certain level (£27,800 in 2005–06) will qualify for a State Second Pension of 20% of qualifying earnings.

You are taxed on your State pensions which are currently payable from age 60 (women) and 65 (men). Over the decade starting 2010/11, the retirement age for women will gradually increase to 65: a woman's retirement age will depend on when she was born.

It has long been possible to defer the state pension which qualifies for a weekly increment for the period of deferment. From April 2005, it will be possible to take the increments as a lump sum after 12 months' deferment. The lump sum will only be taxed at the top rate of income tax that would otherwise have been payable had the lump sum not been taken in that year.

14.2.1 Contracting out of the State Second Pension

Contracting out enables some of your National Insurance contributions to be redirected to a personal or occupational pension scheme so that it can provide an alternative to the State Second Pension.

Whilst some occupational schemes once had to undertake to provide a pension at least equal to an approximate SERPS pension (the 'guaranteed minimum pension'), the only test now is that the pension displays certain features. A personal pension scheme or money purchase occupational scheme will be required to offer 'protected rights' in respect of the National Insurance rebates. The protected rights fund may only provide benefits from age 60 and may only provide an income in retirement. The protected rights fund must make provision for widows'/widowers' pensions where appropriate and must convert to a pension using unisex annuity rates.

Defined benefit occupational schemes must provide benefits that exhibit the features of a 'reference scheme'. Those features include limited inflation proofing of pensions, rules on calculating the minimum accrual rate and, where appropriate, widows'/widowers' pensions.

14.3 Occupational pension schemes (TA 1988 Ss590–617, Sch 23 & FA 1989 Sch 6)

14.3.1 Introduction

From 8 October 2001, it is compulsory for many employers to provide *access* to a stakeholder pension scheme for most employees unless they offer a suitable alternative. This can be an occupational scheme or a grouped personal pension scheme.

Your employer may operate an occupational pension scheme. However, you cannot be compelled to join or remain in the scheme. You could, for instance, opt out in favour of a personal pension scheme (14.6.1) although you would generally be unwise to do so.

If an occupational pension scheme is non-contributory, employees will not be required to make contributions. Otherwise it will be known as a contributory scheme. Directors can be members but there are some restrictions on controlling directors of investment companies (14.3.5).

The schemes have their own trustees and the funds are separate from those of the employer. Smaller schemes are more likely to be run by life assurance companies; larger ones may well have their own investment managers.

In general, your scheme is likely to be 'approved', in which case it obtains favourable tax treatment. However, unapproved schemes may be established providing greater benefits than those permitted under an approved scheme.

An *unapproved scheme* may be funded, in which case your employers get tax relief on their contributions but you are taxed on them as benefits. Contributions now generate a National Insurance liability. Your own contributions (if any) are not deductible for tax purposes. You will be taxed on any pension income taken from a funded unapproved scheme, but not if you take the benefits as a lump sum and tax has already been paid on contributions and on the fund investments.

Under section 397 Income Tax (Earnings and Pensions) Act 2003 you may be liable to income tax on any part of the benefits received under arrangements made or varied after 30 November 1993 from a funded unapproved retirement benefits scheme (FURBS) if the investments have not already been taxed in the UK.

If the scheme is unfunded, your pension will simply be paid out of your employer's general resources at the time. You will be taxed on any pensions and lump sum payments you receive, but there will be no liability to National Insurance.

14.3.2 Obtaining approval

The team responsible for pensions at the Inland Revenue is known as Inland Revenue Savings, Pensions and Share Schemes (IR SPSS). It has previously been called the Pension Schemes Office (PSO) and formerly the Superannuation Funds Office (SFO). To qualify for favourable tax treatment, approval must be sought from the Inland Revenue. It takes two forms, 'approval' and 'exempt approval'.

'Approval' simply prevents you from being taxed on the contributions that your employer makes for you. Most schemes apply for 'exempt approval' which allows a wider range of reliefs. Additional tax benefits include tax relief on your own and your employer's contributions and investment growth in a fund which will usually be free of UK tax on income and capital growth. Note that pension funds may no longer recover tax paid on UK dividends. Exempt approval will only be granted to schemes established under irrevocable trusts.

The Inland Revenue has wide powers to approve schemes. To begin with, certain conditions (TA 1988 S590(2)) must normally be satisfied concerning the pension scheme and these include:

(1) The sole purpose should be the provision of 'relevant benefits' in respect of the service of an employee. These would include any kind of financial benefit, such as pensions or lump sums, connected with your leaving your employment: paid to yourself, your executors, widow, widower, children or dependants. (Benefits given in connection with genuine redundancy are excluded.)

(2) The employer and employees must recognise it and written particulars of the scheme must be given to you if you are a present or potential member.
(3) The scheme must be established in connection with a trade, etc. carried on in the UK by a UK resident person. (However, discretionary approval can be extended to a scheme established by an overseas resident company carrying on part of its trade in the UK.)
(4) A UK resident person must be responsible for administering the scheme according to the rules. Such 'administrator' is normally a trustee or sponsor.
(5) The employer must contribute to the scheme.

Providing the above mandatory rules are satisfied, together with certain other conditions, the Inland Revenue is obliged to approve a scheme. Alternatively, it is able to grant approval on a discretionary basis if certain less stringent requirements are satisfied, and this is the more usual approach. The following are the main features that approved pension funds are likely to have:

(1) Pensions are paid from an age which may be within the range 50 to 75. However, discretionary approval is often granted by the Inland Revenue to schemes allowing retirement at any age due to permanent incapacity caused by illness or accident.
(2) Your pension may be calculated by reference to your length of service and final remuneration. This is known as the *final salary* basis and your pension will be calculated as a fraction of this, typically 1⁄60 for each year of service up to 40. This produces a maximum pension of two-thirds of final remuneration. Under their discretionary powers, the Inland Revenue often allow a shorter service requirement for the maximum pension. Note that an increasingly popular scheme design is to calculate benefits by reference to average career earnings revalued in line with inflation rather than final remuneration.
(3) Since April 1988, *money purchase* schemes are becoming increasingly popular. Broadly, within Inland Revenue limits, your pension is related to the value of the fund created from contributions rather than your final remuneration. This fund will be used to provide your pension and other benefits. Typically, an annuity might be purchased for you on your retirement. It is increasingly common to find schemes that offer a defined benefit (final salary) formula supplemented by a money purchase option. These may be 'hybrid' schemes or may offer an 'underpin'.
(4) On your death after retirement, a pension may be payable to your widow or widower or dependent children. However, the pension will be limited, for instance to two-thirds of your own pension where payable to a surviving spouse. Should you die within five years of taking your pension, a tax free lump sum may also be available.
(5) On retirement, you are normally allowed to exchange part of your pension for a lump sum. The maximum lump sum may be calculated in one of many ways. It will usually be calculated as 3⁄80 of final pay (capped if necessary – 14.3.4) for each year of service and to a maximum

of $^{120}/_{80}$, but may be more generous such as 2¼ times the initial pension before conversion to the lump sum.

(6) Your scheme may provide a lump sum payment of up to four times your final remuneration and a pension for a widow or widower should you die before taking retirement benefits. It may also provide a children's pension, but this is unusual.

A special charge arises where certain small occupational schemes (some schemes with fewer than 12 members), cease to be 'approved' after 1 November 1994. Forty per cent tax is charged on the value of the funds.

14.3.3 **Contributions**

Your employer is obliged to contribute to the scheme and, as indicated, such contributions are in general allowable business expenses. In some cases the employer may pay a 'special' contribution in order to buy benefits in respect of past service. If these special contributions are at least £½ million and exceed the employer's total contribution to the pension scheme for all members then tax relief may be spread over a few years. The contributions must actually be paid for your employer to obtain tax relief (FA 1993 S112).

In some circumstances, you may make a salary or bonus sacrifice to fund your employer's contributions, but of course this will reduce your pensionable remuneration and remuneration for the purposes of calculating disability and death in service benefits.

Whether or not your scheme is contributory (14.3.1) you will have a facility to pay additional voluntary contributions (AVCs) provided that your total personal contribution does not exceed 15 per cent of your total remuneration and that you will not exceed the Inland Revenue benefit limit. Additional voluntary contributions may either be deducted from your pay (net pay arrangement) and invested in your employer's scheme or paid directly by you to a free-standing AVC (14.4).

14.3.4 **Benefits**

As mentioned above (14.3.2), the standard pension scale of one-sixtieth of your final remuneration for each year of service with up to 40 years to count may be increased so that the maximum pension at retirement date (two-thirds of final remuneration) can be achieved with less than 40 years' service. Just what length of service will be required depends on when you joined a scheme with your employer. It could have been as little as 10 years if you joined before 17 March 1987, but since then has been 20 years.

Final remuneration includes benefits taxable under Schedule E and could therefore include, for instance, a taxable car benefit. It is unusual for employers to pension anything other than basic salary although bonuses and other taxable benefits can be pensioned by top-up arrangements including free-standing AVCs (14.4). Final remuneration may be based on the average of three or more consecutive years ending in the last 10 preceding retirement or the best year in the last five. If one year is taken as the basis then any fluctuating earnings such as bonuses must be averaged over at least three years ending with the selected year. The one year basis is not available for directors who control 20 per cent or more of shares in their companies who must always average total remuneration.

If you retire after 16 March 1987 with a salary over £105,600, you can only use the first basis or use £105,600 as your final remuneration. Should you have joined your scheme after 16 March 1987 and before 14 March 1989, your maximum final remuneration for calculating lump sums is £105,600.

Where your scheme was established after 13 March 1989 or if you joined an older scheme after 31 May 1989, earnings capping rules apply. The effect is that your benefits are limited to those appropriate to a given 'cap'. This started as £60,000 for 1989–90 and increases in line with the Retail Prices Index unless otherwise directed.

In recent years the earnings cap has been:

	£
1998/99	87,600
1999/2000	90,600
2000/01	91,800
2001/02	95,400
2002/03	97,200
2003/04	99,000
2004/05	102,000
2005/06	105,600

(Unapproved schemes (14.3.1) are not caught by the earnings capping rules and so offer scope for the highly paid.)

If you are caught by the earnings capping rules, your early retirement benefit position will be improved if you are a 'post 1989' member. Provided you have had at least 20 years of service with your employer, you can have the maximum two-thirds pension on retirement between 50 and 75.

14.3.5 Schemes for directors

Should you be a director, you are normally eligible to join your company's approved pension scheme and enjoy its full benefits. Alternatively, a separate or top-up arrangement might be made for you.

There are certain restrictions. If you control at least 20 per cent of the company's shares your final salary is calculated on a less favourable basis

(14.3.4). Furthermore, if your family owns more than 50 per cent of an investment company or you have at least 20 per cent control of an investment company and are a director, your benefits from its approved pension scheme will be further restricted. (The restrictions on controlling directors of investment companies do not necessarily apply where the company is a holding company.)

14.4 Free-standing additional voluntary contribution (FSAVC) schemes (TA 1988 S591(2)(h))

As mentioned above (14.3.3), you are permitted to make pension contributions of up to 15 per cent of your remuneration each year. If this is not fully used, you can put all or part of the balance into an FSAVC scheme of your own. Some people are ineligible for membership of an FSAVC, most notably directors who control 20 per cent or more of a company's shares. Furthermore, you may only contribute to one FSAVC in respect of each employment in a tax year (although you can contribute to a main scheme AVC and FSAVC at the same time).

Your FSAVC will be free-standing and independent of your employer. However, it is considered together with your occupational scheme when calculating your maximum benefit entitlement. You should note that the FSAVC pension cannot be commuted to produce a lump sum (14.3.2), nor can the pension under a main scheme AVC taken out after 8 April 1987.

FSAVC contributions are paid net of basic rate income tax. If you are a higher rate payer, you will normally obtain the extra relief after you submit your tax return. The FSAVC pension is subject to income tax in the same way as your pension from the main scheme.

When you retire, your combined FSAVC and occupational scheme arrangements may be over-funded. If so, your benefits from the latter are not reduced and your over-funding is repaid to you from your FSAVC scheme, subject to a tax charge. This is 32 per cent if you are a basic rate payer and an effective rate of roughly 48 per cent if you pay higher rate income tax.

14.5 Personal pension schemes and retirement annuity contracts (TA 1988 Ss618–655 & FA 1989 Sch 7)

For many years, there have been pension schemes available where your employer does not operate a scheme for you, or alternatively if you are self-employed. Subject to the rules, full tax relief is available.

The arrangements prior to 1 July 1988 consisted of retirement annuity contracts (14.7). Subsequently, personal pension schemes (14.6) have taken over. New retirement annuity contracts are no longer available after 30 June 1988. However, it is still possible to make further contributions under contracts existing at that date.

Retirement annuity and personal pension schemes are broadly similar. However, there are some important differences, which might cause you to pick one avenue or the other, if you have the choice. For example, higher percentage contributions are sometimes permitted for personal pensions, whereas 'income capping' applies to them but not to retirement annuity contracts.

Stakeholder pension schemes became available from 6 April 2001 and for *tax* purposes they are treated in the same was as personal pension schemes.

14.6 Personal pension schemes (including stakeholder pension schemes)

There are many rules to be satisfied. These include eligibility, contributions, tax relief and benefits. Details are given below.

14.6.1 Are you eligible?

(1) In order to make contributions to a personal pension scheme, you need to have 'relevant earnings' or be a UK resident for tax purposes or a Crown Servant. Relevant earnings are earnings from any employment, in respect of which you do not belong to an approved pension scheme. For these purposes, schemes providing only death in service benefits are ignored.

(2) Earnings are also 'relevant' if they are taxed under Schedule D Cases I and II. Thus self-employed earnings from businesses and professions are included.

(3) You can have two sources of income, one consisting of relevant earnings and the other being from an employment where you belong to the pension scheme.

(4) There is no minimum age for tax purposes, but no contributions may be made from age 75. Contributions may be made on behalf of another individual and in particular by an adult for a child member.

(5) If you are a member of an occupational scheme and have no separate source of earnings then you may only contribute to a personal pension plan if you have not been a controlling director in the last 10 years (in respect of the job supporting the personal pension contribution) and you can identify one of the previous five years (no earlier than 2000–01) in which you earned no more than £30,000 (after deducting any personal contribution to the occupational scheme), again from the job which will support your personal pension contribution.

(6) You are allowed to arrange a personal pension plan to receive a transfer, even though you are not eligible to contribute to it.

(7) If you are a controlling director of an investment company, no remuneration which you receive from it will constitute 'relevant earnings'.

(8) Your maximum permitted contributions may be related to your *net relevant earnings*. These are your 'relevant earnings' less various deductions and subject to an 'earnings cap'. The various deductions are essentially the costs of running the business which are allowed against tax.

14.6.2 **Tax relief**

(1) Your contributions are paid net of basic rate income tax which is then recovered by the scheme from the Inland Revenue and invested for you. If you pay higher rate tax, you can also claim further relief and reduce your tax liability. Higher rate relief is given by increasing the basic rate threshold by the amount of the gross contribution.

(2) If your employer makes contributions, they will be paid gross and, although he can obtain relief, they are not regarded as your taxable income. However, they are counted towards the maximum contributions that you can make.

(3) Your permitted contributions are calculated as a percentage of your net relevant earnings for a 'basis year', or £3,600 (gross) if greater. If you are less than 36 at the beginning of the year of assessment, the percentage is 17.5. Otherwise a higher scale applies (14.6.3). A 'basis year' is nominated by you and is the current tax year or any one of the previous 5 tax years or possibly earlier if you have stopped working.

(4) Where there are no net relevant earnings or you are already a member of an occupational scheme in respect of the same earnings, the maximum gross contribution is £3,600 (you will pay £2,808).

(5) Up to 10 per cent of your contribution to provide pension benefits can be applied in purchasing life cover through a personal pension scheme. A lump sum is payable on your death during the period of cover but no later than 75. These contributions count towards the total (17.5 per cent, etc.).

(6) Since 1989 there has been a limit on the maximum net relevant earnings that you can use to calculate your contributions to a personal pension plan. Originally it was £60,000, but it is indexed, being £105,600 for 2005–06 (£102,000 for 2004–05). So, if you are 30 years old on 6 April 2005, your maximum contribution for 2005–06 is £105,600 × 17.5 per cent = £18,480. Note that by concession the Inland Revenue allow the use of the earnings cap for the year in which relief is being claimed even though the basis year might be an earlier year (see (3) above).

(7) Each of you and your spouse has a separate personal pension scheme allowance. You can each make contributions up to your respective limits.

(8) A contribution to a personal pension plan and a retirement annuity contract will require the earnings cap to be applied to both. If you have income from pensionable employment and net relevant earnings, you can make full personal pension contributions in respect of the net relevant earnings (subject to the cap).

(9) If you ask the Inland Revenue to pay minimum contributions to your personal pension scheme, this enables you to be contracted out of the second state pension (S2P – previously SERPS). Such contributions do not count towards the total (17.5 per cent, etc.).

(10) If you pay contributions before 31 January, you may make an election (no later than the payment) to have some or all of your contributions

paid in that year carried back to the previous one. The effect is that they are treated for tax purposes as if paid in the earlier year. Thus your total tax relief is restricted to your entitlement for the earlier year. Note that carrying back a contribution will not reduce your payments on account for the following year.

(11) Carry-back facilities are not available for employer contributions. A facility to carry forward unused reliefs was withdrawn for personal pension plans on 5 April 2001 and this option is only available in respect of retirement annuity contracts.

(12) Contributions may be made by transferring shares from an approved share option or SAYE scheme within 90 days of exercising the option or transfer. The market value of the shares will be treated as a contribution net of basic rate tax.

4.6.3 Contribution limits

Age at start of year of assessment	Personal pensions*	Retirement annuities
	% of net relevant earnings	
Under 36	17.5	17.5
36–45	20	17.5
46–50	25	17.5
51–55	30	20
56–60	35	22.5
61 and over	40	27.5

* or £3,600 (gross) if greater

14.6.4 Benefits

The benefits available under a personal pension scheme are broadly similar to those provided under an approved occupational pension scheme of the 'money purchase' type. However, there is more flexibility. Thus you secure a pension and have the option of commuting part as a lump sum. This sum may not be more than 25 per cent of the fund providing your pension. The various choices considered apply separately for each of the schemes to which you belong.

You do not actually need to retire before receiving your pension. You can arrange to start receiving it at 50 or over, but not after you reach your 75th birthday. However, an earlier date may be allowed if accident or illness prevent you carrying out your job or one for which you would be suited, or if your occupation is one where it is usual to retire young, such as most sports.

Your pension usually takes the form of an annuity. This is either provided by the life company which arranged the scheme or your fund is used to purchase an annuity on the open market. Either way, it is fully taxable (from 6 April

1995 under PAYE). However, if you buy an annuity with your lump sum, the capital part is tax free (9.14).

If you have included an element of life cover, the lump sum on your death could be written in trust and so be free of inheritance tax. If you die before your pension commences, your estate might be paid a lump sum to cover your original contributions, together with interest and bonuses, etc. More usually, the value of the fund might be paid. The retirement fund may also be written under a trust (or may already be so) and the fund will then by-pass your estate. Alternatively, an annuity might be paid to your widow or other dependants whom you nominate.

The 1995 Finance Act has enabled you to take your tax-free lump sum, but defer buying your personal pension scheme annuity until up to age 75 (FA 1995 Sch 11). Meanwhile you would draw taxable income from the pension fund. The amount must be no less than 35 per cent, nor more than 100 per cent of what the Government Actuary says you would have obtained by buying an annuity. The new rules apply whether or not you opt for a tax-free sum at pension date. If you die within the deferral period, your spouse and dependants can either continue to make income withdrawals, buy an annuity or take a cash lump sum after deduction of tax at 35 per cent (FA 1996 S172).

14.7 Retirement annuity contracts

(1) Higher percentage contributions can be contributed to a personal pension above the age of 35. Indeed, you will often be able to contribute to a personal pension plan even if you have no earnings. You always need net relevant earnings to support a contribution to a retirement annuity contract.

(2) Lower percentages of net relevant earnings can be contributed from age 36 (14.6.3).

(3) No income capping applies to net relevant earnings.

(4) The maximum lump sum which may be taken is three times the pension subsequently payable. However, for each contract you entered into after 16 March 1987, there is a maximum of £150,000.

(5) You must pay the contributions gross and your employer will not be allowed to contribute to your scheme.

(6) Benefits must not normally become payable before age 60.

(7) Most retirement annuities include a facility to take an open market option. This allows the plan holder to move his fund when he takes his benefit to the company offering the best annuity rate. However, if the open market option is taken, then funds must be transferred to a personal pension scheme and the maximum lump sum will be restricted to 25 per cent of the total fund. Retirement annuities can also be transferred to personal pension schemes before age 60 which enable benefits to be taken from the lower age of 50.

(8) You may carry back a contribution to the previous tax year (or even the tax year before that if you had no net relevant earnings in the previous tax year).

(9) A facility to carry forward unused relief enables you to increase your contribution in a current tax year by using unused allowances from the previous 6 tax years. The facility can be combined with the carry-back facility.

14.8 Pension tax reform

The Finance Act 2004 contained very radical legislation to change the tax rules for pensions. This was complemented by the Pensions Act 2004 which changed a number of rules dealing with member protection and introduced a compensation scheme in respect of failed employers.

The Finance Act changes are effective from 6 April 2006 ('A-day'), but some individuals, particularly those with large pension benefits should consider a range of options open to them before then.

The following is a list of the main tax changes:

(1) There will only be one regime for tax purposes. Schemes will not be 'approved', but registered. Approved schemes existing on 6 April 2006 will be automatically registered. Whilst schemes will be structured in many ways to deliver appropriate benefits, there would be no difference for tax purposes between, for example, occupational schemes, personal pension plans or retirement annuity contracts. Complicated eligibility rules will be removed so it will be possible to fund a personal pension from the same earnings as those pensioned by an occupational scheme.

(2) There will be an aggregate annual contribution allowance for each individual of £215,000 in 2006/07 and this will increase over the first five years and probably beyond that. If the allowance is exceeded, the individual will be taxed at 40% on the excess. The allowance is unlimited in the year in which all benefits are taken. Contributions may be made by the employer or the individual and if made by the individual will be further restricted to 100% of earnings to a minimum £3,600 (within the annual allowance of £215,000 etc.). There is a simple factor to ascertain the contribution in respect of each year's accrual under a final salary scheme.

(3) Benefits will be subject to unattractive rates of income tax if in aggregate they exceed a lifetime allowance. The allowance is expressed as a fund and there will be simple factors to 'convert' a pension to its equivalent 'fund' for these purposes. The statutory lifetime allowance will be £1.5 million and this will rise in stages to £1.8 million in 2010–11. If you have already accrued a significant benefit by 5 April 2006, there will be ways of protecting your personal lifetime allowance from the higher rates, but they may entail your not paying any further contributions. *Primary protection* will allow you to pay further contributions or qualify for further accrual, but protection is limited to the value of your benefits at 5 April 2006 increased

to the same extent as the statutory lifetime allowance (that is, 20% over the first five years). *Enhanced protection* will allow full protection of benefits, but on condition that no further contributions are paid (or further pension accrued) after 5 April 2006.

(4) If the lifetime allowance is exceeded, the excess will be subject to a recovery charge (tax) of 25 per cent after which it would be subject to higher rate income tax, that is, a total tax charge on the income and lump sum of 55 per cent. Indeed the rules will allow the excess to be taken as a lump sum after deduction of tax at 55 per cent.

(5) It remains a requirement that the main objective of the pension plan would be to provide an income in retirement although under a new option, an 'alternatively secured pension' or ASP, it will not be necessary to buy an annuity. It will not be possible to pay a lump sum to beneficiaries (other than, possibly, charities) in the event of death after the age of 75.

(6) A lump sum of 25 per cent of the fund would continue to be available (possibly higher in respect of benefits accrued before 6 April 2006). This will continue to be tax-free.

(7) Restrictions on allowable investments would be made the same for small plans and large schemes. The new rules are much more liberal than their predecessors. There are very few restrictions and no ban on transactions with members. However, there may be tax charges if transactions with members (or family) are not undertaken on a commercial basis. For example if the scheme owns a residential property that is used by the member, the member should pay a commercial rent or tax for the use of the property based on the 'benefit in kind' principles. There may also be a tax if a fall in the value of a property owned by the scheme is matched by a corresponding increase in value to a member outside the scheme. There is a range of tax charges whose application is generally dependent on the significance of the transaction in relation to the value of the scheme. The scheme may borrow in order to finance a purchase and borrowing is limited to 50% of the value of net assets as well as commercial principles.

(8) The new rules will increase the minimum retirement age to 55 by 2010 and there will be no early retirement ages for special occupations. However there will be protection for some members of occupational schemes that allowed earlier retirement ages and individuals who had already qualified in a personal pension plan or retirement annuity contract for an early age in a special occupation if they joined the scheme before 11 December 2003.

The objective of the proposals is to make pensions more attractive by making them simpler. Whilst care should be taken not to base financial planning on proposals rather than rules, those with pensions funds exceeding or close to £1.5 million should consider future provision in the light of proposed lifetime allowance.

14.9 Pensions and tax planning

Pension arrangements offer a unique range of tax reliefs. there are tax advantages for contributions by an individual or the employer, on income and capital gains in the fund and in respect of substantial lump sums payable on retirement or death.

The tax reliefs are designed to encourage individuals to invest for the long term and accept restrictions on the way benefits may be taken, primarily as an income.

For most people, pensions continue to be a cornerstone of financial planning, combining tax efficiency with flexibility, convenience and a spread of risk.

Chapter 15

MISCELLANEOUS ASPECTS

15.1 Miscellaneous profits – Schedule D Case VI (TA 1988 Ss18, 69 & 392)

The new consolidating and rewriting Act, ITTOIA (2.10) takes effect from 6 April 2005 for income tax purposes, but does not apply to companies subject to corporation tax. One effect is that all references to classifying income under the various schedules and cases, in particular Schedule D Case VI in this chapter, do not apply. However, the basic rules otherwise remain.

Miscellaneous profits not falling within any of the other cases of Schedule D are charged to income tax under Case VI (prior to 6 April 2005). Such income includes:

(1) Income from underwriting (if not a business). However, Lloyd's underwriting profits (15.9) were assessed under Schedule D Case I.
(2) Income from guaranteeing loans.
(3) Income from dealing in futures. However, this is now more likely to be subject to capital gains tax (20.31).
(4) Certain capital sums received from the sale of UK patent rights.
(5) Post-cessation receipts (11.28).
(6) Certain 'anti-avoidance' assessments (15.10).
(7) Enterprise allowance payments after 17 March 1986. Previously Case I or II applied. Case VI also applies to payments before 18 March 1986 which continue subsequently (11.4).
(8) Profits on the disposal of certificates of deposit.
(9) Gains on certain life policies held by companies.
(10) The surplus from converting from the cash to the earnings basis from 1999–2000 (11.27).

The basis of assessment under Schedule D Case VI is the actual income arising in the tax year. Expenses incurred in earning the income can be deducted in ascertaining the assessable profits.

Losses sustained in any Case VI transaction can be set off against Case VI profits of the same or any subsequent year; they cannot, in general, be set off against income assessable under any other Case or Schedule (TA 1988, S392). However, pre-1995–96 furnished lettings (Case VI) losses may be carried forward to set against the Schedule A pool of income (7.6).

15.2 Tax-free organisations (TA 1988 Ss86, 202, 338–339, 460–467, 505–506 & 683, FA 1990 S24–25, F2A 1997 S35 & Sch 5, FA 1998 S48, FA 1999 Ss56–57 & FA 2000 Ss38–46)

15.2.1 Charities

Approved charities are exempt from tax on any income that is used only for charitable purposes from:

(1) Land and buildings.
(2) Interest dividends and annual payments.
(3) Trades carried on by the beneficiaries of the charity or trades exercised in the course of executing the actual purposes of the charity. Certain lottery income is included from April 1995 (FA 1995 S138).

Under rules which apply from 2000–2001 certain trading and sundry income of a charity up to a limit is exempt from tax, provided it is used for its charitable purposes. The limit for a full year is £5,000, which is increased to the lesser of £50,000 and 25 per cent of all of the charity's incoming resources.

Approved charities are also exempt from capital gains tax.

Since charities are exempted from tax on dividend income, they were able to reclaim the normal tax credit of 20 per cent (25 per cent prior to 6 April 1993). In addition, extra amounts of credit were available to alleviate the sudden drop from 25 per cent to 20 per cent. The transitional tax credit rates were approximately 1993–94 24 per cent, 1994–95 23 per cent, 1995–96 22 per cent and 1996–97 21 per cent (FA 1993 S80).

Further transitional relief applies following the withdrawal of ACT (13.6) and of the ability to reclaim tax credits. Charities were able to reclaim decreasing percentages of the amounts of distribution received.

Gifts to charity out of both capital and income are often afforded favourable tax treatment as described elsewhere in this book. In particular, note capital gains tax (20.29.1), and inheritance tax (22.1).

Gifts of qualifying investments to charities from 6 April 2000 for individuals and 1 April 2000 for companies create tax relief on their value. This covers quoted shares and securities, authorised unit trust units, open-ended investment company shares and offshore fund interests. From April 2002 this relief covers gifts of land and buildings providing the charity agrees to accept it (FA 2002 S97).

Deeds of covenant to charities receive highly favourable tax treatment. As covenantor, you will obtain higher rate tax relief on your gross payments, subject to the rules (6.5). An approved charity (15.2.1) is able to reclaim the basic rate income tax that you will have deducted in making a payment to it under a deed of covenant.

Thus if you covenant to pay a charity £100 gross each year, you will deduct income tax at the basic rate (22 per cent) and only pay £78. The charity will then reclaim the income tax amounting to £22. The charity thus gets a total of £100 each year. Even if the basic rate of income tax is changed, the charity will still get a total of £100 each year from your payment. (By way of contrast, if the covenant is 'net', the charity benefits more when the basic rate is higher.)

Deeds of covenant which are written to last four years or until some later event (for example giving up membership of the charity) previously ceased to be effective for tax purposes after four years. (New deeds of covenant were then required.) However, the rules have now changed to allow tax relief for such covenants to run on, provided you are not empowered to stop payment within the initial four-year period.

From 6 April 2000, deeds of covenant come within the 'gift-aid' rules (see below).

Certain charitable gifts qualify for 'gift aid'. This is income tax or, for companies, corporation tax relief for charitable donations. Basic rate income tax is deducted by the donor and reclaimed by the charity. The donor obtains full tax relief at the higher rate, if applicable. Similarly a company deducts the gross donation from its taxable profits and obtains relief at its corporation tax rate (30 per cent, etc.).

Your 'gift-aid' donations can now be of any size. (Before 6 April 2000, the minimum was £250.) Furthermore, the scheme has been extended to foreign donors, crown servants and members of the armed forces serving overseas. Also, your capital gains tax is taken into account in seeing whether you pay enough tax to cover the relief. One simple 'gift aid' form is needed for each charity to which you give, no matter how many donations you make to each.

Thus, suppose you give under 'gift aid' £1,000 gross to a charity, you deduct 22 per cent basic rate and pay £780, the charity reclaiming the £220. You will also obtain £180 further relief if you are a higher rate income tax payer. Your net cost will then be £600.

Under a special 'millennium gift aid' scheme to help the world's poorest countries, gifts to such countries qualify for relief even if as low as £100 and after 5 April 2000 of whatever amount. From April 1999 this also applies to gifts of money to relieve refugee poverty.

If you make a gift qualifying for 'gift aid' after 5 April 2003, you are able to elect for it to be relieved in the previous tax year (FA 2002 S98). From April 2004, you can nominate a charity to receive all or part of your tax repayments.

A payroll deduction scheme operates from 1987–88. Employees were able to contribute no more than £1,200 each year to charities through an approved agent and obtain tax relief. Employers' expenses in running schemes are allowable business deductions, as are those paid to charitable agencies (FA 1993 S69). From 6 April 2000 the £1,200 limit has been removed and, for 4 years from that date, the charities received a 10 per cent supplement (FA 2003 S146).

Certain anti-avoidance provisions (TA 1988 Ss506–507 & Sch 20) restrict a charity's tax relief if its *funds* are used for non-charitable purposes, or passed to an overseas body without ensuring that it will use the money for charity. Relief is also restricted if the charity lends or invests the funds for the benefit of the original donor unless for charitable purposes. Note that higher rate relief for covenanted donations may be restricted where the charity's own relief is limited. These rules do not generally apply if a charity's taxable income and gains are no more than £10,000 in a year. If you pay more than £1,000 of donations under covenant in a year to charities whose relief is limited as above, your own higher rate relief may be restricted.

The original rules for tax relief on covenanted (or gift-aided) membership subscriptions to heritage and conservation charities were relaxed. The right to free or cheap entry to view the property of the charity does not prevent the member from obtaining tax relief.

15.2.2 **Other tax-free organisations**

Other organisations whose income in certain circumstances may be free of tax include registered and unregistered friendly societies, registered trade unions, mutual associations, pension funds and 'community amateur sports clubs'.

Registered friendly societies are exempt from tax on profits from life assurance business subject to certain limits. The maximum annual premium payable on such a life assurance policy is now £270. The previous limit was based on annual premiums of £200 (FA 1991 Sch 9). Premiums under existing friendly society policies may be increased to the new limit without affecting the tax benefits. In addition, the previous restriction that the cash value on early surrender cannot exceed the premiums paid has also been removed. There remains a limit of £156 annually for each annuity (TA 1988 S464).

Since 31 May 1984, the life business of friendly societies has been treated for tax purposes as being more akin to that of life assurance companies (TA 1988 S466 & FA 1996 S171). The 1992 Friendly Societies Act allows societies to incorporate. The legislation regarding tax exemption now extends to incorporated societies.

Provident benefits paid by *trade unions* to their members are tax-exempt up to certain limits. (Such payments might cover sickness, injury, etc.) The limits which apply from 1 April 1991, are £4,000 for lump sums and £825 for annuities (TA 1988 S467 & FA 1991 S74).

Depending on the exact circumstances, tax exemption may apply to government bodies, foreign diplomats and United Nations Organisation officials in this country and the salaries of the members of visiting forces.

Community amateur sports clubs (CASCs) obtain certain tax reliefs from 1 April 2002 and individuals get reliefs from 6 April 2002 (companies from 1 April 2002). A CASC must be open to the whole community, be organised on an amateur basis and provide facilities for and promote participation in eligible sports.

CASCs will be exempt from corporation tax on interest, the first £15,000 of trading income, the first £10,000 of property income and on capital gains, provided they are spent on qualifying purposes. From 1 April 2004, these thresholds become £30,000 and £20,000 respectively.

Donors to CASCs will benefit from gift aid for individuals, inheritance tax relief, gifts of assets on a no gain/no loss basis for capital gains tax and business gifts of trading stock, plant and machinery (FA 2002 S58 & Sch 18).

From 17 April 2002 investment by companies or individuals in accredited *community development finance institutions* (CDFIs) normally attracts a tax credit of 5 per cent for each of up to five years. The investment can be by way of debt or shares and the CDFIs must use the funds for small businesses and social enterprises working in disadvantaged communities (FA 2002 S57 & Schs 16 & 17).

15.3 Patent holders (TA 1988 Ss520–528)

If you own a patent (11.18) and you grant the right to use it to somebody else he will normally pay you a periodical royalty in respect of the patent user. This royalty is normally subject to tax by deduction at source at the basic rate (22 per cent). If, however, the payer does not deduct tax then you would generally be assessed to income tax under Case VI of Schedule D.

The gross equivalent of any patent royalties that you receive must be included in your total income for income tax purposes (5.2), but you get a credit for the basic rate tax already suffered by deduction at source. Where you receive a lump sum payment, in respect of royalties for the past user of your patent, you can spread the payment backwards over the period of use in order to calculate your income tax liability.

If you sell any patent rights for a capital sum, this will normally be chargeable (prior to 2005–06 under Case VI of Schedule D) provided you are resident in this country. You can, however, spread the payment forward over a period of six years in computing your income tax liability. If, however, you are non-resident, the payer should deduct income tax at 22 per cent in paying you (subject to possible double tax relief and exemptions).

Note that patents acquired or created by companies from 1 April 2002 fall within by the new corporation tax rules for intellectual property (13.29) rather than the above.

15.4 Authors' copyright sales and royalties (TA 1988 Ss534–537B & Sch 4A)

Unlike patent royalties, copyright royalty payments to authors, etc. are made gross without the deduction of any income tax. If you have such receipts and you are an author or composer etc. by profession, then your royalties will be taxed under Schedule D Case II as part of your professional earnings (11.4). Otherwise, any royalties that you receive may be assessed (for years prior to 2005–06) under Schedule D Case VI. Different rules have applied for companies since 1 April 2002 (13.29).

Where you assigned the copyright in the whole or a part of a work, under the previous rules any sum that you received was taxable by reference to the tax year or accounting period in which it was received. If you made the required claim to the Revenue, however, you could normally obtain relief by spreading the payment as follows:

(1) If it took you between 12 and 24 months to prepare the work of art, one half of your proceeds was taxed as if received when paid to you and the other half was taxed as if received one year earlier. If you took more than 24 months in preparing the work, then you were taxed on one third of the proceeds as if received when paid to you, another third as if received one year earlier and the remainder was taxed one year earlier still. Thus a three-year spread was obtained.
(2) If you are the author of an established work and not less than ten years after the first publication you wholly or partially assigned your copyright or grant an interest therein, for a period of at least two years, you could spread any lump sum received. The period over which the sum was spread was the lesser of six years or the duration of the grant or licence.

Income spreading has been replaced by a profits averaging system as follows:

(1) The first years for averaging are 2000–01 and 2001–02.
(2) Individual taxpayers can claim to average the profits of two or more consecutive tax years if the profits are derived from a trade, profession or vocation mainly derived from creative activities.
(3) If the profits of one of the years are 70 per cent or less of the profits of the other, on a claim being made, the average is assessed for each year.
(4) Where the smaller profits (S) are between 70 and 75 per cent of the larger (P), a formula is used to find the adjustment, which is 3D – 0.75P (D = P – S).
(5) An averaging claim may not be made for a year of commencement or cessation.
(6) A claim must be made no later than 12 months after 31 January following the end of the later of the tax years to which it relates.

15.5 Sub-contractors (TA 1988 Ss559–567, FA 1999 S53 & FA 2002 S40)

If you are an independent or self-employed contractor and are not engaged under a contract of employment, you will be taxed as if you are trading, rather than employed. This will normally be advantageous to you because you will be able to deduct various expenses such as travelling from your home or other base of operations to the site, etc. where you are working for the time being.

Special rules apply to payments made by a building contractor or similar organisation in the building trade to a sub-contractor in connection with building and construction work. These extend to non-building firms which spend substantial amounts on construction operations (over £1,000,000 on average for the last three years).

The contractor must deduct tax at the rate of 18 per cent (23 per cent before 6 April 2000) from each payment made to the sub-contractors who work for him excepting those with exemption certificates (see below). The tax deducted must be paid over to the Revenue. Each sub-contractor then prepares accounts under Schedule D Case I which include the gross equivalents of the payments made to him. Income tax is computed on the basis of the accounts (11.4) and the tax already suffered is deducted. If the income tax liability is less than the tax deducted a repayment is obtained. Interest is charged where formal assessments are made on contractors for under-deductions from payments to sub-contractors.

The scheme also applies to certain companies, whilst other rules require the deduction of tax from payments made to temporary agency workers. Companies with a sub-contractor exemption certificate (see below) will need to notify the Revenue of any change in company control.

From 6 April 2002, companies in the Construction Industry Scheme can set off tax deducted from sub-contract payments received against payments due to the Revenue. These include PAYE, national insurance contributions and deductions made as a contractor (FA 2002 S40).

If you are a sub-contractor in the building trade you will normally be able to obtain an exemption certificate from your Inspector of Taxes if you complete the necessary application form and can satisfy certain conditions including having a regular place of business in this country. There is also a turnover test (now £3 million) for which you can include all of your construction income net of materials. Also you must have been either employed (including full-time education or training) or in business in the UK and made full tax returns for a qualifying period of three years up to your application. Mandatory registration cards have been introduced for sub-contractors unable to qualify for exemption certificates.

Up to six months are allowed in the three-year qualifying period for unemployment, etc. at the Inland Revenue's discretion. Relaxations are made to cover periods of working overseas – the three-year qualifying period being allowed to be within the last six years. If you obtain an exemption certificate and show it to a building contractor for whom you do work, then he will be permitted to pay you gross without the tax deduction described above.

As from 6 April 1998, construction workers whose services are supplied by employment agencies, etc., are normally taxed as if they are employees. Hence they are subject to PAYE and NHI deductions.

FA 2004 contains a framework for a new scheme which will take over from the above in April 2006.

15.6 Farming

If you carry on a farming or market gardening business in this country you will be treated as carrying on a trade. You are assessed to income tax (up to 2004–05 under Schedule D Case 1) (11.4).

In addition to the normal Schedule D Case I rules, some special ones apply, including the following:

(1) If you have more than one farm they will all be assessed as one business (TA 1988 S53).
(2) You may receive *deficiency payments* from the Government in respect of certain crops, etc. These are by concession included in your taxable profits for the year when they are received rather than when the crop is sold.
(3) If you have an eligible agricultural or horticultural holding, you may be able to benefit under one of the various Ministry of Agriculture, Fisheries and Food Grant Schemes. Grants received under these schemes are treated as either capital receipts or revenue receipts for tax purposes according to their nature. For example, field husbandry grants are revenue and grants to cover the reclamation of waste land are capital.
(4) Normally all your livestock will be treated for tax purposes as stock-in-trade. If you have any 'production herds', however, you can elect within two years from the end of your first year of assessment that the *herd basis* should apply. 'Production herds' are those kept for the purpose of obtaining products from the living animal (for example, wool, milk, etc.). Where a herd basis election has been made the initial cost of the herd is not charged against your profits but is capitalised together with the cost of any additional animals. The cost of rearing the animals to maturity is also capitalised. (Capital allowances are not available.) Any sales proceeds are taxable and the costs of replacement animals are deductible from your taxable profits. If you sell your entire herd you are not charged to tax on the proceeds (TA 1988 S97 & Sch 5). The herd basis also applies to shared animals.
(5) A special *agricultural buildings allowance* is available (11.14).
(6) If you carry on any farming or market gardening activities without any reasonable expectation of profit on a non-commercial basis you will normally be treated as conducting merely *hobby farming*. The effect of this will be that you will not be granted tax relief for any losses from your farming against your other income. You will, however, be permitted to carry forward any losses from your hobby farming to be set against future taxable profits from the same source (TA 1988 S397). Generally, the restriction applies when you make your sixth consecutive loss.
(7) Relief is available regarding *fluctuating profits* (taken net of capital allowances if under the new scheme – 11.7.3) of individual farmers or partnerships. You are able to claim to average the profits of any pair of consecutive years of assessment, provided you do so within broadly 22 months of the end of the second year. If the taxable profits for either or both years are later adjusted, the original claim is set aside but a new one can be made by the end of the year of assessment following that in which the adjustment is made. Another condition is that the profits in the lower year must be no more than 70 per cent of the profits of the better year. If the lower profits are 70 per cent to 75 per cent of the higher, however,

limited spreading is allowed. Where a loss is made in any year, for the purposes of the spreading rules, the profits are treated as nil and the loss is relieved in the usual ways (11.22) (TA 1988 S96).

(8) Capital gains tax rollover relief (20.25) was extended to include first milk and potato quotas and then ewe and suckler cow premium quotas (TCGA S151 & FA 1993 S86).

15.7 Building society arrangements (TA 1988 S476–483)

From 6 April 1991 building societies (as well as banks, etc.) deduct income tax from interest payments and account for it to the Inland Revenue. The rate was 25 per cent up to 5 April 1996 and then 20 per cent. Non-taxpayers are able to reclaim tax deducted. However, building societies may pay interest and dividends gross to individuals ordinarily resident outside the United Kingdom (8.6). This also applies to payments to charities, friendly societies and pension funds, etc.

Prior to 6 April 1991, if you received any building society interest you included the grossed up equivalent in your total income for tax purposes (5.2) as if income tax at the basic rate had been deducted (8.6). This 'notional' tax deduction could not be reclaimed by you, as a general rule.

15.8 Insolvents

When a person becomes bankrupt, a bankruptcy or interim order is made on a certain date and all income tax and capital gains assessments that have been made by that date for previous years are treated as debts in the bankruptcy. Also any assessments made for the tax year ending on the following 5 April will rank as debts in the bankruptcy provided the assessments were made before the date of the receiving order. PAYE and sub-contractors' deductions made within the previous year will rank as preferential debts. This means that they will be paid in full before any payment is made on the non-preferential debts. The remaining assessments will rank as non-preferential debts.

In the case of VAT (23.11.9) tax payable for the 6 months prior to the date of the order, etc. ranks as a preferential debt.

Any future income of the bankrupt individual will be charged to tax in the normal way. Thus any salary would be subjected to PAYE (10.14) – also income tax would be payable on other income.

15.9 Lloyd's underwriters (FA 1993 Ss171–184 & Schs 19–20, FA 1994 Ss219–230 & Sch 21, FA 1995 S143, FA 1999 Ss82–84 & FA 2000 S107)

The special rules which apply to the taxation of Lloyd's underwriters were substantially altered by FA 1993, FA 1994 for companies and subsequent legislation, the main changes being:

(1) There is a new tax deductible reserve, to replace the limited special reserve. This enables you to put aside profits free of tax to meet future losses. Up to 50 per cent of your profits can be transferred in this way each year, provided the value of the reserve fund is no more than half your overall premium limit. Income and gains within the reserves will be tax-free.

(2) Gains on assets representing your invested premiums are no longer specially treated and are incorporated in trading profits.

(3) In general, your taxable receipts and allowable expenses are now within Schedule D Case I (11.1), together with gains and losses on assets in premium trust funds.

(4) Although syndicate accounts for each trading year are drawn up annually, they are closed off after the third year to allow members to join and leave. At that stage the members for that year pay those for the new year appropriate insurance premiums and the new year's syndicate members take over the outstanding liabilities. This is known as 'reinsurance to close'.

(5) Starting with the 1985 account, 'reinsurance to close' is tax deductible only to the extent that it is shown not to exceed a fair and reasonable assessment of the liabilities. This means aiming at having neither a profit nor loss accrue to the recipient of the premium. These rules were introduced in 1987 and were modified in 1988 and 1993.

(6) For accounting periods beginning after 31 December 1993, profits from corporate membership of Lloyd's are charged to corporation tax under FA 1994. In general, these are treated as trading income except for non-syndicate profits otherwise taxable as income. 'Reinsurance to close' relief is available as for individuals (above).

(7) From 6 April 1999 individual members participating in syndicates through 'members agent pooling arrangements' may treat their shares of the various syndicate capacities so held as being single direct holdings for capital gains tax purposes. Also, capital gains tax rollover relief will apply for all syndicate capacity.

(8) The benefits of tax deferral may be clawed back where provisions for unpaid claims are not properly discounted and those for future claims are overestimated. This applies to individual members of Lloyd's from 2000–2001 and companies' accounting periods beginning after 31 December 2000. (Individuals participating in only a very small proportion of a syndicate's business will be exempted.)

(9) A type of reinsurance is known as a quota share contract. Where a premium is payable under such a contract from 17 April 2002, by a Lloyd's member, tax relief is restricted to take account of that already given for declared but unpaid losses. At the same time, members paying cash calls before entering into share quota contracts will be helped by extending the relief available to losses covered by the cash call.

(10) Lloyd's Names, who after 5 April 2004 transfer their underwriting to a company (or Scottish Limited Partnership in which they are the only

underwriting partner), will be able to obtain relief for trading losses from previous underwriting years against income from the company or limited partnership. Capital gains tax deferment may also be available regarding assets transferred in exchange for shares.

15.10 Anti-avoidance provisions (TA 1988 Ss703–787 etc.)

There is an important distinction between *tax evasion* and *tax avoidance*. Tax evasion refers to all those activities illegally undertaken by a taxpayer to free himself from tax which the law charges upon his income, for example the falsification of his returns, books and accounts. This is illegal and subject to very heavy penalties (16.9.2). Tax avoidance, on the other hand, denotes that the taxpayer has arranged his affairs in such a way as to reduce his tax liability legally – for example, by investing in tax free securities such as national savings certificates.

Tax avoidance is also attempted in more complicated and devious ways with particular use being made of overseas trusts and companies. In order to prevent abuse of the UK tax rules in this way various anti-avoidance provisions have been introduced. Also, certain Court decisions such as *Ramsay* and *Furniss v Dawson* have barred tax relief from artificial circuitous schemes. Much of the legislation is included in TA 1988 Ss703–786, which (in the main) has not been rewritten by ITTOIA (2.10).

Unfortunately, some of the rules introduced to counter sophisticated avoidance schemes penalise quite innocent commercial activities, not carried out with a view to tax saving. It is thus important to consider the anti-avoidance provisions, particularly when involved in overseas operations and company reorganisations or takeovers. The following are some of the more important provisions to consider.

15.10.1 Transactions in securities (TA 1988 Ss703–709)

These provisions charge you to income tax under Schedule D Case VI in respect of any 'tax advantage' that you obtain as a result of one or more 'transactions in securities'. For these purposes a 'tax advantage' is a saving of income tax or corporation tax (including, from 11 October 1996 the payment of a tax credit), but it does not apply to capital gains tax. 'Transactions in securities' include the formation and liquidation of companies as well as purchases and sales of shares, etc. A frequent application of this legislation is to prevent tax savings being effected by obtaining the use of the undistributed profits of companies by means of schemes involving 'transactions in securities'.

You can avoid being assessed under these provisions if you can show that the transactions concerned were carried out for commercial purposes and one of your main objects was not tax saving. If you are planning to carry out certain transactions which you fear may be covered by these provisions you have the right to apply for clearance to the Revenue giving all relevant facts and they must let you know within one month whether such clearance is granted.

15.10.2 **Transfer of assets abroad** (TA 1988 Ss739–746)

The object of these provisions is to prevent you from avoiding tax by transferring some of your assets abroad. The provisions normally, but not exclusively, apply to transfers of assets made by persons ordinarily resident in this country (17.3.1). If as a result of such transfer of assets, income is payable to persons resident or domiciled abroad (to avoid UK income tax) then if anyone ordinarily resident in the UK has the 'power to enjoy' any of the income, he can be assessed to income tax under Schedule D Case VI on all or part of the income. 'Power to enjoy' the income is widely defined.

For income arising from 26 November 1996, confirming normal practice, the legislation applies whatever your ordinary residence status is when you make the transfer, and where a purpose is to avoid any form of direct tax.

There are no provisions under which clearance can be obtained and this particular legislation must be most carefully considered regarding all overseas schemes. You can even be assessed on a benefit if you did not make the original transfer. However, no income can be assessed more than once.

15.10.3 **Sales at undervalue or overvalue** (TA 1988 Ss770–774 & Sch 28AA, FA 1998 Ss108–111 & FA 1999 Ss85–87)

Important rules apply where any sale takes place between people who are connected with each other (this can include partnerships and companies) and the price is less than the open market value of the goods (or services). Then in calculating the tax liability on the trading income of the seller, the sales proceeds must be adjusted to the true value of the goods if the Revenue so direct. This does not apply if the purchase is made by a taxable business in this country as a part of its trading stock. If the purchaser is an overseas trader, however, the sale is not exempted from these provisions.

A similar adjustment must be made for the buyer if the price is more than the open market value of the goods. Other provisions cover capital gains on sales between connected persons. For chargeable periods ending after 1 July 1999, the above transactions are brought within the self-assessment framework. The legislation has been revised in line with international practice and a particular feature is the facility for taxpayers to agree transfer prices with the tax authorities in advance. Advance pricing agreements may be made between taxpayers and the Inland Revenue from August 1999 regarding chargeable accounting periods ending from that time. These enable problems to be cleared in advance so as to remove the risk of extra tax being imposed.

From 1 April 2004, the general transfer pricing rules will encompass thin capitalisation (excessive loan finance between connected companies). Neither will normally continue to apply for small and medium-sized enterprises.

However, the scope of the transfer pricing requirements for other businesses now extends to UK and cross-border transactions, but dormant companies are excluded.

15.10.4 **Sale of income derived from personal activities** (TA 1988 Ss775, 777 & 778)

The object of these provisions is to prevent you from saving tax by contriving to sell your present or future earnings for a capital sum, thereby paying no tax or only capital gains tax instead of income tax at basic and higher rates. Subject to the precise rules, any such capital sum is to be treated as earned income arising when it is receivable and is chargeable under Case VI of Schedule D.

These provisions might apply if you receive a capital sum from the sale of a business which derives part of its value from your personal services. From 6 April 1988, the provisions are not so penal because broadly the same tax rates apply to income and capital gains.

15.10.5 **Artificial transactions in land and 'sale and leaseback'** (TA 1988 Ss776–780)

These provisions are considered in detail in the chapter which deals with income from land and property (see 7.11). Note that tax advantages from sales of land with the right to repurchase are also countered.

15.10.6 **Leasing and capital allowances** (TA 1988 Ss384 & 395, etc. & CAA 2001 Ss213–233)

Complicated anti-avoidance provisions operate concerning the claiming of relief for capital allowances in certain contrived situations. These provisions were designed to counter certain tax saving schemes involving leasing arrangements in group situations and consortia; also leasing partnerships between individuals and companies.

Wider provisions prevent your setting off losses created through claims for capital allowances on leasing assets, against non-leasing income. An exception is made for a leasing trade to which you devote substantially all your time, provided this trade continues for at least six months.

Leasing assets normally qualifies for a 25 per cent writing down allowance (11.9.14). However, the rate is restricted to 10 per cent where the assets are leased to non-residents. Similarly, a writing down allowance of only 10 per cent is available on expenditure after 9 March 1982 where *ships* or *aircraft* were let on charter to non-residents in order to obtain first-year allowances.

Two new measures counter tax-saving through finance leasing schemes. Under a finance lease, a bank, etc., buys an asset and leases it to you so that you have substantially all the benefits of outright ownership.

Also hit are new leases made after 26 November 1996, where the rentals are concentrated towards the ends of their terms. In both cases from that date, for tax purposes, the rentals are as appears in the lessor's commercial accounts, rather than the rentals receivable. Furthermore, the assets concerned do not attract capital allowances (FA 1997 S82 & Sch 12).

FA 2004 blocks capital allowance loopholes with effect from 17 March 2004 concerning sale and leaseback or lease and leaseback of plant and machinery. The new rules are to prevent any double tax advantage to a business from obtaining capital allowances and deductions for lease rentals. They restrict the rental deduction in computing profits. The tax consequences of termination leases are also dealt with.

15.10.7 **Group relief restrictions** (TA 1988 Ss409–413 & FA 1989 Ss97–102)

These provisions can act to restrict or prevent group loss relief being available for one group company (13.13) in respect of trading losses of another. A particular point to watch is that if a group of companies has arranged to sell a loss-making company, relief for the losses of that company may not be available to the other group members for periods prior to the accounting period in which the sale actually takes place.

Special rules apply where companies join or leave a group. Instead of the normal time apportionment to fit the losses or profits to the respective old and new groups, a just and reasonable basis will be substituted in obviously distorted cases. This could involve separate accounts before and after the date of changing groups. Modifications of the rules regarding groups took effect during 1989 and are mentioned elsewhere (13.16).

15.10.8 **Interest schemes** (TA 1988 S787)

Complicated tax avoidance schemes were developed concerning 'manufactured' interest relief. Anti-avoidance rules operate regarding the interest payments.

15.10.9 **Capital gains tax** (TCGA Ss27, 29, 71, 137, 138 & 169 & Sch 7A)

Various rules were introduced for countering the avoidance of capital gains tax in certain situations. The latter include 'value-shifting' schemes, where an allowable loss has been created artificially by moving value out of one asset and possibly into another.

There are also anti-avoidance rules concerning capital gains tax resulting from company reconstructions, takeovers and amalgamations (20.18.6). A clearance procedure applies, however, which is similar to that applying for transactions in securities (15.10.1). Also, the rules do not apply if you can show that the arrangements were carried out for commercial, rather than tax-saving purposes.

Provisions prevent the artificial creation of capital losses by inflating the purchase price of assets for capital gains tax purposes above their true value, so that by selling for the true worth a capital loss results. This artificial effect sometimes resulted from the rule that transactions between connected persons are treated as being for a consideration equal to market value and sometimes through reorganisations of share capital (20.18.6). The capital gains tax cost of the purchaser is only increased to the extent that the capital gains tax position of the vendor is affected.

Gifts relief (20.28) does not apply to non-resident donees. This was being avoided by using certain dual-resident trusts, but from 18 March 1986 these are regarded as non-resident for this purpose.

Capital gains tax rollover relief is not available where a non-resident replaces a business asset within the UK charge with one which is outside it. In general, this new rule applies where the old asset is disposed of, or the new one purchased after 13 March 1989.

With effect from 16 March 1993, tax benefits from buying capital loss companies (13.15) were legislated against. From the same date, capital gains no longer fall out of charge where shares are exchanged for debentures which are outside the tax net.

FA 2004 introduces measures effecting certain disposals after 9 December 2003. Gifts relief (20.28) is withdrawn regarding transfers to a settlement in which the settlor has an interest. Furthermore, private residence relief (20.23) may be lost where gifts relief was obtained on the earlier disposal of the property.

15.10.10 **Commodity and financial futures** (TA 1988 S399 & TCGA S143)

Losses created by means of certain artificial dealing partnerships may not be relieved against general income. (Note that a commodity deal not forming part of a trade is liable to capital gains tax rather than Case VI income tax as previously.)

15.10.11 **Rent between connected persons** (F2A 1992 S57)

Legislation applies to rent accruing after 9 March 1992 between connected persons (broadly close relatives and companies belonging to the same group or under common control). This covers those connected after both that date and when the lease was made. Previously, where the payer obtained tax relief, this was normally on an accruals basis and the recipient was only taxed on the basis of the rent receivable in the period, thus being able to defer tax. Under the rules, the recipient is charged on the rent accruing. This applies where the payer obtains tax relief on the rent and this is paid in arrears.

15.10.12 **Bank lending etc.** (TA 1988 S798)

There are rules to prevent certain tax advantages being obtained by exploiting the double tax relief system. Also, the creation of 'equity loans' where the interest paid is partly dependent on a company's results no longer produces a 'distribution'. This affects banks and the loss-making companies they were able to lend money to at lower rates. The double taxation rules relate mainly to banks.

15.10.13 **Controlled foreign companies** (TA 1988 Ss747–756 & Schs 24 26 etc.)

The Revenue have powers to assess additional tax on certain UK resident companies with interests in controlled foreign companies. Fuller details are given earlier (13.22) but the circumstances where a charge might arise are where a foreign subsidiary in a low tax area is paying insufficient of its profits as dividends, etc. to its UK parent company.

15.10.14 **Offshore funds and other savings income** (TA 1988 Ss757–764 & Schs 27–28, TCGA Ss102, 212 & FA 2003 Ss198–199)

Broadly, if you dispose of an investment in an offshore fund which does not distribute enough of its income, you will be taxed on your entire gain as if it were income under Schedule D Case VI (15.10.2). Gains on switches of holdings in offshore 'umbrella' funds by UK investors, attract capital gains tax. Since 29 November 1994 only 'collective investment schemes' are covered by legislation and the distribution test is waived if the income is no more than 1 per cent of the average value of the assets.

FA 2003 enables certain EU proposals regarding the exchange of cross-border information to be implemented in order to help ensure that savings income is properly reported. However, they do not take effect until after 1 January 2005. Reports will be required regarding non-residents from banks, building societies, other deposit takers, registrars, authorised unit trusts, stockbrokers, etc.

15.10.15 **Dual resident companies** (TCGA Ss159, 160 & 188)

Special provisions apply to prohibit a dual resident investment company from surrendering losses to other members of a UK group (13.13). The companies concerned are UK resident and also taxed in another country because of place of incorporation, management or residence. Furthermore, the definition of such dual resident investment companies extends to those which either do not trade or are mainly used to borrow or to purchase or hold shares in another group member.

Where an asset of a dual resident company ceases to be within the UK capital gains tax charge due to a double tax agreement, the company is deemed to have disposed of the asset. Regarding replacements of business assets (either the disposal or replacement) rollover relief is not available if a UK asset within the capital gains tax charge is replaced by an asset which is not.

Certain dual resident companies are treated as resident outside the UK for some tax purposes. This is to counter avoidance of tax through controlled foreign companies (13.21) and transfers of assets abroad.

Also, rules operate which are designed to prevent a company transferring assets tax-free to a dual resident company in whose hands any gain would be outside the UK tax charge. Similarly, rollover relief (20.25) is denied on the replacement of business assets where one member of a group disposes of an asset and a dual resident group member replaces it with an asset outside the UK tax charge.

15.10.16 **Migration of companies etc.** (TA 1988 S765)

The Taxes Act 1988 S765 contains penal provisions to prevent a UK company from becoming non-resident without Treasury consent being obtained. Such consent is also required to transfer part or all of its business to a non-resident and for certain share transactions. From 15 March 1988, such consent is no longer needed (except for certain share transactions) and it is replaced by a tax charge on unrealised gains. Companies intending to emigrate must notify the Inland Revenue in advance providing an estimate of their UK tax commitments including tax on unrealised gains, and details of arrangements to settle such tax. If the tax is not paid, penalties may be charged. Furthermore, former directors and group companies can be held responsible for tax and interest.

After 30 June 1990, Treasury consent is no longer needed regarding certain transactions relating to companies within the European Community. This applies to issues and transfers of shares and debentures of overseas subsidiaries within the EC. Where special Treasury consent was previously needed, reporting to the Revenue is now required with non-compliance penalties of up to £3,000.

15.10.17 **Capital gains tax – sales of subsidiaries** (TCGA Ss31–34 etc.)

Certain schemes to save tax on capital gains where a group disposes of one or more subsidiaries are blocked. For example, the value of a subsidiary may be reduced before sale by distributing assets to fellow group members at less than market value; such undervalue will be added to the sale proceeds in calculating the capital gain on the sale of the subsidiary. However, the legislation is not intended to catch distributions which could be made out of normal profits and reserves.

The above rules have been widened to catch situations where a subsidiary is sold to another group company which is non-UK resident, which in turn sells it to the eventual non-group purchaser. The new rules apply where the transfer to the overseas group company takes place after 8 March 1999.

Another situation which has been countered, is where the commercial control of a subsidiary is sold, whilst keeping it within the group for capital gains relief on inter-group transfers etc. through using special shares. The benefits of group membership only apply if the parent company of the group has, directly or indirectly, an interest of over 50 per cent in the income and assets of the company.

The sale of a subsidiary can also give rise to capital gains on assets previously transferred to it from other group companies. Conversely, gain buying by groups with losses has been countered. These and similar anti-avoidance rules are considered earlier (13.16).

15.10.18 **Capital gains tax – non-resident trusts** (TCGA Ss80–98 & Sch 5)

From 19 March 1991, sweeping changes have effect regarding the capital gains tax rules relating to offshore settlements. The rules (21.9.1) involve the settlor and beneficiaries. Among other changes, the use of such settlements to delay the onset of capital gains tax has been much curtailed. Further detailed changes, sometimes retrospective to 1991 have been introduced by the 1998 Finance Act.

From 21 March 2000, rules take effect to stop capital gains tax being avoided where an offshore trust is made UK resident and then non-resident again. Also acted against is the situation where gains are sheltered through the double tier of a trust and an offshore company and the existing anti-avoidance laws are set aside by a double tax agreement (FA 2000 Ss94–96).

15.10.19 **Interest within multinational groups** (FA 1993 Ss61–66)

Special rules apply to interest payable within multinational groups to UK companies by non-resident associated companies on certain loans, etc. The interest is taxable as it accrues, rather than when it arises as hitherto. This applies to interest accruing from 1 April 1993.

The rules apply where under the financial arrangements, the interest payable in any 12 month period is less than the amount accruing pro rata to the lender in that period. However, if you can satisfy the Inspector of Taxes that saving tax was not the main motive for using the arising basis and similar terms would have been agreed at arm's length, exemption is available from the rules.

15.10.20 **Capital gains tax – UK trusts**

From 16 June 1999, the avoidance of capital gains tax by purchasing trust losses has been countered. The new rules apply to transfers of trust property to beneficiaries from that day.

The set off of losses against trust gains arising after 20 March 2000 is restricted where gains on the original transfer to the trust were deferred by gifts relief (FA 2000 S93).

Where a beneficiary of a trust sells his interest in it to someone else after 20 March 2000, in certain circumstances there may be a capital gains tax charge. (This particularly applies to UK trusts where the settlor has an interest.) The underlying assets to which the interest relates are treated as disposed of by the trust at market value and immediately reacquired (FA 2000 S91 & Sch 24).

From 21 March 2000, where trustees are in debt and transfer funds to another person and the borrowings have not all been used for trust purposes, the trust assets are in whole or part treated as being disposed of and reacquired at market value, so as to crystallise a capital gain. This is to prevent avoidance schemes involving loans and new trusts (FA 2000 S92 & Schs 25 & 26).

15.10.21 **Manufactured dividends and interest** (TA Sch 23A)

From 17 April 2002, the tax deductibility of manufactured payments made by individuals (and others not charged to corporation tax) has been restricted.

Such payments might arise where the current holder of say loan stock receives a payment of interest or dividend but has agreed to pay an equivalent amount to the original owner. Relief will be restricted to cases where the underlying real payment would be deductible or the recipient is taxed on an equivalent amount from the same UK securities. FA 2004 has strengthened these provisions to ensure that the dividends are taxed at the same rate as relief is given for the manufactured payments and has extended the rules to trusts.

15.10.22 **Avoidance involving partnerships etc.**

Various anti-avoidance measures are included in FA 2004 regarding partnership and related arrangements. Certain of the provisions concern film relief (11.21), licence exploitation, companies in partnership and restricting the loss relief of non-active partners (12.4).

FA 2005 introduces various anti-avoidance provisions regarding partnerships. Ss72–78 limit the amount of relief which partners can claim against their other income and capital gains and give the rules for calculating the excess relief, which is taxable. S79 defines 'capital contribution to the trade' for partners' film relief purposes and enables the countering of avoidance schemes in which partners obtain more tax relief than the capital which they introduced.

15.10.23 **Disclosure of tax avoidance schemes**

FA 2004 includes new disclosure obligations on scheme promoters and taxpayers. The arrangements covered are those where the main advantage is a tax benefit and further conditions, which are being specified, are met. The disclosure rules came into effect on 1 August 2004, but apply to schemes promoted or sold from 18 March 2004, or 23 April 2004 where no promoter or an offshore one is involved.

The promoters are required to provide full details of their tax schemes, which the Inland Revenue will register and allot reference numbers. As a purchaser of such a scheme, you will merely need to enter the reference number in your tax return, unless the promoter is based offshore or no promoter was involved. In those cases, you must provide the scheme details to the Revenue.

The taxes covered are restricted to income tax, corporation tax and capital gains tax. Furthermore, the schemes to be disclosed are limited to those based on employment or financial products, which meet further conditions.

Chapter 16

RETURNS, ASSESSMENTS AND REPAYMENT CLAIMS

This chapter covers administrative matters, largely to be found in the Taxes Management Act 1970 (TMA). With effect from 1996–97, radical changes took effect, with the introduction of the new self-assessment system. This is dealt with below.

16.1 Self-assessment – an overview (TMA Ss7–9D, 12, 12D, 19A–21, 25–41, 42–43, 59A–D & Schs 1–4 etc.)

FA 1994 contains the framework for the self-assessment system which applies for 1996–97 and future years. FA 1995 and FA 1996 contain further relevant provisions, mainly amending those in TMA. Points to note include the following:

(1) Individuals and trustees need to submit their returns to the Revenue by the filing date. This is 31 January after the end of the tax year of the return or if later, three months after its issue. You must include a self-assessment of your tax liabilities.

(2) You need not work out your tax bill if you submit your return by 30 September after the tax year or if later, two months after its issue.

(3) New tax returns are sent to partnerships to show the income and its division between the partners.

(4) Late returns may give rise to penalties including £100 at once and again after six months; also if the Commissioners agree, £60 per day.

(5) The Revenue are able to correct minor errors within nine months of your sending in a return although you can object. You are able to make amendments within one year and the Revenue have the same time for notifying you that they are making enquiries. They may then delay making any repayment reflected in your return.

(6) An enquiry may be limited in scope or so wide as to resemble a back duty investigation (16.9), although confined to the year of the tax return. The Revenue will issue you with a formal notice after completing an enquiry. You are then able to appeal. However, prior to the formal notice, disputes about points of law can be resolved by litigation.

(7) If you have not submitted your return in time, the Revenue are able to make an estimated assessment and you cannot appeal against the tax charge. However, this is displaced when you send in your return and self-assessment.

(8) Your income tax and capital gains tax are normally due for payment on 31 January after the year of assessment. However, except where most of your income is taxed at source, you normally make income tax payments on account on 31 January in the tax year and the following 31 July. These

will generally be of equal amount and based on the final liability for the previous year, but may be reduced to reflect circumstances.

(9) Interest runs from the due date. Also you may incur a 5 per cent surcharge on your unpaid tax for a year of assessment if it is not paid by the next 28 February. A further 5 per cent surcharge may arise on any tax outstanding at the following 31 July. However, the Revenue pay interest on tax over-payments from the original tax payment dates (or due dates if later).

(10) Where a settlement has more than one trustee, each is able to make a return and be accountable for errors and omissions. Any liable trustee can be required to meet liabilities to income tax and capital gains tax.

(11) Your return and self-assessment needs to reflect the taxable position after allowing for claims to reliefs and tax credits. Where the necessary conditions exist for a relief, you are able to claim it in your self-assessment without prior Revenue approval.

(12) You must claim any allowable loss for capital gains tax purposes in relation to the year when it accrues. This means you can include it in your tax return and must claim it within 5 years 10 months of the end of the year of assessment when the loss arises.

(13) Your employers must provide you and the Revenue with details of your expenses payments and benefits in kind, including cash equivalent calculations, unless a dispensation has been given by the Revenue. The deadline is 31 May following the end of the tax year.

(14) In general, in cases where previously the time limit for income tax and capital gains tax claims has been two years, this becomes 31 January after the year following the year of assessment. Thus a claim for 1997–98 was needed by 31 January 2000 instead of 5 April 2000. During this period you are also allowed to revoke or amend any claims and elections made ahead of this time limit.

(15) Various reliefs, such as loss relief, farmers' averaging (15.6), spreading of literary and artistic receipts (15.4) and post-cessation receipts may relate to more than one year. Where this is the case, relief is given in the assessment for the later (latest) year when the claim is made but taking account of the tax figures of the earlier year(s). This will avoid re-opening the earlier years.

(16) There is a wide range of revised time limits applying for income tax and capital gains tax but not corporation tax. In general, the changes involve reductions of just over two months. Thus two years from the end of the year of assessment will become 31 January in the next year but one. Similarly six years thereafter becomes 31 January in the sixth year.

(17) You are required to keep and preserve adequate records on which to base your tax return and failure to do so may result in penalties.

16.2 Your tax return (TMA Ss & FA 1990 S77 & S90)

The Revenue will normally send to you periodically a tax return for completion. If your income includes Schedule A and/or Schedule D income (or their equivalents from 2005–06) you will usually have to submit a tax return each year. If, however, all your income is taxed under PAYE (10.14) you may only be required to complete a return about every three years. Husbands and wives must submit separate returns.

Apart from individuals, trusts, partnerships and companies, etc. also have to submit tax returns. In the case of companies, previously, provided the Revenue received the annual accounts and tax computations they did not normally insist on the submission of corporation tax returns. However, with the introduction of 'pay and file', for the first accounting periods ending after 30 September 1993 (13.4.1), corporation tax returns are mandatory if notices are issued.

If no return is submitted, sources of income and capital gains must broadly be notified to the Inland Revenue. The time limit is one year from the end of the year of assessment or accounting period and there is a penalty of up to the amount of the unpaid tax (FA 1988 Ss120–122).

If you have not been sent a tax return for the previous tax year and you have received income for that year apart from your wages or salary, you should request that the Revenue sends you a return form for completion. This request should be made to the Inspector of Taxes who deals with your affairs – if you are employed it will be the tax district that handles your employer's PAYE affairs.

As well as including details of your income for the previous tax year your tax return also constitutes a claim for income tax allowances and reliefs. Thus your tax return for the year to 5 April 2005 must show your income for the year to 5 April 2005 and the income tax allowances that you are claiming for the year to 5 April 2005. A further reason for you to request a tax return from your Inspector of Taxes is thus to ensure that you are granted all of the income tax reliefs to which you are entitled.

Under the previous system, when a tax return was issued to you it normally stipulated that it must be completed and sent back within 30 days but the Revenue usually allowed further time if required. (However, if you delayed beyond 31 October and had new sources of income unknown to the Inland Revenue, you could be charged interest on the eventual assessment.)

The 1996 and earlier tax returns were comprehensive and consisted of up to 12 pages. Fuller details are included in earlier editions of this book. Your tax returns are now to be completed under the self-assessment rules. You probably receive your return in April each year and it is described below for the year to 5 April 2005.

16.2.1 Your tax return for the year to 5 April 2005

The basic return consists of a ten page form, together with supplementary pages where needed. Green arrows and instructions are provided to guide you through the form.

Page 1 is informative, reminding you that the form should reach the Revenue by 30 September 2005 for them to calculate your tax bill (or include any tax you owe up to £2,000 in next year's tax code). Otherwise, the due date is 31 January 2006. The option of filing electronically is explained and the following warnings are given:

(1) Automatic penalties if your return is late.
(2) Late tax payments attract interest and penalties.
(3) Tax returns to be checked – penalties for false information.

Page 2 is designed to find out if you have the right supplementary pages. There is a series of questions with yes boxes for your answers. Each 'yes' means using particular *supplementary pages*, which are colour-coded and are as follows:

	Circumstances
1. Employment	Employee, director or agency worker.
2. Share schemes	Taxable share options/share related benefits.
3. Self-employment	You are self-employed but not a partner.
4. Partnership	You are a partner.
5. Land and property	You receive UK income from land etc.
6. Foreign	You have taxable overseas income.
7. Trusts etc.	Income from Trusts and deceased's estates.
8. Capital gains	Gains (losses) above the exemptions (20.6).
9. Non-residence etc.	You were not resident/ordinarily resident/domiciled in the UK in all or part of 2003–04.

Page 3 requests details of income on UK savings and investments. This includes interest from banks, building societies, unit trusts, National Savings products and dividends. There are spaces for the amounts after tax, tax deducted tax credit or notional tax and gross income. (The notional tax is not repayable and relates to income such as scrip dividends from UK companies.)

Page 4 covers the remainder of your income. The first section applies if you received UK pensions, retirement annuities or Social Security benefits. You must enter the taxable amounts for 2004–05 of any state pensions and benefits. These include State Retirement Pension, Widow's Pension, Unemployment Benefit, Invalid Care Allowance, Statutory Sick Pay and Maternity Pay and Incapacity Benefit.

The remainder of Page 4 has spaces for the following:

1. Gains on life assurance policies (with/without notional tax).
2. Gains on life policies in voided ISAs.
3. Corresponding deficiency relief.
4. Refunds of additional voluntary contributions (regarding pensions).
5. Other income not entered elsewhere.

Page 5 is for claiming reliefs. The first part relates to pension contributions and includes retirement annuity contracts and self employed/employee contributions to personal pension plans. There are spaces for payments made in 2004–05, used in an earlier year, now to be carried back and brought back from 2005–06.

The following other reliefs are covered, with spaces for the amounts:

1. Interest on qualifying loans.
2. Maintenance or alimony payments under a court order etc.
3. Subscriptions for Venture Capital Trust shares (up to £200,000).
4. Subscriptions under the Enterprise Investment Scheme (up to £200,000).
5. Community investment tax relief.
6. Post-cessation expenses, pre-incorporation losses brought forward and losses on relevant discounted securities.
7. Payments to a trade union or friendly society for death benefits.
8. Qualifying distributions on the redemption of bonus shares or securities.
9. Annuities and annual payments.
10. Payments to employer's compulsory widow's etc. benefit scheme.

Page 6 is for claiming allowances including relief on gifts to charity and the various personal allowances are covered (3.0.1, etc.). Also, spaces are provided for shared claims.

Pages 7 to 10 are headed 'other information'. This includes the transfer of surplus allowances and whether you are liabe to make student loan repayments for 2004–05 on an income contingency student loan. If you wish to calculate your own tax, you must enter the following:

1. Unpaid tax for earlier years included in your 2004–05 tax code.
2. Tax due for 2004–05 included in your tax code for a later year.
3. Student loan repayments due.
4. Total tax, Class 4 National Insurance contributions and student loan repayments due for 2004–05 (put in brackets if an overpayment). A tax calculation working sheet is provided.
5. Unpaid tax for earlier years.
6. Overpaid tax for earlier years.
7. Your first payment on account for 2005–06.
8. 2005–06 tax you are reclaiming now.

If you are claiming to reduce your payments on account you must tick a box provided and give your reasons in the 'additional information' box which is on Page 10.

A repayments section allows you to indicate where and to whom (an agent, etc.) they should be sent and a section for personal details (date of birth, etc.) follows. There is also space to nominate a charity to receive all or part of your repayment.

A box is provided on Page 9 to tick if you do not want tax you owe collected through your tax code. Certain other boxes are to be used together with the 'additional information' section. These cover such matters as provisional figures in your return; claims for trading loss and certain capital loss relief and claiming post cessation or other business receipts to be taxed as income of an earlier year.

The final part of your tax return comprises a declaration for you to sign. You must certify that the return is correct and complete to the best of your knowledge and belief. Also, there are spaces to tick, indicating the supplementary pages which you have completed and enclosed.

16.2.2 **New simplified tax return**

A new simplified four-page tax return form was sent out in April 2004 to about 400,000 taxpayers and 1.5m are planned for 2005. There is no requirement to calculate the tax on the form. It is aimed at those with simple affairs, modest investment and property income including:

- Employees other than directors.
- Self-employed people with turnover under £15,000.
- Pensioners with income from a state, occupational or retirement pension.

16.3 The Tax Inspectors and Collectors (TMA Ss1 & 55)

The overall control and management of income tax, corporation tax and capital gains tax is exercised by the Board of Inland Revenue. (This was merged with HM Customs and Excise on 18 April 2005 by CRCA 2005, creating HM Revenue and Customs). They are responsible for administering the relevant law as contained in the 1988 Income and Corporation Taxes Act and the various Finance and Taxes Acts. The Finance Acts are normally enacted annually about July, the main items having been announced by the Chancellor of the Exchequer in his budget speech in March or April. However, from 1993 to 1996 budgets were in November, with one in March 1993 and a second one in November 1993. The New Labour government had their first budget in July 1997 and then returned to the old system with their Budget on 17 March 1998.

The Board of Inland Revenue is made up of the Commissioners of Inland Revenue. The day-to-day administration, however, is carried out by various Inspectors of Taxes and Collectors of Taxes who are civil servants, appointed by the Board. Inspectors and collectors may be appointed for general purposes or specific purposes, at the discretion of the Board.

The Inspectors of Taxes are organised into various tax districts to one of which you will have to send your income tax return. A district inspector heads each district under whom are a number of inspectors and clerks, who obtain and verify as they think fit the information that is necessary to raise assessments to income tax, capital gains tax and corporation tax.

The Collectors of Taxes have the responsibility of collecting the tax that has been assessed. They normally issue demands or statements of account for the tax that is due (16.8).

The office of the Inspector of Foreign Dividends handles various matters in connection with double tax relief claims.

16.3.1 **The assessment mechanism** (TMA S29)

When you had submitted your income tax return for 1995–96 and earlier years, the Inspector of Taxes issued a 'notice of assessment' to income tax in respect of your various types of income. A capital gains tax assessment was also raised by your Inspector of Taxes (20.15) if appropriate.

If the Revenue had not received sufficient information to raise accurate tax assessments prior to the date on which the tax is due for payment, they would normally make estimated assessments in respect of the taxpayer's sources of income.

Since the introduction of self-assessment, the rules encompass being assessed to tax or being charged under the new regime. For 1996–97 and subsequent years, the self-assessment system applies (16.2). If you submit your return by 30 September 2005, the Revenue can be asked to calculate your 2004–05 tax; otherwise you must do so. Furthermore, if you are required to complete a simplified tax return (16.2.2) you do not need to calculate the tax.

16.3.2 **Due dates for payment of tax** (TA 1988 S5)

For 1996–97 and subsequently, the due dates for paying income tax and capital gains tax are generally 31 January following the year of assessment. For 1997–98 and subsequently, you make payments on account on 31 January and 31 July, each based on half the self-assessed amount for the year before (excluding tax paid at source). (Generally you will not make payments on account if your tax for the previous year is less than £500.)

Your Schedule D Case III income tax for 1995–96 including higher rates was payable on 1 January 1996. Schedule D Case I and Case II assessments on your profits from a trade or profession were payable, however, in two instalments on 1 January in the year of assessment and the following 1 July.

Prior to 1996–97 higher rate income tax on your 'taxed' investment income was payable on 1 December following the year of assessment. This includes tax on interest, etc. taxed at source and dividends. Higher rate income tax on other investment income, however (including rents, etc.), was normally payable on 1 January in the year of assessment. (For due dates of payment of corporation tax see 13.4.)

For assessments issued later than 30 days before the respective date above, however, the date when the tax became due and payable was delayed to a later date. This was normally 30 days after the issue of the assessment. Note, however, the effect of appeals (16.4).

16.3.3 **Discovery** (TMA S29 (3))

Any estimated assessments will be made by the Revenue to as great a degree of accuracy as possible according to any information in their possession such as particulars for previous years. If, however, the Revenue make a *discovery* that:

(1) profits which ought to have been assessed to tax have not been assessed, or
(2) an assessment to tax is or has become insufficient, or
(3) excessive relief has been given

the Revenue may make an assessment in the amount or further amount which ought in their opinion to be charged.

16.3.4 **Time limits for assessments etc.** (TMA Ss30, 34 & 36)

Normally an assessment to corporation tax may be made at any time not later than six years after the end of the chargeable period to which the assessment relates. For income tax and capital gains tax the time limit is five years from 31 January following the year of assessment.

Broadly, the same time limits apply to claims for overpaid tax. FA 2004 legislation aims at preventing any extension of this period for bringing an action based on a mistake in law.

In cases, however, of any fraudulent or negligent conduct by the taxpayer (16.9.1) the Revenue have more time to make assessments.

A special rule applies to the recovery by the Revenue of excessive repayment claims, etc. The time limit is then extended to the end of the tax year when the original repayment, etc. was made or the closing date of any enquiry into the self-assessment return which gave rise to the repayment.

16.3.5 **Tax remission – official error**

If you send in full returns of your taxable income and you receive no assessments, so that you are led to believe that your tax affairs are in order, it is the practice of the Revenue to excuse you all or part of the tax.

For tax arrears notified prior to 11 May 1996, certain income limits applied. However, from that date there are no such limits.

16.4 Appeals against assessments (TMA Ss31D & 44–57)

If you are not in agreement with an assessment to income tax, capital gains tax or corporation tax you may appeal to the Inspector of Taxes within 30 days of the date of the assessment. Your appeal must be in writing and state the grounds on which you object to the assessment; most frequently these are that 'the assessment is estimated and excessive'. Should you not be able to appeal within 30 days for some good reason such as absence from home or ill-health, the Revenue will normally allow you to make a late appeal.

The majority of appeals are settled by agreement. This normally follows when the accounts and/or returns have been submitted to the Inspector of Taxes and any queries that he raises are answered. If, however, you are not able to agree with the Revenue or if you or your accountants have not submitted all of the required information, the appeal will be listed for personal hearing before the Commissioners (16.5).

All the tax charged by an assessment is treated as due and payable (16.3.2) unless, within 30 days, you estimate how much you are being overcharged and apply to the Inspector for the balance to be postponed.

The 30-day time limit is extended where your circumstances change so that your tax liability reduces. It will then be determined by agreement with the Inspector or otherwise by the Commissioners how much of the tax should be held over with only the balance being collected. This collectable balance is payable within 30 days after the Inspector or Commissioners have dealt with the application for postponement. Any unpaid tax normally becomes due 30 days after the date on which, following the agreement of the assessment, the Inspector issues a notice of the tax payable. An interest charge could run from an earlier date, however (16.8.2), especially in the case of a long-drawn-out appeal.

16.5 The Special and General Commissioners (TMA Ss2–6, 46A & 56B–D)

The Commissioners before whom tax appeals are heard are of two kinds, General and Special.

The General Commissioners are not normally paid. They are similar to lay magistrates and the majority of them have no special legal or accountancy qualifications. General Commissioners are appointed in England and Wales by the Lord Chancellor. They are appointed for specific districts each of which has a Clerk to the Commissioners, who is usually a solicitor, to assist them.

The Treasury previously appointed the Special Commissioners who usually had practical experience of taxation matters gained either in private practice or with the Inland Revenue. Now, under rules in the 1984 Finance Act, the Lord Chancellor appoints them only from barristers, solicitors or advocates of at least ten years' standing. The Special Commissioners are full-time civil servants.

Appeals will automatically be heard before the General Commissioners in the district which deals with the tax assessment, except that:

(1) When appealing, you may request that any resulting hearing should be in another district which is more convenient to you.
(2) You may elect within 30 days of the assessment that the appeal should be brought before the Special Commissioners. This does not apply, however, to questions regarding personal reliefs and (under the new rules) delay cases which are always dealt with by the General Commissioners.
(3) Appeals against certain income tax assessments are always heard by the Special Commissioners including those on annual payments not covered by income, transactions in securities (TA 1988 S703), valuations of unquoted securities and transfers of assets abroad (TA 1988 S739).

In many cases you will thus have a choice as to whether the Special or General Commissioners should hear your appeal. As a general rule if your case is good in equity and its justice would commend it to average honest men, you should choose the General Commissioners. If you have a good legal case (that is, one sound according to a strict reading of the law) you should choose the Special Commissioners. However, if you elect for your appeal to be heard by the Special Commissioners this can be opposed by the Revenue if they prove you have no case to present.

There are rules which include giving the Special Commissioners powers to publish their decisions and to award costs where either party has acted wholly unreasonably in pursuing a tax appeal. Also, the Commissioners are given powers to require any party involved in an appeal, including the Revenue, to furnish information.

16.5.1 **Appeal hearings** (TMA Ss44–59)

The Clerk to the Commissioners will advise you of the time and place for your appeal hearing. If you are unable to attend for some good reason or if you or your accountants have not completed the required accounts, etc. it will normally be possible to have the matter adjourned at least once until a later time. If you would like an adjournment you or your agent should raise the question with your Inspector of Taxes who will usually be prepared to arrange this for you if your reasons are in order.

At the appeal hearing you may represent yourself or be represented by an accountant or a solicitor or barrister. If your appeal is on a point of law which you anticipate may go to the Courts (see below) it is wise to be represented at the outset by a barrister who can act for you in the Courts.

The Revenue are normally represented by an Inspector of Taxes but on difficult legal points a person from the Solicitors' Office may act. The proceedings before the Commissioners resemble those in the Courts in many ways – for example, witnesses may be summoned under oath to be examined and cross-examined.

When the hearing has been completed the Commissioners will withdraw to consider their decision. They may confirm or reduce or increase the original assessment. The decision of the Commissioners is final regarding questions of fact.

If either the taxpayer or the Revenue are dissatisfied with a decision of the General Commissioners on a point of law, they should within 30 days 'express dissatisfaction'. The Commissioners should then be requested to supply a 'case stated' which is a document signed by them setting out their decision. A fee of £25 is now charged.

Decisions of the Special Commissioners will always be put in writing and either the taxpayer or the Revenue may appeal within 28 days.

The case will then be taken on appeal to the Courts where it will first be heard before a single judge in the Chancery Division. (It is possible for certain appeals against decisions of the Special Commissioners to be referred direct to the Court of Appeal.) The decision of such a court can be appealed against, following which the case will be heard before the Court of Appeal and on further appeal it may go before the House of Lords.

Before you request a 'case stated' from the Commissioners you should weigh very carefully the strength of your case and the potential tax saving if you succeed in the higher Courts against the high legal costs which would be involved.

16.6 Investigatory powers of the Revenue (TMA Ss20, 20C & Sch 1AA etc., FA 1988 S127 & FA 2000 Ss148–150)

The powers of the Revenue to obtain papers and search premises were strengthened by the 1976 and 1989 Finance Acts. Subject to the consent of the Board of Inland Revenue, the Inspector may require you by notice in writing to supply him with documents in your possession or power, which he considers have a bearing on your tax liability. However, the Board are not to consent unless you have failed or may have failed to comply with any provisions of the Taxes Acts; and as a result your tax position has been seriously affected.

The Inspector may also require documents from certain other people. These other people include your spouse and any of your children. In general these rules do not apply to pending appeals, but they do include access to computer records.

If any of your income comes from a business which you either carried on yourself or you managed, then any person who is or was carrying on a business may be directed to provide documents concerning their dealings with your business. The same applies if your wife carries on a business or manages one.

These rules also apply to a past business and any companies of which you or your spouse are, or were, directors, such companies not needing to be carrying on business. Furthermore, the Director of Savings is within the net.

In order for your Inspector of Taxes to obtain information about your affairs from other people, he must obtain the consent of a General or Special Commissioner (16.5) and the latter must ensure that the Inspector is justified in his request. FA 1994 S255 provides that the same Commissioner cannot later hear an appeal involving the same information. The inspector must tell you why he requires documents unless he can convince a commissioner that disclosure might prejudice collecting the tax.

A barrister, advocate or solicitor cannot be compelled to yield up documents without your consent provided these are covered by professional privilege. This even applies to such a lawyer acting as your tax accountant (see below).

From 27 July 1989 various changes took effect including:

(1) the protection of personal records and journalistic material from disclosure;

(2) a requirement for the Inland Revenue to allow not less than 30 days for requested information to be produced;
(3) the putting of written questions to the taxpayer;
(4) it being a criminal offence to falsify, conceal or destroy documents called for under the Revenue powers.

FA 2000 introduced revised measures to combat serious tax fraud. Where there are reasonable grounds for suspecting this, an Inland Revenue officer may apply for an order from a judge directing that documents needed as evidence are supplied, normally within 10 working days. However, documents subject to legal professional privilege are exempt, whoever holds them. Where this new legislation applies, a search warrant will not be issued. Also covered is an Inland Revenue right to use National Minimum Wage information.

16.6.1 **Tax accountants' papers**

Your tax accountant is not obliged to reveal his working papers to the Revenue subject to the following.

Where a tax accountant is convicted of an offence in relation to tax by a UK court or has a penalty awarded against him for assisting in making incorrect returns, etc. subject to certain rules, an Inspector of Taxes may require him to surrender documents relating to the tax affairs of any of his clients. Notice is required in writing and the permission of a circuit judge, Scottish sheriff or Irish county court judge must be obtained. The power of the Revenue to give this notice generally ceases 12 months after the conviction or penalty award, and does not have effect whilst an appeal is pending.

Not less than 30 days must be allowed for a convicted tax accountant to deliver documents required by the Revenue. Also from that time, personal records and journalistic material are protected as are, in general, audit papers and records of tax advice. At the same time, taxpayers must be notified of requests for information from third parties, unless fraud is involved.

16.6.2 **Entry warrant to obtain documents**

If the Revenue obtain an entry warrant in a case of suspected fraud they may enter specified premises, seizing and removing any documents or other things required as evidence for relevant proceedings. However, note the new judicial order rules introduced by FA 2000 (16.6).

A warrant is valid for 14 days and can only be granted by a circuit judge, etc. who is satisfied on information given on oath by an officer of the Board of Inland Revenue, that evidence concerning a tax fraud is to be found on the premises in question.

The Inland Revenue search powers are broadly restricted to the investigation of 'serious fraud' and are subject to a detailed code of conduct. Also, taxpayers have rights of access to property removed under the search powers.

16.6.3 **Returns of information** (TMA Ss13–19)

The Revenue are empowered to request returns of certain information from traders and others. For example, you may be required to give particulars of any lodgers you may have.

Your bank may be required to return details of interest paid to you during a tax year. Furthermore, the Revenue are empowered to obtain from any business details of its payments of fees, commissions, royalties, etc. exceeding £15 to any person during a tax year.

There is a three-year time limit regarding many of the Revenue powers to request information returns. However, they can extend their enquiries to certain government departments and public authorities.

16.7 Repayment claims (TMA Ss42–43B & TA 1988 S281)

Repayment claims arise in connection with many different facets of taxation. You will normally, however, find that any income tax repayment to which you become entitled arises in one of the following ways:

(1) Most of your income has been taxed at the source and your personal reliefs and allowances exceed your other income. (Also, you may not have received the full benefit of the starting and lower rate income tax bands.) If your income tax return reveals this position and you send in the required simple repayment claim form together with dividend vouchers, etc. in respect of the income tax credits, you will receive an income tax repayment. The repayment will reduce your income tax bill for the tax year to its correct level.

(2) Some of your income has been taxed both in the UK and in another country. You are frequently able to make a double taxation relief repayment claim of either UK tax or overseas tax depending on the circumstances (18.6).

(3) You may have already paid a Schedule A or Schedule D assessment for a tax year and, as described elsewhere in this book, you make an election to the Revenue which results in your assessment for that year being reduced.

(4) You make a business loss which you claim to be offset against your other income for the year (11.22). Some of this income has suffered income tax by deduction at the source and on making the required claim and submitting the tax vouchers or receipts you will be repaid an appropriate amount of such tax, as well as tax credits on dividends.

(5) You discover that an 'error or mistake' has been made in a return or statement or schedule that you have previously submitted as a result of which you have been over-assessed to tax. Within six years after the end of the tax year in which the original assessment was made, you may make a claim to your Inspector of Taxes for the repayment of the tax previously overpaid.

(6) Repayment claims often arise in respect of minors (under 18) all of whom are taxpayers in their own right and so are entitled to at least the personal allowance for a single person. Thus if a minor's only income for 2005–06 consists of non-dividend investment income of say £400 and none of the investments were gifted to him by his parents, then he can reclaim all of the relevant tax credits (that is, $^{20}/_{80} \times$ £400 = £100). Similarly, if the trustees of a settlement apply income for the education and maintenance of a minor, that income is treated as belonging to the child. The income is treated as having suffered basic rate income tax at the source (and additional rate tax if applicable). This enables an income tax repayment claim to be made for the minor unless he has already obtained the full benefit of his tax reliefs and allowances or the settlement had been actually created by one of his parents.

(7) The Revenue may raise an additional assessment and if this is not related to fraud or negligent conduct, you may be able to claim additional reliefs as a result. Such claims, elections, etc., even though out of time according to the normal rules, are valid if made within one year of the end of the tax period in which the assessment is made.

The procedure for making repayment claims is normally very simple. A simple repayment claim form to list your income and allowances (R40) is available. If the Revenue have already received a full return of your income, or in the case of a business or company its accounts and tax computations, it will generally only be necessary to sign a short form in which you claim the tax repayment to which you are entitled.

The self-assessment tax returns have a box to tick if you would like tax overpaid to be repaid to you. There is now also a space to nominate a charity to receive all or part of the repayment. You may be required to send dividend vouchers or tax deduction certificates or receipts to cover the amount of your repayment.

Special forms are usually required for double tax relief claims on which you must enter particulars of the dividends. Special forms are also provided by the Revenue for use in connection with various other repayment claims, for example concerning minors.

Income tax repayment claims should normally be made to your local Inspector of Taxes. If you are, for example, a British subject resident abroad your repayment claims should be made to the Chief Inspector (Claims) at Bootle. The Inspector of Foreign Dividends, however, deals with applications from those residing abroad for the recovery of United Kingdom tax suffered on overseas dividends, etc.

Note that for 1999–2000 and subsequent years, the 10 per cent tax credit on dividends is not reclaimable. However, it is offsettable against other tax so as to reduce your liability.

16.7.1 **Example: Income tax repayment claim**

Miss A is 24 years of age and during the year to 5 April 2006 she only had occasional employment from which her gross earnings were £2,300, no PAYE being deducted. During 2005–06 she pays allowable loan interest of £55. Miss A's only other income for 2005–06 consists of £2,250 dividends (tax credit £250) and an income distribution of £600 (net) from a discretionary trust. Calculate the amount of the income tax repayment claim of Miss A for 2005–06.

Miss A – Income tax repayment claim 2005–06:

Details	£	Gross income £	Tax credits £
Earned income		2,450	
Taxed dividends including tax credit		2,500	250
Trust income – net	600		
Grossed up equivalent at 40%		1,000	400
		5,950	
Less: Personal allowance	4,895		
Loan interest (paid gross)	55		
		4,950	
Taxable amount		1,000	
Total tax credits			650
Less: Income tax liability £1,000 at 10%			(100)
Tax credit restriction (£250 – £100)			(150)
Income tax repayable for 2005–06			400

Note: The repayment excludes any dividend tax credit.

16.7.2 **Repayment supplement** (TA 1988 Ss824–826)

This used to apply if you received a tax repayment more than a year after the end of the year of assessment to which it relates. Interest at the appropriate rate(s) free of tax normally runs from the later of the end of the assessment year in which the tax was paid or 5 April following the year for which repayment is made, until the end of the tax month of repayment.

The interest rate before 6 February 1997 and after 5 February 1996 was 6.25 per cent, prior to which it was 7 per cent. Identical rates also applied for interest on overdue tax (16.8.2) prior to 6 February 1997.

From 6 February 1997, separate repayment supplement and overdue tax rates apply. An important change is that the repayment supplement runs from when you paid the tax. (It remains a requirement that you are UK resident.) The repayment supplement rates are 4 per cent up to 5 August 1997, 4.75 per cent to 5 January 1999, 4 per cent to 5 March 1999, 3 per cent to 6 February 2000 and then 4 per cent to 5 May 2001, 3.5 per cent to 5 November 2001 and then 2.5 per cent to 5 August 2003, 1.75 per cent to 5 December 2003, 2.5 per cent to 5 September 2004 and then 3.5 per cent.

FA 2001 S88 has confirmed that interest is to be added to repayments which arise when relief from one year is set against income of an earlier one. An example is where pension contributions are carried back; also regarding the averaging of profits for farmers and creative artists.

16.8 The collection of tax (TMA Ss60–68)

Under the self-assessment system (16.1), generally applying for 1996–97 and subsequent assessments, once the tax has been ascertained by the Revenue, they will send you a statement of account incorporating a payslip. You should then pay your liability before the respective due dates (normally 31 January and 31 July). However, if you have not received a statement of account, you should pay by the relevant due date so as to avoid interest and particularly surcharge (16.8.3), estimating your liability if necessary.

On being notified of an assessment under the old system (generally pre-1996–97) by the Inspector of Taxes the Collector sends out a first demand. If this is not paid within about a month of its 'due date' a second demand is sent and after about another ten days a final demand follows. The final demand requests payment within seven days under the threat of legal proceedings against the taxpayer concerned.

The Revenue are empowered to take action in Magistrates' Courts for the recovery of tax up to a limit which is currently £250 (FA 1984 S57). Otherwise, action must be in the County Courts (up to the 'County Court limit') or the High Court.

16.8.1 Payments on account

If you receive a large tax demand which you find difficult to meet out of your available funds the Inland Revenue will in cases of hardship allow you to settle the outstanding tax by instalments payable at say monthly or quarterly intervals. You should contact them and explain the position. Interest will probably be payable, however (see below). A standard payments on account system has come in with self-assessment (16.1).

16.8.2 Interest on overdue tax (TMA Ss86–92)

The following rules apply to assessments issued after 31 July 1975 concerning 1995–96 and earlier years. Assessments issued earlier are covered by different rules (even if still unpaid), and details are given in previous editions. For 1996–97 and subsequent tax years, the self-assessment rules apply (16.1). The rules were clarified and modified by the 1989 Finance Act. For example, the mechanics for altering the interest rate have been made more automatic, rather than needing a statutory instrument, as previously.

Interest is payable at the appropriate rate(s) from the 'reckonable date' until the tax is settled. Some recent rates are:

From	Rate %	From	Rate %	From	Rate %
6 September 2004	7.5	6 January 1999	8.5	6 March 1993	6.25
6 December 2003	6.5	6 August 1997	9.5	6 December 1992	7
6 August 2003	5.5	6 February 1997	8.5	6 November 1992	7.75
6 November 2001	6.5	6 February 1996	6.25	6 October 1991	9.25
6 May 2001	7.5	6 March 1995	7	6 July 1991	10
6 February 2000	8.5	6 October 1994	6.25	6 May 1991	10.75
6 March 1999	7.5	6 January 1994	5.5	6 March 1991	11.5

The 'reckonable date' for 1995–96 and earlier assessments, is the date when the tax becomes due and payable (16.3.2) unless you appeal and obtain a deferment of tax. In that case the 'reckonable date' is when the tax becomes due and payable or the date given by the following table whichever is earlier:

Description of tax	Date applicable
(1) Schedules A or D	1 July following the end of the year of assessment.
(2) Additional rates of income tax	1 June following the end of the next year of assessment.
(3) Capital gains tax	1 June following the end of the next year of assessment.
(4) Corporation tax	Usually the normal payment date (13.4).

The above table applies to all amounts, even if not covered by the original assessment.

No interest paid on overdue tax is allowed as a deduction from your taxable income or business profits nor is it allowed as a deduction for corporation tax or capital gains tax purposes.

Interest arises on overdue formal assessments, which have to be raised for PAYE and sub-contractor deductions (15.5). The interest charge runs from 14 days after the end of the tax year to which the assessment relates. With effect from 19 April 1993, interest is chargeable on late payments to the Revenue of PAYE deductions made by employers.

For 1996–97 and subsequently the self-assessment rules apply (16.1). These normally direct that interest runs from the due date for the tax. In general, this means that interest at currently 7.5 per cent (see 16.8.2) applies to overdue income tax and capital gains tax from each due date (31 January, 31 July, etc.).

A special provision removes the interest charge where the Inland Revenue agreed to defer the payment of tax due to the 2001 foot-and-mouth disease outbreak (FA 2001 S107).

16.8.3 **Surcharge on unpaid tax** (TMA S9c)

An additional charge has been introduced under the self-assessment system. Any *balancing* payments unpaid after 28 days from the due date (31 January 1998, etc.) will normally carry a surcharge of 5 per cent. An additional 5 per cent will be levied on tax still unpaid after 6 months.

16.9 Back duty investigations

If you have not disclosed to the Revenue your true income or if you have claimed tax reliefs and allowances to which you were not entitled the discovery of such facts by the authorities might give rise to a 'back duty' case.

It is open to the Revenue to take criminal proceedings against you resulting in a fine and/or imprisonment but this is rare. The normal course will be for the Revenue to obtain full particulars of the income omitted by you and raise assessments on you in respect of the further tax that is due. You will also normally be charged interest on the tax from when it should have been paid if your income had been properly declared. The Revenue may also charge you to penalties (see 16.9.2) depending upon whether your omissions were due to pure carelessness or ignorance or on the other hand were due to some fraudulent intention.

In order to ascertain the amount of your undisclosed income the Revenue will frequently require that capital statements be drawn up at the beginning and end of the period under review. The increase in your net worth between those two dates is then added to your living expenses for the period to give your total income (subject to adjustments for known capital profits, purchases and sales, betting winnings, etc.). Your total income less income already taxed will give your total income requiring still to be taxed. This should be split between the various intervening tax years by considering your assets and living expenses, etc. for each tax year.

16.9.1 **Fraud, wilful default or neglect; fraudulent or negligent conduct** (TMA S36)

Tax lost through the 'fraudulent or negligent conduct' of a taxpayer may be assessed up to 20 years after the end of the period to which it relates. This rule also applies to partners and where agents are culpable. These provisions apply to assessments for 1983–84 onwards and, regarding companies, for accounting periods ending after 31 March 1983.

'Neglect' is defined as 'negligence or a failure to give any notice, make any return or to produce or furnish any document or other information required by or under the Taxes Acts'.

For years of assessment prior to 1983–84 and accounting periods ending before 1 April 1983, the normal six-year time limit for making assessments (16.3.4) is extended indefinitely in any case where there is fraud or wilful default. This does not apply, however, in the case of the personal representatives of a deceased person (21.2).

A statutory offence of evading income tax took effect from 1 January 2001 (FA 2000 S144). This is tried summarily in the Magistrates' Court or on indictment in the Crown Court, with serious penalties (10.9.3).

16.9.2 **Interest and penalties** (TMA Ss55, 56, 70, 86–107 & 283)

Where an assessment has been made for the purpose of making good a loss of tax through fraud, wilful default or neglect, interest at 7.5 per cent (6.5 per cent before 6 September 2004 and 5.5 per cent prior to 6 December 2003 etc.) is charged on the underpaid tax from the date that the tax should have been paid. This also covers tax lost through 'fraudulent or negligent conduct' and was extended from 27 July 1989 to tax assessed late as the result of an incorrect return. Prior to 6 February 1997, various other interest rates applied as for overdue tax (16.8.2).

The maximum penalties are laid down in the legislation but frequently the Board of the Inland Revenue are prepared to accept less according to the particular facts of each case.

Regarding tax years after 1987–88 (or accounting periods ending after 31 March 1989 for companies), relief is given where more than one penalty arises on the same tax. In no case is the total amount of penalty to exceed the maximum possible amount for any one of the penalties involved.

The 1989 Finance Act introduced a simpler procedure for charging default interest and penalties. The Revenue may make formal determinations of the amounts due rather like assessments. You have full rights of appeal to the Appeal Commissioners and Courts. These rules do not apply to the initial penalties under the compliance rules which continue to be awarded by the Appeal Commissioners.

16.9.3 **Penalties – current rules** (TMA Ss93–107)

The following are examples of some of the maximum penalties:

Offence	Penalties
Failure to submit personal tax returns (pre-self-assessment)	£300 plus £60 per day after a court declaration
Failure to submit self-assessment tax returns (limited to tax due)	£100 after the filing date (31 January) and £100 after 31 July (and £60 per day etc.)
Failure to submit return continuing beyond tax year following that in which issued	Additional penalty of up to the amount of tax on income and gain, for year. However, if there is no assessable income or gains, the maximum total penalty is £100

Offence	Penalties
Incorrect returns	100% of tax lost
Assisting in the preparation of incorrect returns or accounts	£3,000
Supplying incorrect information to the Revenue	£3,000
Failure to keep records under self-assessment	£3,000
Failure to give notice of liability to tax	From 6 April 1989 the penalty is the amount of tax if notice is more than one year overdue
Failure to make (when required) a return of information for the Revenue	£300 plus £60 for each additional day in default
Statutory offence of evading income tax from 1 January 2001 (16.9.1)	Summarily in Magistrates' Court, £5,000 and/or 6 months. Indictment in Crown Court, unlimited fine and/or 7 years
Late submission of employers' year-end PAYE returns (10.14.4)	Initial penalty of up to £1,200 per 50 employees and £100 per 50 employees per month for further delays up to one year; beyond which up to 100% of tax underpaid or paid late
Fraudulent or negligent certificate of non-liability to tax re building society or bank deposit	Up to £3,000
False statement made by sub-contractor to obtain exemption from tax deduction (15.5)	£5,000

16.9.4 **Penalties – previous rules** (TMA Ss93–107)

Many of the selected penalties shown in the previous table, (16.9.3), operate from 1989 and others came in with the self-assessment system (16.1). Details of penalties for earlier years are given in previous editions of this book. In general, the fixed penalties were lower. Also, failing to give notice of liability to tax before 6 April 1989 attracted only a £100 penalty, but now if notice is more than one year overdue, the penalty can go up to the amount of the tax.

Chapter 17

DOMICILE AND RESIDENCE

17.1 The importance of domicile and residence

Your domicile and residence have a considerable effect on your liability to UK income tax, capital gains tax and inheritance tax. The position is summarised in the following table and dealt with in more detail in Chapters 18 and 19. (Domicile is defined in 17.2 and residence in 17.3.) Note that after 2004–05, ITTOIA (2.10) generally removes the classification into schedules for income tax purposes, but the basic rules remain.

17.1.1 The tax effects of domicile and residence

Tax	Situation of assets or where income arises	Tax treatment depending on taxpayer's residence and domicile: Taxed on arising basis (18.1.1)	Taxed on remittance basis	Tax free
Income Tax *Schedule D* Cases I & II	UK Abroad	All classes Not normally applicable		
Case III	UK Abroad	Normally all classes Not normally applicable		
Cases IV & V other than trades, professions, pensions, etc.	UK Abroad	Not applicable UK domiciled resident and ordinarily resident	Not applicable Non-domiciled, UK domiciled resident but not ordinarily resident	 Non-resident
Case V relating to trades, professions, pensions, etc.	UK Abroad	Not applicable UK domiciled resident and ordinarily resident (90% pensions)	Not applicable Non-domiciled, UK domiciled resident but not ordinarily resident	 Non-resident
Case VI	UK Abroad	All classes Not normally applicable apart from anti-avoidance rules (15.10)		
Schedule E		See 10.1–10.4		
Capital Gains Tax	UK or Abroad	UK domiciled and resident or ordinarily resident	Non-domiciled but resident or ordinarily resident (UK assets on arising basis)	Neither resident nor ordinarily resident (see note)
Inheritance Tax (residence is normally immaterial)	UK Abroad	UK domiciled or non-domiciled UK domiciled or deemed domiciled (22.4)		 Non-domiciled

Note: If you leave the UK for tax residence abroad after 16 March 1998 an absence of five complete tax years is normally required for this purpose (20.3 & 20.34).

17.2 What is domicile?

Your domicile is the country which you regard as your natural home. It is your place of abode to which you intend to return in the event of your going abroad. For most people it is their country of birth. Everyone has one domicile only. Unlike dual nationality, it is not possible to have two domiciles under English law. There are three main categories of domicile:

(1) Domicile of origin.
(2) Domicile of choice.
(3) Domicile of dependency.

17.2.1 Domicile of origin

You receive a domicile of origin at birth; it is normally that of your father at the date of your birth. In the case, however, of an illegitimate child or one born after the death of his father, his domicile of origin is that of his mother.

Your domicile of origin can be abandoned and you can take on a domicile of choice (see below). You will quickly revert to your domicile of origin, however, if you take up permanent residence again in that country.

17.2.2 Domicile of choice

If you abandon your domicile of origin and go and live in another country with the intention of permanently living there, the new country will become your domicile of choice. You will normally have to abandon most of your links with your original country of domicile (above). However, from 6 April 1996, registration for and voting in UK elections as an overseas elector is disregarded (FA 1996 S200).

If you lose or abandon your domicile of choice, your domicile of origin automatically applies once again, unless you establish a new one.

17.2.3 Domicile of dependency

Certain dependent individuals are deemed incapable of choosing a new domicile and the latter is always fixed by the operation of the law. Dependants for this purpose include infants, married women before 1 January 1974 and mental patients.

A child under 16 years of age automatically has the domicile of his father if he is legitimate, and otherwise that of his mother. If, however, a girl of under 16 marries then she takes on her husband's domicile. (Prior to 1 January 1974 the relevant age was 18.) In Scotland a boy has an independent domicile from age 14 and a girl from age 12.

Prior to 1 January 1974 a wife assumed the domicile of her husband while they were married. After the end of the marriage (by death or divorce) the woman kept her former husband's domicile unless she took on a fresh domicile of choice. Since 1 January 1974, however, a wife's domicile is independent of that of her husband. If married before that date, the husband's domicile remains as the wife's deemed domicile of choice until displaced by positive action.

17.2.4 **Future changes**

A new Domicile Bill was expected which would alter the domicile rules. In particular, it would have been easier for your domicile to be changed and your domicile of origin displaced. In May 1993 the Government said that it had no immediate plans to change the rules, but Budget 2002 announced a review for individuals covering domicile and residence. Furthermore, a background paper was published on this subject in April 2003.

17.3 What is residence?

Your residence for tax purposes is something which is fixed by your circumstances from year to year and you may sometimes be treated as being resident in more than one country at the same time.

Residence depends on the facts of each case and is determined by the individual's presence in a country, his objects in being there and his future intentions regarding his length of stay. The main criterion is the length of time spent in the country during each tax year. Another important point was whether a 'place of abode' is kept in the country (17.3.6).

17.3.1 **What is ordinary residence?**

If you have always lived in this country you are treated as being ordinarily resident here. Ordinary residence means that the residence is not casual and uncertain but that the individual who resides in a particular country does so in the ordinary course of his life. It implies residence with some degree of continuity, according to the way a person's life is usually ordered.

If you come to this country with the intention of taking up permanent residence here, it is Revenue practice to regard you as being both resident and ordinarily resident in the UK from your date of arrival. If, however, you originally did not intend to take up permanent residence here, you would not be considered ordinarily resident unless you stay here for two complete tax years and keep a place to live in this country.

17.3.2 **The residence of an individual** (TA 1988 Ss334–336)

If a person visits this country for some temporary purpose only and not with the intention of establishing his residence here, he is not normally treated as being a UK resident unless he spends at least six months here during the tax year.

An overseas visitor, however, might be treated as acquiring UK residence if he pays habitual substantial visits to this country. The normal requirement would be to come here for at least four consecutive years and stay for an average of at least three months each year. If you wish to remain non-resident you must avoid such habitual visits.

If you come to this country during a tax year with the intention of staying for two years or more, a Revenue concession will apply. You will only be treated as UK resident from your date of arrival, rather than from the beginning of the tax year when you come. A similar concession applies for your year of departure if you leave the UK for permanent overseas residence.

If you pay only short casual visits abroad you will not lose your UK residence, but if an entire tax year is included in any continuous period spent abroad you will normally be treated as being non-resident for at least the intervening tax year (17.3.7).

17.3.3 **The residence of a company** (TA 1988 Ss747, 765–767, FA 1988 Ss66 & 130–132 & Sch 7 & FA 1994 Ss249–251)

Subject to transitional provisions (see below), a company which is incorporated in the UK is treated for tax purposes as being resident here. Prior to 15 March 1988, a company was deemed to be resident where its central control and management were carried out. This was not necessarily where the company was registered although normally the central control and management would be exercised in the country in which the company was registered.

Where a company simply had its registered office here but carried on all its business from offices abroad and held its board meetings abroad, it was non-resident. Such companies did not come within the new rules for determining residence until 15 March 1993, provided they were already non-resident on 14 March 1988 or became non-resident later with Treasury consent. (In general, such companies needed to continue to carry on business.)

Under the controlled foreign company rules (13.21), where a company is resident abroad, it is necessary to establish in which country. Broadly, it is regarded as resident in the country where it is liable to tax because of its domicile, residence or place of management.

If a company registered abroad transacts some of its business in this country, it will not normally be treated as being UK resident provided its management and control are exercised abroad, which includes all board meetings being held abroad.

Taxes Act 1988 S765 contains certain penal provisions to prevent a UK company from becoming non-resident without Treasury consent being obtained. Fuller details are given earlier (15.10.16).

Where a company is resident in two countries, the double tax agreement often determines which residence applies for its purposes. If such a dual resident company is non-UK resident under the double tax agreement, it is so regarded for all UK tax purposes from 30 November 1993.

17.3.4 **The residence of a partnership** (TA 1988 S112)

Where any trade or business is carried on by a partnership and the control and management of the trade is situated abroad, the partnership is deemed to be resident abroad. This applies even if some of the partners are resident in this country and some of the trade is carried on here (12.8).

17.3.5 **The residence of a trust**

A trust is generally treated for capital gains tax purposes as being resident and ordinarily resident in the UK unless its general administration is ordinarily carried on outside this country and a majority of the trustees are neither resident nor ordinarily resident here. Stricter rules generally apply for income tax. For these purposes, special rules apply where at least one trustee is UK resident and one is not, depending on the settlor's status when he created the settlement or introduced further funds. If the settlor was then resident, ordinarily resident or domiciled in the UK, for determining the residence of the trust, all of the trustees are treated as being UK resident. Otherwise, they are all treated as being resident outside the UK. (A similar rule concerns the residence of executors, etc.) (FA 1989 Ss110 & 111).

17.3.6 **Place of abode in the UK** (TA 1988 S335 & FA 1993 S208)

Prior to 6 April 1993, if you maintained a house or flat in this country available for your occupation this was usually a factor towards deciding that you were resident here. Your residence position, however, was decided without regard to any place of abode maintained for your use in the UK in the following circumstances.

(1) You worked full-time in a trade, profession or vocation no part of which was carried on in this country.
(2) You worked full-time in an office or employment, all the duties of which (ignoring merely incidental duties) were performed outside the UK.

For 1993–94 and subsequent years of assessment, your residence position may not be affected by your having a place of abode here. Such accommodation will be ignored in considering whether or not you have come to the UK for a temporary purpose (17.3.2). However, if you leave the UK and retain a home here, your reasons for this may be a factor in deciding your residence.

17.3.7 **The effect of visits abroad** (TA 1988 S334)

If you are a citizen of the Commonwealth or the Republic of Ireland and your ordinary residence has been in the UK you are still charged to income tax if you have left this country only for the purpose of occasional residence abroad. In order to obtain non-residence for UK tax purposes your overseas residence must be more than merely occasional, it must have a strong element of permanency. The normal Revenue requirements are as follows:

(1) A definite intention to establish a permanent residence abroad.

(2) The actual fulfilment of such intention.
(3) Normally a full tax year should be spent outside this country before you are considered non-resident. Short periods in the UK may be disregarded by the Revenue, however. Thus if you left the country permanently on 30 September 2004 you will only be confirmed as non-resident after 5 April 2006. If you go abroad for the purposes of employment or to carry on a trade, once you are accepted by the Revenue as being no longer resident here, your non-residence is made retrospective to the day after your date of departure. In other cases of permanent departure, non-residence will normally run from the day after departure, but in some instances may run only from the following 6 April. In general, the Revenue have less stringent rules regarding those working abroad under contracts of employment.

17.4 How to change your domicile and residence

As has been already indicated, domicile and residence normally run together but domicile is much more difficult to change.

The way in which to change your residence is summarised on the previous page. You simply establish a permanent residence abroad and remain out of this country for a complete tax year. (In certain circumstances short visits to the UK are allowed.) After that you must avoid returning to this country for as much as six months in any one tax year, averaging less than three months here every year. Even if you do not work abroad, it is now less necessary to avoid having a place of abode available for you in the UK (17.3.6).

The general rule is that you will be charged to UK tax for the entire year of assessment as being either resident here or non-resident. However, in certain circumstances, by Inland Revenue Concession, the year of assessment is split for this purpose, namely where, being not ordinarily resident:

(1) You come to the UK to take up permanent residence or stay at least two years (previously three years).
(2) You cease to reside in the UK because you have left for permanent residence abroad.

The concession (A11) also applies if you go abroad under a contract of employment which includes a complete tax year. However, you may not spend 183 days or more in the UK in any tax year, nor an average of 91 days over a maximum period of 4 years.

In order to establish a fresh domicile, you should take as many steps as possible to show that you regard your new country as your permanent home.

The following points are relevant to establishing a particular country as your new domicile:

(1) Develop a long period of residence in the new country.
(2) Purchase or lease a home.
(3) Marry a native of that country.

(4) Develop business interests there.
(5) Make arrangements to be buried there.
(6) Draw up your will according to the law of the country.
(7) Exercise political rights in your new country of domicile (17.2.2).
(8) Arrange to be naturalised (not vital).
(9) Have your children educated in the new country.
(10) Resign from all clubs and associations in your former country of domicile and join clubs, etc. in your new country.
(11) Any religious affiliations that you have with your old domicile should be terminated and new ones established in your new domicile.
(12) Arrange for your family to be with you in your new country.

The above are some of the factors to be considered and the more of these circumstances that can be shown to prevail, the sooner you will be accepted as having changed your domicile.

Chapter 18

TAX ON FOREIGN INCOME

18.1 Overseas income from investments and businesses (TA 1988 Ss18 & 65–67)

If you obtain any income from investments and businesses situated overseas, you will normally be charged to income tax under Case IV or Case V of Schedule D. Case IV applies to income from 'securities' unless the income has already been charged under Schedule C or its successors (8.2). Case V applies to income from 'possessions' outside the UK. This includes businesses but does not cover emoluments from any overseas employment (18.5).

Your income assessed under Case IV and V of Schedule D will be included in your total income for tax purposes (5.2). After 2004–05, the classification into schedules for income tax purposes no longer applies in view of ITTOIA (2.10). However, the basic rules remain.

Frequently your overseas income will have already suffered tax in its country of origin. If you also have to pay UK income tax on this income you will normally be entitled to some relief to limit the extent that you are taxed doubly on the same income (18.6).

If you are UK resident and suffer 'special withholding tax' on savings income from abroad, you will be able to credit it against your UK tax liability and have any excess repaid. Also you can ask the Inland Revenue for a certificate for the paying agent to pay you gross. 'Special withholding tax' is broadly levied under an EU directive of 3 June 2003 or corresponding legislation of a non-EU state.

From 1997–98, the normal basis of assessment under Cases IV and V of Schedule D is the amount of income arising in the year of assessment. For 1996–97, a transitional basis applied (18.2). Before that, for sources of income existing prior to 5 April 1994, there was a 'previous year' basis. In the opening and closing years of a source of income, however, special rules applied (18.2.1 and 18.2.2).

In certain special circumstances the 'arising basis' is not used and the normally more favourable 'remittance basis' applies. If you are UK domiciled and ordinarily resident, however, your assessments on overseas pensions are based on only 90 per cent of the income arising.

18.1.1 What is the remittance basis?

Under the remittance basis you are only taxed on the amount of income actually brought into this country, in the year of assessment (whilst you still possess the source of overseas income). Remittances from sources opened before 6 April 1994 were assessable on the basis of the amounts for the previous tax year. However, 1996–97 was a transitional year, for which you were assessed on half your remittances in 1995–96 and 1996–97. If you are assessed on the remittance basis and bring income into the UK in a tax year after the source has come to an end, you are not liable to UK tax on it at all (18.1.2). Remittances can be made in cash or kind (18.1.3).

If you make no remittances you will have no liability to UK tax on your overseas income that is taxable on the remittance basis, no matter how high your income is in any year, although you might well suffer foreign tax.

18.1.2 **When does the remittance basis apply?** (TA 1988 S65)

Your Case IV and V and subsequent assessments will be based not on the 'arising' basis but on the remittance basis:

(1) If you are resident in this country but not domiciled here (17.3.2); or
(2) If you are a British subject or a citizen of the Republic of Ireland and are resident in this country but not ordinarily resident here.

You may have some overseas income that is taxed on a remittance basis and some that is taxed on an arising basis. In this case you should clearly segregate the two sources of income by using separate bank accounts since income from the latter can be brought into this country without paying any additional tax here because it has already been charged to UK tax.

If you are not resident in this country (17.3.2), you will not normally be charged to tax in respect of your Case IV and Case V and subsequent income, even if it is remitted here.

18.1.3 **What are classed as remittances?** (TA 1988 S65)

Whilst you have any continuing sources of overseas income in respect of which income arising abroad has not been fully transmitted to this country, any sums brought into the UK will normally be first considered to be remittances of overseas income.

The above will not apply if you keep separate bank accounts for income and capital, bringing in funds from the latter only (possibly giving rise to capital gains tax).

As well as cash and cheques, any property imported or value arising here from property not imported will be classed as remittances. Thus if you buy a car abroad out of your overseas profits and bring it into this country this is a remittance (although strictly speaking the second-hand value of the car at the time of importation should be used instead of the cost of the car). Similarly, if you hire an asset abroad out of unremitted overseas income, any use that you get from the asset in this country should be valued and treated as a remittance.

If you borrow money against sums owing to you for overseas income and bring the former into this country, this is a remittance. Similarly, if you borrow money here and repay it abroad out of overseas profits, this is known as a 'constructive remittance' and is taxable. Other forms of 'constructive remittances' include the payment out of overseas income of interest owing in this country, and the repayment out of such income, of money borrowed overseas which was made available to you in this country.

If you use non-remitted overseas income to buy shares in UK companies this is normally treated as a remittance unless a third party abroad actually acts as the principal in the transaction.

You are able to use non-remitted overseas income to cover the costs of overseas visits (including holidays) and provided you bring none of the money back to this country there is no taxable remittance. For this purpose the Revenue allow you to receive traveller's cheques in this country provided they are not cashed here.

If overseas profits are remitted to the Channel Islands or the Isle of Man this is not treated as a taxable remittance since those countries are not regarded as part of the UK for taxation purposes. They were, however, treated as being part of the UK for the purposes of exchange control. It was a UK exchange control rule that income earned abroad should be remitted to the UK and this was satisfied by sending the money to, say, Jersey or Guernsey without in turn incurring any UK income tax liability. The UK exchange control rules were generally withdrawn from 24 October 1979 and you are now free to keep money in other countries, subject to their own regulations.

18.2 The basis of assessment under Schedule D Cases IV and V (and subsequently) (TA 1988 Ss65 & 391, FA 1994 S207)

As previously mentioned the normal basis of assessment had been the amount of income arising in the tax year preceding the year of assessment. In certain cases, however, the assessment was based on the remittances in the previous tax year (18.1.2).

Legislation in the 1994 Finance Act abolished the preceding year basis from 1996–97. The assessment for each subsequent tax year is generally based on your actual income within it. Your 1996–97 assessment was normally based on half your income (or remittances) for that year and 1995–96. However, new sources arising after 5 April 1994 are immediately assessed on the new (actual) basis.

If you have an overseas business and the remittance basis does not apply, the assessment rules will generally follow those for Schedule D Cases I and II (11.7.1). Thus you are assessed on the adjusted profits for your accounts year ending in the year of assessment. However, the assessment for the first year is based on the actual profits to 5 April.

Under the current system, income from property outside the UK has been aligned with that within the UK by importing some of the new Schedule A rules (7.6). Thus interest payable on a loan to purchase property is allowed as a deduction. Income from overseas property remains assessable under Schedule D Case V and separate from your UK property income pool. However, from 6 April 1997, your overseas property income is pooled.

A few deductions are allowed in computing the income arising including the following:

(1) Any annuity paid out of the income to a non-resident of this country.
(2) Any other annual payment (not being interest) out of the income to a non-resident.
(3) Normal trading expenses against the income from any trade, etc. which you have abroad.
(4) Normal maintenance costs against rental income arising abroad.
(5) Ten per cent of any pensions.
(6) If you pay any overseas taxes for which you get no form of double tax relief then you can deduct such payments in computing your overseas income arising.
(7) If your overseas pension (or part of it) arises under the German or Austrian law relating to victims of Nazi persecution, the deduction was 50 per cent up to 1985–86. Subsequently such income is totally exempt. This includes cases where refugees from Germany were later credited with unpaid social security contributions thereby getting higher pensions.

18.2.1 **Special rules for fresh income – old system** (TA 1988 S66)

(1) For the tax year in which the income first arose your assessment was based on the income for that year.
(2) Unless the income first arose on 6 April, the assessment for the second tax year was on the actual income arising in that year.
(3) Your assessment for the third tax year was based on the income arising in the preceding tax year. However, if income first arose on 6 April your assessment for the second tax year was based on that arising in the previous year.
(4) You could elect that your first assessment on a preceding year basis should instead be on the income actually arising in the respective tax year.
(5) In case of income assessable on a remittance basis (18.1.1) the above rules were applied by substituting the remittances during the tax year for the income arising during that year.
(6) These rules do not apply for sources of income taxed under the current system (18.2).
(7) For fuller details of the commencement and cessation rules under the old system, please see earlier editions of this book.

18.2.2 **Special rules where source of income ceases – old system** (TA 1988 S67 & FA 1995 Ss124 & 125)

(1) If an overseas source of income ceased in a given tax year then your assessment for that year was on the income arising in it.
(2) Your assessment for the tax year preceding that in which the source ceases was increased to the actual income arising if this was greater than the original 'preceding year' assessment.
(3) The above rules applied to income assessed on a remittance basis – you simply used the remittances during the tax year instead of the income arising.
(4) Where you are assessed on the remittance basis (18.1.1) you are not liable to UK tax on any income that you bring into this country during a tax year later than the one in which your overseas source ceases.
(5) Under the current system (18.2), some of the above rules are not needed, since assessments are generally on an actual basis.
(6) A special rule covers where you trade overseas in whole or part and cease being UK resident. This results in your being taxed as if your trade or profession ceases and recommences. It took effect generally from 1997–98 and if your business started after 5 April 1994, for 1995–96 and 1996–97 also. A similar rule applies for partnerships (FA 1995 Ss124 & 125).

18.3 Professions conducted partly abroad

If you are engaged in any profession or vocation that is conducted partly within this country and partly overseas, you will normally be assessed on your entire 'global' profits under (prior to 2005–06) Case II of Schedule D. It is only if you conduct a separate profession or vocation entirely abroad that what was previously Schedule D Case V will apply.

This rule is particularly applicable to actors and entertainers, etc. who travel widely in the conduct of their professions. The rule does not apply, however, to income from an office or employment the duties of which are conducted entirely abroad.

18.4 Relief for overseas trading by individuals

From 1978–79 to 1984–85 inclusive special relief applied against assessments under Schedule D Cases I and II on trades, professions or vocations including partnerships. If you carried on such a trade, etc., resided in the UK and were absent from it for at least 30 'qualifying days' in a year of assessment, you were able to claim the relief. You deducted from your assessment a percentage of the proportion relating to your total 'qualifying days' working abroad. From 1978–79 to 1983–84, the relief was 25 per cent, for 1984–85 it was 12.5 per cent and nil thereafter.

18.5 Earnings from overseas employments (TA 1988 Ss19, 132, 192 & 193 & Sch 12)

From 6 April 1974 to 5 April 1984, you were normally assessed to tax under Case I of Schedule E on 75 per cent of your earnings from any overseas employments. For 1984–85, the taxable proportion was 87.5 per cent, after which the relief was totally abolished. However, subject to certain rules, a 100 per cent deduction applied for extended periods of absence (18.5.1). But this relief was withdrawn for all except seafarers, for periods after 16 March 1998.

18.5.1 The 100 per cent deduction up to 16 March 1998

Before 17 March 1998 you were not normally liable to UK tax on any income from *overseas employments* which you earned during a 'qualifying period' of absence from this country of at least a year. This did not need to be a tax year and you were allowed to spend here up to one-sixth of the period, but no more than 62 days in any one visit. Otherwise the required continuous 'qualifying period' was broken. This meant that you had to start reckoning your qualifying period from when you return overseas again.

Also, the one-sixth test applied to all periods cumulatively from the start of your 'qualifying period' until the end of each overseas visit. Thus if you started your overseas service by being away for 20 days, came back for 20 days and returned for 20 days, your 'chain' was broken because you had spent one-third of the 60 days in the UK instead of the maximum of one-sixth.

An *overseas employment* is one the duties of which are performed outside this country. If an employment is performed partly here and partly abroad, you will normally be taxed on the income arising under what was previously Case I of Schedule E (10.1). Special rules (19.1.7) apply, however, if you are not domiciled here (17.2). Any duties that you perform in this country which were purely incidental to the performance of your overseas employment were normally disregarded and so the special treatment would apply.

If you worked on a ship, from 1988–89 the 62-day period was increased to 90 days and the fraction was one-quarter (FA 1988 S67). Seafarers have longer permitted periods in the UK which apply where at least part of a UK visit between two periods of absence is after 5 April 1991. The new limits are respectively 183 days and half the total period (FA 1991 S45).

From 6 April 1992, your overseas earnings must be calculated net for the purposes of the relief. Deductions must be made for appropriate pension contributions, expenses and capital allowances. Previously, faultily drawn legislation allowed gross earnings to be used.

18.5.2 The 100 per cent deduction after 16 March 1998

With effect from 17 March 1998, the general foreign earnings deduction (100 per cent relief 18.5.1) has been removed. However, the relief remains for seafarers, excluding those employed on offshore installations for oil/gas exploration or extraction. The rules for seafarers are broadly as before, with permitted visits to the UK of up to half of the 'qualifying period' (18.5.1) including no more than 183 consecutive days.

18.5.3 **Remittances**

The rules concerning the remittance of Schedule E income are exactly the same as for income assessable under what was previously Cases IV and V of Schedule D (18.1.2). The remittance basis now broadly only applies for overseas employments if you are UK resident and not domiciled here and/or not ordinarily resident. Note that you are assessed on remittances made after 5 April 1990 whether or not the employment has ceased.

Remittances of income from overseas employments are not taxable here in either of the following situations:

(1) If made during a tax year in which you are not resident here (whether or not you are ordinarily resident in this country).
(2) If made when you are UK domiciled and ordinarily resident (normally taxed on an arising basis).

18.5.4 **Expenses concerning work overseas** (TA 1988 Ss80–81 & 193–195)

Provided your employer ultimately bears the cost, normally you are not taxed as a benefit on any of the following expenses concerning overseas employments:

(1) Travelling to take up your overseas employment or returning on its termination. (Expense relief is available if you bear the cost yourself.)
(2) Board and lodging overseas.
(3) Certain visits by your family (10.6.4).
(4) Unlimited outward and return journeys between your overseas employment and the UK.

Similar rules apply to the travel and subsistence of UK residents with businesses carried on wholly abroad. The rules cover travel between overseas trades as well as between the UK and abroad.

18.6 Double taxation relief (TA 1988 Ss788–816)

The UK government has entered into agreements with the governments of other countries for the purpose of preventing double taxation under the UK tax law and under the tax law of such other countries in respect of the same income (This can now apply even if the UK does not recognise the other government (FA 2002 S88)). A further object of certain of those agreements is to render reciprocal assistance in the prevention of tax evasion.

Under particular double taxation conventions certain classes of income are made taxable only in one of the countries who are party to the agreement, for example, that in which the taxpayer resides. Certain other income is taxable in both of the countries concerned but in the case of UK residents, the overseas tax is allowed as a credit against the UK tax. If after 16 March 1998 your overseas tax on such income is reduced, you must tell the UK Revenue (FA 1998 S107).

Double tax relief is restricted for UK banks lending to non-residents to 15 per cent of the gross interest. However, it is now necessary to look at each loan separately. Foreign tax credit relief is only to be offset against the corporation tax on a particular loan.

If there is no double tax convention between this country and another one then 'unilateral relief' may be available. This means that if you are a UK resident and obtain income from the other country, you are normally allowed to set off any overseas tax suffered against your UK tax liability on the same income. If you are not allowed to do so then you can deduct the overseas tax in computing the overseas income taxable in this country.

Various changes have effect after 31 March 2000 regarding mainly multinational companies. For example, the rate of underlying tax attributable to an inter-group dividend is capped at 30 per cent (45 per cent against other dividends not themselves capped). The on-shore pooling rules are extended from 1 April 2001 to allow relief for foreign tax rates paid up to 45 per cent even if this is at more than one level in a chain of companies. FA 2005 Ss85–89 make rule changes. These include denying underlying tax relief if a tax deduction is given in another jurisdiction calculated by reference to the relevant dividend.

Double tax agreements may include provisions for the exchange of information about taxpayers, between the UK and the overseas country concerned. This is particularly aimed at countering tax evasion.

18.6.1 Double taxation relief – list of countries which have general agreements with the UK

Antigua
Argentina
Australia
Austria
Azerbaijan
Bangladesh
Barbados
Belarus
Belgium
Belize
Bolivia
Botswana
Brunei
Bulgaria
Burma (Myanmar)
Canada
Chile
China
Cyprus
Czechoslovakia
Denmark
Dominica (terminated 1987)
Egypt
Estonia
Falkland Islands
Fiji
Finland
France
Gambia
Georgia
Germany
Ghana
Gilbert Islands (Kiribati and Tuvalu)
Greece
Grenada
Guernsey
Guyana
Hungary
Iceland
India
Indonesia
Irish Republic
Isle of Man
Israel
Italy
Ivory Coast
Jamaica
Japan
Jersey
Jordan
Kazakhstan
Kenya
Korea
Kuwait

Latvia
Lesotho
Lithuania
Luxembourg
Malawi
Malaysia
Malta
Mauritius
Mexico
Mongolia
Montserrat
Morocco
Netherlands
Netherlands Antilles (ceased 31.3.89)
New Zealand
Nigeria
Norway
Oman
Pakistan
Papua New Guinea
Philippines
Poland
Portugal
Romania
Russian Federation
Seychelles (terminated 1993)
Sierra Leone
Singapore
Solomon Islands
South Africa
South West Africa (Namibia)
Spain
Sri Lanka
St Kitts & Nevis
St Lucia (terminated 1988)
St Vincent (terminated 1987)
Sudan
Swaziland
Sweden
Switzerland
Taiwan
Tanzania (terminated 1980)
Thailand
Trinidad & Tobago
Tunisia
Turkey
Uganda
Ukraine
USA
USSR*
Uzbekistan
Venezuela
Vietnam
Yugoslavia (Croatia & Slovenia)
Zambia
Zimbabwe

* The convention with the USSR has become known as being with the Russian Federation, but also applies to most other states which used to make up the USSR until superseded by new agreements. However, from April 2002, Armenia, Georgia, Kyrgyzstar and Moldova are excluded.

Note: In addition to the above general agreements, arrangements of a more restricted kind have been entered into with Brazil, Jordan, Lebanon and Zaire covering the double taxation of profits from shipping and air transport. Agreements with Algeria, Cameroon, Ethiopia, Iran and Saudi Arabia cover only air transport and one with Hong Kong covers only shipping.

Chapter 19

NON-RESIDENTS, VISITORS AND IMMIGRANTS

19.1 On what income are non-residents liable to UK tax?

If, for a given tax year, you are not a UK resident (17.3.2) you will normally be liable to UK income tax only on income arising in this country. If your income arising here is also taxed in your country of residence you will in many cases be entitled to double taxation relief (18.6). Should there be a double taxation agreement between your country of residence and the UK (18.6.1) this agreement may provide that certain categories of income arising in this country should only be taxed in your own country and not here. The following paragraphs cover the position if such relief is not obtained. Remember that for tax years after 2004–05, classification into schedules for income tax purposes normally no longer applies, in view of ITTOIA (2.10). However, the basic rules remain.

19.1.1 Business profits in the UK (TA 1988 S18 & FA 1995 S126 & Sch 23)

If you are non-resident but carry on a business in this country you will be charged to tax here on your profits. You will be assessed to income tax under Schedule D Case I (11.2) at the starting rate (10 per cent), basic rate (22 per cent) and higher rate (40 per cent) if your total income liable to UK tax is sufficiently high (2.2).

If your UK business is operated by a manager, etc., he is charged to the tax on your behalf but if your only business in this country consists of selling through a broker or agent who acts for various principals, you will not be chargeable. From 6 April 1996, your branch or agent in the UK is made jointly responsible with you for all that needs to be done concerning the self-assessment of the profits.

19.1.2 Income from property and land in the UK (TA 1988 S15)

Income tax under Schedule A is charged on this income (7.1). If you are non-resident you will nevertheless have to pay UK income tax on this income; the basic rate normally should be deducted at source by the tenant or agent in paying you. Furthermore such income is frequently not covered by the relevant double taxation agreement.

19.1.3 Interest received from sources in the UK (TA 1988 Ss18, 66 & 349)

You are liable to income tax under Schedule D Case III on this income (8.5). If you are not ordinarily resident, you can sign a declaration and obtain your interest gross from banks, building societies and other deposit takers.

19.1.4 **Interest on UK securities** (TA 1988 Ss44–52)

Income tax at 20 per cent (25 per cent before 6 April 1996) will be withheld from interest payments made to you unless some lower rate (or nil rate) is specified in any double taxation agreement (18.6). (See also exempt gilts, 19.2.)

19.1.5 **Dividend payments to non-residents** (TA 1988 Ss232, 811 & 812)

If you are non-resident, your dividends from UK companies normally carry no tax credits unless you get relief under TA 1988 S278 (19.7) or under certain double taxation arrangements (see below). Thus if you receive a dividend of £90, you will normally pay overseas tax on this amount with no deduction for the £10 tax credit which you would have got, if you were a UK resident. You may be liable, however, to the excess of the higher rate income tax over the tax credit (5.0.1) on the actual dividend payments. Such tax would qualify for relief against your overseas tax subject to the relevant double tax arrangements (18.6).

Provided the relevant double tax agreements have been revised to permit it, special arrangements can be made between UK companies and the Board of Inland Revenue. These enable a UK company, when paying a dividend to an overseas resident, also to pay him an amount representing the excess over his UK tax liability on the dividend of the UK tax credit to which he is entitled under the relevant double tax agreement (18.6.1). Comparable rules apply to companies. However, from a date to be fixed, the right of certain non-resident companies to payments of tax credits will be subject to withdrawal. This broadly covers various situations involving 'unitary taxation'.

19.1.6 **Investment managers acting for non-residents** (TMA S78, FA 1991 S81 & FA 1995 Ss126 & 127 & Sch 23)

Casual agents and brokers, investment managers, such as banks and other financial concerns, are exempted from any tax liability as agents for non-residents. The exemption applies provided, for example, the agent is in the business of providing investment management services to a number of clients, on a normal commercial basis. It extends to stocks and shares, interest on deposits and futures, commodities, financial futures and options contracts (not involving land).

Generally from 6 April 1996 (and in some cases 1995) a Revenue concession became law, which may be of benefit to you if you are non-resident. Your UK income tax is then limited to that deducted at source regarding investing and trading through a broker, investment manager, etc. A condition is that the investment manager acts as your independent agent.

19.1.7 **Income from employments in the UK** (TA 1988 S19, etc.)

If you are not resident in this country (or not ordinarily resident) you are assessed to UK tax (previously under Schedule E) in respect of any emoluments during the relevant tax year regarding duties performed here. Non-domiciled employees obtain relief for travel expenses between their UK jobs and their countries similar to that afforded to UK personnel working abroad (10.6.4). However, the relief is only available for five years from the arrival of the employee in the UK (TA 1988 S195).

19.1.8 Higher rate income tax

If you are not resident in this country but are liable to UK income tax on part or all of your income, this may be taxed at the starting, lower, basic and higher rate. This will depend on the amount of your income liable to UK income tax. Thus if for 2005–06 this is earned and comes to £40,000 after allowable deductions, you will pay income tax at 10 per cent on £2,090, 22 per cent on £30,310 and 40 per cent on £7,600. Thus your total UK income tax will be £209 + £6,668.20 + £3,040 = £9,917.20 (subject to possible double tax relief).

19.2 Interest paid to non-residents in respect of certain UK government securities (TA 1988 S47, FA 1996 S154 & 155 & Sch 28)

From 6 April 1998, 'free of tax to residents abroad' (FOTRA) status extends to all gilts (8.2). Previously, the interest on certain specified UK government securities (19.1.4) could be paid to you gross without the deduction of any UK income tax provided certain conditions were satisfied.

19.3 Rules for taxation of visitors' income (TA 1988 S336)

If you come to this country as a visitor only and you do not intend to establish your residence here, you will not normally be charged to UK income tax on income arising elsewhere. This applies provided you have not actually been in this country for more than six months during the relevant tax year.

As a general rule you are not subject to UK income tax unless you are chargeable as a person resident here (17.3.2).

Even if you are not resident in this country during a given tax year you will normally be chargeable to UK income tax on your income arising from sources within the UK. However, interest on certain government bonds is exempted if you make the required application to the Revenue (8.2). You may also be entitled to double taxation relief in respect of your income arising in this country (18.6).

19.4 When does a habitual visitor become a UK resident?

If you are a visitor to the UK you are treated as resident here for tax purposes in any year of assessment in which you spend more than six months in this country.

Even if you do not stay for six months in any tax year, you will be regarded as becoming resident if you come here year after year (so that your visits become in effect part of your habit of life) and those visits are for a substantial period or periods of time. The Revenue normally regard an average of three months as being substantial and the visits as having become habitual after four years. Further, if your arrangements indicated from the start that regular visits for substantial periods were to be made the Revenue would regard you as being resident here in and from the first tax year.

If, however, a place of abode was maintained for you in this country, subject to certain specified exceptions, you were regarded by the Revenue as being resident here for any year in which you paid a visit to the UK. This was relaxed from 1993–94 (17.3.6).

19.5 The position of visiting diplomats (TA 1988 Ss320–322)

Special tax exemptions are given to visiting diplomats including agents-general, high commissioners, consuls and official agents. Consular officers and employees of foreign states who visit this country are afforded certain tax exemptions here, even if they stay in the UK for sufficiently long normally to be treated as resident here.

Regarding consular officers and employees of foreign states, the conditions for the exemptions to apply are that:

(1) the individual is not a citizen of the UK or colonies;
(2) he is not engaged in any trade, profession or employment in this country (apart from his diplomatic duties); and
(3) he is either a permanent employee of the foreign state or was not ordinarily resident in the UK immediately before he became a consular officer or employee here.

The tax concessions which apply when appropriate arrangements have been made with the foreign state concerned, include the following:

(1) Any income of the individual which falls under Cases IV and V of Schedule D (18.2) is not subject to income tax here.
(2) Certain overseas dividends and interest on securities are not taxed in this country.
(3) Emoluments of the individual from his consular office or employment are not taxed here.
(4) No capital gains tax (20.3) is payable on disposals of assets situated outside the UK.

19.6 Visiting entertainers and sportsmen (TA 1988 Ss555–558)

Rules apply from 1 May 1987 under which UK appearances by non-resident sportsmen and entertainers are taxed at once. Payments of £1,000, or more, are subjected to basic rate (22 per cent) income tax at source. However, it is possible to agree a lower or nil rate with the Inland Revenue where it can be established that the eventual UK tax liability will be less than 22 per cent.

19.7 The entitlement of certain non-residents to UK tax reliefs (TA 1988 S278)

Unless you are resident here or fall within the categories listed below,you will not obtain any UK personal reliefs and allowances (3.0.1) against your income tax liability in this country.

If you fall within the undermentioned categories, however, you will qualify for personal relief against your income taxable in this country.

(1) Subjects of Great Britain or the Republic of Ireland.
(2) Employees of the Crown or Crown protectorates or missionary societies.
(3) Residents of the Isle of Man or the Channel Islands.
(4) Previous residents of the UK who have gone abroad for reasons of their own health or that of a member of their families.
(5) Widows of Crown servants.
(6) A national of any European Economic Area state.

To get this relief, you must submit a claim to the Revenue giving details of your UK and world income. From 6 April 1990 full personal allowances are available for those in the above specified categories.

19.8 Immigrants

If you come from abroad to this country with the intention of taking up permanent residence here the following tax consequences will result:

(1) You will normally get full UK personal reliefs and allowances for income tax for the entire tax year during which you arrive.
(2) If you have any British government securities on which you had been receiving interest gross as a non-resident (8.2) as soon as you arrive here you will be liable to tax on this interest.
(3) You will not be taxed here on any lump sum payment that you receive from a former employer or overseas provident fund in respect of termination of an overseas employment.
(4) If you have any income assessable under what was previously Case IV or V of Schedule D on a remittance basis (18.1.1) and the source ceases before you arrive here, you will have no liability on any sums remitted. If the source ceases in your year of arrival but after you take up permanent residence here, your liability is on the lower of your total remittances in the tax year and the income arising from your date of arrival until the date that the source closed.
(5) If you had a source of income outside this country before coming here, this source is not treated as being a fresh one on your arrival. Thus if you had possessed the source for some years the preceding year basis will normally apply.
(6) Subject to the above comments, you will generally be taxed here only in respect of income arising from your date of arrival.

Chapter 20

CAPITAL GAINS TAX

20.1 Introduction

Subject to the specific rules that are summarised in the following pages, you will be charged to capital gains tax in respect of any chargeable gains that accrue to you on the disposal of assets during a given tax year. You deduct from your capital gains any allowable capital losses (20.13) and then indexation allowance (20.11) and/or taper relief (20.12). (The taper relief system applies for realisations from 6 April 1998.) For individuals, capital gains tax is charged at the same rates as on investment income (10 per cent, 20 per cent and 40 per cent for 2005–06).

An annual exemption of £8,500 applies for individuals and broadly £4,250 for trusts (21.6). Companies pay corporation tax at corporation tax rates on their capital gains (13.15), subject to special rules for authorised investment trusts and unit trusts (20.18.7).

Most references throughout this chapter are to the Taxation of Chargeable Gains Act 1992 which consolidates the relevant legislation.

20.2 What is a chargeable gain? (TCGA S15)

A chargeable gain is a gain which accrues after 6 April 1965 to a taxpayer (including a company, trust, partnership, individual, etc.) such gain being computed in accordance with the provisions of the relevant legislation. There must, however, be a disposal of an asset in order that there should be a chargeable gain.

20.3 Who is liable? (TCGA Ss2, 10 & 12)

Any taxpayer (including a company, trust, partnership, individual, etc.) is chargeable to capital gains tax on any chargeable gains accruing to him in a year of assessment during any part of which he is: (a) resident in this country (17.3), or (b) ordinarily resident here (17.3.1).

Also, even if neither resident nor ordinarily resident here, a taxpayer who carries on a trade in the UK through a branch or agency is generally liable to capital gains tax accruing on the disposal of: (a) assets in this country used in his trade, or (b) assets held here and used for the branch or agency. This rule extends to professions and vocations, as well as trades (20.32).

If you are resident or ordinarily resident here during a tax year you will be liable to capital gains tax on realisations of assets throughout the world. An exception is made, however, if you are not domiciled in this country (17.2); in that case you are only charged to capital gains tax on your overseas realisations of assets to the extent that such gains are remitted here (18.1). For these purposes, if you are non-domiciled and have a non-sterling bank account, this is treated as located outside the UK unless both the account is held at a UK branch and you are UK-resident (TCGA S275).

20.3.1 **Temporary non-residents** (TCGA Ss9 & 10A)

If you leave the UK for tax residence abroad (17.3) after 16 March 1998, stiffer capital gains tax rules apply regarding sales of assets you had owned when you depart. You will be liable to capital gains tax on such disposals if you become neither resident nor ordinarily resident for less than five tax years. However this does not apply unless you were a UK tax resident for any part of at least four of the seven tax years before departure.

Your gains as above in the year that you leave are charged for that year and otherwise for the tax year when you resume UK residence. Gains made on assets acquired after you become tax resident abroad and before your return, will normally be exempt.

20.4 Capital gains tax rates from 6 April 1988 (TCGA Ss4–6)

Originally, capital gains tax was charged by means of a single rate of 30 per cent. This was changed from 6 April 1988 and further modified from 6 April 1992, with the introduction of the lower rate band and then from 6 April 1999:

(1) Individuals now suffer capital gains tax at 10 per cent, 20 per cent and 40 per cent, the same as the income tax rates on investment income. (For 1999–2000, the rates were 20 per cent and 40 per cent).

(2) From 6 April 1992 to 5 April 1999, the capital gains tax rates for individuals were 20 per cent, 23 per cent and 40 per cent.

(3) The rate for accumulation and maintenance trusts and discretionary settlements from 2004–05 is 40 per cent (previously 34 per cent) (21.6).

(4) Other trusts in general paid 23 per cent up to 5 April 1998, then 34 per cent and now 40 per cent from 2004–05. However if the settlor or his or her spouse has any interest in or rights relating to a settlement, any capital gains will be subjected to his or her rates (21.6).

(5) The capital gains of companies continue to bear corporation tax at the appropriate rate (13.15).

(6) To find the rate or rates payable by an individual, you take the total gains less losses (20.13) for the tax year, deduct capital losses brought forward and the annual exemption, considering this together with taxable income after reliefs and allowances. (From 1991–92, certain trading losses may also be deducted – 20.13.) For 2005–06, the first £2,090 is taxed at 10 per cent, the next £30,310 is taxed at 20 per cent and the remainder attracts 40 per cent. (Your income is taxed at your lower rates first and your capital gains attract your highest rates.)

(7) Thus, if your taxable income after allowances for 2005–06 is £24,000, you have £32,400 – £24,000 = £8,400 of your 20 per cent rate band

unused. This means that if your net capital gains for 2005–06 are £18,500, this is reduced to £10,000 by your annual exemption (£8,500). Your capital gains tax is thus:

£	£
8,400 at 20%	1,680
1,600 at 40%	640
	2,320

20.5 Annual exemptions (TCGA S3 & Sch 1)

The previous system for relieving small gains was changed from 6 April 1980, when an annual exemption was introduced. The following rules apply and the rates shown are for 2005–06.

(1) The first £8,500 of your net gains is exempted from capital gains tax. This applies no matter how high are your total gains for the year.
(2) Any set-off for losses from previous years (20.13) is restricted to leave £8,500 of gains to be exempted. In this way your exemption is protected and you have more losses to carry forward. All losses for the year must be deducted, however, in arriving at the net gains.
(3) These rules apply to personal representatives for the tax year of death and the next two years.
(4) The rules also apply to trusts for the mentally disabled and for those receiving attendance allowance.
(5) For other trusts set up before 7 June 1978 the first £4,250 of net capital gains each year is exempt (21.6).
(6) Trusts set up after 6 June 1978 by the same settlor each have an exemption of £4,250 divided by the number of such trusts. Thus if you have set up two trusts since that date, they each have an exemption of £2,125. In any event each trust obtains an exemption of at least £850.
(7) Any set off for trust losses from previous years is restricted so that the appropriate exemption (£4,250, etc.) is not wasted.
(8) The above figures apply to future years subject to indexation in line with the increase in the Retail Prices Index. This applies unless Parliament otherwise directs.
(9) From 1990–91 onwards, husband and wife each have their own annual exemptions and the above rules apply to their own gains and losses alone. Previously, unless they were separated, only one annual exemption applied to their combined net gains.
(10) The corresponding annual exemption figures for previous years have been:

	Individuals, etc. £	Trusts £
1992–93 to 1994–95	5,800	2,900
1995–96	6,000	3,000
1996–97	6,300	3,150

	Individuals, etc. £	Trusts £
1997–98	6,500	3,250
1998–99	6,800	3,400
1999–2000	7,100	3,550
2000–01	7,200	3,600
2001–02	7,500	3,750
2002–03	7,700	3,850
2003–04	7,900	3,950
2004–05	8,200	4,100

20.6 What assets are liable? (TCGA Ss21–27)

Subject to various exemptions (see 20.8.1) all forms of property are treated as 'assets' for capital gains tax purposes including:

(1) Investments, land and buildings, jewellery, antiques, etc.
(2) Options and debts, etc.
(3) Any currency other than sterling (special rules for companies – 13.25).
(4) Any form of property created by the person disposing of it or otherwise coming to be owned without being acquired. (This would cover any article which you made or work of art created by you.)

20.7 What assets are exempted? (TCGA – see below)

The following classes of assets are exempted from charge to capital gains tax subject to the relevant rules:

20.7.1 Assets exempted from capital gains tax

(1) Private motor vehicles (S263).
(2) Certain gifts covered by an election (20.27).
(3) Your own home – this is known as your 'main private residence' (20.23).
(4) National Savings Certificates, Defence Bonds, Development Bonds, Save-as-you-earn, etc. (S121).
(5) Any foreign currency which you obtained for personal expenditure abroad (S269).
(6) Any decoration for gallantry (unless purchased) (S268).
(7) Betting winnings including pools, lotteries and premium bonds (S51).
(8) Compensation or damages for any wrong or injury suffered to your person or in connection with your profession or vocation (S51).
(9) British government securities (S115). Disposals prior to 2 July 1986 were only exempt if the 'gilts' had been held for at least one year, or had passed to you on death or from a trust.
(10) Life assurance policies and deferred annuities provided that you are the original owner or they were given to you. If you bought the rights to a policy from its original owner you may be liable to capital gains tax on the surrender, maturity or sale of the policy, or death of the life assured (S210). Certain policies assigned after 25

June 1982 may give rise to income tax instead of capital gains tax, however (TA 1988 Ss540 & 544).

(11) Chattels sold for £6,000 or less (20.24).
(12) Assets gifted to charity (20.29.1).
(13) The gift to the nation of any assets (for example, paintings) deemed to be of national, scientific or historic interest; also land, etc. given to the National Trust (S258).
(14) The gift of historic houses and certain other property of interest to the public, provided they are given access – also funds settled between 2 May 1976 and 6 April 1984 for the upkeep (S258). (Now covered by the gifts exemption – 20.28.)
(15) Tangible movable property which is a wasting asset (that is, with a predictable life of 50 years or less). This includes boats, animals, etc., but not land and buildings (S45) nor assets qualifying for capital allowances.
(16) Disposals by a close company (13.17) of assets on trust for the benefit of its employees (S239).
(17) If you sell a debt this is not liable to capital gains tax provided you are the original creditor and the debt is not a 'debt on a security' (a debenture, etc.). Otherwise capital gains tax applies. The 'debt on security' requirements do not apply, however, to certain business loans (excluding those from associated companies) made after 11 April 1978. Loss relief may be available on such debts and also on certain business guarantees made after that date (S251).
(18) Land transferred after 5 April 1983 from one local constituency association to another, which is taking over from it, as a result of the Parliamentary constituency boundaries being redrawn (S264).
(19) Certain corporate bonds issued after 13 March 1984 which you held for more than 12 months (20.19). Disposals after 1 July 1986 are exempt without time limit (Ss115–117).
(20) Transactions in futures and options in gilts and qualifying corporate bonds after 1 July 1986 (S115).
(21) Business expansion scheme shares issued to you after 18 March 1986, provided you are the first holder of those particular shares (11.25).
(22) Certain 'deep discount' (8.8) and from 14 March 1989, 'deep gain' securities (S117).
(23) Profits from the sale of timber and uncut trees (TCGA S250).
(24) Sales of PEP units, subject to the rules (8.10).
(25) Venture Capital Trust shares held for at least three years (five years if issued before 6 April 2000), subject to the rules (8.13).
(26) EIS shares held for at least three years (previously five), in accordance with the rules (11.26.).

20.8 What constitutes a disposal? (TCGA Ss21–26)

The following are examples of circumstances in which you will be treated as making a disposal or a part disposal of an asset:

(1) The outright sale of the whole asset or part of it.
(2) The gift of the asset or a part of it – the asset must be valued at the date of gift and this valuation is treated as the proceeds. An election for holding-over the gain is sometimes possible (20.28).
(3) If an asset is destroyed, for example, by fire, it is a disposal.

(4) If you sell any right in an asset, for example, by granting a lease, this is a part disposal although if you obtain a fair rent there is normally no capital gains tax liability.
(5) If any capital sum is received in return for the surrender or forfeiture of any rights, this is normally a disposal. For example, you may receive a sum of money for not renewing a lease in accordance with a renewal option which you possessed.
(6) If you die, you are deemed to dispose of all of your assets at your date of death but no capital gains tax is payable. Whoever inherits your assets does so at their market value at your death.
(7) A part withdrawal from a life policy of the original owner and for which you gave money or money's worth (TCGA S210).

The following are not treated as disposals of assets for capital gains tax purposes:

(1) If you give or sell an asset to your spouse this is not treated as a capital gains tax disposal, provided he or she is living with you during the relevant tax year. In that case your spouse is charged to capital gains tax on any subsequent disposal that he or she makes of the asset as if bought when you originally acquired it at the actual cost to yourself (plus any indexation allowance – 20.12). From 5 December 2005, this also applies to transfers between civil partners in accordance with the Civil Partnership Act 2004 (6.9).
(2) If you transfer an asset merely as security for a debt but retain the ownership this is not a capital gains tax disposal. This would apply, for example, if you mortgage your house.
(3) If you transfer an asset to somebody else to hold it as your nominee, this is not a disposal provided that you remain the beneficial owner.
(4) Gifts of assets to charities are effectively not treated as disposals (20.29.1).

20.9 How your chargeable gains are computed (TCGA Ss15–20 & 37–40)

The following general rules should be followed:

(1) If the asset sold was originally acquired before 7 April 1965, special rules apply (20.17).

(2) Special rules also apply in the case of leases and other wasting assets (20.29.2).

(3) Ascertain the consideration for each of your disposals during the tax year – this will normally be the sale proceeds but in the following cases it will be the *open market value* of the assets (20.16):
    (a) Gifts of assets during the tax year.
    (b) Transfers of assets (by gift or sale) to persons connected with you including your business partner and close relations other than your wife. This also applies to other disposals of assets not at arm's length. (Anti-avoidance rules operate to prevent losses being manufactured artificially in this way (15.10).)

(c) Transactions in which the sale proceeds cannot be valued, or where an asset is given as compensation for loss of office, etc. to an employee. If, for example, you give your friend a picture from your collection on condition that he paints your house each year for the next ten years, then since this service cannot be accurately valued you are treated as disposing of your picture for its market value.

(4) Deduct from the disposal consideration in respect of each asset its original cost (or value at acquisition) together with any incidental expenses in connection with your original acquisition and your disposal of each asset. For disposals after 5 April 1988, if it gives a better result, you normally deduct the value at 31 March 1982 instead of the cost (20.10). Also deduct any 'enhancement' expenditure, that is, the cost of any capital improvements to the assets not including any expenses of a 'revenue nature' (2.6).

(5) Deduct (if applicable) indexation allowance (see below).

(6) Apply taper relief as appropriate for periods after 5 April 1998 (20.12).

(7) Your incidental costs of acquisition and disposal (see (4) above) include surveyors', valuers' and solicitors' fees, stamp duty, and commission in connection with the purchase and sale. Also the cost of advertising to find a buyer and accountancy charges in connection with the acquisition or disposal. No expenses are deductible, however, if they have already been allowed in computing your taxable revenue profits (2.6).

20.10 Re-basing to 31 March 1982 values (TCGA Ss35–36 & Schs 3–4)

If you dispose of an asset after 5 April 1988, which you owned on 31 March 1982, its base value is automatically taken as its value at that date, provided this exceeds the cost. Thus, if you bought some shares for £1,000 in 1970 and they were worth £4,000 on 31 March 1982, you use £4,000 as their base value for capital gains tax purposes. Assuming you sell the shares for £10,000 in August 2005, your capital gain is £10,000 – £4,000 = £6,000 (ignoring indexation and taper relief).

Re-basing to 31 March 1982 does not increase a gain or loss compared with what it would have been under the old rules. Furthermore, where there is a gain under the old system and a loss through re-basing, or vice versa, the transaction is treated as giving rise to neither gain nor loss. For example, if you sell an asset for £1,000 which had cost £500 and was worth £1,500 at 31 March 1982, ignoring indexation you had a gain of £500 under the old rules and a loss of £500 through re-basing; you are therefore treated as having no gain and no loss.

The existing rules for assets held at 6 April 1965 can themselves give rise to disposals being treated as producing no gain and no loss (20.17). This is not affected by re-basing.

Even if you did not hold an asset at 31 March 1982, it may still qualify for re-basing if you received it from someone else in circumstances that there was neither a gain nor loss under the rules and their acquisition was before that date. A particular example is where one spouse acquires an asset from another.

If you held assets at 31 March 1982, but subsequently realised them in circumstances such that your gain was deferred, re-basing does not apply. However, special relief is available regarding disposals after 5 April 1988 (excluding no gain/no loss disposals). Provided you make a claim to the Inland Revenue within two years of the end of the year of assessment in which the disposal is made, your original held-over, rolled-over or deferred gain is halved (TCGA S36 & Sch 4).

You had the right to elect that all of your assets were re-based as at 31 March 1982. There was a two year time limit for this irrevocable election (that is, before 6 April 1990). However, this is extended to two years after the end of the tax year in which you make your first sale after 5 April 1988.

20.11 Indexation allowance (TCGA Ss53–57 & Sch 7A & FA 1998 S122)

If your disposal is after 5 April 1982 (31 March 1982 for companies) the original cost and enhancement expenditure may be increased by *indexation*. For disposals between 5 April 1985 (31 March for companies) and 6 April 1988, you had the option of basing indexation on the value of the asset sold, at 31 March 1982. After 5 April 1988, disposals are automatically re-based to their 31 March 1982 values if this is beneficial and so indexation is taken on the base value (20.10).

Indexation does not apply after April 1998 (20.12) except for companies. Thus if you sell an asset after 6 April 1998 which you acquired before that date, you obtain indexation up to April 1998 only.

The expenditure is scaled up in proportion to the increase in the Retail Price Index from the month of acquisition (or March 1982, if later) until the month of disposal. Values for the *Retail Prices Index* are shown in 20.11.1.

For disposals from 6 April 1986 to 29 November 1993, you obtained the full benefit of indexation relief, even to the extent that it created or enlarged a loss (20.13). Special rules apply regarding assets held on 6 April 1965 (20.17) and shares (20.14). Any disposals that you make after 29 November 1993 will obtain full indexation relief if the end result is a gain. However, subject to transitional relief for individuals and trustees, indexation no longer creates or increases a capital loss. The transitional relief applied to disposals from 30 November 1993 to 5 April 1995. Up to £10,000 of loss relief due to indexation could be obtained during that period, but not carried forward to 1995–96.

Transactions between husband and wife do not normally give rise to capital gains tax (20.9). Thus if you acquire an asset from your spouse, your deemed acquisition cost is taken to be his or hers, augmented by any indexation

20.11.1 **Retail prices index (adjusted)**

	1982	1983	1984	1985	1986	1987	1988	1989	1990	1991	1992	1993	1994	1995	1996	1997	1998	1999	2000	2001	2002	2003	2004	2005
January		82.6	86.8	91.2	96.2	100.0*	103.3	111.0	119.5	130.2	135.6	137.9	141.3	146.0	150.2	154.4	159.5	163.4	166.6	171.1	173.3	178.4	183.1	188.9
February		83.0	87.2	91.9	96.6	100.4	103.7	111.8	120.2	130.9	136.3	138.8	142.1	146.9	150.9	155.0	160.3	163.7	167.5	172.0	173.3	179.3	183.8	189.6
March	79.4	83.1	87.5	92.8	96.7	100.6	104.1	112.3	121.4	131.4	136.7	139.3	142.5	147.5	151.5	155.4	160.8	164.1	168.4	172.2	174.5	179.9	184.6	190.5
April	81.0	84.3	88.6	94.8	97.7	101.8	105.8§	114.3	125.1	133.1	138.8	140.6	144.2	149.0	152.6	156.3	162.6	165.2	170.1	173.1	175.7	181.2	185.7	
May	81.6	84.6	89.0	95.2	97.8	101.9	106.2	115.0	126.2	133.5	139.3	141.1	144.7	149.6	152.9	156.9	163.5	165.6	170.7	174.2	176.2	181.5	186.5	
June	81.9	84.8	89.2	95.4	97.8	101.9	106.6	115.4	126.7	134.1	139.3	141.0	144.7	149.8	153.0	157.5	163.4	165.6	171.1	174.4	176.2	181.3	186.8	
July	81.9	85.3	89.1	95.2	97.5	101.8	106.7	115.5	126.8	133.8	138.8	140.7	144.0	149.1	152.4	157.5	163.0	165.1	170.5	173.3	175.9	181.3	186.8	
August	81.9	85.7	89.9	95.5	97.8	102.1	107.9	115.8	128.1	134.1	138.9	141.3	144.7	149.9	153.1	158.5	163.7	165.5	170.5	174.0	176.4	181.6	187.4	
September	81.9	86.1	90.1	95.4	98.3	102.4	108.4	116.6	129.3	134.6	139.4	141.9	145.0	150.6	153.8	159.3	164.4	166.2	171.7	174.6	177.6	182.5	188.1	
October	82.3	86.4	90.7	95.6	98.5	102.9	109.5	117.5	130.3	135.1	139.9	141.8	145.2	149.8	153.8	159.5	164.5	166.5	171.6	174.3	177.9	182.6	188.6	
November	82.7	86.7	91.0	95.9	99.3	103.4	100.0	118.5	130.0	135.6	139.7	141.6	145.3	149.8	153.9	159.6	164.4	166.7	172.1	173.6	178.2	182.7	189.0	
December	82.5	86.9	90.9	96.0	99.6	103.3	110.3	118.3	129.9	135.7	139.2	141.9	146.0	150.7	154.4	160.0	164.4	167.3	172.2	173.4	178.5	183.5	189.9	

* At January 1987 the index base was changed to 100.0 and the above table shows figures before that date adjusted to the same base.

§ From April 1998, indexation only applies to companies.

allowance attaching to it at the transfer date. When you sell the asset, you obtain full indexation allowance on your deemed acquisition cost, from the date you took over the asset from your spouse. Similar treatment applies to company intra-group transfers (13.15) and certain reconstructions. Legatees obtain indexation allowance as if they had acquired the assets at the date of death. (Apart from assets held by companies, indexation only runs to April 1998.)

20.11.2 **Example: Computation of chargeable gain – pre-6 April 1998**

Mr A sells a block of flats on 15 July 1997 for £260,000. The flats were bought in May 1981 for £100,000 and subsequent capital expenditure amounted to £17,000 (all pre-April 1982). Also £10,000 had been spent on decorations and maintenance. The legal costs on purchase were £1,500 and stamp duty was £1,000. Surveyors' fees prior to purchase amounted to £500. At 31 March 1982, the market value was £115,000*. £100 was spent in advertising the sale and agents' commission amounted to £6,000. Legal costs on sale were £900. Assuming that Mr A's profit is taxed as a capital gain, what tax will he pay on it? Assume also that for 1997–98 Mr A has no other capital gains or losses and that his taxable income after all reliefs and allowances is £18,000. Assume also that the July 1997 indexation figure is 156:

	£	£
Cost of block of flats		100,000
Add:		
Enhancement expenditure		17,000
(decorations and maintenance not relevant)		
Legal costs on purchase		1,500
Stamp duty on purchase		1,000
Surveyors' fees on purchase		500
Total cost		120,000*
Add:		
Indexation £120,000 x (156 – 79.4)/79.4		115,768
		235,768
Proceeds		260,000
Less:		
Cost and indexation as above	235,768	
Advertising	100	
Agents' commission	6,000	
Legal fees on sale	900	
		242,768
Chargeable gain		17,232
Less: annual exemption		6,500
		10,732
Capital gains tax at 23% (on 26,000 –18,000 = 8,000)		1,840.00
at 40% 2,732		1,092.80
		2,932.80

* If the market value at 31 March 1982 had been more than £120,000, the property would be re-based to this value and this would also be used in calculating indexation.

20.12 Taper relief (TCGA Sch A1, FA 2000 Ss66 & 67, FA 2001 S78 & Sch 26, FA 2002 Ss46–48 & Sch 10 & FA 2003 S160)

A new time-related relief system regarding the capital gains of individuals, trustees and personal representatives, applies from 6 April 1998. However, the old system continues for companies for the time being. The following basic rules are subject to certain anti-avoidance provisions.

(1) Under the new rules, indexation does not apply for periods after 5 April 1998. Thus if you sell an asset after that date which you acquired beforehand, you obtain indexation up to April 1998 only.

(2) Taper relief applies to gains realised after 5 April 1998, subject to the rules. According to the number of complete years that the asset has been owned after that date, a percentage only of the gain will be chargeable. New rules apply to business asset disposals from 6 April 2000 and 2002. Different percentages apply for business and other assets as follows:

Gains on disposals of business assets				**Gains on disposals of non-business assets**	
Number of whole years in qualifying holding period	Percentage of of gain chargeable. Disposal date			Number of whole years in qualifying holding period	Percentage of gain chargeable
	pre-6.4.00	from 6.4.00 to 5.4.02	from 6.4.02		
1	92.5	87.5	50	–	–
2	85	75	25	–	–
3	77.5	50	25	3	95
4	70	25	25	4	90
5	62.5	25	25	5	85
6	55	25	25	6	80
7	47.5	25	25	7	75
8	40	25	25	8	70
9	32.5	25	25	9	65
10 or more	25	25	25	10 or more	60

(3) Any assets which you acquired before 17 March 1998 and dispose of after 5 April 1998 have an extra year added for taper relief purposes. Thus if you bought an asset in 1990 and sell it in June 1999, you will obtain taper relief as if you had held the asset for two complete years after 5 April 1998. However, this rule does not apply to business asset disposals after 5 April 2000.

(4) Business assets which attract increased taper relief are broadly defined as those used in your own or your partnership's trade (including profession) or your 'qualifying company'. Also included are assets held for the purposes of a qualifying full-time employment and shares which you hold in a 'qualifying company' (see below). The business asset rules extend to those held by trustees and personal representatives. For owner

ship and sales from 6 April 2004, qualifying business assets also include those used for trade by an individual (or partnership etc. but not company) other than the owner.

(5) A 'qualifying company' is a trading company or the holding company of a trading group in which you hold shares giving you 5 per cent of the voting rights, provided you are a full-time working officer or employee of that company, or otherwise 25 per cent.

(6) From 6 April 2000, the rules for determining whether shareholdings qualify as business assets for taper relief purposes are improved, so as to include all shares and securities in:
(a) unquoted trading companies including AIM companies;
(b) a listed trading company where you are an officer or employee;
(c) a listed trading company where you have at least 5 per cent of the voting rights.

(7) The scope of business assets qualifying for relief has been further broadened to include the shares of employees in non-trading companies in which they work; also assets other than shares used in a business in which a trust is a partner. (An employee must not have a material interest of more than 10% in the company.)

(8) Taper relief applies to your net gains for a tax year after deducting any losses for that year and then previous losses (20.13). Your losses are allocated on the basis that produces the lowest tax charge. Your annual exemption (£8,500) is set off after taper relief.

(9) If you transfer an asset to your spouse, taper relief on a later disposal will be based on the combined period for which you both held it. However, in the case of other no gain/no loss disposals and gifts hold-over relief, you only take the holding period of the new owner. Regarding business assets rollover relief, you consider the holding period of the replacement asset. An exception is where one EIS investment is replaced by another (11.26) when the combined holding period qualifies for taper relief (TCGA S5BA).

(10) In the case of reinvesting in a Venture Capital Trust before 6 April 2004 and other instances where your gain on an asset is deferred, taper relief is based on the holding period of your original asset.

(11) The rules for computing gains on shareholdings (20.18–20.20) have been changed to reflect the new system. In particular, shares etc. acquired from 6 April 1998, are no longer pooled.

(12) FA 2002 Sch 10 contains minor amendments, including taper relief no longer being restricted by a change of activity by a close company. Also, the range of debentures attracting taper relief was increased and the threshold for qualifying shareholdings in joint venture companies fell from 30 to 10 per cent.

20.12.1 **Example: Capital gains computation after 5 April 1998**

Mr B bought as an investment some shares in C plc in May 1982 for £5,000 and sells them for £28,000 in June 2005, having no other gains for 2005–2006. Mr B has capital losses of £3,000 for 2005–2006 but none brought forward. Assuming indexation relief to April 1998 of 100% and taking current rates and allowances, the capital gains for 2005–2006 on the C plc shares are:

	£	£
Proceeds		28,000
Less: cost	5,000	
indexation to April 1998, say 100%	5,000	10,000
		18,000
capital losses		3,000
Capital gain before taper		15,000
8 complete tax years rank for taper (including extra year for pre-17 March 1998 asset)		
Percentage of gain chargeable (20.12)	70%	10,500
Annual exemption, say		8,500
		2000
Capital gains tax at, say, 40%		800

20.13 Capital losses (TCGA Ss2, 16, 111 & 253–255 Schs A1 & 7A)

If your capital gains tax computation in respect of any disposal during the tax year produces a loss, such loss is normally deductible from any chargeable gains arising during the year. Any remaining surplus of losses is then available to be carried forward and set off against any future capital gains. For 1989–90 and previous tax years, any unrelieved losses were offset against gains of your spouse in the same year. Any surplus losses were then carried forward to offset against your respective gains.

'Qualifying loans' made to traders which later prove irrecoverable rank as capital losses, subject to the rules. However, after 19 March 1990, any amounts subsequently recovered are taxed.

Your net capital gains are reduced by losses brought forward down to the tax free amount of currently £8,500 (20.5) and any balance of the losses is carried forward (TCGA S3(5)).

In computing your capital losses note the special rules for assets owned at 6 April 1965 (20.17). Also note that losses may be reduced by 1982 re-basing (20.11). For disposals before 30 November 1993 but (apart from transitional relief) not subsequently, indexation allowance could both create and augment a loss (20.12).

The 1995 Finance Act (S100) introduced the necessity to claim capital gains tax loss relief, which can be done through your tax return. (A special section is included in the supplementary page dealing with capital gains.) You must claim your losses within five years and 10 months of the end of the year of assessment when they arose. (For companies, this period is 6 years from the end of the relevant accounting period.)

A new rule applies where you make a loss after 9 April 2003 on disposing of an unascertainable 'earn out' right to deferred consideration (20.18.6). Subject to certain conditions, you will be able to elect to take the loss back to the tax year of the original gain on the asset sale (FA 2003 S162).

Before computing taper relief (20.12) you must reduce your chargeable gains by losses for the same tax year and then losses carried forward. However, the set-off is in the order that produces the best result for you and only so as to reduce the untapered gain to the amount of your annual exemption. Thus losses would first be set against gains not eligible for taper and then against those with the least entitlement such as perhaps non-business assets.

20.13.1 **Relief for trading losses against capital gains** (FA 1991 S72 & FA 2002 S48)

For many years, companies have been able to set off trading losses against capital gains (13.15), but not vice versa. A similar relief operates from 1991–92 for individuals with losses from unincorporated businesses.

If you make a loss in your trade, profession or vocation and do not have enough income to cover it, you can elect for the unused losses for say 2005–06 to be set against your capital gains for that year. Any trading losses still unused would then be carried forward to 2006–07 and any not covered by your income for that year are available against 2006–07 capital gains. The relief does not cover 'hobby farming' and other businesses not carried out on a serious commercial basis.

Previously, the gains available to be relieved by trading losses were after taper relief. However, for 2004–05 and subsequent trading losses, the available gains are taken before taper relief and for 2002–03 and 2003–04, you have the right to elect for the new treatment to apply.

20.14 Losses on unquoted shares in trading companies (TA 1988 Ss573–576)

Beneficial rules apply to disposals of shares in 'qualifying trading companies'. Provided you were the original subscriber, you can elect to obtain income tax relief (11.22) for any loss on a fully priced arm's length sale, liquidation, etc.

For disposals in 1994–95 and subsequently, losses on unquoted shares in trading companies are available against your income of the current or preceding year. You must claim within 12 months from 31 January following the tax year of disposal.

A 'qualifying trading company' is broadly one which has always been UK resident but never quoted and has traded for at least six years, or from within a year of incorporation if less. The company is permitted to have stopped trading within the previous three years provided it has not become an investment company in the meantime. 'Trading' excludes dealing mainly in shares, land or commodity futures with retrospective effect, qualified trading companies now exclude building societies and registered industrial and provident societies. The relief applies to individuals and certain investment companies.

20.15 Assessment and payment of capital gains tax (TMA S29, TCGA Ss7, 48, 59B–59C & 279–281)

Assessments to capital gains tax were raised on the taxpayer concerned in respect of each tax year as soon thereafter as the Revenue obtained the necessary information. In the case of a company, however, its gains are included in its corporation tax assessment which is due for payment according to the special company rules (13.2).

Prior to 6 April 1990, in assessing the tax, the losses of one spouse could be deducted from the gains of another. Also, the wife's gains were assessed on the husband. Both of these rules ceased to have effect from 6 April 1990, with the introduction of independent taxation.

Your capital gains for 1996–97 and subsequent years comes within the new self-assessment rules (16.1). Your capital gains tax is then payable by 31 January following the tax year of the gains.

Your capital gains tax assessment for 1994–95 was due for payment on 1 December 1995 or 30 days after the assessment was issued, if later. A similar interval applied for 1995–96 gains and those for earlier years.

The date on which a capital gain arises is the actual date of sale or gift, etc. In the case of a transaction in which a sales contract is used such as the sale of shares or property it is the date of the contract which applies. It is not the completion date if this is different. Similar considerations apply to fixing the date of acquisition for capital gains tax purposes.

Certain gifts after 13 March 1989, for which gifts relief is not available (20.28) qualify for the payment of any capital gains tax by instalments. The assets concerned are land, unquoted shares and controlling holdings of quoted shares. Subject to making an election, the tax becomes payable by ten equal yearly instalments. If the instalments are paid on time, the tax on gifts of agricultural property will carry no interest, otherwise, interest runs from the normal date when the total liability would have been due.

Normally, even if the sales consideration is paid by instalments over a number of years the gain is assessed for the tax year in which the sale arises. If, however, you can satisfy the Revenue that you would otherwise suffer undue hardship, payment of the tax can be spread over the period of the instalments (maximum eight years).

20.16 Valuations (TCGA Ss272–274 & Sch 11)

It is necessary to value assets in various circumstances for capital gains tax purposes including gifts, transactions between connected persons, acquisitions on death and valuations at 6 April 1965. However, the most important date for valuations is 31 March 1982, for re-basing purposes (20.10).

The general rule for valuing assets for capital gains tax purposes is that you must take the 'market value' of the assets at the relevant time. 'Market value' means the price which the assets might reasonably be expected to fetch on a sale in the open market.

It is necessary to value only the assets actually being disposed of even though they form part of a larger whole. This is particularly important regarding the shares in a non-quoted company. Suppose you hold 90 per cent of the shares in such a company which are together worth £90,000. If you gift 10 per cent of the company's shares to your son you might assume that their value is £10,000. This would, however, probably not be true since your 90 per cent holding carried with it full control of the company whereas 10 per cent of the company's shares is a minority holding which would be normally worth considerably less than £10,000 in the circumstances mentioned. The true market valuation of the gifted 10 per cent holding might only be £1,000 depending on the profits of the company and dividends paid. Note that different valuation rules apply for inheritance tax purposes (22.12).

A revenue concession applies where you acquire shares on a no gain/no loss transfer from your spouse, who had held them at 31 March 1982. It also applies to transfers in similar circumstances between group companies. Two years' written notice is needed from the end of the year of assessment or accounting period of the disposal. The 31 March 1982 value will then be taken as a proportionate part of the value of the transferor's *entire* holding at that time. This applies to disposals after 15 March 1993 and assessments open at that time. If notice is not given, the shares may be valued at 31 March 1982 as if held by the *transferee*.

Unquoted share valuations must take account of all information which a prudent arm's-length purchaser would obtain.

Particular rules relate to the valuation of quoted securities such as shares and debenture stocks. (These apply in most cases, including 31 March 1982 valuations.) In this case you must normally take:

(1) the lower of the two prices shown in the Stock Exchange Official Daily List plus one-quarter of the difference between them, or
(2) halfway between the highest and lowest prices at which bargains (other than at special prices) were recorded in the shares or securities for the relevant day.

In valuing quoted shares at 6 April 1965, however, you must take the *higher* of:

(1) midway between the two prices shown in the Stock Exchange Official Daily List (that is, the middle market price), and
(2) halfway between the highest and lowest prices at which bargains (other than at special prices) were recorded in the shares or securities for 6 April 1965.

Apart from quoted shares other valuations will normally require to be agreed with the Revenue valuation officers such as the district valuers who are concerned with valuing land and buildings.

20.17 Relief on sales of assets owned on 6 April 1965 (TCGA Sch 2)

Although a short term capital gains tax operated from April 1962 until April 1971 when it was repealed, the present-day system of capital gains tax only operates regarding sales after 6 April 1965. Rules were, therefore, introduced with the purpose of relieving such part of your capital gains as can be related to the period before 7 April 1965. Following the introduction of 1982 re-basing (20.10) these rules are of far less importance since in most cases, a lower gain (or greater loss) will result from re-basing. However, a better result sometimes comes from applying the old rules and these are then used, unless you have elected for all of your assets to be valued as at 31 March 1982.

The general rule is that you assume that your asset increased in value at a uniform rate and you are relieved from capital gains tax on such proportion of the gain as arose on a time basis prior to 7 April 1965. This is known as the 'time apportionment' method. Thus if your total gain is G and you held an asset for A months prior to 6 April 1965 and B months after that date until the date of sale, your taxable chargeable gain is G x B/(A + B). (Any loss is similarly reduced). Your time apportionment benefit is limited to 20 years prior to 6 April 1965. Thus if you acquired an asset before 6 April 1945 you are treated as having acquired it on that date.

Where indexation relief is available, this must be applied before time apportionment. Thus the indexation benefit is reduced. This follows a case decision in the House of Lords in March 1993 (*Smith* v *Schofield*).

Instead of using 'time apportionment' you have the option of substituting for the cost of the asset its market value at 6 April 1965 (Sch 2(17)). In order to do this you must make an election to this effect to the Revenue within two years of the end of the tax year in which you make the disposal. (In the case of a company the election must be made within two years of the end of the accounting period in which the disposal is made.) It is very rare indeed that the market value of an asset at 6 April 1965 exceeds its value at 31 March 1982. Thus 6 April 1965 valuations are mainly relevant when you disposed of assets before 6 April 1988.

The rules do not allow you to increase a capital loss by means of a 6 April 1965 election. Also, if the effect of an election is to convert a gain into a loss, you are regarded as having no gain and no loss on the transaction.

Once you make an election it is irrevocable, even if it results in your paying more tax than on a 'time apportionment' basis. If you make an election, any indexation allowance to which you are entitled (20.11) is calculated on the 6 April 1965 value and not cost. This is now subject to your right to elect for indexation to be taken on the value at 31 March 1982 (20.10).

The 'time apportionment' basis *does not* apply to quoted shares and securities (20.18). Nor does it apply to land with development value when sold (or which has been materially developed after 17 December 1973). Such land is normally automatically dealt with on the 6 April 1965 valuation basis.

20.18 Quoted shares and securities (TCGA Ss104–117)

The following rules do not apply to *UK government securities* which are exempt from capital gains tax if sold (or otherwise disposed of), nor do they create allowable losses. However, any compensation stock received on a nationalisation after 6 April 1976 may give rise to a gain or loss on sale reflecting that on your original shares up to the date of issue of the compensation stock.

20.18.1 'Pooling' – pre-6 April 1998 acquisitions

All shares of the same company and class that you held prior to 6 April 1982 (1 April for companies) were put into a 'pool'. With the introduction of indexation allowance, however, pooling no longer applied to new purchases. However, pooling was reintroduced regarding share *disposals* after 5 April 1985 (20.18.3) for individuals and trusts, etc. (after 31 March 1985 for companies). You now are treated as having one pool of shares purchased after 5 April 1982 and another before that time.

Shares which you acquire after 5 April 1998 are no longer to be pooled (20.18.4). However, this does not apply to companies.

The 'pool' is considered indistinguishable regarding the various numbers of shares that it comprises. Thus if you bought 100 ordinary shares in A Limited on 1 May 1976 for £200 and another 200 ordinary shares in A Limited on 30 September 1980 for £1,000 your total pool cost is £1,200 (that is, £4 per share). If you then sell 100 shares they are not treated as being the original ones which you bought for £200; they are treated as coming from your 'pool' at the average pool cost of £4 per share giving a cost of £400.

However, where you introduce shares into a single company PEP (8.10) from a 'pool', you are able to identify the shares. This is to facilitate computing the gain on the remainder, when sold (FA 1993 S85).

'Pooling' does not apply to shares purchased on or before 6 April 1965 unless you elected for all your shares to be valued as at that date (20.18.8). In the absence of this election, you allocated any sales prior to 6 April 1982 first against your holdings at 6 April 1965 on a 'first in first out' basis. After these shares were eliminated you then went to the 'pool'.

Each separate purchase or sale of shares of the same company and class results in adjustments to the 'pool' except that if you bought and sold shares on the same day the respective sale and purchase are first matched against each other. Any surplus or deficit was then added to or deducted from your 'pool'. This rule ceased to apply for transactions from 6 April 1982 (1 April 1982 for companies – subject to a parallel pooling system), but was re-introduced from 6 April 1985.

20.18.2 **Identification – sales from 6 April 1982 to 5 April 1985** (FA 1982 Ss88 & 89 & Sch 13 & FA 1983 S34 & Sch 6)

If you disposed of quoted shares and securities between 5 April 1982 and 6 April 1985 special identification rules applied. Similarly, shares purchased between those dates were no longer pooled.

20.18.3 **Indexation and identification – sales from 6 April 1985 to 5 April 1998** (TCGA Ss104–114)

Revised rules apply to share disposals by individuals after 5 April 1985 and by companies after 31 March 1985. However, securities covered by the accrued income provisions to combat bond-washing (8.3) only came within the indexation and identification rules after 27 February 1986.

As previously mentioned indexation ran immediately (20.11). An exception was where you bought and then sold the same shares within 10 days; your transactions were matched and you obtained no indexation relief.

Under the revised rules, you kept separate pools of shares acquired after 5 April 1982 (and before 6 April 1998) and those obtained from 6 April 1965 to 5 April 1982. Furthermore, acquisitions prior to 6 April 1965 must be kept separately (20.18.1), unless there is a pooling election (20.18.8), in which case they are included in the 31 March 1982 pool.

If you sold shares after 5 April 1985 and before 6 April 1998, they are to be identified with your acquisitions of the same shares on a 'last in first out' basis. They are thus first identified with your post 5 April 1982 pool, then with your pre-6 April 1982 holdings and finally with your unpooled pre-6 April 1965 holdings. (For companies the pools run to and from 31 March 1982 and 1 April 1982.) If it produces a better result for you, disposals out of your pre-April 1982 and pre-April 1965 pools will be re-based (20.10), the market value at 31 March 1982 being taken.

From 19 March 1991, disposals of 'business start up scheme' (11.25) shares cannot be pooled with shares of the same type.

Indexation was calculated separately on the different parts. Holdings acquired before 1 April 1982 could be valued at 31 March 1982 for indexation purposes if you made the required election (20.11). By a concession dated 25 May 1989, the Revenue treat holdings of the same class held at 31 March 1982 as a single holding for re-basing and indexation. This applies whether the shares, etc. were bought before or after 6 April 1965. Subsequent acquisitions cannot be treated in that way.

Every additional purchase will carry indexation relief until sale. This is done on a pooled basis by adding indexation relief to the pool prior to each purchase or sale. The total indexation relief in the pool is then found by deducting the total cost and the relief on the sale is simply the proportion appropriate to the number of shares sold.

20.18.4 **Share identification – sales after 5 April 1998** (TCGA Ss104–110)

Pooling (20.18.1) ceased for share acquisitions after 5 April 1998 by individuals and trustees (but not by companies). New rules also apply for disposals after that date, which are to be identified with acquisitions in the following order:

(1) acquisitions on the same day
(2) acquisitions within the next 30 days (countering 'bed and breakfasting')
(3) previous post-5 April 1998 acquisitions on a 'last in first out' basis
(4) shares in the pool at 5 April 1998 (if any)
(5) any shares held at 5 April 1982
(6) shares acquired before 6 April 1965
(7) subsequent acquisitions (that is more than 30 days later).

Regarding a part disposal after 5 April 2002 of shares acquired on the same day after that date, some of which came from an employee share scheme, you can elect on the earliest disposal that shares with the smaller gain are disposed of first.

20.18.5 **Example: Share identification and indexation**

Mr A carried out the following share transactions in the ordinary shares of quoted company B Ltd:

	Date	Number	Cost or Proceeds £
Purchases	20.6.78	2,000	3,000
	10.5.80	1,000	2,000
	10.7.83	2,000	4,000
	10.9.84	4,000	11,000
Sale	20.4.2005	9,000	45,000

The value of B Ltd shares at 31 March 1982 was £1.80. Calculate Mr A's capital gain assuming the following (very approximate) indexation figures: ▶

March 1982 to April 1998	100%
July 1983 to September 1984	10%
September 1984 to April 1998	80%

(1) The shares sold are taken first out of the post 5 April 1982 pool:

	£
Cost of 2,000 shares 10.7.83	4,000
Indexation July 1983 to September 1984 10%	400
	4,400
Cost of 4,000 shares 10.9.84	11,000
	15,400
Indexation September 1984 to April 1998 80%	12,320
Cost and indexation for 6,000 shares	27,720
Proceeds of 6,000 shares	30,000
Capital gain on 6,000 shares from post-5 April 1982 pool	2,280

(2) The remaining shares sold are then identified against the pre-6 April 1982 pool:

	£
Cost of 3,000 shares (£1.67 each)	5,000
Re-based to £1.80 per share	5,400
Add indexation relief from March 1982 to April 1998 100%	5,400
	10,800
Proceeds of 3,000 shares	15,000
Capital gain on 3,000 shares	4,200

TOTAL GAIN 2005–06	£2,280 + £4,200	6,480
CAPITAL GAIN 2005–06 after taper relief (7 + 1 years) 70%		4,536

20.18.6 **Bonus issues, take-overs and company reorganisations** (TCGA Ss116, 117 & 126–140 & 251)

If you receive a free scrip (or bonus) issue of shares of the same class as those that you already hold, you must treat the additional shares as having been bought when your original shares were bought. Thus if you bought 100 shares in A Limited for £2 each in 1960 and you now receive a bonus issue of 100 shares you will have 200 shares at a cost of £1 each which are all treated as having been bought in 1960. Note, however, the special rules for scrip dividend options (8.9).

Your company may have a capital reorganisation, in the course of which you receive shares of a different class either instead of or in addition to your original shares. You are not normally charged to capital gains tax on any old shares in your company which you exchange for new ones. Any capital gains tax is only payable when you sell your new holding. The rules for reorganisations including bonus issues hold good under the 'indexation' system unless new consideration is given.

If you take up 'rights' to subscribe for additional shares in a company of which you are a shareholder, your rights shares are treated as having been acquired when your original shares were purchased and the cost of the rights shares is added to the original cost of your holding. If you sell your 'rights' on the market without taking up the shares this is considered to be a 'part disposal' of your holding and accordingly is charged to capital gains tax (20.21). If the proceeds are small (normally no more than 5 per cent) in relation to your holding, however, you can elect not to pay tax then but set off the proceeds against the original cost of your holding. Under the indexation rules (20.18.4), however, any new consideration (for rights shares, etc.) is treated effectively as a new acquisition so that indexation runs accordingly.

Anti-avoidance rules act to prevent you from obtaining capital gains tax loss relief artificially from reorganisations. Any increase in the capital gains tax acquisition value of shares which you obtain through the reorganisation is limited to the actual increase in value.

In the case of a take-over you may receive cash for your shares in which case this is taxed as an ordinary disposal. If, however, you receive shares or loan stock, etc. in the acquiring company, you will not normally be liable to pay capital gains tax until you actually sell your new shares or loan stock, subject to certain conditions and anti-avoidance laws (15.10). One of the conditions is that the acquiring company already held, or obtains as a result of the take-over over 25 per cent of the ordinary share capital of the other company.

If you receive qualifying corporate bonds (20.19) on the take-over of your shares, the above relief is modified. You are treated as disposing of your shares at that time, but your gain is deferred until you sell the bonds. From 16 March 1993, these rules extend to certain debentures which are not debts on security (and so previously may have escaped tax). Securities later becoming QCBs may also be covered (20.19(11)).

Sometimes, the consideration for the sale of a company might include an element which is deferred and unascertainable, perhaps related to future profits ('earn out rights'). Broadly, from 26 November 1996, a previous concessional treatment is legislated for. This concerns an 'earn out right' being treated as a security for capital gains tax purposes including deferment.

From 10 April 2003, treating 'earn out rights' as a security will apply automatically, subject to certain conditions and an election to disapply them (FA 2003 S161).

All of the above rules concerning bonus issues, take-overs and company reorganisations apply equally to unquoted shares (20.20).

20.18.7 **Investment trusts and unit trusts** (TCGA Ss99–103)

Special rules apply regarding all disposals both of shares owned *by* the trusts and of shares and units *in* the trusts by their shareholders and unit holders. Authorised unit and investment trusts are exempt from tax on their capital gains. However, any disposals which you make of units and investment trust shares carry full capital gains tax with no credit (subject to your £8,200 annual exemption).

From 20 March 1990, capital gains tax indexation does not apply to units in certain unit trusts and offshore funds. This mainly applies to gilt funds and sterling money funds, with at least 90 per cent invested in such funds or building society shares.

20.18.8 **Holdings at 6 April 1965** (TCGA Sch 2)

'Time apportionment' (20.17) does not apply to quoted shares. Instead you must consider the mid-market price at 6 April 1965 (20.16). Subject to the election described below, your gain on any sales after 6 April 1965 of shares held at that date is the difference between the proceeds and the higher cost of the shares and their value at 6 April 1965. Similarly any allowable capital loss on such share sales is the difference between the proceeds and the lower of the cost of the shares and their value at 6 April 1965. However, for disposals after 5 April 1988, 1982 re-basing (20.10) is likely to occur. As a result, the value at 31 March 1982 would be used.

If the price at which you sell the shares held at 6 April 1965 is between their value at that date and their cost then you are treated as having no gain and no loss for capital gains tax purposes (subject to the election described below). For indexation purposes, if the value at 6 April 1965 is used to compute a capital gain, then the allowance is calculated on that value (20.11). However, for disposals after 5 April 1985, you can elect for your indexation relief to be taken on the values at 31 March 1982 (20.11).

As regards disposals of quoted shares and securities which you held at 6 April 1965 you have the right to elect that any capital gains or losses on such disposals shall be calculated by substituting the 6 April 1965 values for the original costs in all cases. The election for each category is irrevocable, and has to be made within two years of the end of the tax year (or accounting year for a company) in which the first sale after 19 March 1968 is made (but see new rules below). Thus in most cases the election time limit will have expired by now. Full details are given in earlier editions of this book.

A further opportunity was introduced to allow you to elect to have pooled, quoted securities, which you acquired before 6 April 1965. The time limit is two years after the end of the year in which your first disposal occurs after 5

April 1985 (31 March 1985 for companies). The effect is that your various quoted securities become part of your respective pre-April 1982 share pools.

20.19 Exemption for corporate bonds (QCBs) (TCGA Ss115–117 & 132)

The exemption for capital gains tax for gilt edged securities (20.8.1) was extended to certain QCBs satisfying the following conditions:

(1) The bonds were acquired or issued after 13 March 1984.
(2) They are debentures, loan stocks or similar securities, not necessarily secured but 'debts on security'.
(3) They are normal commercial loans, expressed in and redeemable in sterling. Denomination in foreign currency is being allowed with the introduction of the FOREX scheme (13.25).
(4) At least some of the shares or debentures of the issuing company are quoted.
(5) The bonds are capable of being marketed but are not issued by a company to another company in the same group.
(6) Disposals after 1 July 1986 are exempt regardless of the time for which the bonds have been held. Similarly losses have ceased to be available. Prior to that date, normally exemption only applied if you held the securities for at least one year before disposal.
(7) If you sustain a loss on a QCB held on or issued after 14 March 1989, you will obtain relief where part or all of the loan is irrecoverable. However, this relief has been withdrawn regarding loans issued after 16 March 1998.
(8) Regarding disposals after 18 March 1991, bonds convertible into other QCBs are exempt. However, those convertible into shares or securities of the issuing company's quoted parent are not.
(9) From 29 November 1994, the QCB capital gains tax exemption no longer applies to certain indexed securities which are linked to an index of quoted share prices.
(10) Where shares are exchanged for a mixture of cash and QCBs, the cash is liable to capital gains tax but re-investment relief (20.25.2) is available on appropriate share purchases. This relief is also available where a held-over gain comes into charge on a QCB disposal.
(11) After 26 November 1996, the change of status of a security from a non-QCB to a QCB (and vice versa) is treated as a conversion of securities (20.18.6). This could give rise to a capital gains tax charge where the terms of a security change. FA 1999 (Ss59 & 60) expanded this to cover artificial options.

20.20 Unquoted shares (TCGA S273 & Sch 2)

Many of the above points regarding quoted shares and securities apply also to unquoted shares but the following special rules should be noted:

(1) Regarding holdings of shares at 6 April 1965 the 'time apportionment' rule normally applies to sales after that date subject to the right of election for valuation at 6 April 1965 (20.17). This is not a 'blanket' election for all your non-quoted shares as is the case for quoted shares. (For disposals after 5 April 1988, 1982 re-basing is likely to prevail – 20.10.)

(2) If after 6 April 1965 there is a capital reorganisation or take-over regarding a non-quoted company in which you have shares 'time apportionment' normally stops at that time and on any future sales you have a time apportioned gain or loss to the date of reorganisation or takeover and the full gain or loss after that time. This does not apply, however, in the case of a bonus issue of the same class of shares (20.18.6).

(3) If a reorganisation or takeover as in (2) above occurred before 6 April 1965 any shares still held at that date must automatically be valued at 6 April 1965 and the time apportionment does not apply. You still consider, however, the cost of your original holding when computing any capital gain or loss on a future sale.

(4) Prior to 6 April 1982 (1 April for companies) the 'pooling' rules (20.18.1) applied to shares acquired after 6 April 1965 but not to acquisitions before that time which must be separately considered on a 'first in first out' basis.

(5) The indexing and identification rules (20.18.4–7) apply to non-quoted shares as for quoted ones. The rule in (4) above regarding shares held at 6 April 1965 was modified, however, so that the 'last in first out' basis applied for disposals between 5 April 1982 and 6 April 1985.

(6) Any relief which you obtain against your income, for business expansion scheme investment (11.25) is not also available to create a capital loss. Thus if you eventually sell the shares at a profit, you will obtain full relief for the cost in calculating your capital gain, but not if you sell at a loss.

(7) Subject to the rules (20.25.2) rollover relief applied on reinvestment where qualifying shares in one company were sold after 15 March 1993 and qualifying shares in another were purchased before 6 April 1998.

20.21 Part disposals (TCGA Ss42 & 242–244 & Sch 3)

Where part of an asset is disposed of (including part of a 'pool' holding of shares in a particular company) it is necessary to compute the cost applicable to the part sold. This is normally done by multiplying the original cost by the fraction A/(A+B) where A is the consideration for the part disposed of and B is the market value of the remaining property at the date of the part disposal. If indexation applies (20.11), the cost apportionment formula is applied before computing the indexation allowance and the same applies for taper relief (20.12). No indexation is calculated on the costs attributable to the undisposed of part (until that is sold).

For part disposals after 5 April 1988, the fraction A/(A + B) is applied to the value at 31 March 1982 if more than the cost. If a part disposal has already taken place between 31 March 1982 and 6 April 1988, the gain on a further disposal after 5 April 1988 must be computed on the basis that 1982 re-basing applied to the earlier part disposal.

A special rule applies to small part disposals of land (only a small part of the whole being sold, etc.). Provided that such proceeds during the tax year do not exceed £20,000, you may deduct the proceeds from your base cost rather than pay tax now. For disposals after 5 April 1986, this rule applies where the proceeds do not exceed ⅕ of the total market value of the land.

20.22 A series of disposals (TCGA Ss19 & 20)

Before 20 March 1985, if you acquired a series of assets (shares, etc.) from one or more people connected (20.9) with you, all of the assets were valued together to find the relevant proceeds and your acquisition figure. After 19 March 1985, however, the rule operates only from the viewpoint of a person splitting up an asset or collection of assets by two or more transactions to connected persons. The transactions must be within a total period of six years.

20.23 Private residences (TCGA Ss222–226)

The house or flat where you live is normally exempt from capital gains tax when you sell it, subject to the following rules:

(1) The house must have been your only or main residence during the time that you owned it subject to various allowable periods of absence (see below). You ignore all periods before 6 April 1965 for these purposes.

(2) You are allowed to be absent from the house which is your main residence for the following maximum periods without losing your exemption:
   (a) The last 36 months of ownership. For disposals before 19 March 1991, this period was 24 months.
   (b) Periods of absence totalling three years.
   (c) Any period throughout which you worked abroad.
   (d) Any periods up to four years in aggregate when you are prevented from living in your house due to your employment being elsewhere.
   (e) Any period during which you live in job-related accommodation, but intend to return to your main residence.

   Provided you have no other residence which you claim to be exempt during the above periods they are taken cumulatively and so you could have a long period of absence and still not lose your exemption. You must, however, return to your main residence at the end of periods (b), (c) and (d) above or else you will lose part of your relief.

(3) Any periods of absence subsequent to 31 March 1982 in excess of the periods allowed (see above) result in the relevant proportion of your sale profit being charged to capital gains tax. (For disposals before 6 April 1988, all periods of absence after 6 April 1965 must be considered.) For example, if you bought your house in June 1996 and sold it in June 2005 at a profit of £8,000 having lived elsewhere for reasons unconnected with your employment for the middle six years, your chargeable gain is £8,000 × ⅛ = £1,000. (You are only allowed three years of absence and the last three in any event, leaving one year taxable.)

(4) If a specific part of your house is set aside for business purposes then that proportion of your profits on sale of the house will be taxable. Thus if you have eight rooms of which two are wholly used for business purposes you would normally claim 25 per cent of your house expenses against your business profits and when you sell your house you will pay capital gains tax on 25 per cent of your total gain (arising after 6 April 1965). If, however, you use no rooms exclusively for business purposes you will not normally be liable for any capital gains tax if you sell your house even though you claim part of your house expenses against your business profits.

(5) If you dispose of your main residence and part has been let for residential purposes, you obtain some exemption for the let portion. This is not to exceed the exemption on the part occupied by you, or £40,000 if smaller (£20,000 before 19 March 1991). Note that you will be exempt for the periods mentioned in 2(a)–(e) in any event.

(6) If you have two residences you can give written notice to the Revenue within two years as to which of the two should be treated as your main private residence and thereby be exempted from capital gains tax. The election should be given within two years of acquiring your second residence. If you do not elect then the Revenue will decide in the light of the time that you spend at each of your residences which of these is your main private residence.

(7) For the purposes of the exemption, your main residence is taken to include land of up to half of a hectare (including the site of the house). If the house is large and its character requires a larger garden, this is likely to be allowed. Note that the exemption covers the disposal of part of your main residence; for example a strip of your garden. However, take care not to sell the house before the garden, since this would not then be part of your main residence.

(8) For disposals after 9 December 2003 by an individual or settlement, private residence relief is not generally available where, in computing the gain, account must be taken of gifts relief in respect of an earlier disposal.

Previously, you also obtained capital gains tax exemption on no more than one residence owned by you and occupied by a dependent relative, rent-free and without any other consideration. Relief was withdrawn for disposals after 5 April 1988 unless the dependent relative had remained in occupation from an earlier date (TCGA S226).

20.24 Chattels sold for £6,000 or less (TCGA S262)

A chattel is an asset which is tangible movable property such as a chair, a picture, or a pair of candlesticks. For these purposes a set is treated as one chattel. If you dispose of a chattel for no more than £6,000 you pay no capital gains tax and if your proceeds exceed £6,000 your capital gain is restricted to ⅝ of the excess. Thus if you sell a set of antique chairs for £6,300 (original cost £500) your capital gain is restricted to ⅝ × (£6,300 – £6,000) = £500.

If you bought a chattel for more than £6,000, and sold it for less than £6,000, your allowable loss is restricted to the excess of the cost over £6,000.

20.25 Replacement of business assets – rollover relief (TCGA Ss152–160 etc.)

You are liable for capital gains tax in respect of any sales of assets used in your business. Similarly a company is liable on any sales of its business assets. If further business assets are purchased within one year preceding and three years after the sale, 'rollover' relief is obtained as a result of which the gain on the disposal is deducted from the cost of the new business assets. Thus, the gain is 'rolled over' and no tax is paid until the new business assets are sold, unless the latter are in turn replaced. (Note the special 50 per cent reduction for certain rolled-over pre-31 March 1982 gains – 20.10.)

To obtain rollover relief, both your old and new assets must be 'qualifying'. This implies being within the following classes:

(1) (a) Land and buildings (but not trading stock).
    (b) Fixed plant and machinery not forming part of a building.
(2) Ships, aircraft and hovercraft.
(3) Goodwill.
(4) Satellites, space stations and spacecraft, etc.
(5) Milk and potato quotas.
(6) Ewe and suckler cow premium quotas.

Note, however, that regarding plant and machinery, rollover relief is only available if it is fixed and so, for example, motor vans and fork lift trucks do not qualify.

To get the relief you must use the old and new assets in the same business. However, if you carry on several trades, they are treated as one for this purpose. (Relief is still available if you cease one trade and start another.) Also, rollover relief applies regarding purchases and sales by you of personally owned assets used in your 'family company' (20.29).

If you are non-resident and replace a business asset chargeable to UK tax with one which is not, rollover relief is generally no longer available. This covers the situation where you sell an asset used in your business in the UK and buy one overseas.

Note that to obtain total relief, the entire proceeds must be invested, otherwise you pay tax on your capital gain up to the extent of the shortfall.

If the new business asset is a wasting asset (20.29.2) it must be replaced by a non-wasting asset within ten years. Otherwise the rolled-over gain becomes chargeable. This also applies to assets which will become 'wasting' within ten years, such as a lease with 59 years to run. However, this clawback does not apply to a held-over gain arising before 31 March 1982 and becoming chargeable after 5 April 1988 (TCGA Sch 4).

'Rollover' relief is applicable to companies (13.16). Also a special extension of the rules covers 'gilts' obtained by companies in exchange for group companies in the aircraft and shipping industries on compulsory acquisition through nationalisation. An election is required within four years of the exchange and then the normal new compensation stock rules do not apply.

Dual-resident companies obtain no rollover relief where they replace a UK business asset with one overseas. Also rollover relief is denied where the replacement asset is outside the UK tax charge and is acquired by a dual resident group member (15.10.15).

To fit in with the new self-assessment rules, provisional rollover relief claims will be allowed, including on compulsory purchase (20.25.1). You will need to declare in your tax return that you intend to re-invest the proceeds in qualifying assets and will lose your relief unless you reinvest within 3 years of the disposal.

20.25.1 **Rollover relief on compulsory purchase** (TCGA Ss247 & 248)

A form of rollover relief, similar to that available on business assets (20.25) applies to certain land which is sold to local authorities. The property must either be compulsorily bought from you or the purchasing local authority must have compulsory acquisition powers. The relief is available if your replacement property is business or non-business land but not if it qualifies for main residence relief (20.23).

20.25.2 **Rollover relief on reinvestment** (TCGA Ss164A–164N)

An important extension to rollover relief (20.25) applied regarding the disposal of certain shares in unquoted trading companies after 15 March 1993. You needed to have owned at least 5 per cent of the voting shares (making it your 'personal company') and broadly qualify for retirement relief (apart from the age requirement) (20.29).

The relief extended to any assets of which you disposed. Also, your new investment could be in any number of ordinary shares in the 'qualifying company' before 6 April 1998. Note:

(1) The shares purchased needed to be in 'qualifying' companies. These had to carry on 'qualifying trades' and not be controlled by another company etc., whilst any subsidiaries had to be directly owned and trading.
(2) From 27 November 1996, relief was available for purchases of shares in a holding company with non-UK subsidiaries provided the trades were carried on wholly or mainly in the UK. Eligibility for relief depended on the group activities as a whole.
(3) Where there was a share for share exchange, you could elect that this was a disposal so that the new relief took effect.
(4) The definition of 'qualifying trades' was similar to that for EIS companies (11.26), with some changes.
(5) Your replacement expenditure was first allocated to your gain. Thus your relief was the lower of your gain and the cost of the new asset. However, you could claim a lower amount of relief.
(6) The relief needed to be claimed, but is lost if you emigrate, sell the new shares without qualifying replacement, or if within three years of your share purchase the new company's trade ceases to qualify.
(7) Rollover relief was withdrawn for re-investment in shares after 5 April 1998, but improved EIS relief is available (11.26).

20.25.3 **Re-investment into EIS and VCT units**

Subject to the rules, a type of reinvestment relief is available where you subscribe for EIS (11.26) and VCT (8.12) units. You could defer capital gains on other assets by investing up to £150,000 in EIS shares and up to £100,000 in VCT shares each tax year. However, for 2004–05 the EIS limit became £200,000 and the VCT deferal facility was withdrawn.

For EIS relief, the capital gains must arise no earlier than 29 November 1994 and the EIS shares purchased within one year before and three years after the disposals. With VCT reinvestment, gains must be after 5 April 1995 and the VCT units purchased within one year before and one year afterwards, but no later than 5 April 2004.

20.25.4 **Rollover on transfer of business to a company** (TCGA S162 & 162A)

If you carry out a business and incorporate it, you may be entitled to automatic rollover relief, related to the proportion of the consideration which you take in shares. However, for business transfers after 5 April 2002, you are able to elect that the rollover does not apply, which might increase taper relief. This opt-out election rule also applies where trustees incorporate a business which they carried on.

20.26 Gifts of business assets

A form of 'hold-over' relief applied to certain transfers of assets, other than bargains at arm's length, made after 11 April 1978. The assets covered were any used in your trade or 'family company' (20.29); also shares in such a company. A claim was required from both parties, similar in effect to that for general gifts (next page).

A more general relief applied for individuals after 5 April 1980 and for settlements after 5 April 1981 (next page). The old relief still applied for gifts to companies. From 14 March 1989, the old rules for gifts of business assets were expanded (20.28), following the cancellation of the general relief for gifts (20.27).

20.27 General relief for gifts

In general, transfers of assets which you made after 5 April 1980 and before 14 March 1989, other than bargains at arm's length, were covered by comprehensive 'hold-over' rules. Only UK resident or ordinarily resident individuals (17.3.1) were covered up to 5 April 1981 but after that date, gifts *to* UK trusts were included. From 6 April 1982 gifts *from* trusts were also included. There was a special 50 per cent reduction for certain held-over pre-31 March 1982 gains (20.10).

The general gifts relief rules were cancelled regarding gifts made after 13 March 1989. The business asset gifts provisions were expanded from that date (20.28).

20.28 Gifts relief from 14 March 1989 (TCGA Ss165–169 & 260 & Sch 7 & FA 2000 S90)

With the removal of general gifts relief from 14 March 1989, the business gifts relief (20.26) was expanded so that it now includes other items. The scope is now:

(1) Business assets used in a trade, profession or vocation carried on by the giver or his family company, etc.
(2) Certain agricultural property (normally where the giver has vacant possession).
(3) Shares and securities in family trading companies or non-quoted trading companies. (These categories include the holding companies of trading groups.)
(4) Gifts of heritage property and to maintenance funds.
(5) Gifts to political parties which qualify for inheritance tax exemption.
(6) Gifts which give rise to an immediate charge to inheritance tax, for example, into (or out of) a discretionary settlement (22.30.2). Potentially exempt transfers (22.3) do not qualify for this relief. However, if a gift is

covered by the nil rate band and exemptions for inheritance tax but would otherwise be taxed, the gifts election is available.

(7) Distributions of capital from accumulation and maintenance settlements may also qualify for the election. However, the beneficiary must not obtain the capital later than the income entitlement.

(8) Subject to an election by donor and recipient, gifts to a housing association (TCGA S259).

(9) Certain assets not mentioned above, which are not eligible for gifts relief may qualify for the tax on disposal to be paid by instalments (20.15).

(10) The relief is only available if the donee is UK resident and/or ordinarily resident.

(11) Should you receive some consideration the claim covers only the gift element, if this is less than your total gain. If you are entitled to retirement relief (below) this reduces the held-over gain.

(12) If you received a gift and made the election, then the held-over gain may be assessed on you, should you become neither resident nor ordinarily resident in the UK before having disposed of the asset. However, this only applies if emigration is within six years of the end of the year of assessment of the gift.

(13) From 9 November 1999, the relief is not available on transfers of shares or securities to companies.

(14) Gifts relief is generally denied regarding disposals to settlor-interested trusts after 9 December 2003. (Such a trust is one for which you both provided settled property and have an interest).

20.29 Business retirement relief (TCGA Ss163–165 & Sch 6)

If you were over 50 and disposed by gift or sale of the whole or part of a business which you had owned for the past ten years, you were exempted from capital gains tax on the first £250,000 of any gain arising before 6 April 1999 in respect of the 'chargeable business assets' of the business. However, the relief has been phased out after 5 April 1999 (20.29.1). If you had several businesses your total relief was restricted to £250,000.

Note that you did not actually need to retire to obtain the relief. 'Chargeable business assets' included assets used for the trade, etc. of the business, and also goodwill but not assets held as investments.

For disposals after 5 April 1988, not only was the first tranche of gains exempted from capital gains tax; the second tranche was given 50 per cent relief. For 2002–03, the second tranche was £150,000.

You were also able to obtain relief if you retired younger than the required age (50, etc.) for reasons of ill-health. You had to show that you were likely to remain incapable of performing your previous work and would require a medical certificate. You must claim relief in this case and this must be done not later than two years after the tax year of your disposal.

For share disposals after 15 March 1993, a ‘personal company’ was necessary. It was simply necessary to own five per cent of the voting shares. Also from that time, the relief extends to any ‘full-time working officer or employee’.

Only the proportion of the gain on the shares attributable to the ‘chargeable business assets’ of the company compared with its total chargeable assets qualified for the relief. Note that shares in subsidiary companies were regarded as ‘chargeable business assets’.

Reduced relief was available concerning disposals of the whole or part of a business which you have owned for less than ten years. You obtained 10 per cent of the full relief if you owned the assets for at least one year prior to disposal, 20 per cent relief for at least two years of ownership and so on.

If your wife complied with the requirements, she too was eligible for the relief if she sold her business or shares in a ‘family company’.

The relief also covered disposals by a settlement of assets used by a beneficiary for his own or his family company’s business. Also shares in a family trading or holding company were covered. The beneficiary must have had an interest in possession in the settlement, withdrawn from the business and retired.

From 1999–2000 onwards, capital gains tax retirement relief was withdrawn as follows:

20.29.1 **Withdrawal of retirement relief**

Year	100% relief on gains up to: £	50% relief on gains between: £	£
1998–99	250,000	250,001	1,000,000
1999–2000	200,000	200,001	800,000
2000–2001	150,000	150,001	600,000
2001–2002	100,000	100,001	400,000
2002–2003	50,000	50,001	200,000
2003–2004	nil	nil	nil

20.30 Charities (TCGA Ss256 & 257)

Charities are exempted from capital gains tax in respect of any gains on the disposal of assets provided that such gains are applied to charitable purposes.

If you make a gift of an asset to a charity you pay no capital gains tax on this disposal. If the gifts are of qualifying investments, you also obtain income tax relief (15.2.1).

20.31 Leases and other wasting assets (TCGA Ss45, 240 & Sch 8)

A 'wasting asset' is defined as an asset with a predictable life not exceeding 50 years, not including freehold land and buildings, etc. Leases with no more than 50 years still to run are a special kind of wasting asset and are separately treated for capital gains tax (see below).

'Wasting assets' which are also movable property (chattels) are normally exempted from capital gains tax. In the case of other wasting assets apart from leases, you must reduce their original costs on a straight line time basis over the respective lives of the assets. Thus if you buy a wasting asset for £10,000 with an unexpired life of 40 years and sell it after 20 years for £20,000, assuming the residual value after 40 years would have been nil, your allowable cost is £10,000 × $^{20}/_{40}$ = £5,000; thus your chargeable gain is £20,000 – £5,000 = £15,000.

In the case of a lease with no more than 50 years of its original term unexpired (including leases for shorter terms) the original cost must be written off according to a special formula under which the rate of wastage accelerates as the end of the term of the lease is reached. If you sell such an interest in property and lease back the premises at a lower rent for less than 15 years, you may be taxed on all or part of the proceeds either as a trading receipt or other income (prior to 2005–06 under Schedule D Case VI) (19.1.2).

From 6 April 1996, capital sums paid to a landlord for varying, waiving or surrendering a lease, or commuting the rent are taken into account in the year when payable. Previously they were related to the year when the lease was first granted.

20.32 Traded options (TCGA Ss115, 143, 144A, 148 & 271)

Options to buy or sell quoted shares are dealt with on the Stock Exchange. They are not treated as wasting assets, which means that the entire cost is deductible on sale. The abandonment of a traded option is treated as a disposal so that its cost is an allowable loss. This treatment extends to all traded options quoted on the London International Financial Futures Exchange and recognised stock exchanges.

Transactions in futures and options in gilts and qualifying bonds are exempt from capital gains tax. A further rule provides that if you write a traded option and later extinguish this obligation by buying another option, the cost is allowable against the original sale. From 30 November 1994, it is made clear that where options are settled in cash, such expenditure is fully allowable.

20.33 Commodity and financial futures (TCGA Ss72, 143 & 271)

Profits from futures which are not part of a trade less losses which you realise are normally covered by capital gains tax and not income tax. This rule applies to commodity futures or financial futures dealt in on a recognised futures exchange.

There is broadly similar capital gains tax treatment for commodity and financial futures and qualifying options (20.32), which are dealt in 'over-the-counter'. Income and gains from futures and options are exempt from tax in authorised unit trusts and pension schemes. From 30 November 1994, where financial and commodity futures are settled in cash, full relief is given for this expenditure.

20.34 Overseas aspects (TCGA Ss9–14, 25, 80–98, 140, 159–160, 185–188, 275–279 & Sch 5)

As already mentioned (20.3) provided you are resident and/or ordinarily resident in this country (or your non-residence is only temporary (20.3.1)), you are liable to tax on capital gains anywhere in the world. An exception is where assets are realised in a country which will not allow the proceeds to be remitted to the UK. You can then claim that your gain is deferred until the year when it becomes possible to remit the proceeds. If you are non-domiciled in the UK, you are only liable to capital gains tax on overseas gains to the extent that they are remitted here (18.1).

Non-residents carrying on a trade in the UK through a branch or agency are liable to capital gains tax on assets used in the business. This also covers professions and vocations; however, assets are re-based to their values at that date. Furthermore from that date deemed disposals may take place for capital gains tax purposes. This happens if the assets are moved out of the UK or the trade, etc. ceases.

If you are UK domiciled, the Revenue have powers to apportion to you the capital gains of certain overseas trusts from which you benefit (21.9) and companies. This extends to overseas companies owned by foreign trusts. Regarding overseas companies, relaxations applying from 7 March 2001 include exemption if your interest is no more than 10 per cent.

The *market value* rule (20.9) applies in general to gifts and other dispositions of overseas assets for less than full consideration involving neither resident nor ordinarily resident persons (FA 1984 S66).

Where a company is being 'exported' (17.3.3), there is a deemed disposal of all of its assets at market value for capital gains tax purposes. This broadly applies to companies migrating after 14 March 1988, from which time only those incorporated outside the UK are able to become non-resident. Furthermore, rollover relief (20.25.1) does not apply where assets are sold before and replaced after migration. If a company which migrates continues to trade in the UK through a branch or agency, any connected assets will be exempted from the deemed disposal.

If a foreign registered 75 per cent subsidiary of a UK company migrates, tax on the capital gains attributable to its foreign assets can be deferred. Parent and subsidiary must make a joint election and the tax becomes payable if any of the foreign assets are sold or if the parent–subsidiary relationship ceases.

If a dual-resident company owns an asset which ceases to be within the UK capital gains tax charge through a double tax agreement, it is deemed to have disposed of the asset. Thus a capital gain may result. Also, for disposals after that date by a non-resident company, tax on the capital gains can be collected from other companies in the same group or from controlling directors. This applies if the original company does not pay within six months of the due date.

If you are a UK resident investor in an offshore 'umbrella fund' you will be subjected to a capital gains tax charge when you switch holdings.

Non-resident companies may transfer their UK branch or agency business to UK resident companies without any immediate capital gains tax charge. This hold-over relief applies if the companies are in the same world-wide group.

Sweeping changes operate from 19 March 1991 regarding the capital gains tax rules for overseas trusts and the rules are now being extended to earlier settlements. These are considered later (21.9.1) as are subsequent changes (21.9.2).

With effect from 1 January 1992, various relieving provisions came into effect regarding cross-border reorganisations of businesses within the EC. As a result, capital gains tax may be deferred where there is a share exchange and on transfers of UK and non-UK trades, subject to the rules. For a share exchange, voting control must be acquired for shares with not more than 10 per cent of the nominal value in cash. Regarding a UK trade, this must be transferred from a company situated in one EC country to one situated in another, in exchange for securities.

The FOREX legislation (13.25) (now being absorbed into the loan relationships legislation – 13.27) came into force for the accounting periods of companies beginning after 22 March 1995. One result is that capital gains tax will no longer be charged on monetary assets in foreign currency. Legislation has been introduced for asset disposals from 1 January 1995, to block saving tax from the new rules coupled with no gain/no loss transfers (FA 1995 S131).

Chapter 21

THE TAXATION OF TRUSTS AND ESTATES

21.1 Trusts

A trust is brought into existence when a person (the settlor) transfers assets to trustees for the benefit of third parties (the beneficiaries). Another word for a trust is a settlement. A trust may also be created under a will when a person (the testator) sets aside the whole or a portion of his estate to be administered (by trustees) for the benefit of his heirs or other beneficiaries. (Where an individual declares himself to be a trustee of certain of his assets a trust will also come into existence.)

21.2 Trusts – new tax system

For 2004–05 and subsequent years, the tax rates applying to various trusts, including discretionary and accumulation ones, are a 40 per cent 'rate applicable to trusts' and a 'dividend rate' of 32.5 per cent. From 2005–06, the first £500 of the income of such trusts will be charged only at the income tax rate appropriate to that slice of income and if tax was deducted at source, no more might be payable. For example, suppose that for 2005–06, a trust chargeable at the special trust rates receives (1) £200 income from property, (2) £250 building society interest (less £50 tax deduction) and (3) £270 dividend income, on which the non-repayable tax credit is £30. The tax payable is:

	£		£	
(1)	200	at 22%	44.00	
(2)	250	at 20%	50.00*	
(3)	50	at 10%	5.00*	
	250	at 32.5%	81.25	£180.25
* Deducted at source or covered by tax credit				£ 55.00
Net amount payable				£125.25

Capital gains tax is charged on any capital gains of the trust (21.6).

Retrospectively to 6 April 2004, certain trusts with 'vulnerable beneficiaries' (21.2.2) can elect that the trust's tax is no more than it would have been, had the income and gains gone directly to such beneficiaries.

The tax assessments etc. are normally made in the joint names of the trustees who pay the tax out of the trust funds.

Any income distributed to beneficiaries is added to their total income for tax purposes (5.2) The income distributions are normally treated as being net of income tax at the appropriate rate(s). Thus they carry a corresponding tax credit. In the case of discretionary trusts, etc. (21.3.4) tax must be paid by the trustees to bring the tax credit up to 40 per cent. (Special rules apply to dividends from 6

April 1999 – 21.2.1.) The trustees should issue with each payment a form R185E which sets out the amount paid and the relevant tax credit. They will then account for the 40 per cent on the distributions after setting off any tax suffered, including that on the first £500.

21.2.1 **Dividend income of trusts** (FA 1993 Ss77–79 & Sch 6)

The following rules apply for dividend income after 5 April 1993, whether or not the settlor is living. If you have an 'interest in possession' in the trust, so that for example you receive the income as of right, the trustees receive tax credits of 10 per cent (20 per cent before 6 April 1999) and are charged no further tax on the dividends. When these are distributed to you, the net income carries with it a tax credit of 10 per cent (20 per cent before 6 April 1999). This treatment normally extends to Scottish interest-in-possession trusts with UK resident trustees.

If the trust had other income as well as dividends, this carried a credit of 25 per cent. Distributions to you were regarded as coming first out of the other income carrying 25 per cent tax credit and then out of dividend income, with a 20 per cent credit. However, with effect from 6 April 1996, a tax credit rate of 20 per cent applied to most savings income (2.2).

The trustees of accumulation and maintenance (21.4) and discretionary settlements (21.5) normally pay the 'rate applicable to trusts' on their income of 40 per cent from 2004–05 (previously 34 per cent). There is a special rate of 32.5 per cent on dividend income from 6 April 2004 (25 per cent for the five prior years). This is to take account of the notional tax credits on the dividends. As a beneficiary you have a 40 per cent tax credit (34 per cent before 6 April 2004) on any income distributions.

21.2.2 **Trusts with vulnerable beneficiaries** (FA 2005 Ss23–45 & Sch 1)

(1) From 2004–05 tax relief is available for 'qualifying trusts' with vulnerable beneficiaries.
(2) Particularly covered are trusts for disabled persons (mentally or physically) and children who have lost a parent.
(3) To obtain tax relief, all trustees and the relevant vulnerable beneficiary must so elect by the next 31 January but one after the relevant tax year. Thus for 2004–05, election is needed by 31 January 2007.
(4) Income tax relief will operate by bringing the trust's liability into line with that of the beneficiary, calculated as if the latter had received the income direct and taking account of personal relief and lower tax rates.
(5) Capital gains tax will be charged directly on UK-resident vulnerable beneficiaries where the trustees are UK-resident or ordinarily resident. However, if the beneficiary is non-resident, the trustees will account for the tax, computed as if the gain arose to the former. (The new regime does not cover gains of the trustees if they are not UK-resident or ordinarily resident.

21.3 Trusts where the settlor is still living (TA 1988 Ss660–685)

The taxation of trusts where the settlor is still living follows the general rules outlined above except that in certain circumstances the settlor himself is assessed to tax on the income of the trust. In order to avoid such assessment various rules should be observed including the following.

From 6 April 1995, new and simplified rules apply which broadly have the same effect as the previous ones. However, material changes were proposed regarding the taxation of capital sums paid to the settlor (21.3.6), particularly concerning loans between him or her and the settlement. After widespread objections this part of the new legislation was withdrawn but is expected to reappear in modified form in the future. Meanwhile the original rules apply.

21.3.1 **Period** (TA 1988 S660)

The settlement must be set up for a period which is capable of exceeding six years.

21.3.2 **The settlor must not have an interest** (TA 1988 Ss673, 677 & 683)

In the event that the settlor has retained an interest in the income or assets of the trust, he will be assessed to income tax on the income of the settlement to the extent that it remains undistributed. (The settlor has retained an interest in the trust if he or his wife can obtain some benefit from it.) Furthermore, if the income is distributed to others, subject to certain exceptions, the settlor and not the recipient will be charged to the excess of higher rate tax over the income tax on the distribution. For trusts made after 13 March 1989, in which the settlor retains an interest, with some exceptions, he or she is taxed on all of the income at the basic and higher rates. (This applies to the income from existing settlements arising from 6 April 1990.)

For 1990–91 and subsequent years, simple outright gifts and pension allocations between husband and wife are not to be treated as settlements for the purposes of these rules. However, this does not apply to gifts of property which do not carry a right to all of the income or where a right to income alone is given.

21.3.3 **The settlement must be irrevocable** (TA 1988 Ss671 & 672)

If the settlor or his wife has power to revoke the settlement or partially revoke it, he is assessed to income tax on its income.

21.3.4 **Discretionary settlements** (TA 1988 S674)

Discretionary settlements are those under which the application of the income and/or capital of the trust is left to the discretion of the trustees. Under such a trust the settlor or his wife must not be able to benefit from the income, or else he will be assessed to income tax on that income, whether or not any of it is actually paid to him. This does not apply if only the widow or widower of the settlor may benefit.

21.3.5 **Settlements for benefit of own children** (TA 1988 Ss600B, 660B, 663–670 & FA 1999 S64)

Under a trust created by the settlor, his own unmarried minor children (under 18 years of age) must not receive any income nor must it be used for their upkeep or education. Otherwise the settlor will be assessed to income tax on such income. This does not apply to income which is accumulated, however (see 21.4) nor to income not exceeding £100 per child each tax year.

The above rules are extended to any bare trust which you set up after 8 March 1999, for your unmarried minor children, so that they are entitled to the income and capital. Additions to existing settlements are also caught. You will be taxed on the income whether it is accumulated or paid for the benefit of your children.

21.3.6 **Capital sums paid to the settlor** (TA 1988 S677)

Where 'capital sums' from a settlement (including loans and loan repayments) are paid to the settlor, he is assessable to income tax. The assessments are limited to the undistributed trust income and the balance is carried forward for matching against future income. The carry forward period is limited to 11 years from the 'capital sum' payment and no income is assessable for any period subsequent to the repayment by the settlor of a loan from the settlement.

The rules extend to companies connected with the settlement (normally where the trustees are participators and the company is close – 13.17). A 'capital payment' from the company to the settlor gives rise to the assessment of trust income on him or her, if there is an associated capital payment or asset transfer within five years from the trust to the company.

Note: In all of the above cases there are rules to prevent the double taxation of the trust income so it will not be assessed both on the settlor and the beneficiaries. Usually, 20 per cent income tax is paid by the trust or it has already been deducted at the source as in the case of, for example, interest on government securities. Dividends received by the trust carry with them tax credits which are effectively transferred to beneficiaries who are given income distributions. Also, if the trust is subject to additional rate correspondingly higher tax credits attach to income distributions to beneficiaries (21.5).

21.4 Accumulation settlements for the benefit of the settlor's children

If you wish to create a trust for the benefit of your minor (unmarried) children without being assessed to income tax on its income (see above) this can be done by means of an accumulation settlement. The income of the settlement should be accumulated for each child until at least the age of 18 and no payments should be made for their benefit until that age. (The trust deed normally states that the trustees are empowered to accumulate income.) If it is wished to distribute income to adult beneficiaries this can be done, but the income shares of the settlor's minor children must be accumulated, or else the settlor is liable to higher rate income tax on such income.

21.5 Income of discretionary trusts etc. (TA 1988 Ss686–687, 809, FA 1993 Sch 6, FA 1995 S86 & FA 2005 Ss14, 23–29 & 34–45)

The trustees normally pay on their income the 'rate applicable to trusts' of 40 per cent from 2004–05 (34 per cent for the previous five years). There is a special rate of 32.5 per cent on dividend income from 6 April 2004 (25 per cent for the five prior years). This is to take account of the notional tax credits on the dividends. From 2005–06, the first £500 of income is chargeable at lower rates (21.2). Trusts with vulnerable beneficiaries have relief from 2004–05 (21.2.2).

The position from 6 April 1993 to 5 April 1996 was broadly similar in effect. The settlement bore income tax of 35 per cent but obtained tax credits of 20 per cent on its dividend income and 25 per cent on other income where suffered. Trust management expenses gave rise to relief at 15 per cent (35–20) if they were allocated to dividends and 10 per cent (35–25) otherwise. The expenses were first to be allocated to dividend income. The position for 1996–97, 1997–98 and 1998–99 was that the full tax rate was 34 per cent, leaving 14 per cent to pay after allowing for 20 per cent tax credit relief.

The above applies to trusts where the income is accumulated or is payable at the discretion of the trustees but not where the income is treated for tax purposes as being that of the settlor; nor where a person is absolutely entitled to the income.

Where income distributions are made to beneficiaries, the amounts received by the latter are treated as being net of tax at 40 per cent from 2004–05 (previously 34 per cent). The recipients can reclaim part or all of this tax if their incomes are low enough. For example, if for 2004–05 a discretionary trust pays £600 to your child (or for his maintenance) and he or she has no other income, there is a tax credit of £600 × $^{40}/_{60}$ = £400 which is all reclaimable.

From 6 April 1999 the trustees do not receive credit for the 10 per cent (notional) tax credit on dividends when distributing income. However, they must still account for the 'rate applicable to trusts' amounting to 34 per cent up to 5 April 2004 and subsequently 40 per cent, after setting off 25 per cent or 32.5 per cent respectively on any dividends. This limits the amount of dividend income that can be distributed in many cases, thus reducing the income of the beneficiaries. (This may influence the investment policy of the trustees).

Bank interest on deposits belonging to discretionary and accumulation trusts was previously paid gross. However, from 6 April 1996, it is paid net of tax at 20 per cent. Overseas trusts with no connection to the UK will be able to continue receiving gross interest provided the trustees give the bank a signed declaration.

21.6 Trusts' capital gains tax (TCGA Ss4, 5, 68–76, 165–167 & Sch 7)

Regarding realisations by trusts, a 40 per cent capital gains tax rate applies from 2004–05 (previously 34 per cent), including discretionary and accumulation trusts and personal representatives. Relief may apply where there are vulnerable beneficiaries (21.2.2). Prior to 6 April 1998, 23 per cent applied except for discretionary and accumulation trusts for which the 34 per cent rate applied. Where the settlor (or spouse) has an interest in or rights relating to a settlement, the rate may be increased to the settlor's top rate. Also, the settlor's annual exemption (£8,500) would apply if not used up (TCGA Ss77 & 78).

The full (£8,500) annual exemption (20.6) applies to trusts for the mentally disabled and those receiving attendance allowance. (From 6 April 1981 only broadly half the property and income need be applied to the disabled.) Other trusts normally obtain exemption at half the rate (£4,250). However, regarding trusts formed after 6 June 1978, the exemption is split between those with the same settlor. Thus if you had settled two such trusts they each have an annual exemption of £2,125. If there are more than five, however, they each still have an exemption of £850.

For recent years the corresponding exemptions are:

	Disability trusts £	Other trusts £	Minimum £
1998–99	6,800	3,400	680
1999–2000	7,100	3,550	710
2000–01	7,200	3,600	720
2001–02	7,500	3,750	750
2002–03	7,700	3,850	770
2003–04	7,900	3,950	790
2004–05	8,200	4,100	820
2005–06	8,500	4,250	850

When any chargeable assets are introduced into the trust by the settlor this is a realisation by him on which he pays capital gains tax if applicable (20.10). For example, if A bought 1,000 shares in B Ltd for £1,000 in May 1988 and gifts them in June 2005 to a settlement that he created, the shares must be valued at that time. If the shares are then worth £2,000 he has a chargeable gain of £1,000 for 2005–06 (subject to indexation to April 1998 and taper relief). If, however, the shares are worth only £600 at that time, he has an allowable loss of £400 (£1,000 – £600), subject to taper, which he can only set off against any capital gains resulting from other transactions between A and his trust. This is because they are treated as being 'connected persons' (20.10).

There are trust rules, whereby if you are the settlor, you may be taxed on the capital gains, particularly where you have or are treated as having an interest in the trust. The rule covers both UK resident settlements (TCGA Ss77 & 78) and non-resident ones (TCGA Ss86 & 86A). The tapered gains would be attributed to you at present, with no personal loss relief. However, under new rules (FA 2002 S51 & Sch 11) from 2003–04, the gross gains will be attributed to you and you can then offset losses, before applying taper relief. Also, until 31 January 2005, you can elect for similar treatment for any of the three earlier years (2000–01 to 2002–03).

21.7 Trusts' capital gains tax – business assets, gifts etc.

Where, after 11 April 1978, business assets, including shares in 'family companies' were settled, the trustees and settlor could jointly claim for any gain on the assets to be held over (20.26). The effect was that the settlor had no capital gains tax to pay on the settled business assets, etc. and the acquisition value for the trustees was correspondingly reduced. From 6 April 1981 to 13 March 1989, the general gifts relief (20.27) applied to disposals *to* trusts. Regarding gifts *by* trusts, the old business assets rules applied for 1981–82, after which the general gifts relief applied up to 13 March 1989. From 14 March 1989, the old business assets rules apply with some extensions (20.28), for instance concerning discretionary settlements.

From 6 April 1985 capital gains tax retirement relief was extended to cover certain trust disposals of business assets (or family company shares). This particularly applies where a beneficiary of the trust with a life interest in possession (other than for a fixed term), who previously carried on the business, withdraws from it and retires (20.29).

Rollover relief on reinvestment (20.25.2) applied in certain limited cases to shares sold by trusts after 15 March 1993 where the proceeds were reinvested before 6 April 1998. A typical situation would have been that you were a beneficiary with an interest in possession in the shares disposed of. You would need to have been a full time working officer and own personally at least 5 per cent of the voting shares. In addition, the normal rules must be satisfied.

For disposals made after 29 November 1993 by most trusts, the wider exemption applied (20.25.2). Thus all chargeable gains of trusts were eligible for relief if reinvested in ordinary shares in qualifying companies. The exception was where the beneficiaries included those who were neither individuals nor charities. Rollover relief on reinvestment in shares does not apply after 5 April 1998.

21.8 Trusts' capital gains tax – disposals of interests and distributions

The disposal of an interest in the trust by one of the original beneficiaries is normally exempt from capital gains tax. However, this does not apply to non-resident settlements.

Where a *life interest* ends in a settlement otherwise than on death, capital gains tax does not arise on the excess of its value over the base cost. However, on a subsequent disposal the original base value must be used. Where a *life interest* in a settlement ends on death, there is similarly no capital gains tax. However, the capital gains tax base value of the assets is adjusted to their market value at that time.

Where a capital asset of a trust is distributed to a beneficiary this is a chargeable event which can give rise to a capital gain in the trust. (This even applies for minors, etc. who are not yet legally able to own the property.) Thus if a trust bought 1,000 shares in B Ltd for £2,000 in April 1995 and it distributes them to beneficiary C in July 2005 when their market value is £3,000 the trust will have a capital gain of £1,000 (£3,000 – £2,000), which is assessable for 2005–06 subject to the annual exemption, some indexation and taper. (An exception to this rule is where a beneficiary under a will receives his entitlement – 21.10.3.) The beneficiary normally has a base value equivalent to the market value of the asset.

Various anti-avoidance rules apply (15.10.20). For example, where a beneficiary sells his interest in a trust to someone else after 20 March 2000, in certain circumstances there may be a capital gains tax charge. This particularly applies where the settlor has an interest. The underlying assets to which the interest relates are treated as disposed of by the trust at market value and immediately reacquired, giving rise to trust capital gains accordingly (TCGA S76A & Sch 4A).

21.9 Foreign trusts (TCGA Ss13, 76, 76B, 80–90, 96 & 97 & Sch 5 & 5A)

For taxation purposes a trust is generally treated as being resident abroad if a majority of the trustees are so resident and its administration and management is carried out overseas. Such a trust was generally exempt from capital gains tax on realisations of assets in the UK and elsewhere. However, sweeping changes took effect from 19 March 1991 and that rule no longer applies in certain cases (21.9.1). Further important changes apply from 1998 and 1999 (21.9.2).

For income tax purposes, broadly, for 1989–90 (with some exceptions) and subsequent years if at least one trustee is UK resident and at least one is not, special rules apply (17.3.5), depending on the settlor's status when he introduces funds into the settlement. If the settlor was then resident, ordinarily resident or domiciled in the UK, the non-resident trustees are treated as UK resident for determining the trust's residence for income tax purposes. Otherwise, all of the trustees are treated as non-UK resident.

If the settlement arises on death, the residence, etc. of the deceased at the date of death applies for deeming the residence of the trustees and a similar rule applies concerning the personal representatives.

There are rules under which the Revenue can sometimes assess UK resident beneficiaries with their shares of any capital gains (provided that the settlor is UK domiciled and resident or ordinarily resident either when he made the settlement or when the capital gain is made). UK beneficiaries are only taxed to the extent that they receive *capital payments* attributable to such gains. Where the *capital payments* and trust capital gains are in different tax years the beneficiary is taxed in the later one. *Capital payments* made to beneficiaries after 5 April 1992 may attract a supplementary charge (21.9.1).

There are rules to prevent capital gains tax being avoided by transfers between settlements and by a trust changing its residence. For the purposes of the rules, the term 'settlement' includes dispositions, arrangements and agreements; whilst 'settlor' takes in those making reciprocal arrangements or undertakings to provide funds indirectly. From 19 March 1991, there are rules to charge to tax, trust capital gains on settlors who have any interest in the settlement (21.9.1 & 21.9.2).

Where a beneficiary obtains an asset from a foreign trust, his base value is taken to be the market value of the asset, as a general rule. However, from 10 March 1981 to 5 April 1983, his base value was limited to the amount of any consideration which he actually gave for the asset, except in certain cases where the foreign trust was liable to UK capital gains tax.

UK income of foreign trusts is charged to income tax here along roughly the same lines as non-resident individuals are so charged. There is no higher rate liability, however, unless distributions are made to beneficiaries resident in this country or if the anti-avoidance provisions apply regarding transfers of assets abroad (15.10.2). In the latter event, in certain circumstances, the Revenue may charge any beneficiaries who are resident in this country with basic and higher rate income tax on the trust income.

Regarding the UK dividends received by foreign discretionary and accumulation trusts after 5 April 1993 and before 6 April 1999, a notional tax credit of 20 per cent of the gross (20/80) was added. This was then allowed as a credit against the full 'rate applicable to trusts'. However, this tax credit was not repayable. From 6 April 1999, the notional tax credit became 10 per cent.

21.9.1 **Foreign trusts – capital gains from 19 March 1991** (TCGA Ss80–87 & 98A & Sch 5 & 5A)

Rules operate from 19 March 1991 aimed at increasing the application of UK capital gains tax to foreign trusts. These rules include a capital gains tax charge when the trustees of a settlement cease to be UK resident after 18 March 1991. This is based on the values of the assets which fall out of the UK capital gains tax net when the trustees change residence (not assets used in a UK trade). The trustees are not able to cover such gains by rollover relief through buying new assets outside the UK tax charge.

As the settlor of a non-resident settlement, you will be charged to capital gains tax if certain conditions are satisfied including the following:

(1) You are UK domiciled and resident or ordinarily resident (17.2 and 17.3).
(2) You have an 'interest' in the settlement. This covers being able to benefit, now or in the future, from the income or property of the settlement. You are also caught if your spouse, children or their spouses can benefit (also in some circumstances grandchildren – 21.9.2).
(3) The rules apply to your settlement, if you set it up after 18 March 1991. Earlier settlements may also be caught, where, for example, property or income is provided otherwise than by way of arm's length bargains. Other instances include the trustees ceasing to be UK resident after that date and a member of your immediate family ((2) above) becoming a beneficiary for the first time.
(4) Any capital gains and losses made by your settlement before 19 March 1991 are not caught by the new rules. However, subject to the conditions being satisfied, you will be assessed on the subsequent net gains. Also, you will have an obligation to notify the Inland Revenue of events which may involve a charge to tax.

If you are a beneficiary of a non-resident settlement and receive a *capital payment* after 5 April 1992, you may be liable to pay a *supplementary charge* in addition to the normal capital gains tax. The rules include the following:

(1) You must be UK domiciled and resident or ordinarily resident (17.2 and 17.3). Originally the settlor had to have this status when you received the payment or when the trust was established. For gains and capital payments after 16 March 1998, this charge applies regardless of the residence or domicile status of the settlor.
(2) Your capital payments will be matched with trust gains on a 'first in first out' basis.
(3) The supplementary charge runs from 1 December in the tax year following the one when the gain arose, to 30 November following the year of assessment in which your capital payment is made.
(4) You will not be charged if your capital payment fails to be matched with trust gains of the same or immediately preceding tax year.
(5) The supplementary charge will be 10 per cent of the tax for each year up to six. Thus, if the top rate remains 40 per cent, the maximum supplementary charge will be 24 per cent making a total of 64 per cent.

The Revenue must be provided with information where a non-resident trust is set up after 18 March 1991; property (other than at arm's length) is transferred to an earlier trust; or a trust ceases to be UK resident. This is normally limited to where the settlor is UK resident and/or domiciled and now applies whether or not the settlor has an interest. However, after 16 March 1998, the information rules extend to anyone who transfers property (other than at arm's length) to an offshore trust.

21.9.2 **Foreign trusts – capital gains changes from 1998** (TCGA Ss76, 79A–B, 85–88, 96, 97 & Sch 5)

(1) Regarding disposals after 5 April 1999, the rules for settlements set up after 18 March 1991 (21.9.1) generally extend to earlier trusts. Thus if you created such a trust and you, your spouse or children can benefit, you will be taxed on the trust gains. This will not apply if you are non-domiciled and not resident and/or not ordinarily resident, nor in certain other cases, such as where children are under age 18 at 5 April 1999.

(2) If you set up a foreign trust after 16 March 1998 from which your grandchildren (or those of your spouse) can benefit, you may be charged on the trust gains. This also applies to earlier trusts where capital is subsequently settled, or after 16 March a trust is exported or varied regarding grandchildren.

(3) Any gain realised after 5 March 1998 from the disposal by a beneficiary of an interest in a trust which is or had been located offshore is no longer exempt.

(4) From 21 March 2000, rules take effect to stop capital gains tax being avoided where an offshore trust is made UK resident and then non-resident again. There will be no uplift in the value of any beneficiary's interest in the trust assets if the trust had a stockpile of gains not attributed to the trust beneficiaries.

(5) Also acted against from 21 March 2000 is the situation where gains are sheltered through the double tier of a trust and an offshore company and the existing anti-avoidance laws are set aside by a double tax agreement.

21.10 Estates of deceased persons

21.10.1 **The tax liability of the deceased** (TMA Ss40, 74 & 77)

When a person dies, income tax and capital gains tax must be settled on all his income and capital gains up to the date of his death. Any of this tax that is not paid during his lifetime must be settled by his executors or administrators out of his estate.

If the deceased has not been assessed to tax on all his income or capital gains prior to his death, the Revenue are allowed to make assessments on such income and capital gains within three years after 31 January following the end of the tax year in which death occurred. The Revenue may make assessments in this way in respect of any tax years ending within six years before the date of death in cases of fraud, wilful default or neglect of the deceased but no earlier years can be assessed (16.9.1).

21.10.2 **Income tax during the administration period** (TA 1988 Ss695–720)

The administration period of an estate is the period from the date of death of the deceased until the assets are distributed to the beneficiaries according to the will of the deceased or according to the rules of intestacy. Where, however, a trust is set up under a will the administration period only normally lasts until the trust takes over the residue of the estate.

During the administration period, the executors or administrators pay any lower or basic rate income tax assessable on the income arising in that period. The tax paid by self-assessment or deduction at source is subtracted from the amounts of income paid to those entitled to the income of the estate. Non-trading expenses of the executors are also deducted, but normally, any trading expenses will have been deducted from trading income in arriving at its net taxable amount.

The beneficiaries include the income that they receive in their tax returns when the payments are made to them. They must return the gross equivalents allowing for income tax at the 20 per cent lower rate (for income under Schedule F) and/or basic rate (22 per cent). Any distributions of estate income out of post 5 April 1993 dividends (21.2.1) and post 5 April 1996 savings income (2.2) must be grossed up at the lower rate (20 per cent) and carry a 20 per cent tax credit. However, distributions from dividends received after 5 April 1999 must be grossed up at 10 per cent.

Once the total income payable to each beneficiary has been ascertained, it is allocated to the respective tax years for which it arose and they pay (if applicable) higher rate tax on that basis. However, different rules apply to estates in the course of administration at 6 April 1995 and new ones. From that date, income payments made to the beneficiaries are taxable in the year of receipt, any balance normally being taxable on completion of the administration and not subject to spreading.

21.10.3 **Capital gains tax during the administration period** (TCGA Ss3, 4 & 62)

Although before 31 March 1971 all of the chargeable assets of the deceased were considered for capital gains tax purposes to be disposed of at the date of his death, no such liability arises regarding deaths on or after that date. The executors or administrators of the estate are regarded as acquiring the assets at their market value at the date of death and if they later sell any of the assets during the administration period, the estate is assessed to capital gains tax on any surplus. The rate was 30 per cent up to 5 April 1988, 25 per cent to 5 April 1996, 24 per cent for 1996–97 and 23 per cent for 1997–98. From 1998–99 the rate was 34 per cent, increasing to 40 per cent from 2004–05.

Thus if part of the estate of A deceased consisted of 1,000 shares in B Ltd whose value at his death on say 30 June 2001 was £2,000, if those shares are sold on 1 November 2005 for £3,000 (in order to pay inheritance tax for example), the estate is assessed to capital gains tax on £1,000 (£3,000 – £2,000) for 2005–06 (subject to taper relief and annual exemption).

If, however, assets of the estate are given to beneficiaries in settlement of their entitlements under the will of the deceased, no capital gains tax is charged on the estate on such transfers of assets. Instead, each beneficiary is treated for capital gains tax purposes as if he had acquired the assets at the same time as the personal representatives acquired them and at the same value.

Thus in the example mentioned above, if instead of selling the 1,000 shares in B Ltd for £3,000 on 1 November 2005 the executors gave them to C on that day in satisfaction of a legacy provided by the will of A deceased, C is treated as having acquired the shares on 30 June 2001 for £2,000 only. (The value of £2,000 was the probate value of the shares at the date of death.) Thus no capital gains tax is payable by the estate in respect of the transfer. If, however, C then sells shares on 1 December 2005 for £3,500 his chargeable gain (subject to taper relief) will be £1,500 (£3,500 – £2,000), although the shares have only gone up in value by £500 since he received them. This is because his entitlement to the legacy is considered for capital gains tax purposes to extend back to the date of death.

Deeds of variation (which effectively rewrite the provisions of wills or intestacies) can be made for the purposes of both capital gains tax and inheritance tax (22.29.6). Previously an election was needed, but variations made after 31 July 2002 which so direct, will apply automatically for capital gains tax and inheritance tax purposes (FA 2002 S52).

For the year of assessment in which death occurs and the next two years, the full personal annual exemption is applied to the net gains (£8,500, etc. – 20.6).

See Chapter 22 (22.30) for guidelines to the inheritance tax rules concerning settlements.

Chapter 22

INHERITANCE TAX

22.1 Introduction

This chapter deals with what was originally known as capital transfer tax, but following sweeping changes in the 1986 Finance Act was renamed inheritance tax. The name applies from 25 July 1986. However, the inheritance tax rules cover transfers on and after 18 March 1986.

The tax is highly complicated and technical. Although many of the basic capital transfer tax rules remain, important innovations such as potentially exempt transfers (PETs) were introduced (22.3). Many of its complexities are beyond the scope of this book. The following is thus only a brief outline.

The rules for inheritance tax are contained in the Inheritance Tax Act 1984 (ITA) and subsequent Finance Acts. The tax covers transfers on death and certain lifetime transfers, particularly to discretionary settlements. However, lifetime transfers between individuals and to certain trusts are only taxed if death occurs within seven years (22.3).

Before capital transfer tax there was estate duty, which did not apply to deaths occurring after 12 March 1975 (22.14). Where property passed on deaths after 12 November 1974 and before 13 March 1975, estate duty applied at capital transfer tax rates. For details of estate duty, reference should be made to Chapter 19 of the 1974–75 *Hambro Tax Guide* and earlier editions.

22.2 Property chargeable (ITA 1984 Ss1–3 & 103–114)

Subject to various exceptions and reliefs (22.15) inheritance tax will be charged on *chargeable transfers* which you make during your lifetime, as well as on the value of your estate when you die. However, with the introduction of the inheritance tax regime, the scope for tax on lifetime gifts was much reduced by the rules concerning *potentially exempt transfers* (22.3). These escape tax unless death occurs within seven years. As a result, most inheritance tax is payable following death.

Chargeable transfers are evaluated by taking the decrease in your assets less liabilities brought about by the transfer and deducting certain exemptions (22.17). Normally, arm's length transactions are ignored if they are not intended to convey any gratuitous benefit. Any capital gains tax which you pay is ignored in calculating the decrease.

If you are domiciled (17.2) in the UK or deemed domiciled (22.4) here, inheritance tax applies to all of your property, wherever situated. Otherwise it only applies to your property in this country.

22.3 Potentially exempt transfers (ITA S3A & FA 1986 S101 & Sch 19)

If you make gifts to other individuals, or to accumulation and maintenance settlements (22.30.1) or trusts for disabled persons, they are classed as 'potentially exempt transfers' (PETs). This means that inheritance tax will not be payable on these gifts unless you die within seven years. Should that happen, however, the PETs (less exemptions) become *chargeable transfers*. Your tax must then be recalculated as later indicated (22.5.1) but using the rate scale applying at death and subject to possible tapering relief (22.6).

The scope of PETs includes lifetime transfers concerning interest in possession trusts. These are broadly trusts where one or more beneficiaries have the income or use of property as of right. Transfers into such trusts are PETs as are transfers out, except on death. If you make a PET, no inheritance tax return is required.

22.4 Deemed domicile (ITA 1984 S267 & FA 1996 S200)

You are deemed to be domiciled in the UK if one of the following applies:

(1) You were domiciled here on or after 10 December 1974 and within the three years preceding the date of the chargeable transfer.
(2) You were resident here on or after 10 December 1974 and in not less than 17 of the 20 years of assessment ending with that in which you made the chargeable transfer.

22.5 Rate scale (ITA 1984 S7 & Sch 1 & FA 2005 S98)

The inheritance tax scheme applying from 18 March 1986 has a seven year limitation on cumulation. Also, as previously mentioned (22.3) lifetime transfers (excluding transfers to discretionary settlements, etc.) are not cumulated unless you die within seven years. There are, however, various exemptions from the general rules (22.17).

Capital transfer tax was charged on the cumulative total of all your lifetime transfers after 26 March 1974 together with the property passing on your death. There was a ten year limitation on cumulation (22.7).

Inheritance tax is charged according to the following table (22.5.1) which applies to *chargeable transfers* and property passing on death after 5 April 2005. The threshold is now £275,000, compared with £263,000 for 2004–05. (Fuller details appear later – 27.4.)

The threshold for 2006–07 has been enacted as £285,000 and £300,000 for 2007–08.

There is only one scale but lifetime gifts which are not PETs (22.3) are charged at 50 per cent of the rate. This applies basically to transfers into discretionary settlements, charges on such settlements (22.30.2) and chargeable transfers arising from close company transactions. Tax is paid on such transfers soon after they are made, cumulating them with others within the previous seven years to calculate the amount. If death occurs within seven years, however, tax is adjusted using the full rates, with possible tapering relief (22.6) where death is later than three years after the transfer. However, the adjustment does not operate to reduce the original tax.

On death within seven years of a PET (22.3) inheritance tax must be calculated by treating it as a *chargeable transfer* and cumulating with any earlier chargeable transfers within seven years of the PET. Tax is calculated using the value of the gift when made but using the scale current at the date of death. On gifts more than three years before death, some tapering relief will be available (22.6).

22.5.1 **Inheritance tax rate after 5 April 2005**

Slice of cumulative chargeable transfers	Cumulative total £	% on slice	Cumulative total tax £
The first £275,000	275,000	Nil	Nil
The remainder		40	

In general, the current rate scale applies to chargeable transfers and on deaths after 5 April 2005. Previously the rate scales have been modified periodically. Each time the burden has been slightly reduced. The full tables appear in Chapter 27.

22.6 Tapering relief (ITA 1984 S7)

Where an individual dies within seven years of making a potentially exempt transfer (PET) (22.3) a proportion of the full tax is payable as follows:

Death in years	%
1–3	100
4	80
5	60
6	40
7	20

If a transfer is within the nil rate band, so that it attracts no inheritance tax, no benefit is obtained from tapering relief in that instance. Regarding those lifetime transfers which attract inheritance tax immediately at half the full rates (22.5), the tax is increased to full rates if death occurs within three years. Otherwise, the above tapering scale is applied to the rates current at death unless this produces a lower charge than that originally paid. In that case the original basis holds good.

22.7 The ten-year cumulation period

FA 1981 introduced a ten-year limitation on cumulations (superseded by a seven year limit from 18 March 1986). If you made a chargeable transfer it was added to all chargeable transfers which you made in the previous ten years and any made before that time dropped out.

22.8 The seven-year cumulation period (ITA 1984 S3A)

Regarding chargeable transfers and deaths occurring after 17 March 1986, the cumulation period was reduced to seven years. This meant that any transfers which you made in the three years to 17 March 1979 immediately fell out of cumulation regarding transfers after 17 March 1986.

Remember that only a limited category of transfers come into charge immediately (22.5). PETs (22.3) are only cumulated and charged to inheritance tax if you die within seven years. Then the PETs become *chargeable transfers* and are brought into cumulation with previous chargeable transfers within seven years of each PET (including the PETs within seven years of death). The estate left at death (22.14) is then added to the chargeable transfers in the last seven years in order to compute the inheritance tax on those assets.

22.9 Indexation of rate bands (ITA 1984 S8)

For each year to 5 April, the inheritance tax rate or rates (22.5) are to apply subject to indexation. The threshold and the various rate-bands will be increased in proportion to the rise in the retail prices index from September to September and each new threshold will be rounded up to the nearest £1,000. This applies unless the Treasury otherwise directs.

22.10 Valuation (ITA 1984 Ss160–170, 222 & 242)

For inheritance tax purposes your assets are normally valued at their open market value at the transfer date. If the value of an asset which you keep is affected by the transfer, you will need to value your 'estate' both before and after the transfer in order to calculate its resultant fall. Your liabilities must be taken into account in valuing your total 'estate'. Regarding appeals as to the value of land, the Special Commissioners are able to refer to the Lands Tribunal.

22.11 Quoted securities passing on death (ITA 1984 Ss178–189)

Relief is available where quoted securities are sold for less than their probate values within 12 months of death. This applies where any quoted shares or securities or holdings in authorised unit trusts are realised within one year of death. The persons liable to pay the inheritance tax can claim that the total of the gross sale prices should be substituted for the original probate values of the investments. Where, however, the proceeds are re-invested by those persons in quoted shares or unit trusts after the death and within two months after the last sale, the above relief may be reduced or lost.

For deaths after 15 March 1992, the relief is extended to investments cancelled within 12 months of the date of death; also where quotation is suspended in the 12 months after death. It is necessary that at the date of cancellation or first anniversary, the shares are still held by the person liable for the tax.

22.12 Valuation of related property (ITA 1984 S161)

Where the value of any of your property is less than the appropriate portion of the value of the aggregate of that and any 'related property' you must value your own property as the appropriate portion of the value of that aggregate.

'Related property' is property belonging to your spouse. It also includes property belonging to a charity, charitable trust, housing association, etc. or which had belonged to it during the last five years, and came from an exempt transfer from you or your spouse after 15 April 1976.

This rule is particularly relevant to the valuation of unquoted shares. For example if you and your wife each have 40 per cent of the shares of an unquoted company, then the value of 80 per cent of the shares is normally much higher than twice the value of 40 per cent of the shares. This is because an 80 per cent holding carries with it full control of the company.

Thus the successful estate duty saving device of splitting a shareholding in a non-quoted company between your wife and yourself so that neither of you has control, is not effective (so far as the first transfer is concerned) in producing a lower aggregate value for inheritance tax purposes.

If you inherit any related property, a special relief applies where you sell the property within three years of the death for less than the value on which tax was originally paid. Subject to various conditions including the requirement that the sale is at arm's length for a freely negotiated price, you can claim for the related property in question to be revalued at death on the basis that it was not related to any other property.

22.13 Land sold within four years of death (ITA 1984 Ss190–198)

Where the person paying the capital transfer tax or inheritance tax arising on death after 15 March 1990 on land or buildings sells them within four years of the death for less than their probate value, he can claim that the sale proceeds are substituted in the tax calculations. For sales before 16 March 1993, the period was three years.

There are a number of conditions including the requirement that the shortfall is at least the lower of £1,000 and 5 per cent of the probate value of the land. Relief is extended regarding a compulsory purchase notified before the end of three years from death.

22.14 Inheritance tax on death (ITA 1984 S4 & FA 1986 Sch 19)

The general rule is that if you are domiciled (or deemed domiciled – 22.4) in the UK at the time of your death, all of your assets, wherever they may be situated, form part of the *gross value* of your estate for the purposes of determining the inheritance tax payable. (The same applied for capital transfer tax.)

If you are not domiciled in the UK at your death then the tax is only chargeable on those assets which are situated in the UK (22.28).

The *net value* of your estate is determined by making certain deductions (22.14.2) from the *gross value* of all the property passing on your death.

The tax on your death is charged as if immediately before your death you made a chargeable transfer equal to the *net value* of your estate, subject to certain adjustments and exemptions (22.15) if appropriate.

For deaths after 17 March 1986, the inheritance tax rules apply and the tax is calculated from the single scale taking account of your cumulative lifetime gifts within *seven* years of death. These gifts include PETs (22.3) on which no tax was previously paid. As previously explained, death may lead not only to tax on the estate but also on lifetime gifts (22.6).

Your executors will need to apply for probate of your will. Otherwise, if you die intestate, letters of administration must be obtained. In either case, it will be necessary for an inheritance tax account to be completed (normally on CAP Form 202 or 200). At least a provisional amount of tax will need to be paid at that time. Further administrative rules appear later in this chapter (22.24).

22.14.1 **Gross value of estate** (ITA 1984 S5)

The gross value of your estate includes all your property situated anywhere in the world, such as land, shares, the goodwill of a business, debts owing to you, etc., apart from *excluded property* (22.15).

Certain other amounts must also be included in your gross estate, even though they do not belong to you or only arise after your death, such as the proceeds of a life policy held by you on your own life, or any death benefit under a pension scheme which is payable to your estate (rather than under the more usual discretionary disposal clause contained in most pension schemes).

Other amounts to be included in your gross estate are various interests in trusts (22.30). In these cases the trustees may pay the appropriate tax but the rate is calculated by reference to the value of the estate including the trust funds.

22.14.2 **Net value of estate**

The more common deductions which are made from the gross value of your estate in order to arrive at its net value are as follows:

(1) Certain exempt transfers (22.17.3).
(2) Funeral expenses.

(3) Debts owing by you at the date of death which are payable in the UK. However, certain debts may be disallowed in whole or part if you had made connected gifts to the creditors, or the liability had not been incurred for full consideration for your benefit. (FA 1986 S82).
(4) Debts due to persons outside the UK are normally only deductible from the value of assets situated outside this country.
(5) Whilst legal and other professional fees owing at the death may be deducted as debts, no deduction is given for probate and executors' expenses.
(6) Liabilities for income tax and capital gains tax up to the time of death, whether or not assessments were made before that time. No deduction can be made for inheritance tax payable on your death, however, nor can tax liabilities be deducted regarding income and capital gains arising for periods subsequent to your death.

22.15 Excluded property (ITA 1984 S6)

The following 'excluded property' must be left out of the value of your estate for capital transfer tax and inheritance tax purposes, regarding both lifetime transfers and property passing on death:

(1) Property outside the UK if you are neither domiciled nor deemed domiciled in this country.
(2) A reversionary interest unless either you bought it or it relates to the falling in of a lease which was treated as a settlement (22.30). Certain anti-avoidance rules apply to prevent misuse.
(3) Cash options under approved retirement pension schemes (14.3.2), provided an annuity becomes payable to your dependants instead of the cash option itself.
(4) Originally, certain UK government securities on which interest may be paid gross to non-residents (8.2), provided you are neither domiciled, deemed domiciled, nor ordinarily resident here. From 6 April 1998 all of your gilt-edged securities are excluded property and thus free of inheritance tax if you are neither UK domiciled nor deemed domiciled.
(5) Certain overseas pensions from former colonies, etc. including death payments and returns of contributions.
(6) Savings such as national savings certificates and premium bonds, if you are domiciled in the Channel Islands or the Isle of Man.
(7) Certain property in this country belonging to visiting forces and NATO headquarters staff.

22.16 Double taxation relief (ITA 1984 Ss158 & 159)

Various other countries also operate systems of capital transfer tax/inheritance tax and the government of the UK is empowered to enter into agreements with them for the avoidance of the double payment of such tax both here and in the other country.

Concerning capital transfer tax or inheritance tax payable on death, relief is continued for estate duty payable on the same property in other countries if there was a 'double estate duty' agreement with the countries in question as at 12 March 1975. The following countries have agreements with the UK covering estate duty and/or capital transfer tax or inheritance tax:

France	Pakistan
India	South Africa
Ireland	Sweden
Italy	Switzerland
Netherlands	United States of America

Unilateral double taxation relief is available for overseas tax paid on death or a lifetime transfer. The tax must be of a similar nature to inheritance tax and if the property is situated in the overseas country, a credit is given against the UK tax of the amount of the overseas tax. If the property is either situated *both* in the UK and the overseas country, or in *neither* of those places, the credit against the UK tax is C × A/(A + B). A is the amount of inheritance tax, B is the overseas tax and C is the smaller of A and B.

22.17 Exempt transfers (ITA 1984 Ss18–27)

Broadly, exempt transfers can be divided between those which apply both on death and during your life and those which are only exempt if the transfers are during your life. The first category includes transfers between your wife and yourself.

22.17.1 Transfers between husband and wife

Transfers between your wife and yourself both during your lives and on death were exempt from capital transfer tax and are exempt from inheritance tax. (Thus lifetime gifts are not even treated as PETs – 22.3.) From 5 December 2005, this also applies to transfers between civil partners in accordance with the Civil Partnership Act 2004 (6.9).

Full exemption does not apply, however, if the recipient of the property is not domiciled (or deemed domiciled) in this country (17.2) (unless the donor is also neither domiciled nor deemed domiciled here). In this case, only the first £55,000 transferred to the non-domiciled spouse is exempt. This resembles the previous estate duty relief.

Under the estate duty rules, if you left property in trust for your wife for life, when you died duty was paid; but none was payable on her subsequent death. (If her death is after 12 November 1974, no capital transfer tax or inheritance tax applies.) If, however, the first death occurs after 12 November 1974, the new relief applies and so no tax is payable on property passing to the surviving spouse. For this reason, when the latter dies, full inheritance tax is payable on the trust property.

22.17.2 Exempt transfers – lifetime gifts

The following transfers are only exempt if made by an individual during his life. They do not normally apply to transfers made by trustees nor to assets passing on death. In any one fiscal year to 5 April, you can make all of these exempt transfers cumulatively and so can your wife. The rules apply not only to chargeable transfers but also to PETs (22.3). Thus if a transfer which would otherwise be a PET is an exempt transfer, it will not attract inheritance tax, even if you die within seven years.

(1) *Transfers each year up to a value of £3,000.* If you do not use up the full £3,000 allowance in one year, you can carry the unused part forward for one year only. If your transfers taken against this exemption reach £3,000 in one year, you have nothing available to carry forward, even though you may have had £3,000 carried forward from the previous year.

For example if you made no chargeable transfers in the year to 5 April 2005, you have £6,000 available for exempt transfers under this category in the year to 5 April 2006. If, however, you transferred £500 in the year to 5 April 2005 you have £2,500 carried forward and so can transfer £5,500 in the year to 5 April 2006.

In any year to 5 April, your annual exemption first reduces those lifetime transfers which are not PETs; and then your PETs (FA 1986 Sch 19). (Deaths within seven years may cause the reallocation of your annual exemptions, particularly regarding amounts originally set against your 'non-PETS' for the following year.)

(2) *Small gifts.* Outright gifts to any one person not exceeding £250 for each year to 5 April are exempt. The £250 exemption cannot be used against gifts larger than that amount. Thus you can make an unlimited number of exempt gifts of £250 to different people but any gifts of £251 or more must be set against the £3,000 and other exemptions with the excess being potentially taxable (if the nil rate band has been exhausted).

(3) *Normal expenditure out of income.* To qualify under this exemption, a transfer must be part of your normal expenditure. This means that there must be an element of regularity. Life assurance premiums (9.2) are particularly suited for this. Further conditions are that the transfer is out of your after-tax income and you are left with enough income to maintain your usual standard of living.

Life policy premium payments will not qualify for this exemption, however, if they are made out of an annuity purchased on your life, unless you can show that the policy and the annuity were effected completely independently of each other. This rule even applies if you make gifts out of your annuity receipts and the donee pays the premiums on the policy on your life.

If you buy an annuity, and make transfers from it, only the income proportion of the annuity (9.14) is treated as your income for the purposes of the normal expenditure rule, the capital element is not.

(4) *Gifts in consideration of marriage* made to one of the partners of the marriage or settled on the partners and their children, etc. The limits are £5,000 if the donor is a parent of one of the marriage partners, £2,500 if a grandparent or great-grandparent or one of the parties themselves, or otherwise £1,000. (Eligibility for relief extends to marriage gifts from settlements where an interest in possession ends (22.30).)

22.17.3 **Other exempt transfers**

Subject to the particular rules, the following transfers are exempt both if made during your life and on death. They also apply to trusts (22.30).

(1) *Transfers in the course of trade, etc.* are exempt if allowed as deductions in computing the profits for income tax purposes (11.3). This applies equally to professions and vocations, as well as allowable deductions against other forms of profits or gains for the purposes of income tax and corporation tax.
(2) *Gifts to charities* are exempt without limit. Gifts to settlements for charitable purposes are covered by the exemption, as are gifts to charities from other trusts.
(3) *Gifts to political parties* are wholly exempt. For these purposes, a 'political party' is one with at least two members sitting in Parliament or one member and not less than 150,000 votes for its candidates at the last General Election.
(4) *Gifts for national purposes, etc.* made to the National Trust, National Heritage Memorial Fund, National Gallery, British Museum and similar organisations including universities and their libraries as well as museums and art galleries maintained by local authorities or universities.
(5) *Gifts for public benefit* of property deemed by the Treasury to be of outstanding scenic, historic, scientific or artistic merit including land, buildings, pictures, books, manuscripts, works of art, etc.
(6) *PETs (22.3) of property held for national purposes, etc.* This exemption applies where, prior to the death of the recipient, the property is sold by private treaty (or gifted) to an organisation as mentioned in (4) previously.
(7) *Gifts of shares* to an employee trust provided it will then hold at least half of the ordinary shares of the company (ITA 1984 S28). Exemption now extends to share ownership plans (FA 2000 S134).
(8) *Gifts to housing associations* or sales of land to them at under-value (ITA 1984 S24A).

22.18 Relief for business property (ITA 1984 Ss103–114)

In general, 'relevant business property' qualifies for business property relief. 'Relevant business property' includes a business or part of a business; shares and securities owned by the controller of a company; unquoted minority shareholdings and land, buildings, plant and machinery used in your partnership or a company which you control. Control of a company for these purposes includes shareholdings which are 'related property' (22.12) in relation to your own shares.

Normally, investment company and land or share-dealing company shareholdings do not qualify for the relief. However, UK stockjobbing and 'market making' qualify for the relief. You must normally own the business property, or property which has directly replaced it for at least two years prior to the transfer or else it is not 'relevant business property' and so no relief is due.

The rates of relief are 100 per cent and 50 per cent. Prior to 10 March 1992 the relief was 50 per cent and 30 per cent. The scope of the 100 per cent relief became wider on 6 April 1996.

Relief is available as follows (pre-6 April 1996 figures in brackets where different):

(1) The whole or part of a business:	100 per cent
(2) Quoted shares or securities in a trading company which you control:	50 per cent
(3) Property transferred by you which is used in a trade by a company controlled by you or partnership in which you are a partner:	50 per cent
(4) Unquoted shares in a trading company	
Over 25 per cent voting power:	100 per cent
25 per cent or less without control (including related property):	100 per cent (50 per cent)
(5) Holding in a USM company	
Over 25 per cent voting power:	100 per cent
25 per cent or less without control (including related property):	100 per cent (50 per cent)

The 50 per cent relief category is extended to cover the transfer of land or buildings owned by a trust. Immediately before the transfer, the assets must have been used in his own trade by a person beneficially entitled to an interest in possession in the trust.

Business property relief is available against PETs which fall into charge following the donor's death within seven years. However, the relief is lost if the recipient disposes of the property before the donor's death. But relief is not lost if the gifted business property is disposed of, but replaced by other qualifying assets within three years. Also, the property must remain 'relevant business property' during the seven-year period. If these conditions are satisfied for only part of the property, the relief is proportionately reduced. These rules also apply to other lifetime transfers within seven years of death.

Where part of an estate is left to the surviving spouse and thus attracts no tax, and part to others, the allocation of business property relief and relief for agricultural property (22.21) was open to abuse. However, from 18 March 1986 specific gifts of such property must be reduced by the relief. Otherwise, the relief is spread proportionately over the estate.

22.19 Waivers of dividends and remuneration (ITA 1984 Ss14 & 15)

If you waive any remuneration to which you are entitled this normally does not produce any capital transfer tax or inheritance tax liability, provided the amount waived would otherwise have been assessable to income tax under Schedule E (10.1) and your employer obtains no income tax or corporation tax relief for the waived remuneration.

No inheritance tax accrues on the waiver of any dividend to which you have a right, provided you waive the dividend within the 12 months before it is due. These waiver rules apply from the inception of capital transfer tax.

22.20 Conditional exemption for certain objects and buildings etc. (ITA 1984 Ss27, 30–32A, 57A, 78–79A & Sch 4)

Property similar to that mentioned in (4) and (5) above (22.17.3), is exempted from inheritance tax on death provided the recipient undertakes to keep it in the country, preserve it and allow reasonable access to the public. If it is later sold the tax is payable unless the sale is to an institution such as the British Museum, National Gallery or National Trust.

For relief claims made after 16 March 1998, there is normally a 2 year time limit. Furthermore, chattels associated with heritage buildings will need to be of pre-eminent quality and future undertakings must give access to the public without prior appointment.

A similar relief applies to lifetime transfers subject to various conditions. The recipient must give the required undertaking. The relief extends to historical and artistic buildings and objects comprised in settlements. It also applies to settlements set up to maintain historic buildings and now objects historically associated with them, together with land of outstanding interest. Such settlements must tie up the capital for at least six years for maintenance purposes only. But after that funds may be withdrawn subject to inheritance tax in certain circumstances.

Special rules apply regarding maintenance settlements for approved objects and buildings, etc. Provided the Board of the Inland Revenue (previously the Treasury) are satisfied that the trusts and trustees comply with certain requirements, transfers to such a settlement are exempt (22.17.3) for inheritance purposes. In general the trust funds must be used for the maintenance of approved assets for at least six years.

The exemption also applies where someone with a life interest in a trust dies and within two years the property goes into a heritage maintenance fund. Heritage property can be offered in lieu of inheritance tax and, from that date, there is the option of calculating the value of the property at the date of the offer instead of acceptance.

Land is exempted which is essential to a building of historic or architectural interest. Previously exemption depended on the land touching the building, but this is no longer necessary.

22.21 Relief for agricultural property (ITA 1984 Ss115–124A)

Under the rules which apply after 9 March 1981 you must have either occupied the property for the purposes of agriculture for at least two years before transferring it, or owned it for seven years up to that time, with others farming. The rules are relaxed where you inherit the property or where you have replaced one agricultural property by another. Agriculture includes stud farming for the purposes of the relief and also (from 29 November 1994) the cultivation of short rotation coppice (FA 1995 S154). From 26 November 1996, farmland which has been dedicated to wildlife habitats will also be eligible for relief subject to the rules (FA 1997 S94).

The relief is 100 per cent if you enjoy the right to vacant possession or can obtain this within the next 12 months. 100 per cent relief also applies to transfers of tenanted farmland where the tenancy starts after 1 September 1995. Where a tenancy is acquired by succession following the previous tenant's death, it is treated as a tenancy starting from the date of death.

Otherwise, the relief is normally 50 per cent, which applies to existing tenanted situations, etc. Prior to 10 March 1992, the rates were 50 per cent and 30 per cent. If you qualified for the higher relief under the old but not the new rules, you still obtain this regarding property held at 9 March 1981 and transferred after that date, up to the old limit of £250,000 or 1,000 acres if more valuable. The excess is then relieved at the lower rate which is now 50 per cent.

By concession, 100 per cent relief (not 50 per cent) applies on your transfer of tenanted agricultural land, where you have the right to vacant possession within 24 months; also where the value transferred is broadly the vacant possession value of the property. This concession applies for transfers after 12 February 1995 and earlier cases which were still open. Another concession, operative from the same time, allows 50 per cent relief on certain farm cottages even though the occupier has retired.

The grant of a tenancy of agricultural property is not to be treated as a transfer of value if it is made for full consideration (ITA 1984 S16).

Similar rules to those for business property relief apply regarding lifetime gifts within seven years of death and the allocation of relief to partially exempt estates (22.18). Thus the relief is lost if the recipient disposes of the agricultural property before the donor's death unless it is replaced within three (previously one) years by other agricultural property.

22.22 Woodlands (ITA 1984 Ss125–130)

Inheritance tax relief against the charge at death on growing timber is available, provided you either owned the woodlands for at least five years, or you acquired them by gift or inheritance.

Under the relieving provisions, provided the inheritor elects within two years of it, tax is not charged on your death. If, however, before the recipient dies, the timber is sold or given away, tax is charged on the proceeds or value of the gift. The tax rate is found by adding such proceeds to the estate at your death. Remember that the relief applies only to the timber and not the land on which it grows.

Business property relief is normally available on woodlands which are managed on a commercial basis.

Where the disposal follows a change in tax rates the respective new rates (26.4) are applied, even if the death was before they took effect.

22.23 Quick succession relief (ITA 1984 S141)

This relief applies to reduce the tax payable on death where the deceased himself received chargeable transfers on which the tax was paid within five years of his death. The deduction is broadly a proportion of the original tax, being 100 per cent, 80 per cent, 60 per cent, 40 per cent or 20 per cent, depending on whether the period between the transfer and the death is one, two, three, four or five years or less in each case. Where there are more than two transfers of the same property within five years of each other, special rules apply.

22.24 Administration and collection (ITA 1984 Ss215–261, etc.)

Inheritance tax (and capital transfer tax) are under the care and management of the Board of the Inland Revenue. Generally speaking the rules for administration, appeals and penalties resemble those for income tax (16.9.2).

Chargeable transfers must be reported to the Inland Revenue in an inheritance tax return within 12 months from the end of the month of transfer or death.

The tax chargeable on death must be paid on at least an estimated figure before probate is granted (22.14). However, this does not apply to estates worth no more than £240,000 (£220,000 before 1 August 2003), which qualify for a much simpler inheritance tax return. Such inheritance tax is payable out of the residuary estate unless there is a contrary direction in the will. However, property situated outside the UK continues to bear its own tax. Recipients of PETs are primarily responsible for the relevant tax.

From 31 March 2003, an optional electronic transfer method has been introduced for paying inheritance tax from bank and building society accounts owned by the deceased.

FA 2004 includes certain changes to the IHT penalty regime. For example, where fraudulent or negligent material is submitted, there will be no penalty if no additional IHT results. Late delivery of an IHT account will involve a penalty of £100, unless the tax is less or there is a reasonable excuse.

Interest on unpaid tax runs from when the tax is due. The due date is six months after the end of the month in which death occurs. For lifetime transfers it is six months after the end of the month in which the transfer is made. In the case of transfers between 5 April and 1 October, the due date is 30 April in the following year.

From 16 December 1986, a single rate of interest applies to overdue inheritance tax. This is currently 4 per cent and has varied as follows:

From	Rate %	From	Rate %
6 June 1987	6	6 January 1994	4
6 August 1988	8	6 October 1994	5
6 October 1988	9	6 March 1999	4
6 July 1989	11	6 February 2000	5
6 March 1991	10	6 May 2001	4
6 May 1991	9	6 November 2001	3
6 July 1991	8	6 August 2003	2
6 November 1992	6	6 December 2003	3
6 December 1992	5	6 September 2004	4

The interest is not deductible for income tax purposes. If you overpay inheritance tax or capital transfer tax you will get non-taxable interest at the same rates, up to the date on which the repayment of the excess tax is made.

FA 1999 updated and strengthened certain inheritance tax administration and collection provisions. For example, personal representatives now need to provide information regarding gifts during the seven years before death. Also, the Revenue's charge for unpaid tax has been tightened and their information seeking powers increased.

Higher penalties were introduced. For example, incorrect information provided by those liable to inheritance tax can give rise to penalties of up to £3,000 plus the extra tax in cases of fraud or up to £1,500 plus the extra tax concerning negligence.

FA 2004 enables the simplification of the accounts rules. Except for large estates and a few others, an IHT account will only be necessary if tax is to pay. Otherwise, the Probate Service will deal with the formalities for both tax and probate.

22.25 Payment by instalments of tax on death (ITA 1984 Ss227–229 & FA 1986 Sch 19)

Inheritance tax on death on certain assets may be paid by annual instalments over ten years. This applies to land and buildings, controlling holdings of shares in companies and certain other unquoted shares, as well as business assets. Also, shares dealt in on the USM are included. (PETs which become chargeable only qualify for the instalments basis if the recipient had kept the property until the death of the donor.)

Instalments paid on time concerning the shares and business assets mentioned above are free of interest. Land and buildings qualify for this relief only if they are held as business assets, otherwise interest is payable, currently at 4 per cent. Tax in respect of property qualifying for agricultural relief may be paid in interest free instalments as above.

22.26 Payment of tax on lifetime gifts by instalments

The above provisions apply to lifetime transfers if the donee bears the tax and for settled property which is retained in a settlement. If interest is payable it is currently at 3 per cent. The interest free category is extended to include lifetime disposals of timber. In the case of minority holdings of unquoted shares, these must be worth at least £20,000, in order to qualify for the instalments option; also being at least 10 per cent holdings. The instalments basis may also be allowed where paying the tax in one sum would cause undue hardship and the recipient keeps the shares.

22.27 Inheritance tax and life assurance

Life assurance policies can be used to create a fund to pay future inheritance tax and to facilitate gifts to your beneficiaries.

If you effect a policy on your life for your own benefit, the proceeds payable on your death will be taxable as part of your net estate (22.14.1).

22.27.1 Policies written in trust

You may effect a policy in a non-discretionary trust for some other person or persons, such as for example your wife and children. In this case the policy proceeds will not be paid into your own estate but will be paid to the trustees for the beneficiaries. Each premium payment, however, will constitute a separate potentially exempt transfer (22.3) by you. Thus they could be taxable if you die within seven years, unless an exemption applies such as the £3,000 or £250 reliefs (22.17.2), or the normal expenditure rule (22.17.2), or the policy is for your wife. If premiums are paid to a discretionary trust, each premium will be chargeable at the time and if no exemption applies, may give rise to recalculation of tax if death occurs within seven years (22.5).

22.27.2 **Gifts of policies**

Where you write a policy in trust, this is one way of gifting it. Another way is to assign the policy. Unless it is covered by exemptions (22.27.1) there will usually be a potentially exempt transfer. The transfer value is normally the greater of your gross premium payments and the surrender value of the policy. Your assignment will be potentially exempt if it is to an individual or certain kinds of trust (interest in possession, accumulation and maintenance, or for the disabled). If you make cash gifts to cover subsequent premiums, these gifts will normally be potentially exempt.

However, for policies effected after 17 March 1986, the gifts with reservation rules (22.29.4) may apply. Broadly if you have a retained benefit in the policy the proceeds will form part of your estate at death.

22.27.3 **'Life of another' policies**

If someone else effects a policy on your life and pays the premiums, then the proceeds are not taxable on your death. This is known as a 'life of another' policy. If the person who effects the policy predeceases you, however, then the surrender value of the policy at the date of death of that person is normally included in his taxable estate.

22.28 Property outside Great Britain

Since if you are neither domiciled nor deemed domiciled (22.4) in the UK, you will only normally pay inheritance tax on your assets situated here, it is important to ascertain the situation of particular property. The situation of property for inheritance tax purposes is normally deemed to be as follows:

(1) Cash – its physical location.
(2) Bank accounts – the location of the bank or branch (see also below).
(3) Registered securities – the location of the share register.
(4) Bearer securities – the location of the title documents.
(5) Land and buildings – their actual location.
(6) Business assets – the place where the business is conducted.
(7) Debts – the residence of the debtor.

Foreign currency accounts with UK banks are exempted from inheritance tax if the deceased is not UK domiciled. This also applies if the deceased had an interest in possession (22.30) in a settlement with such an account, unless the settlor was UK domiciled, resident or ordinarily resident, when he made the settlement or the trustees were so situated immediately before the death (ITA 1984 S158).

22.29 Miscellaneous points

22.29.1 **Close companies** (ITA 1984 Ss94–102 & FA 1986 Sch 19)

There are rules under which inheritance tax may be charged where a close company (13.17) makes a transfer of value. Broadly, tax may be charged on the company as if each of the participators (13.17.2) had made a proportionate transfer according to his or her interest in the company. The rules are extended to cover close companies being owned by trusts or being their beneficiaries.

Transfers of values arising as above from alterations in the capital and associated rights in a close company may attract inheritance tax at once. They are not PETs (22.3).

22.29.2 **Free loans** (ITA 1984 S29)

From 6 April 1976 to 5 April 1981, subject to various exceptions, if you allowed someone else the use of money or property at no interest or less than the market rate, you were treated as making a chargeable transfer for each year to 5 April that the arrangement continued. These provisions ceased to have effect after 5 April 1981 although interest-free loans for a fixed stated period can still be treated as a chargeable transfer under general principles.

22.29.3 **Associated operations** (ITA 1984 S268)

Special rules enable the Revenue to treat two or more transactions related to a certain property as forming one 'chargeable transfer'. Where transactions at different times are treated as associated operations, the chargeable transfer is treated as taking place at the time of the last of these transactions.

22.29.4 **Gifts with reservation** (FA 1986 S102–102C & Sch 20)

If you make a gift after 17 March 1986 but reserve some benefit, this will normally result in the property remaining yours for inheritance tax purposes on your death. (This could also apply if you later enjoy the benefit of the gifted property.) However, if you subsequently release the reservation, you will be treated as making a PET (22.3) or chargeable transfer at that time. In contrast to PETs, the Capital Taxes Office may require a return to be made for a gift with reservation.

A particular example is where you gift a house but remain living there. The rule does not apply if your benefit is minimal (for example, you do not live in the house but only pay occasional visits). If you give full value for any benefit (for example, pay a full rent for the house), the rule is also set aside. There is also an exception where the reservation represents reasonable provision by a relative for the care and maintenance of an elderly or infirm donor whose circumstances have changed since making the gift.

The rules regarding gifts of homes have been strengthened with effect from 9 March 1999. If you make such a gift, it will be treated as being 'with reservation' if there is an arrangement for you to occupy the property to a material degree without paying full consideration. Exceptions include where you are only allowed to occupy the property once the interest which you gifted has come to an end.

The rules do not normally catch regular premium insurance policies made before 18 March 1986 and not altered since then.

It was held in a decided case (*CIR* v *Eversden*), that gifts made by a married person were not caught if routed through a trust for the spouse. However, such gifts with reservation made after 19 June 2003 are caught.

22.29.5 **Family maintenance** (ITA 1984 S11)

If you make any of the following gifts during your life, they are exempt:

(1) For the maintenance, education, etc. of your child, former wife or illegitimate child.
(2) For the maintenance or education of a child not in his parent's care, who has been in your care during substantial periods of his minority.
(3) For the care or maintenance of a dependent relative.

22.29.6 **Deeds of family arrangement** (ITA 1984 S17)

Inheritance tax is not charged on certain variations in the destination of property passing on death. Nor is it charged on the disclaimer of title to property passing on death. The variation or disclaimer must be within two years of the death. An election to the Revenue was required within six months of a variation. However, provided a variation made after 31 July 2002 states that it is to take effect for inheritance tax purposes, no election is needed. (The same applies for capital gains tax – 21.10.3.)

This exemption operates similarly, but without time limit, where a surviving spouse's life interest under an intestacy is redeemed. It also applies if an interest in settled property is disclaimed unless there is some consideration in money or money's worth.

Disclaimers are effective for inheritance tax purposes. These involve one or more beneficiaries disclaiming their entitlement. As a result, the assets return to the estate and are dealt with according to the directions of the will or as on intestacy.

22.29.7 **Pre-owned assets**

Legislation in FA 2004 (Sch 15) takes effect from 2005–06 and operates by imposing an income tax charge to counter certain estate planning benefits. The rules may catch you if you have disposed of assets since March 1986, but continue to enjoy benefits from them; also where you have funded the purchase of an asset for a third party. The stated objectives are contrived arrangements, but there are various exemptions and the rules are complicated.

An annual cash value will be quantified for your chargeable benefits for 2005–06 and subsequent years, which will be ignored if no more than £5,000, otherwise being added to your taxable income. Market rentals are to be used for land, with imputed percentages of capital value applying for chattels and intangible assets.

If you are caught by the above, you can elect by 31 January 2007, that the charge shall not apply for 2005–06 and subsequent years. You will then be regarded for IHT purposes as if the property in question forms part of your estate. This resembles the 'gifts with reservation' rules (22.29.4). Otherwise, you may prefer to wind up your original arrangements.

22.30 Settled property (ITA 1984 Pt III)

The rules concerning inheritance tax (and previously capital transfer tax) in relation to settled property are most detailed and the following are just a few guidelines:

(1) Broadly any settlement is subject to the inheritance tax rules on its worldwide assets, if at the time it was made the settlor was domiciled in the UK. Otherwise only assets situated in this country (22.28) are caught.
(2) The settlement of any property after 26 March 1974 is itself treated as a chargeable transfer by the settlor. However, after 17 March 1986, settlements on accumulation and maintenance trusts (22.30.1) or for the disabled are classified as PETs (22.3). Thus any property which you settle in this way only attracts inheritance tax if you die within seven years.
(3) If you have an interest in possession in any settled property for the time being (for example, you receive the income as of right), the property itself is treated as yours for inheritance tax purposes. Thus if your interest ends, you will be treated as making a transfer of the value of the property concerned. The tax is calculated on the basis of your cumulative transfers to that time. You can deduct your £3,000 annual exemption (22.17.2) and marriage allowance if applicable (ITA S57).
(4) From 17 March 1987 lifetime transactions involving interest in possession settlements are classed as PETs. This covers gifts setting them up, transfers out and changes in the beneficial interests.
(5) No inheritance tax is payable if you obtain an absolute interest in property in which you previously had a life interest (or other interest in possession). Similarly, tax normally is not payable on the reversion to you in your lifetime (or your spouse within two years of your death) of property which you previously settled. However, this rule normally no longer applies to discretionary settlements (22.30.2).
(6) Special rules apply to trusts where there is no interest in possession – particularly discretionary trusts, etc. and accumulation and maintenance settlements (22.30.1).
(7) Quick succession relief is given if an interest in possession comes to an end within five years of a previous chargeable transfer of the settled property. The relief is now allowed against the tax due on the later trans-

fer, etc. but is calculated as a *percentage of the tax payable* on the first transfer. The percentage is 100 per cent, 80 per cent, 60 per cent, 40 per cent or 20 per cent where the interval is not more than one, two, three, four, or five years respectively.

(8) Superannuation schemes and charitable trusts are normally exempted from inheritance tax as are employee and newspaper trusts (ITA Ss76, 86 & 87); also certain 'protective trusts' and trusts for the mentally disabled (treated as having a life interest in property settled for them after 9 March 1981). Where property is held temporarily on such trusts, the tax charge is proportionately reduced on a time basis (FA 1984 S102).

22.30.1 **Accumulation and maintenance settlements**

Accumulation and maintenance settlements with no fixed interests in possession for one or more beneficiaries up to an age not exceeding 25 are not subjected to the periodic charge (22.30.2); nor is inheritance tax charged on the capital distributed to those beneficiaries. This relief covers for example a settlement under which your son obtains an interest in possession at the age of 25 and at 35 gets the capital, the income being accumulated up to 25 apart from various payments for his maintenance. No inheritance tax is payable during the currency of the trust, nor when your son becomes entitled to the income at 25 nor the capital at 35.

Relief broadly only applies if either not more than 25 years have passed since the original settlement date (or when it first became accumulating); or if all beneficiaries are grandchildren of a common grandparent (or their widows, widowers, children, step-children, etc.).

Any payments into accumulation and maintenance settlements after 17 March 1986 are PETs (22.3). Thus no inheritance tax can be payable regarding their creation unless the settlor dies within seven years.

22.30.2 **Discretionary trusts etc.**

The following rules apply where there is no interest in possession in *all or part of the property.*

(1) The principal charge to inheritance tax (previously capital transfer tax) is the *periodic* charge. This usually falls on every tenth anniversary of the date of the settlement occurring after 31 March 1983. (Where a transfer requiring court proceedings was made in the year to 31 March 1983, the onset of the periodic charge was delayed until after that date.) The charge is at 30 per cent of the life-time inheritance tax rate (itself now half of the full 40 per cent rate) which would apply to the assets held on discretionary trusts (taking the $N/40$ fraction for additions during the ten year period – see (3) below).

(2) In calculating the rates of tax which apply, you must accumulate transfers made by the settlor in the seven years immediately prior to the

creation of the settlement and other settlements made by him on the same day; but this does not apply to a pre-26 March 1974 trust. For periodic charges before 18 March 1986, you needed to accumulate transfers by the settlor in the *ten* years before the creation of the settlement.

(3) For a settlement made between 26 March 1974 and 9 March 1982, distributions of capital made in the preceding ten years are taken into account in calculating the rate of tax on the first periodic charge. An exemption applies for transfers to charities and benevolent funds for employees (this also applies to pre-27 March 1974 trusts).

(4) Interim charges are made on distributions of capital to beneficiaries between periodic charges, but only N/40 of the full tax is charged on each distribution. (N is the number of completed three month periods for which the property has been held on discretionary trusts during the current ten year period – see (1) above.)

(5) Previously, tax was charged on the value of the trust property leaving the trust. However, after 8 March 1982, the charge is based on the reduction in the value of trust property, which could be greater.

(6) If property becomes settled under a will or intestacy it is taken to enter the settlement at death. Where the death is after 12 March 1984 any such property which is distributed within two years of death to a charity, employee trust, etc. is treated as if distributed at the time of death (FA 1984 S103).

(7) Property passing directly from one discretionary settlement to another is treated as remaining in the first for the purposes of the discretionary settlement rules. However, after 14 March 1983 this does not apply to certain reversionary interests existing before 10 December 1981 (FA 1984 S104).

(8) Non-resident trustees are liable for the periodic ten-year charge (see above).

(9) Transfers into discretionary settlements are charged to inheritance tax at half the rates applicable at death. If death occurred within three years and the original transfer was before 18 March 1986, the tax was increased by using the full rates at death (22.5.1). Subsequent to that date, if death occurs broadly within five years of a post-17 March 1986 transfer, the tax is likely to be increased, subject to tapering relief (22.6). 100 per cent of tax at full rates is due if death is within three years of the transfer, 80 per cent in the fourth year and 60 per cent in the fifth year.

22.31 Avoiding double charges (FA 1986 S104)

Rules were introduced to prevent double charges to inheritance tax on transfers of value and other events occurring after 17 March 1986. The rules in part take the place of the previous rules regarding mutual transfers. The situations covered include where a PET (22.3) becomes chargeable and immediately before the death the estate includes property acquired from the person who received the PET for less than full price.

22.32 Example: Calculation of inheritance tax payable

Mr A, having made no gifts relevant for capital transfer tax or inheritance tax, gives £56,000 to his son on 30 June 2002 and £100,000 to his wife on 15 September 2002. He dies on 31 May 2005 leaving an estate valued at £470,000, bequeathed as to £50,000 to his wife, £30,000 to charity and the remainder to his son, including his non-quoted shares in a family trading company valued at £120,000.

Inheritance tax is payable as follows:

	£	£
30 June 2002 – gift to son		56,000
Less: Annual exemption 2001–02 brought forward	3,000	
Annual exemption 2002–03	3,000	6,000
Potentially exempt (22.3)		50,000
15 September 2002 – gift to wife is exempt provided she is UK domiciled (17.2)		
Estate at death 31 May 2005		470,000
Less: Bequests free of inheritance tax:		
To wife	50,000	
To charity	30,000	80,000
		390,000
Less: Business property relief (22.18) 100% x £120,000		120,000
		270,000
Potentially exempt transfer 30 June 2002		50,000
		320,000
Inheritance tax on £320,000 : £275,000	Nil	–
£45,000	40%	£ 18,000

Chapter 23

AN OUTLINE OF VAT

23.1 Introduction

VAT was introduced into the UK on 1 April 1973 with an original rate of 10 per cent. A rate of 15 per cent replaced the previous 8 per cent standard rate and 12½ per cent higher rate on 18 June 1979. The rate was increased to 17½ per cent from 1 April 1991 (5 per cent now applying in isolated cases). All other countries now in the European Community have introduced a similar tax and the coverage, but not the rates, has been (at least in theory) harmonised. It is beyond the scope of this book to give more than a brief outline of the provisions of VAT. VAT is under the control and management of HM Customs and Excise, now to be known as HM Revenue and Customs following its merger on 18 April 2005 with the Inland Revenue (CRCA 2005).

VAT in the UK is imposed:

(1) on imports of goods by any person into the UK (subject to special EC rules – 23.17);
(2) on the supply (such as sale, hire and HP) of goods and services (which together comprise virtually all supplies) by a business in the UK; and
(3) in certain circumstances the import of services by a business.

Hence the tax is payable whenever goods or services pass from one business to another or to a private consumer, although in the former case it is frequently refunded.

After the end of each accounting period for the tax (usually a period of three months) each business has to render a *return* to Customs and Excise of all its 'outputs', that is, the supplies of goods and services it has made during the period to other businesses or to consumers; and has to account to Customs and Excise one month after the end of the period for VAT on the prices (before tax) of those outputs. Each business is, at the same time, normally allowed a credit for the VAT on its 'inputs' in that period, that is, goods imported by it and goods and services supplied to it for the purposes of the business. Unlike income tax or corporation tax, no distinction is made between capital or revenue inputs; the credit generally extends to the tax on its capital purchases as well as on its purchases of stock in trade.

The total tax on the inputs of a business is ascertained from the tax invoices given to it by every other business which has supplied it with goods or services. Amongst other details a typical tax invoice shows:

	£
Goods	100.00
VAT at 17½%	17.50
Price payable	117.50

At the end of each accounting period the business will total all the tax invoices it has received for its inputs in that period, which it must keep for production to Customs and Excise when required, together with its vouchers for tax imports; it will also total all its outputs for the period (keeping copies of all tax invoices it has rendered to other businesses) and a typical return for an accounting period will show:

	£	£
Total outputs during the period	50,000	
VAT thereon		8,750
Total inputs for the period	20,000	
VAT thereon		3,500
Balance payable to Customs and Excise		5,250

The effect of the credit mechanism is that although VAT is charged on each business in the chain of import, production and distribution, each business in the chain gets a credit for the tax on its inputs, so that the whole tax is passed on to the consumer on the final sale to him. This is best shown by an example which uses the original 10 per cent rate for simplicity:

	Price (ex-VAT) £	VAT £	£
Manufacturer imports raw materials	10	1	
Manufacturer accounts to Customs and Excise on import			1
Manufacturer sells product to wholesaler	100	10	
Manufacturer accounts to Customs and Excise for VAT			9 (10–1)
Wholesaler sells product to retailer	150	15	
Wholesaler accounts to Customs and Excise for VAT			5 (15–10)
Retailer sells to consumer	200	20	
Retailer accounts to Customs and Excise for VAT			5 (20–15)
Consumer bears VAT of		20	
Customs and Excise collect			20

This example, however, only shows how VAT is collected and borne over a series of transactions; it is not necessary to trace each item in this way, as the return at the end of each accounting period will cover all the inputs and outputs of the period. Credit for the VAT on unsold stock will have been given on its purchase and it will therefore be held tax free until sale.

Because of the credit mechanism outlined above a business does not normally bear much tax; it mainly acts as a collection agency. The ultimate consumer bears all the tax, which is why VAT is described as a sales tax. The difficulty of having a retail sales tax lies in determining when the final retail sale takes place. With VAT it does not matter; if the purchaser is a VAT registered business, he will generally get credit for the tax as input tax, and if he is not he will bear it. Another advantage of the credit mechanism is that the effect is neutral between supplies which go through a number of stages and those where the supplier is vertically integrated. In both cases the tax is on the amount of the final price to the consumer.

A turnover tax charges tax on tax and therefore encourages vertical integration which is not usually in the public interest.

As will be seen later (23.3), businesses which make some 'exempt' supplies do not normally get credit for the VAT on their inputs relating to these supplies.

23.2 VAT in practice

All businesses (23.4), except for the very small, are normally required to be registered with Customs and Excise and they have to make returns every three months. Some businesses which are likely to have repayments of tax, however, because they make zero-rated supplies, are allowed a one-month period. The return has to be completed and the tax paid by the end of the following month. Any amounts due to you will be paid but payments made to you in error may be recovered by assessment.

If Customs and Excise unreasonably delay any repayment to you, a repayment supplement of the greater of 5 per cent of the tax and £50 (previously £30) will be due. Also, you have the statutory right to claim interest on your overpayment of VAT due to the error of Customs and Excise. In future, interest rates will correspond more exactly with the Inland Revenue rates (16.8.2).

As from 18 July 1996, the powers of Customs and Excise to assess for undeclared VAT is limited to three years, except in cases of fraud and certain other cases, like 'do it yourself' housebuilders. Furthermore, the right to claim back overpaid VAT is restricted to a maximum of three years. Interest payable by the authorities is similarly limited (FA 1997, Ss44–49).

Businesses with annual turnovers under £660,000 which have been registered for at least one year are able to elect for annual VAT accounting. They make nine equal payments on account by direct debit and a tenth balancing amount with their annual return. Another arrangement open to businesses with outstanding VAT of not more than £5,000 and turnovers under £660,000 is to account for VAT on a cash rather than an invoice basis. This new limit (previously £600,000) applies from 1 April 2004. Businesses already within these schemes can remain until their turnover reaches £825,000 (previously £750,000).

The voluntary annual accounting scheme is improved for businesses with turnovers below £150,000 from 10 April 2003 (£100,000 from 25 April 2002) who do not need to wait for one year. Such a business has the option of making quarterly interim payments, but normally nine interim monthly payments will be followed with a balancing payment. However, if this total is below £2,000, no interim payments need be made.

From 1 October 1992, very large taxpayers make monthly VAT payments. This applies to those with VAT of at least £2 million for their four quarters up to 31 March 1991 and they make VAT payments on account of the first two months each quarter. Other businesses join the scheme once it can be seen that their VAT liability will exceed the threshold. As from 1 June 1996, monthly payments are 1⁄24 of the annual liability, with an option to pay the true VAT monthly. However, all payments must be made by electronic means and cleared by the month-end.

23.2.1 Penalties

There are penalties which may be imposed by the Courts for overdue VAT returns and payments. Naturally, far heavier penalties apply in cases involving dishonesty.

The 1985 Finance Act contained stern provisions to counter VAT evasion and speed up tax payment. For example, failure to pay tax on time or submit returns could involve a 'default surcharge'. From 1 April 1993, the maximum penalty is 15 per cent of the VAT involved. However, from 1 October 1993, a new minimum rate of 2 per cent applies for the first default after a surcharge liability notice. (For businesses with an annual turnover of no more than £150,000 there is no longer an automatic penalty on late VAT payments.)

From 1 January 1995, the penalties on late registration for VAT are 5 per cent, 10 per cent and 15 per cent of the tax. These rates apply where registration is late by no more than nine months, 18 months and more than 18 months respectively.

A 'serious misdeclaration penalty' at 15 per cent of the tax operates from 11 March 1992. There is a 'period of grace' extending to the due date for the next return. Also, the penalty will not now normally apply where misdeclarations are compensated for in the next return, nor where the undeclared tax is less than the lower of £1,000,000 and 30 per cent of the 'gross tax'. 'Gross tax' means your VAT on both inputs and outputs.

There is also a 15 per cent penalty on 'persistent misdeclaration resulting in understatements or overclaims'. This penalty will now only be used where a person has under-declared or over-claimed tax three times within twelve accounting periods and a written warning has been issued. Also, the misdeclaration in each period must be at least 10 per cent of the 'gross tax' or £500,000 if less. (Where a penalty is imposed for 'serious misdeclaration', it will also be included in the reckoning for 'persistent misdeclaration' penalty.)

Giving incorrect certificates of entitlement to zero-rating regarding supplies of fuel and power, new buildings or construction services is liable to a civil penalty. However, this is now subject to mitigation.

23.2.2 Allocation of outputs and inputs to periods

There are rules determining into which period a supply falls. For goods it is normally the date when the goods are removed or made available, and for services it is the date of performance. (There are special rules where VAT rates change.) There are two exceptions. If an invoice (which must contain specified information) is issued within 14 days after that time, the date of the invoice is taken. In practice this will usually apply and the advantage is that the VAT return can be made up from the copy invoices.

The other exception is for payments in advance when it is the date of invoice or payment which counts. This is the only time payment is relevant; normally it is the invoice which matters (see below under 'Special Cases' for the position of bad debts). An arrangement can also be made with Customs and Excise to use the last day of the calendar month or of a VAT accounting period as the time of supply.

The same rules apply for determining into which period the inputs fall. Consequently, relief for input tax will normally be available before the invoice has been paid. The invoices will need to be kept as proof. The VAT return will be a summary of invoices issued and invoices received. If tax is due to Customs and Excise, it will be paid with the return. Inputs of goods and services incurred prior to registration may subsequently be recovered in certain circumstances.

Strictly speaking, tax on *imports* by a business is due at the date of import. However, in practice the VAT is payable by the 15th of the month following importation. (Payment must be by direct debit and covered by bank guarantee.) No tax is due so long as the goods are in a bonded warehouse. Taxable persons pay no VAT on temporary imports for repair, modification etc., provided ownership does not change. Where the reverse happens, VAT on the re-import only applies to the repairs, etc. plus freight and insurance. Imports from EC countries are subject to special rules from 1 January 1993 (23.17).

23.3 Zero-rating and exemption

So far we have assumed that all the inputs and outputs of a business are taxable at a positive rate. Certain types of supply are treated specially either because they are 'zero-rated' or because they are 'exempt'. Details of these types are set out in Schedules 8 and 9 to the Value Added Tax Act 1994 and summaries of these Schedules are given later in this chapter.

If a supply is *zero-rated* this means that no tax is charged on the supply but credit is given to the supplier for all tax on his inputs relating to that supply. *Exports* of goods, for instance, are often zero-rated so that these leave the country free of VAT in the UK, although they may be liable to VAT in the country into which they are imported if that country imposes a VAT. However, exports to non-VAT registered customers in other EC member states may be taxable in the UK.

A business which exports most of its products will probably find that its returns for an accounting period show more tax on its inputs than on its outputs (the majority being zero-rated). In that event, the business can claim back the difference from Customs and Excise. Zero rating also applies to goods shipped for use as stores on a voyage or flight to a destination outside the UK, or for retail sale in transit. However, this does not apply to private voyages and flights.

The EC requires its members to have a VAT with a similar structure although different rates are allowed. One of the reasons is that the similar treatment of imports and exports ensures equality between home-produced and imported goods. Exports to EC countries are subject to special rules from 1 January 1993 (23.17).

In addition to exports, food and many other items sold within the UK (23.14) are also zero-rated. However, *exports of services* (for example professional advice) are often treated as supplied where the recipient resides, thus being outside the VAT net.

Exemption of a supply of goods or services is not so favourable as zero rating, for whilst this means that there is no VAT on the supply (as with zero-rating), there is no credit allowed for the corresponding tax on the inputs of the business. Thus life assurance is one of the exempt items (23.16) so that there is no tax on a premium on a life policy but the life assurance company can get no credit for the tax on those inputs which it uses for its life assurance business. This introduces a hidden tax cost to its business.

A business which supplies both taxable (including zero-rated) and exempt goods and services is a 'partly exempt' business and will have an accounting problem. When claiming credit for the tax on the inputs from Customs and Excise, it is entitled to credit for the tax on those inputs which it uses for its taxable supplies but it is not entitled to credit for the tax on those inputs which it uses for its exempt supplies.

Normally, a proportion of the business's input tax corresponding to its taxable supplies is allowed. (After 17 April 2002, this is subject to anti-avoidance rules which may adjust the allowable input tax to reflect the use made of the purchases.) However, if exempt input tax is less than £7,500 per year credit for input tax is not restricted. A requirement from 1 December 1994 is that the exempt input tax is no more than 50 per cent of total input tax. VAT is only recoverable if attributable to:

(1) business taxable supplies;
(2) supplies outside the UK which would have been VATable or zero-rated if made here;
(3) business supplies of certain warehoused goods disregarded for VAT;
(4) overheads supporting the above.

23.4 Business

Central to the working of VAT is the definition of 'business' because the credit mechanism is applied only to a business. It is defined to include any trade, profession or vocation. It also includes clubs and associations, such as sports clubs and members' clubs. The charging of admission fees, for example by the National Trust, is also taxable as a business. VAT is not charged on subscriptions to political parties, trade unions or professional bodies. In general, such subscriptions are now exempt.

23.5 Small traders

23.5.1 Registration

From 1 April 2005 a person whose taxable (including zero-rated) supplies are not more than £60,000 (previously £58,000 from 1 April 2004) per annum is not liable to be registered, although he can apply to be registered voluntarily. A business is required to register if the value of taxable supplies in the past 12 months exceeded £60,000. Alternatively, registration is required if there are reasonable grounds for believing that the value of taxable supplies will exceed £60,000 in the next 30 days.

A small trader who is not registered is in the same position as a business making only exempt supplies. He does not charge tax to his customers and has to bear any input tax.

From 1 April 2005 *deregistration* is in general allowed if Customs and Excise are satisfied that the taxable supplies for the ensuing year will not exceed £58,000 (previously £56,000).

23.5.2 Flat-rate scheme (FA 2002 S23)

From 25 April 2002, a new optional scheme operates under which, subject to the rules, you can elect to calculate your VAT due for each period by applying a fixed percentage to your total VAT-inclusive turnover. The rates have been improved from 1 April 2004. The actual percentage depends on your trade or profession and the following are examples:

	%
Retail – food, tobacco, newspapers, children's clothing and post offices	2
Public houses	5.5
Agriculture not listed elsewhere	6
Retail of goods not listed elsewhere and wholesaling agricultural products	6
Retailing vehicles and fuel	7
Building where materials supplied	8.5
Fishing, travel agencies, storage, freight, couriers and taxis	9
Hotels or accommodation, publishing	9.5
Estate agency, property management	11
Entertainment, laundry services	11
Financial services	11.5
Restaurants, hairdressing, real estate not listed elsewhere	12

▶

Computer repairs, professionals such as accountants, architects, lawyers etc.	13
Computer and IT consultancy, data processing	13
Building – labour only	13.5

Note:
With effect from 1 April 2004, the above rates are reduced by 1 per cent in each case in your first year of VAT registration. This is subject to your notifying your liability to register on time.

You can elect for the scheme to apply if your expected taxable turnover for the next 12 months is no more than £150,000 (£100,000 before 10 April 2003). Also, your total business turnover, including exempt supplies (23.3) and other non-taxable income must not be more that £187,500 (£125,000 before 10 April 2003). For example, suppose you are a travel agent and your total VAT-inclusive sales in a quarter are £22,000. If you have elected to join the scheme, you will simply pay 10% × £22,000 = £2,200, instead of your actual VAT on outputs, less that on your inputs.

23.6 Zero-rated supplies

A person whose supplies are all zero-rated can apply to be exempted from registration. He will not then be able to claim a refund of his input tax but he will not have to make VAT returns.

23.7 Groups and divisions of companies

A group of companies may be registered as a single business and supplies between members of the group will be ignored. The requirement that the companies should be UK resident has now been widened to include overseas companies with a fixed establishment in the UK. One company in the group is responsible for making returns for all the members of the group. Alternatively, a company which is organised in divisions can register each division separately.

The Commissioners of Customs and Excise can direct that separately registered entities are treated as one for VAT purposes. This applies for companies and other traders. The object is to combat artificially splitting a single business to avoid registration. Similarly, ineligible companies can be removed from groups. Certain avoidance schemes involving the movement of a company or the transfer of assets in or out of a group from 29 November 1995 are also countered. Further anti-avoidance measures take effect from 27 November 1996 and 1 August 2004 regarding groups. The latter makes it more difficult to join a VAT group in limited cases and prevents a company being in two such groups at the same time.

From 1 April 1990, capital items, such as computers, land and buildings over specified value limits are excluded from the VAT self-supply charge (23.11.3), which otherwise arises when assets are transferred to a partly exempt VAT group as part of the transfer of a going concern.

23.8 Local authorities

Local authorities are in the position of being both in business and also carrying on non-business activities, such as welfare services. Their business activities are treated in the normal way but the input tax on any non-business activities is refunded. In this way there is no hidden tax burden in the rates.

23.9 Charities

Sales in charity shops, fêtes, coffee mornings, etc. of donated goods are exempted. This applies to up to fifteen events of each type in a year in one location, not counting small-scale events, with weekly income no more than £1,000. Apart from this, business supplies of a charity are treated in the normal way; there is no exemption for charities. Non-business supplies such as distribution of free goods are outside the tax unless they are exported when they are zero-rated. Where a branch of a charity makes business supplies, for example sales at a fête, it may be treated as a separate entity from the charity and be entitled to the £60,000 limit before it is taxable. See zero-rating (23.14) for certain reliefs applicable to charities. The list of zero-rated items related to charities is being increased over the years. Further details may be found in VAT leaflet 701/1/92.

A new scheme enables national museums and galleries to reclaim VAT from 1 April 2001, even though they allow free admission to the public.

23.10 Retailers

Because retailers often cannot record each sale separately there are special schemes for calculating the amount of the tax which they pay. The schemes also deal with the difficulty of retailers which sell both zero-rated goods (for example, food) and standard-rated goods (for example, kitchen equipment). Details of the schemes are contained in Customs and Excise Notice No 727 and supplements describing each scheme.

23.11 Special cases

23.11.1 Motor cars

No deduction of input tax on motor cars is allowed on cars acquired for use in the business. This also applied to the acquisition of hire cars and taxis, except London-type taxis. However, VAT is recoverable for vehicles used in their businesses by private taxi and self-drive firms and driving schools. Businesses may recover input tax on cars used for a demonstrably wholly business purpose, primarily leasing, but must charge VAT on any cars sold.

The VAT on the hire charge is available for credit as input tax. However, this is restricted by 50 per cent where the car is leased from a business which has recovered the VAT and the car is partly used for private motoring. A car dealer is not affected and can claim a credit for input tax in the normal way, but if he takes a car out of stock and uses it in his own business, tax must be paid and it is not available for credit (see 'Self-supply', below). The definition of 'motor car' for this purpose excludes commercial vehicles, vans without rear side windows and vehicles accommodating only one or more than 9 persons.

From 12 May 2001, a 5 per cent VAT rate applies to children's car seats.

Petrol supplied at below cost by companies and partnerships etc. for private journeys is not allowable for VAT purposes so far as the input tax is concerned. This creates problems in computing the disallowance and a quarterly scale corresponding to the income tax figures (10.6.5) is used for each person concerned. (There is also a monthly scale.) The company, etc. is charged VAT on the scale figures which effectively cancels the appropriate input tax. The basic scale figures are as follows:

Quarterly Scale

Cylinder capacity	Accounting periods beginning on or after 1.5.03		1.5.04		1.5.05	
	Petrol £	Diesel £	Petrol £	Diesel £	Petrol £	Diesel £
Up to 1400cc	237	225	232	216	246	236
1401–2000cc	300	225	293	216	311	236
over 2000cc	442	283	432	273	457	300

If a car is wholly used for business purposes, the scale charge does not apply; nor does it apply where a car is used entirely for private purposes, in which case input tax is not deductible.

Rules being introduced later this year will affect motor dealers and manufacturers who allow employees to use demonstration cars privately at a nominal fee. In future, VAT will be charged on the open market value.

23.11.2 Business entertainment

Input tax on business entertainment is not deductible. Entertainment includes meals, accommodation, theatres and sporting facilities. This does not, however, prevent deduction of input tax on subsistence expenses refunded to employees.

23.11.3 Self-supply

It is advantageous for a business which makes exempt supplies to produce its own goods since no input tax will be charged for which it will be unable to obtain a credit. To prevent distortion, an order charging printed stationery to tax even though supplied to oneself has been made. Thus a bank, which is exempt, printing its own stationery would be charged tax on the value of the stationery and it could not obtain relief for the tax. An order also applies to cars to prevent avoidance of the non-deduction of input tax mentioned above.

Regulations may be made to restrict the recovery of input tax on self-supplies by partly exempt businesses. Recovery will only be allowed to the extent governed by the business's partial exemption method. However, from 1 June 2002, partly exempt businesses which produce printed matter for their own use valued above the VAT registration limit no longer have to account for VAT under the self-supply rules.

Developers of certain non-residential *buildings* may be treated as making self-supplies in various circumstances. This applies where, for example, a lease is granted which is an exempt supply; also, when the developer is not a fully taxable person and occupies the building.

In such cases VAT is chargeable based on the land and taxable construction costs, subject to certain exclusions. These include where the value is less than £100,000 and where the construction was completed before 1 August 1989; also, if the freehold had already passed and the non-residential building is new.

23.11.4 **Second-hand goods**

Second-hand goods are chargeable to tax in the normal way, except that there are special provisions relating to cars, motorcycles, caravans, boats and outboard motors, original works of art, antiques over 100 years old, collectors' pieces, electronic organs and aircraft, which provide that VAT is payable only on the dealer's mark-up. Except in the case of cars these provisions apply only when no tax was charged on the dealer's acquisition or when tax was charged on another dealer's mark-up. Where goods are taken in part-exchange, full VAT is still payable on the new goods supplied.

From 1 January 1995, the dealer's mark-up is chargeable to VAT for all second hand goods, works of art, antiques and collectors items apart from precious metals and gems. VAT is computed on a global basis and other changes have since been made.

Goods obtained under the special VAT rules for transferring a business as a going concern can now only be sold under the margin scheme if they were so eligible in the hands of the previous owner.

23.11.5 **Sales on credit**

A separately disclosed credit charge is exempt from VAT.

23.11.6 **Gifts**

Business gifts of goods are taxable on the cost price but items costing in aggregate under £50 (£15 before 8 March 2001) can be ignored. This applies to samples in general unless more than one identical item is supplied to one person, in which case relief is limited to one item. Gifts of services are not taxable. From 1 October 2002, the £50 rule applies to a series of gifts within a 12-month period not exceeding such aggregate.

23.11.7 Personal use

If a person acquires goods in the course of business and uses them for his own personal use, for example, a shopkeeper who takes goods off the shelf, tax is payable on the cost price of the goods.

23.11.8 Accommodation for directors

VAT on repairs, refurbishments and other expenses relating to domestic accommodation provided for directors and their families does not rank as deductible input tax. This applies where the accommodation is provided by a business for domestic purposes but not to any rooms used specifically for business where a proportion of the total VAT would be deductible.

23.11.9 Bad debts

Relief for bad debts exists where the debtor goes bankrupt or goes into liquidation. The amount excluding VAT is claimed from the liquidator, etc. and the VAT from Customs and Excise. Retailers in effect obtain bad debt relief as the special schemes are based on payments. (Relief extends beyond cases of formal insolvency.)

Automatic bad debt relief is now available on debts which are more than six months old (from payable date), and have been written off in the accounts. If you have reclaimed VAT on inputs for which you do not pay, you needed to repay this if your supplier has claimed bad debt relief (FA 1997 S39). However, FA 2002 (S22) removes the connection between the repayment of input tax on unpaid invoices and the supplier claiming bad debt relief. The relief extends to non-monetary (barter) transactions (FA 1998 S23).

23.11.10 Tour operators

Previously, the services of tour operators regarding overseas package holidays were not liable to VAT in the UK. However, FA 1987 S16 introduced a special VAT margin scheme. UK based tour operators buying in services pay VAT on the margin between their buying and selling prices. This applies if the services are used in the EC, including the UK. Furthermore they are not able to recover any VAT charged by suppliers for those services.

23.11.11 Fuel and power

Fuel and power were originally zero-rated but commercial use was standard rated from 1 April 1989 (23.15). FA 1993 provided that domestic fuel and power were to remain zero-rated until 31 March 1994, then being taxable at 8 per cent for the year to 31 March 1995. After that, the standard rate of VAT (17.5 per cent) was to have applied but Finance Act 1995 kept the rate at 8 per cent and from 1 September 1997 it is 5 per cent. This rate now applies to the installation of energy-saving materials and from 1 June 2002, certain grant-funded heating equipment in homes. From 1 June 2004, ground-source heat pumps are also included. This extends to air source heat pumps and micro-combined heat and power units in residential accommodation and certain charity buildings from 7 April 2005.

From 1 January 2005, VAT on wholesale supplies of natural gas and electricity is to be accounted for where the customer receiving the supply is established. Otherwise, the place of supply will be where it is consumed. Other changes include relieving natural gas and electricity from VAT when imported from outside the EC.

23.11.12 Registration of racehorse owners

Subject to the Jockey Club changing the Rules of Racing to allow owners to seek sponsorship and appearance money, racehorse owners will be able to register for VAT purposes. This has retrospective effect to 16 March 1993.

23.12 Documentation

The legislation contained in FA1972 and nearly all the subsequent Finance Acts was consolidated into the Value Added Tax Act 1983. In turn this together with further legislation in Finance Acts has been consolidated into the Value Added Tax Act 1994. Also a large number of statutory instruments have been made under powers contained in the Acts, all of which are available from HMSO.

Detailed information is contained in various Notices issued by Customs and Excise. However, these are constantly updated and the titles often change. They are available free from any Customs and Excise VAT office and include the following:

Number			
48	Extra-statutory concessions	719	Refund of VAT to 'do-it-yourself' builders
700	The VAT guide	723	Refunds of VAT in the European Community and other countries
700/21	Keeping records and accounts	725	The single market
700/50	Default surcharge	727	Special schemes for retailers
700/56	Insolvency	728	Motor vehicles, boats, aircraft: intra EC movements by private persons
700/62	Self-billing	730	Investigations – Statement of Practice
701/1	Charities	731	Cash accounting
702	Imports and warehoused goods	732	Annual accounting
703	Exports	741	International services
704	Retail exports	742	Property ownership etc.
705	Personal exports of new motor vehicles (outside EC)	744	Passenger transport, international freight, ships and aircraft
706	Partial exemption	749	Local authorities and similar bodies
708	Buildings and construction		
714	Young children's clothing and footwear		

It should be emphasised that these Notices are in general guides, and, with certain exceptions such as No 727, they do not have any legal force. Several of the Notices are supported by numerous leaflets on specific topics.

23.13 Appeals

Independent VAT tribunals deal with appeals about the matters listed below. (From a date to be appointed, these are to be known as VAT and duties tribunals, with wider coverage.) There are tribunals in London, Edinburgh, Belfast and Manchester. The tribunal consists of a chairman who can sit alone or with one or two other members. The procedure is explained in a leaflet printed by the President of VAT Tribunals which is available from Customs and Excise VAT offices. The 1985 Finance Act (S27 & Sch 8) contains certain rules about VAT Tribunals. For example chairmen must be barristers or solicitors (advocates in Scotland) of seven years' standing.

The matters over which the tribunals have jurisdiction are as follows:

(1) Registration.
(2) Registration of groups of companies.
(3) Assessment of VAT by Customs and Excise.
(4) The amount of VAT chargeable.
(5) The amount of the deduction of input tax.
(6) Apportionment of input tax by a partly exempt person.
(7) Special schemes for retailers.
(8) The value of certain supplies.
(9) The provision of security.
(10) Repayment of VAT on certain imports.
(11) Refunds to do-it-yourself builders.
(12) Bad debt relief.
(13) Voluntary registration of a person whose turnover is below the limit.
(14) Appeals against certain Commissioners' decisions which in turn depend upon prior unappealable decisions which they made.

There is an appeal from the tribunal on a point of law (there is no appeal on a question of fact) to the High Court and from there to the Court of Appeal. There is a final appeal to the House of Lords if leave to appeal is obtained. In Scotland appeals go to the Court of Session and thence to the House of Lords.

23.14 Zero-rating (VATA Sch 8)

The following is a list of the important items. Full details are contained in the General Guide (VAT Notice No 700) available from Customs and Excise. The group numbers have been changed in some instances by VATA 1994.

- *Group 1: Food* All food except pet foods, alcoholic drinks and certain food products (such as ice cream, chocolate, confectionery including cereal bars, soft drinks and potato crisps). Meals out are, however, taxable and this includes hot take-away food and drink.

- *Group 2: Sewerage services and water* Water except for distilled water and bottled water; emptying cesspools. (Standard rated from 1 July 1990 if for industrial use – 23.15.)
- *Group 3: Books etc.* Books, newspapers, magazines, music, maps. But diaries and stationery are taxable.
- *Group 4: Talking books and tape recorders for the blind and handicapped and wireless sets for the blind*, including (from 1.4.92) their repair and maintenance.
- *Group 5: Construction of dwellings etc.* Sale of the freehold or grant of a lease for more than 21 years of a building by a builder; construction, and demolition of buildings but not repairs (now basically dwellings for your own, charity and community use – 23.15). Sales by a builder's merchant, and architects' and surveyors' fees are, however, taxable. A person building his own house can reclaim tax paid on items purchased. (Conversions, reconstructions, alterations and enlargements for industrial and commercial use are normally standard rated and sales of reconstructed buildings are exempt.) From 1 August 2001, the sale of renovated houses which have been empty for over 10 years is zero rated. From 1 June 2002, new annexes constructed partly for charitable use will be proportionately zero-rated.
- *Group 6: Protected buildings* This includes alterations and reconstructions of listed buildings, ancient monuments and listed churches.
- *Group 7: International services* Exports of services, such as an agent arranging the export of goods or certain services outside the EC for a named principal (see also 23.3). Also carrying out work on goods from abroad subsequently exported outside the EC.
- *Group 8: Transport* Passenger transport (inland and international) including travel agents (except in relation to hotels in the UK or package tours), and international freight transport. Taxis and hire cars are, however, taxable, as are pleasure boats and aircraft. Lifeboats and slipways, etc. are all included as are spare parts, etc. for lifeboats and for zero-rated ships and aircraft.
- *Group 9: Caravans and houseboats* Caravans which are too large to be used as trailers on the roads (22.9 feet in length or 7.5 feet in breadth). But smaller caravans are taxable.
- *Group 10: Gold* Transactions on the London Gold market.
- *Group 11: Bank notes*
- *Group 12: Drugs, medicines, medical and surgical appliances* Drugs dispensed by a registered pharmacist on a doctor's prescription. Other drugs purchased without a prescription are taxable. Medical and surgical

appliances for the disabled. Donated computer equipment is zero-rated, as are lifts and distress systems for the handicapped and necessary work on bathrooms, etc. in private homes and in bathrooms for the handicapped in charity residential homes, day centres and other charity premises. More general relief is available for medical equipment, ambulances, etc. purchased out of charitable funds or donated. This extends to the sale of donated goods and printed media advertising costs.

- *Group 13: Imports, exports etc.* This group has limited application.
- *Group 14: Tax-free shops* Relating to travellers to other EC countries making purchases on planes, ships, at airports and ports within the limits (1 litre of spirits, 2 litres of wine, 60 ml of perfume, 200 cigarettes etc. and £71 of other goods to be carried in personal luggage).
- *Group 15: Charities* (23.9) This includes non-classified advertising (all advertising from 1 April 2000), medical video or refrigeration equipment and motor vehicles with from seven to fifty seats. Also, drugs and chemicals used in medical (and veterinary) research by a charity are zero-rated, also welfare vehicles for the terminally ill and certain rescue equipment. The sale of donated goods is generally included, as is fund-raising and educational advertising on television, radio and cinema. Also covered are toilet facilities in charity-run buildings and boats adapted for the handicapped.
- *Group 16: Clothing and footwear* Clothing for young children, industrial protective clothing (provided meeting UK or EC safety standards and bearing mark) and motor-cyclists' and pedal cyclists' crash helmets. (Protective boots and helmets are standard-rated if supplied to employers for their employees – 23.15.)
- *Export of goods* (23.3) This does not include exports to Northern Ireland, which is part of the UK, or to the Isle of Man.

Note: Zero-rating has priority over exemption if a supply falls into both categories.

23.15 Changes to zero-ratings

On 21 June 1988, the European Court of Justice ruled that certain zero-ratings did not comply with European Community Law. As a result, the following items are *standard-rated (17.5 per cent)*, details being introduced by the 1989 Finance Act and now included in VATA 1994:

(1) construction of buildings for industrial and commercial use;
(2) supplies after 31 March 1989 of fuel and power other than to final consumers for domestic use (domestic use taxable from 1 April 1994 – 23.11.11);
(3) sewerage services and water supplies to industry after 30 June 1990;
(4) supplies after 31 March 1989 of news services insofar as they are not provided to final consumers;

(5) protective boots and helmets supplied to employers after 31 March 1989 for use by their employees.

All contracts entered into before 21 June 1988 continue to be zero-rated. Owners of non-domestic property have the option to elect to charge VAT on rents, and on sales of certain used buildings, from 1 August 1989. Owners can obtain no input tax relief before the election has effect, subject to transitional relief. Certain transactions in non-residential buildings may be treated as self-supplies giving rise to VAT.

23.16 Exemptions (VATA Sch 9)

The following is a list of the more important items. Full details are contained in the General Guide (VAT Notice 700) available from Customs & Excise:

- *Group 1: Land* Sales, leases and hiring out of land and buildings (unless within zero-rating Group 8 or taxable). Examples of taxable items are hotels (excluding conference facilities), holiday accommodation, camping, parking, timber, mooring, exhibition stands, sporting rights and the sale and construction of new non-residential buildings and civil engineering works (23.15).
- *Group 2: Insurance* All types of insurance and insurance brokers and agents. Both premiums and the payment of claims are exempt.
- *Group 3: Postal services* Post, except telegrams. But telephones and telex are taxable.
- *Group 4: Betting, gaming and lotteries* Bookmakers, charges for playing bingo. But admission or session charges, club subscriptions and takings from gaming machines are taxable.
- *Group 5: Finance* Banking, buying and selling stocks and shares and charges from credit card companies to retailers etc. accepting the cards; also making arrangements and certain intermediary services. But stockbrokers' commissions and unit trust management fees are taxable.
- *Group 6: Education* Schools, universities, non-profit-making institutions teaching pupils of any age, or providing job training; private tuition by an independent teacher; government funded training programmes (including from 1 April 1993 where provided for profit).
- *Group 7: Health* Doctors, dentists, dental workers, nurses, midwives, registered health visitors, registered opticians (including spectacles supplied in the course of treatment), chiropodists, dieticians, medical laboratory technicians, occupational therapists, orthoptists, physiotherapists, radiographers and remedial gymnasts, hearing aid dispensers, registered pharmaceutical chemists, medical and surgical treatment (except health farms, etc.).
- *Group 8: Burial and cremation* Undertakers, crematoria.

- *Group 9: Trade unions and professional bodies.*
- *Group 10: Sports competitions.*
- *Group 11: Certain works of art etc.*
- *Group 12: Fund-raising events* Supplies of goods and services by charities and other qualifying bodies (including certain subsidiaries) in connection with fund-raising events.

Note: Zero-rating has priority over exemption if a supply falls into both categories.

23.17 Trading within the EC

F2A 1992 Sch 3 made detailed provisions related to the introduction of the Single Market from 1 January 1993. From that date, import procedures are abolished for movements of goods within the EC. Instead there is a concept of 'acquisition'. Supplies of goods between persons registered for VAT in EC countries continue to be zero-rated. However, the acquirer must account for local VAT in the member state to which the goods are sent.

If you supply goods to persons registered for VAT in other EC countries, you will need to submit quarterly EC Sales Lists. (Supplies between the UK and non-EC countries remain largely as before.)

Private individuals normally effectively bear VAT at the appropriate rate in the member state of the supplier. However, VAT in the member state of the purchaser (and not the supplier) applies to mail order purchases, new motor vehicles, motor cycles, boats and aircraft; also supplies to non-VAT registered businesses and non-taxable institutions.

If you supply goods from another EC member state to non-VAT registered customers in the UK and are responsible for delivery, this is known as 'distance selling'. Should your annual turnover from distance selling reach £70,000, you must register for UK VAT.

Different rules apply to the supply of services from one EC country to another. In some cases these can require local VAT to be paid in the country of receipt or performance.

Fiscal warehousing operates from 1 June 1996. New provisions allow VAT free trading within fiscal warehousing regimes for qualifying commodities, such as specified foodstuffs, metals and chemicals. When these are removed from the regime, VAT becomes payable.

A new requirement to register for VAT operates from 21 March 2000 in certain circumstances regarding overseas businesses. The aim is to stop goods being sold free of VAT in the UK where the seller (or a previous owner of the business) has reclaimed the VAT paid on the goods under the rules which allow unregistered overseas businesses to do so (FA 2000 S136 & Sch 36).

23.18 Optional rate for farmers (VATA S54)

From 1 January 1993, farmers can choose whether to register for VAT or opt to become flat rate farmers. If your taxable supplies are below the registration level (£60,000) you will still have the option of not registering for VAT, nor will you have to become a flat rate farmer.

As a flat rate farmer, you will be outside the VAT system and so obtain no relief for purchases. However, to compensate you, a fixed rate is to be added to your sales and retained by you. The actual rate is 4 per cent. However, you will not be eligible if you would stand to gain £3,000 or more in a year by participating in the scheme.

23.19 Renovations and conversions of residential properties (VATA Sch A1)

From 12 May 2001, a reduced VAT rate of 5 per cent applies to the cost of the following:

(1) renovating dwellings that have been empty for at least 3 years
(2) converting a residential property into a different number of dwellings (for example, flats)
(3) converting a non-residential property into one or more dwellings
(4) converting a dwelling into a care home or house in multiple occupation.

From 1 June 2002, the 5% rate also covers:

(1) converting a non-residential home into a care home or multiple occupancy building (for example, bedsits)
(2) renovating or altering a care home, etc. not lived in for at least 3 years
(3) renovating or altering a multiple-occupancy building not lived in for 3 years or more
(4) constructing, renovating or converting a building which qualifies for the 5 per cent rate into a garage.

23.20 Avoidance schemes – disclosure (VATA S58A & Sch 11A)

Businesses with turnovers upwards of £600,000 is required to inform Customs and Excise if they use certain VAT avoidance schemes, which are recorded on a statutory list. This must be done within 30 days after the first return becomes due which is effected by the scheme after it is listed. A penalty of 15 per cent of the tax avoided will apply if you fail to disclose.

Broadly similar rules will apply to businesses with turnovers over £10 million who use schemes with some of the 'hallmarks of avoidance'. However, in those cases, the non-disclosure penalty is a flat rate of £5,000.

There are also provisions for the promoters of VAT avoidance schemes voluntarily to register those which have the 'hallmarks of avoidance' with Customs and Excise. Provided it has been given the relevant reference number, a business using such a scheme does not need to notify the authorities.

Chapter 24

STAMP DUTY

24.1 Introduction

Stamp duty is perhaps the most modest of capital taxes although the 'take' is increasing. However, even though the rates are very low, stamp duty is likely to arise on some of your major capital transactions and could involve significant sums. Therefore a brief outline is given below. This concentrates on the *ad valorem* duties, which are charged according to the value of a transaction, rather than the less important *fixed duties*.

The stamp duty rules are contained in the Stamp Act 1891, Stamp Duties Management Act 1891 and subsequent Finance Acts. The 1984 Finance Act (S105) halved the rates of some of the main *ad valorem* duties to 1 per cent from 20 March 1984 (12 March 1984 for most Stock Exchange transactions). The 1985 Finance Act removed certain fixed duties (S79) and abolished contract note duty. Also, *gifts* ceased to be liable to *ad valorem* duty; along with deeds of family arrangement (22.29.6) and divorce transfers. The duty on share transfers was further reduced to 0.5 per cent by the 1986 Finance Act (S58). Also, a new stamp duty reserve tax was introduced (24.5).

Stamp duty is essentially a charge on documents (instruments). (These must be delivered as well as signed.) It is not charged on the transactions and so if you carry out a transaction without documenting it, no duty should be chargeable. Furthermore if you later make a separate written record of an oral contract, this should not involve stamp duty. However, the Inland Revenue are re-appraising their attitude towards stamp duty avoidance and certain rules regarding shares are being changed. For example bearer letters of allotment are no longer exempted. In addition from 8 December 1993 surrenders of leases are dutiable whether or not they are documented.

The payment of stamp duty is confirmed by a stamp being impressed on the document. The stamp office may need to adjudicate the value of a transaction for duty purposes and you could need to supply balance sheets and other details. If documents are not stamped, you will not always be open to action by the Revenue but the instruments will not be admitted in evidence in court. Also, you may be liable for fines if you present the instrument late for filing – in practice after 30 days from when the instruments are first executed (or brought into the UK).

Anti-avoidance provisions are being introduced regularly and more are expected. For example, from December 1993, exchanges of land interests are now treated as sales. Also, land interests must be valued if the price payable on transfer cannot then be ascertained. FA 1999 includes stiffer penalties, for example for late stamping and changes the interest rules. FA 2002 contains a series of anti-avoidance measures regarding commercial property transactions. From 1 December 2003 stamp duty land tax broadly replaced stamp duty on land transactions.

24.2 Exemptions

The following table lists some of the more important exemptions from stamp duty.

24.2.1 Exemptions from stamp duty

- Transfers of Government Stocks ('Gilts')
- Transfers of units in certain authorised unit trusts invested in UK government securities, etc.
- Transfers of short term loans (no more than five years)
- Transfers of certain fixed rate non-convertible loan stocks
- Transfers of bearer loan capital
- Transfers of certain non-sterling loans raised by foreign governments or companies
- Conveyances, transfers or leases to approved charities (FA 1982 S129)*
- Conveyances, transfers or leases to the National Heritage Memorial Fund*
- Transactions effected by the actual operation of law
- Documents regarding transfers of ships (or interests in them)
- Transfers brought about by will (testaments and testamentary instruments)
- Articles of apprenticeship and of clerkship
- Customs bonds, etc.
- Certain legal aid documents
- Contracts of employment
- Certain National Savings documents
- Deeds of Covenant and bonds
- Policies of insurance and related documents (excluding life assurance up to 31 December 1989)
- One life assurance policy which is substituted for another according to the rules (FA 1982 S130)
- Transfers (and issue) of certain EC Loan Stocks
- Transfers of Treasury guaranteed stock
- Property put into unit trusts (FA 1988 S140)
- Agreement pursuant to Highway Acts
- Appointment, procuration, revocation
- Letter or power of attorney
- Deeds not liable to other duties no longer liable to 50p duty
- In Scotland, resignation, writ, etc.
- Warrants to purchase Government stock, etc. (FA 1987 S50)
- Transfers to a Minister of the Crown or the Treasury Solicitor (FA 1987 S55)
- Life assurance policies after 31 December 1989
- Superannuation contracts or grants after 31 December 1989
- Transfers of insurance business under a demutualisation scheme (FA 1997 S96)
- Conversions and mergers of open-ended investment companies and authorised unit trusts up to 30 June 1999
- Certain on-exchange transactions by intermediaries

- Units in a unit trust from 1 February 2000, when liable to stamp duty reserve tax (FA 1999 S122)
- Transactions in intellectual property from 28 March 2000 (FA 2000 S129 & Sch 34)
- Purchases and leases of land and buildings by registered social landlords (FA 2000 S130)
- Transfers of assets to the Northern Ireland Assembly Commission (FA 2000 S132)
- Certain shares in open-ended investment companies and unit trusts held within individual pension accounts (FA 2001 Ss93 & 94)
- Purchase by employees of partnership or dividend shares from an AESOP trust (FA 2001 S95)
- Documents transferring goodwill from 23 April 2002 (FA 2002 S116 & Sch 36)
- Registered social landlords granting short-term tenancy agreements from 1 January 2000 (FA 2003 S129).

* Not treated as duly stamped unless they have a stamp denoting not chargeable to duty.

24.3 Relief for take-overs and within groups

Relief applied from *ad valorem* stamp duty (FA 1985 S78) up to 24 March 1986, where a company issued shares, etc. in exchange for those of another company, in the course of obtaining control, or if it already had control. *Relief normally remains*, however, where there is a company reconstruction with no real change in ownership unless redeemable shares are involved (FA 2000 S127). Also, relief applies for transfers between associated companies (broadly 90 per cent common control). FA 1995 Ss132–134 extended the relief to leases granted by one associated company to another and generally reduced the requisite control to 75 per cent, the definitions now following the corporation tax rules (FA 2000 Ss123 & 124).

24.4 *Ad valorem* duties

The most important stamp duties with which you may be involved are those which increase according to the consideration involved. These are known as *ad valorem* duties. Normally, *ad valorem* duties are charged at a fixed percentage but this is sometimes expressed in bands, so that the 0.5 per cent on share transfers, etc. is 50p for every £100 or part thereof. Also, for some duties, sliding scales apply for small transactions.

The following table gives the basic percentage rates of various *ad valorem* duties:

24.4.1 *Ad valorem* stamp duties

	Rate (%)
Capital duty (1% before 16 March 1988)	Nil
Conveyance or transfer on sale other than share transfers*	See 24.4.2
Share transfers	½
Certain non-exempt loan transfers	½
Exchanges or partitions of freehold land	1
Inland bearer instruments‡	1½
Overseas bearer instruments‡	1½
Conversion of UK shares into depositary receipts (24.5)	1½
Lease premiums	1

Leases: *Ad valorem* duty on rents pre-1 December 2003

Term	Annual rent	Duty for every £50 or part thereof
Not exceeding 7 years or indefinite	Not exceeding £5,000ø	Nil
	exceeding £5,000ø	£0.50

Term	Annual rent	Duty for every £50 or part thereof
7–35 years	–	£1
35–100 years	–	£6
over 100 years	–	£12

ø £500 before 28 March 2000.

* Includes land, etc. For most categories including houses, no duty is payable if the value is certified at no more than £120,000 (24.4.2).

‡ Bearer loan capital exempt.

24.4.2 *Ad valorem* duty on transfers of property other than shares (FA 1998 S149)

In general, the rate for land and buildings was 1 per cent, but there was normally a £60,000 threshold, at or below which no duty was payable. However, increases from 8 July 1997, 24 March 1998, 16 March 1999 and 28 March 2000 produced new scales as follows for property other than shares:

Price £	8.7.97 to 23.3.98 £	24.3.98 to 15.3.99 £	16.3.99* to 27.3.00 %	28.3.00 to 16.3.05 %
Up to 60,000	Nil	Nil	Nil	Nil
60,001–250,000	1 per 100 or part	1 per 100 or part	1	1
250,001–500,000	1.50 per 100 or part	2 per 100 or part	2.5	3
Above 500,000	2 per 100 or part	3 per 100 or part	3.5	4

* A new calculation basis applies from 16.3.99.

Note that SDLT (24.4.3) generally took over for land transactions from 1 December 2003 but the above rates still apply with the threshold for commercial property increasing to £150,000 and from 17 March 2005, that for residential property to £120,000.

Transfers and leases of property in the most disadvantaged areas of the UK are now exempt from stamp duty (FA 2001 S92 & Sch 30 & FA 2002 S110). This applies from November 2001 regarding all property transfers of no more than £150,000. From 10 April 2003, all non-residential property in such areas is exempted. However, from 17 March 2005 the relief regarding commercial properties is generally withdrawn.

24.4.3 **Changes operating from 1 December 2003** (FA 2003 Ss125–126 & Schs 19–20)

(1) Stamp duty land tax (SDLT) generally replaced stamp duty in respect of land transactions with effect from 1 December 2003 and minor technical changes have been made subsequently.
(2) For commercial property, the zero rate band upper limit increased from £60,000 to £150,000.
(3) A modernised scheme started and stamp duty was generally abolished on transactions involving land.
(4) New leases bear duty at 1 per cent of the discounted net present value of the rent payments where this exceeds £120,000 (previously £60,000) for residential and £150,000 for non-residential property.
(5) SDLT is charged on certain transactions relating to land and partnerships which were not previously covered, including land which is transferred into a partnership by an existing partner or in exchange for a partnership share.

24.5 Stamp duty reserve tax (FA 1986 Ss86–99, FA 1996 Ss186 & 189 & FA 1999 Ss116–123 & Sch 19)

A charge called stamp duty reserve tax applies at 0.5 per cent on certain transactions in securities otherwise not liable to stamp duty. The charge broadly operates from 27 October 1986 but does not apply to securities exempt from sale duty (for example gifts) or traded options, etc. Examples of when the tax applies are renounceable letters of allotment and sometimes where there is no transfer document (for example closing transactions within Stock Exchange accounts). A special rate of 1.5 per cent applies to the conversion of UK shares into depositary receipts after 18 March 1986.

From 1 July 1996, transfers of shares into electronic transfer systems are exempted from stamp duty. However, if the transfers are made for consideration in money or money's worth, the underlying agreement will be liable to stamp duty reserve tax.

A new stamp duty reserve tax framework operates from 1 February 2000 regarding transfers of units in unit trusts. The rate is 0.5% unless the trust is shrinking, when a lesser rate may apply. A similar scheme will apply for open-ended investment companies.

24.6 Abolition of stamp duty on shares etc. (FA 1990 Ss107–111 & FA 1991 Ss110–117)

It was intended that stamp duties on shares would be abolished from a date to be announced. This was to coincide as far as possible with the introduction of paperless dealing under the new Stock Exchange share transfer system. At the same time, stamp duty charges on property other than land and buildings would go, including on patents, goodwill and debt. However, the proposed 'Taurus' scheme having been abandoned, stamp duty on share transfers (except gifts) remained.

From 1 July 1996, transfers of securities into an electronic transfer system are exempt from stamp duty. However, stamp duty reserve tax (24.5) may apply, according to the rules.

The duties to be abolished include the 0.5 per cent stamp duty on individual share transfers, 1.5 per cent where UK shares are transferred into clearance services or converted into depositary receipts, stamp duty reserve tax (24.5), stamp duties on bearer shares and unit trust unit transfers.

A number of documents are still to be liable to a fixed amount of stamp duty amounting to 50p per document. However, from October 1999, the rate increases generally to £5. All of these are to be relieved from stamp duty at the same time as the *ad valorem* duty on shares is abolished. After that, stamp duty will apply only to land transactions.

Chapter 25

SOCIAL SECURITY

25.1 Introduction

The main social security legislation is now comprised in the Social Security Acts of 1992 and supporting statutory instruments and amendments. The subject is a wide one and only an outline is given below.

Arguably, social security contributions are not a tax but their effect is very similar. Although ultimate benefits such as retirement pensions are secured, when you pay the contributions, you must normally do so out of your after-tax income. Social security contributions payments do not reduce your taxable income any more than do income tax payments.

25.2 National Insurance contributions

Contributions are payable under four categories known as 'Class 1' (employees), 'Class 2' (self-employed), 'Class 3' (voluntary) and 'Class 4' (self-employed earnings related). Classes 2 and 3 are flat rate contributions and Class 4 is dealt with subsequently (25.5). The following points should be noted regarding Class 1:

(1) Contributions are graduated according to earnings up to a certain level and are collected together with income tax under the PAYE system (10.14). They are not allowable for income tax purposes.

(2) Your employer supplements your contributions. Your employers' contributions are deductible for tax purposes.

(3) No contributions are payable if the weekly earnings are less than £91 but once this level is reached, your entire wages (up to £610) carry percentage contributions.

(4) There is no upper earnings limit for employers. They pay contributions on the total earnings of employees.

(5) If your employers operate an approved pension scheme which is contracted out of the state scheme, lower contributions will be due. If you contract out via a Personal Pension Plan, you still pay full National Insurance contributions. The rebate is paid direct to the pension plan.

(6) You will not have to pay contributions if you have retired and passed normal retirement age (60 for a woman and 65 for a man). If you are still working beyond age 65 you will not be liable for contributions. Your employer remains liable, however.

(7) If you have a company car and earn no less than £8,500 annually, your employer will pay Class 1A National Insurance contributions at currently 12.8 per cent on your taxable benefits. These comprise both your car scale benefit and fuel benefit, where applicable. This is an annual charge, payable for 1991–92 and subsequent tax years normally by the following 19 July.

The following tables give details concerning the rates of contribution.

25.2.1 National Insurance contributions

	Tax year	
	2004–05 £	2005–06 £
'Class 1' – employees aged 16 and over		See 25.2.2
'Class 2' – self-employed pw	2.05*	2.10*
'Class 3' – voluntary pw	7.15	7.35
'Class 4' – self-employed earnings related	8% on annual earnings between 4,745 & 31,720 1% above 31,720	8% on annual earnings between 4,895 & 32,760 1% above 32,760
* Small earnings exemption	4,215	4,345

25.2.2 Class 1 National Insurance contributions

2004–05			2005–06		
	Not contracted-out	Contracted-out		Not contracted-out	Contracted-out
Employee weekly earnings	%	%	**Employee weekly earnings**	%	%
Below £91	Nil	Nil	Below £94	Nil	Nil
Above £91			Above £94		
£0–90.99	Nil	Nil	£0–93.99	Nil	Nil
£91–610	11	9.4	£94–630	11	9.4 (2)
Over £610	1	1	Over £630	1	1
Employer weekly earnings	%	%	**Employer weekly earnings**	%	%
Below £91	Nil	Nil	Below £94	Nil	Nil
£91–610	11.8	9.3	£94–630	12.8	9.3 (1) (2)
Above £610	11.8	11.8	Above £630	12.8	12.8

Notes:
(1) The rebate shown refers to salary-related schemes. For money-purchase schemes, the rebate is 1 per cent.
(2) The respective rebates apply to earnings within the £82–94 (employees) and £82–94 (employers) bands.

25.2.3 National Insurance contributions reforms

Important reforms to the National Insurance contributions scheme run from April 1999 and later, including the following:

(1) Employers and employees only pay contributions on earnings above the starting point.
(2) The previous 2 per cent rate for employees goes and all pay less than before.
(3) From 2000–01 the starting point for employer contributions was lined up with the income tax personal allowance and there is a single rate of 12.2 per cent, reduced to 11.9 per cent for 2001–02 but increased to 12.8 per cent from 2003–04.
(4) The Contributions Agency transferred from the Department of Social Security to the Inland Revenue.
(5) Class 1A National Insurance contributions apply to a far wider range of benefits in kind from 2000–01, similar to those liable to income tax. Contributions will only be payable by employers and details are included in the forms P11D (10.7), due by 6 July each year, the first payments being due by 19 July 2001.
(6) The contribution rates for 2003–04 were raised substantially.

25.3 Social security benefits

A wide range of benefits is payable. Some of these are summarised in the following tables and split between those which are taxable and those which are not.

25.3.1 Taxable social security benefits

	From 12.4.04 to 10.4.05 £	From 11.4.05 £
Retirement pension		
– Single	79.60	82.05
– Wife (or other adult dependant)	47.65	49.15
Old person's pension (non-contributory) (over 80)	47.90	49.40
Carer's allowance		
– Single	44.35	45.70
Severe disablement allowance (only taxable if paid with retirement pension)		
– Higher rate	15.55	16.05
– Middle rate	10.00	10.30
– Lower rate	5.00	5.15
Widow's benefit (bereavement benefits)		
– Pension – basic (variable below 55)	79.60	82.05
– Widowed parent's allowance	79.60	82.05

	From 12.4.04 to 10.4.05 £	From 11.4.05 £
Jobseekers allowance		
– Single person under 18	33.50	33.85
– Single person 18–24	44.05	44.50
– Single person 25 or over	55.65	56.20
Incapacity benefit		
– Short term (higher rate) (under pension age)	66.15	68.20
– Long term (over pension age)	74.15	76.45
Statutory maternity pay (maximum)	102.80	106.00

25.3.2 Non-taxable social security benefits

	From 12.4.04 to 10.4.05 £	From 11.4.05 £
Severe disablement allowance		
– Single	44.80	46.20
Attendance allowance		
– Higher rate	58.80	60.60
– Lower rate	39.35	40.55
Child benefit		
– First child	16.50	17.00
– Each other child	11.05	11.40
Increases for children – child's special allowances and guardian's allowances	11.05	11.40
Disability living allowance (replaces mobility allowance)		
– mobility component – higher	41.05	42.30
– lower	15.55	16.05
Industrial disablement pension (maximum)	120.10	123.80
– incapacity benefit – long term	74.15	76.45
Maternity allowance		
– standard rate	102.80	106.00
– adult dependant	34.60	35.65
Bereavement payment – lump sum	2,000.00	2,000.00
Housing benefits – various		
War pension – death benefit, disablement, widow's pension, widower's pension – various		

Note: In addition, earnings related unemployment benefit supplement is exempt from income tax.

25.4 Statutory sick pay (SSP)

Employers generally pay up to 28 weeks SSP for each employee in any tax year. (The employee does not need to have paid National Insurance contributions.) Only after that is any sickness benefit paid direct by the State. Employers can deduct their SSP payments in any month from the total National Insurance contributions payable to the authorities, subject to the rules.

SSP is paid at the following weekly rates (daily rates are calculated proportionally):

Normal weekly earnings	2004–05 £	Normal weekly earnings	2005–06 £
Less than £79.00	Nil	Less than £82.00	Nil
£79.00 or more	66.15	£82.00 or more	68.20

25.5 Class 4 National Insurance contributions

Self-employed persons and others liable to Schedule D income tax under Cases I and II may be charged, in addition to their normal flat-rate Class 2 contributions, an earnings related amount under Class 4. The following should be noted.

(1) The contribution rate for 2005–06 is 8 per cent which applies to your Cases I and II income between £4,895 and £32,760. The maximum on this is thus 8 per cent x £27,865 = £2,229.20. In addition, the excess over £32,760 is charged at 1 per cent.

(2) The rates, etc. for recent years were as follows:

Year	% rate	From £	To £	Maximum payable £
1996–97	6.0	6,860	23,660	1,008.00
1997–98	6.0	7,010	24,180	1,030.20
1998–99	6.0	7,310	25,220	1,074.60
1999–2000	6.0	7,530	26,000	1,108.20
2000–01	7.0	4,385	27,820	1,640.45
2001–02	7.0	4,535	29,900	1,775.55
2002–03	7.0	4,615	30,420	1,806.35
2003–04	8.0	4,615	30,940	2,106.00*
2004–05	8.0	4,785	31,720	2,158.00*

* From 2003–04 1 per cent is payable on excess earnings

(3) Prior to 6 April 1975, the charge did not apply.

(4) Class 4 is payable on your Schedule D assessments under Cases I and II for the tax year, after capital allowances, but with no deduction of personal allowances, pension contributions, etc. Your share of partnership income is thus included.

(5) If your wife has self-employed earnings, these are separately charged to Class 4.
(6) Class 4 does not apply to men over 65 at the end of the previous year of assessment and women then over 60.
(7) Your contributions for each year of assessment are normally collected through your income tax assessment on your self-employed earnings. Thus it is normally payable in two instalments (16.3.2).
(8) It is possible to defer your Class 4 payments in certain cases, such as where you also pay Class 1 contributions.
(9) If you are not resident in the UK (17.3) Class 4 will not apply.
(10) From 6 April 1985 to 5 April 1996, but not subsequently, half of your Class 4 contributions were deductible in computing your taxable profits (11.29).
(11) The rate for 2003–04 was increased by 1 per cent (25.2.3). (A 1 per cent rate now applies to the excess earnings above the normal limit.)

Chapter 26

TAX-SAVING HINTS

26.1 Tax planning

The following pages deal with various ways in which you can arrange your affairs to reduce your tax bill. This should not be done by tax evasion which is completely illegal (15.10) and may result in your tax bill being increased by the addition of interest and penalties (16.9.2). You should always fully disclose your taxable income to the Revenue in your income tax return (16.2).

You are fully entitled, however, to arrange your affairs legally in such a way that your tax liability is reduced. This is known as tax avoidance (15.9). There are various anti-avoidance rules (15.9) but providing you are able to steer clear of these provisions you can make substantial tax savings by sensible planning. This chapter covers numerous tax-saving hints with references to fuller explanations later in the book.

Tax planning is a very complex subject and many complicated schemes have been evolved. Such schemes are outside the scope of this book and in any event should be treated with great caution, following certain court decisions (*Ramsay, Furniss* v *Dawson*, etc.). Furthermore, have regard to the new rules for the disclosure of tax avoidance schemes (15.10.3). If you have substantial income and/or assets you should obtain professional advice on tax planning if you have not already done so.

26.1.1 Tax planning don'ts

(1) DON'T save tax at the expense of commercial benefits. (It is no good losing money in your business just to pay no tax.)

(2) DON'T cause unhappiness to yourself and your family in order to save tax. (Don't emigrate if you know you will not like your new country.)

(3) DON'T enter into tax-saving schemes which run on for a long time. These may be effective when you set them up but could be the target of future anti-avoidance legislation before they are completed.

(4) DON'T jeopardise your future financial security. (Do not give away all of your money just to reduce inheritance tax.)

(5) DON'T make inflexible arrangements. It is always necessary to review your tax planning in the light of changes in your financial position and family. You must also take full account of changes in the tax system, such as the drastic cuts in tax rates.

(6) DON'T forget that the law may change. Particularly remember that with inheritance tax on death it will be the law at your death and not necessarily the law now that will govern the liability.

(7) DON'T rigidly segregate capital and income. Good tax planning sometimes involves saving income and sometimes spending capital. Each has its own taxes and you should aim to maximise both after tax.

26.1.2 **A basic plan**

Before examining in detail ways of saving income tax, capital gains tax and inheritance tax, the following general guidelines are given, which are applicable to the tax and financial planning of many people:

(1) Buy your own house when you marry, or as soon afterwards as you can afford. If you remain single, house purchase is also desirable in appropriate circumstances. Although tax is no longer saved on *mortgage interest payments* (4.7), your home is likely to prove a good long-term tax-free investment.
(2) Divide your assets and income with your spouse so that the best use is made of the independent taxation rules (6.1). Savings of both income tax and capital gains tax can be made in this way.
(3) Arrange to have the maximum pension cover possible in your particular circumstances. If you are self-employed, etc. you should pay *personal pension contributions* (14.6).
(4) Arrange adequate *life cover* (9.2) to protect your family.
(5) If you have spare funds when your children marry, make outright gifts to them. Provided you survive for seven years no inheritance tax (22.3) will be payable, even if the marriage and other exemptions are exceeded.
(6) When your children have married, if your house is larger than you need, consider selling it and investing part of the proceeds for your retirement.
(7) If you have spare funds over and above your retirement needs you and your wife should each make outright gifts to and settlements on your children and others. In order to cover inheritance tax, which might be payable if you die within seven years (22.3), appropriate term life assurance is advisable.
(8) Subject to there being sufficient funds for your spouse, leave at least £275,000 in your will to others (26.4.5), otherwise the £275,000 *nil rate inheritance tax band* (22.5) may be wasted.

26.2 Income tax saving

26.2.1 **Personal reliefs and allowances**

Always claim all of the *personal reliefs and allowances* (3.0.1) to which you are entitled. Notify the Revenue as soon as you qualify for an additional allowance. If possible, make sure your spouse and yourself have sufficient income to cover your respective personal reliefs.

26.2.2 **Businesses**

Make sure that you claim all *business expenses* (11.3) to which you are entitled. If you are able to use your car in *your business* (11.9.11) you can claim a reasonable proportion of the running costs (it is sometimes better if your business, etc. actually owns the car).

26.2.3 **Capital allowances**

Do not overlook *capital allowances on plant and machinery* (11.9) and *industrial buildings* (11.11). Bear in mind that 100 per cent initial allowance is still available on buildings in certain recent enterprise zones (11.12).

26.2.4 **Incorporation**

Once your business profits bring your top income tax rate above 22 per cent, consider incorporation. Operating as a limited company will involve the 19 per cent *small companies corporation tax rate* (13.6), until the limit is passed. (An exception would be if your company is a close investment holding company (13.18) when 30 per cent may be payable.) The corporation tax starting rate may increase the attractions of incorporation, particularly since this is now nil per cent (13.7).

You will probably become a director and thus be employed by your company, although you might take some of your income as dividends. The National Insurance burden will change, but on balance, tax savings are likely particularly in view of the hefty National Insurance increases from 2003–04. Also, you can normally improve your pension cover. However, if you take dividends from a company whose profits are taxed at less than 19 per cent, this will be increased in view of the new non-corporate distribution rate (13.7.1).

26.2.5 **Employments**

Make sure you claim all *allowable expenses* (11.3). Try to obtain part of your wages or salary in tax-free ways such as profit related pay (10.15) or luncheon vouchers. Tax savings may result if for example you have a company car or are given an interest-free loan or join your firm's pension scheme. However, watch changing tax rules such as the higher car benefit scales (10.6.5). If you are not covered by an *occupational scheme* (10.11) you should consider effecting a *personal pension scheme* (14.6).

26.2.6 **Saving tax for your employees**

If you are an employer you can enhance the after-tax income of your employees by various means including the following:

(1) Have a *canteen* for your staff or supply *luncheon vouchers* (10.6.3).
(2) Provide *business cars* (10.6.5) for employees (including wives who are employees) where appropriate and tax effective. However, the new system based on car list prices from 1994–95, together with subsequent increases, may lessen the tax advantages.
(3) Grant *interest free loans* to staff (but see 10.6.9 for restrictions).
(4) Provide *housing accommodation* (10.6.13) if the employees have to live close to their work.
(5) Operate *pension schemes* for staff (10.11). Remember that employers can contribute to personal pension schemes.

(6) Provide workplace *sports and recreation facilities* for your staff – the cost is normally a business expense and the employees will not be taxed on the benefit (10.6.17).
(7) If appropriate, operate a *share option* scheme, particularly since the scope is widening (10.9.2).
(8) If you wish to make leaving payments to any employees make the payments in such forms as to qualify for relief from tax under the *'golden handshake' provisions* (10.12 and 10.12.1).
(9) Provide *childcare facilities* (10.6.15).

Note that (2), (3) and (4) above are subject to the fringe benefit rules for *directors and employees earning over £8,500 annually* (10.6.2). It is still of considerable value to provide such benefits in most cases, however. For example, normally a *car* will involve the appropriate *scale charge* (10.6.5) and employer's National Insurance contributions (25.2) but the employee may obtain a larger benefit from having the use of the car. This includes its capital value, insurance, car tax, repairs and, subject to an additional scale charge (10.6.5), any petrol bought for him.

26.2.7 **Repayment claims**

If you are entitled to make any income tax *repayment claim* (16.7), make sure that you do so at your earliest opportunity. In any event you should not allow the relevant time limit to expire. (This is normally six years after the end of the tax year concerned but is sometimes earlier.)

26.2.8 **New businesses and fresh sources of Schedule D income etc.**

By 1996–97, with the introduction of self-assessment, the previous year basis had been phased out (11.7.4). This removed the commencement and cessation opportunities under the previous rules. However, making your accounting date early in the tax year will effectively delay the payment of tax.

If you make a *loss in a new business* (11.23), make the best use of it, not forgetting the option of relieving general income going back up to three years before you started to trade. This is particularly useful where income tax rates fall, since your new business losses might be offset against more highly taxed income for previous years.

26.2.9 **Using your home as an office**

If you use your home as an office, make sure that you obtain tax relief as appropriate. If you are an employee, you will need to show that your business use is wholly, exclusively and necessarily required for the purposes of your job. If, on the other hand you have your own business, the 'necessity' test is dropped.

You should be able to claim a proportion of such items as council tax, light and heat, cleaning, insurance and repairs. The proportion is normally calculated on the basis of the main rooms (excluding kitchens and bathrooms) used for your work. A different fraction would be appropriate for claiming your telephone bills. Of course, any expenses reimbursed to you by your employer cannot be claimed.

One word of warning. By claiming that a fixed part of your home is used for business, you might lose your capital gains tax main residence exemption (20.23). However, if you use no rooms exclusively for business purposes, this is understood not to apply.

26.2.10 **Spouse's earnings**

If you have a business, pay your husband or wife properly for any work that he or she does for it. In view of independent taxation, it is important that both spouses have adequate income, so as to use their allowances, starting rate (10 per cent), lower rate (20 per cent) and basic rate income tax bands. Also, appropriate pension arrangements can be made.

You must be careful that your business does not pay your spouse more than the job is worth, or else the Revenue might seek to disallow part of the spouse's wages and so you will be taxed on the amount as a disallowed business expense. Also note that if the spouse's wage is £94 per week or more, National Insurance contributions must be paid.

The separate taxation of husband and wife is automatic and, as a result, the wife's earnings election (6.4) is no more. However, it is even more advantageous than before for each spouse to have income, because the wife is now taxed on her investment as well as earned income.

A satisfactory arrangement is to form a business partnership with your spouse which will give him or her an entitlement to a share in the profits, normally treated as earned income, and to a personal pension plan. However, note that if your spouse's share of the annual profits is over £4,895 the excess is charged at 8 per cent (maximum £2,229.20) under the *Class 4 National Insurance Contribution Scheme* (25.5). Above £32,760, a 1 per cent rate applies.

From 5 December 2005, similar comments apply to civil partners under the CPA (6.9).

26.2.11 **Independent taxation – investments**

Ensure that you and your spouse split your investments between you so that you each have investment income and capital gains. In this way, the one with the lower income will be better placed to use his or her allowances, starting rate (10 per cent), lower rate (20 per cent) and basic rate bands.

A valuable opportunity arises with dividend income, where say you are a higher rate payer and your spouse pays tax at no more than the basic rate. In that situation, you pay an extra 32.5 per cent on each grossed up dividend. However, your spouse pays no more tax, being liable for only 10 per cent on each gross dividend, which is covered by the tax credit (8.1.2). Hence you can make worthwhile tax savings by transferring shares to your spouse. But remember that the 10 per cent tax credit attaching to dividends is not repayable.

The above extends to most other investment income apart from where it arises from property. The maximum rate from 2000–01 on this savings income in the hands of a basic rate (22 per cent) tax payer is 20 per cent. Thus where you pay 40 per cent and your spouse no more than 22 per cent, transfer investments such as gilts, and building society and bank deposits to him or her.

26.2.12 **Independent taxation-elections**

Make sure that you use the elections under the independent taxation scheme to the best effect (6.1). If you and your spouse jointly own assets, you can elect for the income to be split between you in the ratios that you own them, otherwise the income is split equally for tax purposes.

This election enables taxable income to be diverted to the spouse with unused allowances or a lower income tax rate, thus saving tax. However, the split follows ownership automatically regarding jointly owned shares in close companies (6.1).

26.2.13 **House purchase**

The removal of tax relief for mortgage interest on your main residence, generally from 2000–01 reduces the advantages of buying compared with renting. However, current low interest rates and freedom from capital gains tax (20.23) on any gain support buying and you should carefully consider the most favourable way to finance this. However, you should act prudently.

As a basic method, you could select the conventional mortgage repayments system. Under this you will normally make monthly payments to the building society etc., partly consisting of the capital advanced to you and partly of interest.

If you have a comfortable income you might consider tying your mortgage to a life assurance endowment policy. Under this system you borrow a fixed sum from a building society or insurance company for a given term (20 years, etc.).

You effect a life assurance endowment policy for the sum borrowed, the policy being held by the lender as security. Every year you pay the mortgage interest and policy premiums. At the end of the term your life endowment policy matures and the capital sum is paid to the lender in settlement of the mortgage.

Your policy can be with or without profits. The latter is cheaper but the former might prove a better investment. Make sure that the policy is adequate and monitor it regularly.

An advantage of this system is that your life is covered automatically so, if you should die, the mortgage is automatically discharged. You obtain income tax relief at 12.5 per cent in respect of the life assurance policy if taken out before 14 March 1984.

Note, however, that under the endowment system you pay rather more in the earlier years than under a repayment mortgage. Inflation exaggerates this effect because the earlier payments are made in 'dearer' money. Therefore if you are able to invest the difference more profitably, there is a case for choosing a repayment mortgage. A particular instance would be if otherwise you could not afford your total permitted *personal pension* contributions (14.6).

If you make regular *personal pension* payments you may be able to have an interest only mortgage. The capital sum will then be repaid out of the *cash sum on retirement* (14.6.4) which you can receive. This method is attractive for tax purposes since the *personal pension* contributions (14.6) which you pay qualify for tax relief at your highest earned income rates, subject to the rules.

A more recent development was the use of personal equity plans (PEPS) to repay the capital element in a mortgage. With the annual amount allowed to be invested in PEPS being £6,000 plus £3,000 in single company PEPS (8.10), there was ample scope for ongoing schemes to be set up to repay quite substantial mortgages. However, since ISAs have taken over from PEPS from 6 April 1999 (8.12) the amount allowed to be invested is less, being £7,000 at present.

26.2.14 **Tax-free investments**

Various forms of tax-free income are given in a table in Chapter 2 (2.6.1). Avail yourself of the opportunities open to invest in tax-free situations. However, weigh up the interest you might receive tax-free with the after-tax interest on other investments.

Particular investments on which the income is tax-free are PEPS (8.10), TESSAs (8.11) and ISAs (8.12). PEPS (personal equity plans) provided an attractive way to invest in equities, unit trusts, etc. and also carry capital gains tax exemption. TESSAs (tax exempt special savings accounts) took effect from 1 January 1991. Their freedom from income tax on the interest, subject to the rules (8.11), made TESSAs very competitive.

ISAs have taken over from PEPS and TESSAs from 6 April 1999 and your annual investment is limited to £7,000, this level now being retained until 5 April 2010. So if it is economically sound, hang on to any PEP and TESSA investments which you made prior to that date. However, take account of the removal from 6 April 2004 of the ability of PEPs and ISAs to reclaim the 10 per cent tax credit on dividends.

26.2.15 **Enterprise Investment Scheme (EIS)**

EIS investment normally saves you tax at 20 per cent (11.26). Thus, if you invest say £1,000, the net cost is £800. Provided you are able to select sound investments, the tax advantages are most attractive. These include capital gains tax exemption, tax relief for any losses and the option to carry back part of the relief to the previous tax year (11.26). Even more advantageous, is the facility for rolling over capital gains into the purchase of EIS shares (1.3.6). From 2004–05, your annual EIS investment is limited to £200,000.

26.2.16 **Venture Capital Trusts (VCTs)**

Unlike with EIS investment, VCTs now save you tax at 40 per cent (8.12). But you are no longer able to hold over gains by investing in VCTs (1.3.6). VCTs have the advantage of being dealt with on the Stock Exchange. This means that once you have held them for the required five-year period, disposal should be straightforward. The annual investment limit from 2004–05 is £200,000.

26.2.17 **Life assurance (9.2)**

As well as in connection with house purchase, life assurance provides a valuable method of coupling profitable investment with life cover. Subject to the rules (3.2.6) you obtain 12.5 per cent tax relief on qualifying premiums for policies effected before 14 March 1984. Normally, the 12.5 per cent would be deducted from your premiums on payment. Since relief is not available for policies effected subsequently, any existing at that date should be continued so that relief is obtained on the premiums. (Of course this does not apply to policies no longer appropriate to your needs.)

There are many schemes in which life assurance is linked to property bonds, unit trusts, shares and combinations of these, under which you obtain life cover. Despite the withdrawal of tax relief on premiums, life assurance policies remain attractive as investments (quite apart from the life cover they provide) because of their ability to provide tax-free proceeds and a wide spread of investments for a small outlay, etc.

26.2.18 **Personal pensions (14.6)**

If you have earned income in any year, regarding which you are not in an occupational pension scheme, and on which you pay income tax, you obtain full relief from such tax in respect of any personal pension contributions paid, up to the permitted maximum. The full rules are set out later in this book (14.6), subject to which you obtain relief from income tax in respect of the entire contributions paid. Thus you can obtain relief of up to 40 per cent of your contributions if your income is sufficiently high. This is a most valuable form of relief and so if you are eligible, personal pensions should feature prominently in your planning.

You obtain relief at the highest tax rates attributable to your income. Thus suppose on the top £1,000 of your income you pay income tax of £400; if you pay an allowable contribution of £1,000 under a personal pension scheme, you will obtain £400 tax relief and so your net cost is effectively only £600 (£1,000 – £400). This will secure for you a pension at retirement when your top tax rate may well be lower. Personal pension annuity contracts provide a very cheap way of obtaining life cover. This is because part of the available limit each year can be applied in *temporary* (term) *life assurance cover* (14.6). Again, full tax relief at your top rate is obtained on the contributions paid.

There are rules which enable you to defer taking your annuity. For the deferral period, you can take taxable income from the pension providers. This is a valuable new feature which you can use to good advantage where annuity rates are currently low. Subject to the withdrawals, your fund will be available to buy your annuity when rates improve.

Over the years, the personal pension contributions limits have, in general, been increased, particularly at higher income levels (14.6). You should take full advantage of the increased facility particularly bearing in mind that with current trends you will probably need to provide for a higher pension to compensate for inflation.

At least as valuable is the rule allowing contributions paid in one tax year to be treated as paid in the previous one. This is particularly useful if you can elect for contributions to be taken back to a year when your top tax rate was higher than for the year when the contributions are paid.

From 1 July 1988, the personal pensions relief provisions absorbed the old rules for retirement annuities (14.6). Also, some improvements took place, such as in permitted contribution levels for those in their fifties (as from 6 April 1987). In addition there is the facility for *employees* to pay *personal pension* contributions net of basic rate income tax.

The 1989 changes to the personal pension rules have important planning implications. The more beneficial contribution limits ranging up to 40 per cent of earnings at age 61 (14.6.3), should enable all but very high earners to increase their contributions. However, the limit on earnings qualifying for cover may mean that if you come within this category, you would do better to pay increased contributions on existing retirement annuity contracts. You will then only be able to pay up to the old limits ranging up to 27.5 per cent of earnings at age 61 (14.6.3), but you will not be subject to the £105,600 earnings limit (£102,000 for 2004–05).

The operation of the stakeholder pension rules from 6 April 2001 has increased the tax-planning opportunities. All personal pension contributions are now paid net of basic rate tax so you generally obtain some relief earlier. Also, since at least £3,600 can be paid each year, lower earners and retired people can generally contribute at that level or more.

Because of the tax advantages, you should maximise your pension contributions, provided that you can afford them. At the same time, you should take full account of the radical new rules taking effect from 6 April 2006 (14.8). These may profoundly affect your future contributions.

26.2.19 **Pension schemes for controlling directors**

If you are a controlling director of a family company, it can implement a *pension scheme* (14.3.5) for you. Contributions paid by the company will enjoy tax relief as a deductible business expense and you can be provided with similar benefits to those of any employee under an occupational pension scheme, such as a pension of up to two-thirds of final salary, or a tax-free cash lump sum and a reduced pension, a pension for your widow in the event of death either before or after retirement and substantial life assurance cover for your family in the event of death in service.

26.2.20 **Deeds of covenant (6.5)**

Subject to the rules (6.5) deeds of covenant effected after 14 March 1988 in favour of individuals produce no tax savings. This makes it important to keep in force those existing at that date. (New deeds in favour of charities carry full relief.)

The covenantor who makes the payments under a pre-15 March 1988 deed deducts basic rate income tax and pays the net amount to the beneficiary. If the latter is not liable for income tax because his income is less than his tax allowances, he reclaims income tax deducted by the covenantor (6.5).

Payments under *deeds of covenant to charities* (15.2.1) are of benefit to them since they reclaim the basic rate income tax which you deduct on payment. Furthermore, charitable covenants qualify if they are capable of exceeding three years; and you obtain higher rate tax relief for any such payments (15.2.1). However, from 6 April 2000, the £250 gift aid minimum (15.2.1) has been removed. As a result, you are now able to make smaller tax-efficient single payments and need not use deeds of covenant.

26.2.21 **Gifts and settlements**

If you are a higher rate taxpayer and have more income and capital than you need, you can divest yourself of the surplus altogether and thereby save yourself the income tax on the income concerned. You can probably arrange that the income ends up in the hands of individuals with lower tax rates than yourself. Alternatively the income may be *accumulated in a trust* (21.1) where no more than 34 per cent income tax was payable. However, this became 40 per cent from 6 April 2004. If trusts are created you should take care that the *settlor* is not *taxed on the income* (21.3). Note that inheritance tax may apply in some circumstances (22.30). Similarly watch the effect of *inheritance tax on gifts* (22.1).

This facility for moving income to lower rate taxpayers, such as grandchildren, remains important even though the trust rate is 40 per cent. For example, accumulation and maintenance settlements can be used to produce worthwhile income tax savings by making payments for the education and maintenance of beneficiaries. Income tax repayment claims are then likely covering the excess of income tax at the 40 per cent trust rate on the distributions, over the lower rates and personal reliefs of those beneficiaries (to the extent not used).

Trusts tax planning has been made more attractive by two measures in FA 2005. These are the £500 lower tax band (21.1) and new rules for taxing trusts' income and gains where there are vulnerable beneficiaries (21.2.2).

Gifts to charities under 'gift aid' carry full tax relief. You deduct basic rate tax and the charity reclaims this. At the same time the gross gift carries higher rate tax relief. (Before 6 April 2000 there was a £250 minimum (15.2.1).)

26.2.22 Lower and starting rate bands

The introduction of lower rate bands modestly increased the scope for income tax saving. You should see that your spouse and, where practicable, children have sufficient income to cover their respective lower rate bands. This depends upon each child being at least 18 years old or married if younger (6.6).

The position is now more complicated and for 2005–06 there is also a £2,090 starting rate band taxed at 10 per cent. At the same time, the upper limit of the 20 per cent lower rate band applying to savings income has become £32,400. Thus if you are a 40 per cent tax payer, useful savings can result from transferring income to your spouse and children as appropriate. (From 5 December 2005, these stratagems also apply to CPA partners – 6.9.)

26.2.23 The use of overseas income, taxable on the remittance basis

Generally speaking the *remittance basis* (18.1.1) only applies in certain limited cases. If, however, you obtain any *income overseas* which is taxable here under *Schedule D Case IV or V* (18.1), or under *Schedule E Case III* (18.5.1), and such income is taxed on the remittance basis, do not bring the income into the country unless you need it to cover your living expenses. Note, however, that any *bank deposit interest* (8.7) or other income derived from any investment made with the funds is normally liable to UK tax on an arising basis, if you are *resident and domiciled* in the UK, subject to the detailed rules. (From 2005–06, the split into schedules and cases goes, but the underlying rules remain.)

You can use your overseas deposits for spending on holidays abroad, etc. (18.1). Furthermore, once your overseas source of income has come to an end you can bring your funds into this country in a subsequent tax year without any charge to income tax.

26.3 Capital gains tax saving

A number of simple ways are open to you for saving capital gains tax. Some of these are described on the following pages.

26.3.1 £8,500 net gains exemption

Make the best use of this relief. If your sales of chargeable assets produce net gains which are not normally far in excess of £8,500 in any tax year, try to spread your realisations so that your net gains are no more than £8,500 each year – you will then pay no capital gains tax.

Remember that your spouse and each of your minor children can also realise up to £8,500 of net gains each year and pay no capital gains tax. It is thus a good idea to spread any share dealings, etc. throughout your family. This is made easier by *capital gains tax gifts relief* (20.28) which now applies in certain circumstances, subject to the necessary election. However, gift elections are no longer normally of use regarding quoted shares, etc. (26.3.3).

Under the system for taxing husband and wife, you each have a capital gains tax exemption now of £8,500. In order to make full use of both reliefs, split your investments between you.

If your net gains are less than £8,500 in any tax year, realise further profits by share sales. The previous 'bed and breakfast' arrangement, under which you could buy back the shares the following day and establish a gain or loss was stopped from 17 March 1998. You now have to wait for at least 30 days, or the sale and purchase are matched. So if you want to keep the shares, your spouse could buy them back or you could buy shares in another company.

26.3.2 Loss relief

Make sure that you keep a proper record of all your capital losses. These are relievable against any capital gains in the same tax year and any balance is carried forward to be used in future years.

If you make a loss in your non-incorporated trade or profession, do not overlook claiming to set this against your capital gains. Trading losses can now be offset against capital gains for the same and next tax years (11.22).

26.3.3 Capital gains tax gifts election

Since the scope for capital gains tax gifts elections is restricted (20.28), it is important to structure your gifts to avoid a capital gains tax charge, if possible. For example, make gifts of cash or quoted securities on which you have little or no capital gains, as well as gilts and loan stocks. Also, chattels worth no more than £6,000 each and gifts within your £8,500 annual exemption.

Furthermore, make gifts still within the scope of the election. These include certain unquoted and family company shares and other business assets (20.28); also gifts which involve immediate inheritance tax. This last category includes discretionary settlements and applies even if no tax arises because the nil rate band has not been exceeded. However, remember that gifts relief is generally denied for disposals to settlor related trusts (20.28).

26.3.4 **Husband and wife**

Sales and gifts of assets between yourself and your spouse are not normally liable to capital gains tax (20.9). This enables you to redistribute your assets for inheritance tax purposes without paying any capital gains tax. This also applies to partners within CPA (6.9) from 5 December 2005.

26.3.5 **Retirement relief**

1998–99 was the last year for which full capital gains tax retirement relief (20.29) was available. After that it was phased out so that none is granted for 2003–04. However, you will normally obtain taper relief of up to 75 per cent.

26.3.6 **Rollover relief**

Another important capital gains tax relief related to businesses is rollover relief (20.25). If you sell a business or business assets, consider replacing them within one year before and three years after the disposal. Subject to the rules, you will then pay no capital gains tax until you dispose of the replacements.

Rollover relief is available where shares in one qualifying unquoted trading company are sold and shares in another are acquired, subject to the rules (20.25.2). This is known as *reinvestment relief.* You originally needed to have held at least 5 per cent of the shares for at least a year and be a full-time working director or employee.

Furthermore, gains on any assets can now be rolled-over into the purchase of shares in qualifying unquoted trading companies (20.25.2). There are no requirements as to working in the companies or as to the number of shares to be held. However, you should take care that investing into any particular company makes commercial sense.

Purchases of EIS shares (1.2.15) afford re-investment relief for post-28 November 1994 gains. From 6 April 1998, reinvestment relief and the EIS have been combined into a new but more restricted unified scheme.

26.3.7 **Timing**

Timing your sales of shares or other chargeable assets can have an important bearing on your capital gains tax. If you postpone a sale until after 5 April it means that you delay the payment of your tax for one year. Also if you know that you will be incurring a capital loss during the next tax year you should defer making any potential capital profits until that year because, although capital losses can be carried forward, they cannot be set off against capital profits in earlier tax years.

Similarly if you have already made a lot of capital profits during the current tax year you should consider incurring *capital losses* during the same year which can then be offset. You should not normally sell investments unless it is sound to do so from a commercial point of view.

26.3.8 **Indexation**

Pay careful attention to the effects of the *indexation rules* (20.12) on your capital gains tax position. In choosing which investments to sell, have regard to the indexation relief available due to the level of base cost and time held. However, indexation does not apply to assets acquired after 31 March 1998. If you sell an asset after that date which you acquired before it, you obtain indexation up to April 1998 only.

Subject to the transitional rules, indexation relief can no longer be used to create or increase a loss on disposal (20.13). Thus consider holding shares which are likely to improve. If you are able to sell these at a profit, your indexation relief will no longer be lost.

26.3.9 **Taper relief**

From 6 April 1998, indexation has been replaced by taper relief (20.12). For business assets disposed of during 1998–99 and 1999–2000, including shares in your business company, you obtained relief of 7½ per cent of the gain for each year. For other investments the relief is 5 per cent of the gain for each of years three to ten. Thus you have a strong incentive to delay selling.

Disposals of business assets during 2000–01 and 2001–02 obtained better relief of up to 75 per cent after four years and such disposals after 5 April 2002 obtain 75 per cent relief after two years.

Regarding assets held at 17 March 1998, you are credited with an extra year towards the maximum of ten (but not regarding the new four-year or two-year taper). However, regarding non-business assets such as quoted shares, subject to investment considerations, you should hold these for approaching ten years to maximise your taper relief.

Note that unlike indexation, taper relief is calculated on the gain, rather than the base cost. This means that the bigger your gain, the higher your relief. This provides an incentive for you to keep your better investments longer.

26.3.10 **Charities**

Gifts made to charities are completely free of capital gains tax. Thus if you wish to make a generous gift to a charity of a capital amount (rather than recurring annual amounts under deed of covenant) you will save yourself future capital gains tax if you gift a chargeable asset on which you have a large potential profit. For example if you wish to give £20,000 to a charity and own shares in A Ltd which cost £4,000 in 1993 and are now worth £20,000 you should gift those shares. (If you sold the shares and donated cash they would only produce £13,600 net of 40 per cent capital gains tax – assuming you are a 40 per cent taxpayer and ignoring indexation, taper relief and any annual exemption.)

From 6 April 2000, an even more valuable relief applies regarding gifts to charity of certain investments, including quoted shares or securities, authorised unit trusts and open-ended investment companies (15.2.1). The market value of your gift is deducted from your taxable income.

26.3.11 **Main private residence**

Ensure that you gain the maximum benefit from this exemption (20.23). If you have two residences (even if one is rented), claim within two years of the date of purchase of your second abode which should be treated as your main private residence to be free of capital gains tax. You have a free choice in this matter and so should select the house or flat likely to increase in value the most.

26.4 Inheritance tax planning

The essence of inheritance tax planning is the conservation of wealth. Remember that most lifetime gifts are free of inheritance tax provided you survive for seven years (22.3). Thus timely action is advisable. Also, bear in mind that future reforms could radically change the system and make it much harsher.

In broad terms you should aim to spread assets amongst your family to minimise the effects of these two taxes. Do not make gifts which you cannot afford, however, nor give too much money outright to young or irresponsible children. Also, you should have regard for anti-avoidance rules, such as those concerning pre-owned assets (22.29.7).

26.4.1 **Reducing your assets by gifts**

Take advantage of the various *exempt transfers* (22.17). By this means you can gift to your children, and others, considerable amounts over a period of years, free of any inheritance tax charge, even if you die within seven years. Gifts to your wife (or partner under the CPA from 5 December 2005) are normally free of inheritance tax in any event (22.17.1).

If you have funds surplus to your requirements, you can make gifts totalling £3,000 in any year (22.17.2). In addition, you can make outright gifts of up to £250 each year to any number of other individuals and, furthermore, if you have surplus after-tax income you can make *normal expenditure gifts out of income* (22.17.2). Do not overlook the reliefs applied to *marriage gifts* (22.17.2) for your children and grandchildren, etc.

By means of all the above transfers you can reduce your estate without risking any inheritance tax liability on your premature death. Furthermore, by making the required election any capital gains tax on the gift (20.28) of certain assets will be held over until the recipient's disposal. The scope of capital gains tax gifts relief now mainly applies to gifts of business assets including shares in family companies, etc. (20.28).

Another important category of gifts qualifying for the relief is those on which inheritance tax may be immediately payable.

Remember that the above exemptions apply to both your wife (or CPA partner from 5 December 2005) and yourself. Also, do not forget that unused portions of the £3,000 limit can be carried forward for one year only. Thus your wife should also make gifts, and if her resources are insufficient you should put her in funds. But watch the associated operations rules (22.29.3).

26.4.2 **Larger gifts and settlements**

If you have a large estate, you should consider making more substantial gifts which will entail the payment of inheritance tax, should you die within seven years. The rate would be nil for the first £275,000 of chargeable transfers, however (22.5). Your relief would effectively be more if *business property relief* (22.18) or *agricultural property relief* (22.21) applies. Subject to the inheritance tax charge if you die within seven years, large gifts are now the most tax-efficient method of passing on wealth in many cases. Provided the recipients are sufficiently mature to look after the money, etc. large outright gifts are to be strongly recommended. Unless you are in poor health or of advanced years, the contingent inheritance tax liability can be covered by temporary life assurance (26.4.10) at moderate cost.

For elderly people with smaller estates it is not necessarily advisable, however, to gift the £275,000 tax-free band since this is equally tax-free on death and it could be better to retain this sum for contingencies.

It may be desirable to make larger gifts in the form of settlements, but if these are discretionary the *periodic charge* (22.30.2) would normally apply at some future time, as well as the tax which you pay when you make the settlement and further tax when benefits are paid to the beneficiaries. Also, you are liable for inheritance tax at half the death rates when you set up the trust.

However, *settlements* (22.30) set up within your £275,000 nil rate band are not likely to give rise to significant inheritance tax liability, subject to the detailed rules. *Small* discretionary settlements of this kind are thus useful for passing funds to your dependants whilst maintaining a degree of flexibility. (Note that you should not be a beneficiary under a new settlement.) A further advantage regarding discretionary settlements is that they qualify for capital gains tax gifts relief (26.3.3). This is true whether or not any inheritance is paid on the capital introduced.

Accumulation and maintenance settlements (22.30.1) are useful for the benefit of your minor children and grandchildren. Provided you survive for seven years after establishing the settlement, you pay no inheritance tax. Furthermore, if the beneficiaries obtain fixed interests (for example, in the income) which they become entitled to when they are no more than 25 years old, then no subsequent inheritance tax is payable (22.30.1), even if the payment of the ultimate capital is deferred to an older age. (An exception is where a beneficiary with a life interest dies.)

Fixed trusts are also of use if you wish your grown-up children to have income but no capital until a stipulated time. Thus, if you settle money on your 26-year-old son giving him an entitlement to the annual income until he is 35 and then the capital, you are immediately divested of the capital. The amount which you settle is treated as a potentially exempt transfer, so that inheritance tax applies if you die within seven years. Your son eventually gets the capital at age 35 and no more inheritance tax is payable. Your son is fully taxed on the income, however, and if his other income becomes high as he matures, his income tax burden could be heavy.

In establishing settlements unless they are discretionary remember that capital gains tax gifts relief will be limited. Thus either settle cash or assets which will give rise to no capital gains tax, unless you are able to settle assets still qualifying for gifts relief (20.28). Also, remember that higher tax rates now apply to trusts, except where income is distributed.

26.4.3 **Gifts to charities etc.**

Gifts to charities and political parties are completely free from inheritance tax. Thus you should consider making such gifts during your lifetime and bequests in your will. Both will reduce the value of your estate for inheritance tax purposes, and capital gains tax relief applies concerning charitable dispositions (20.29.1).

26.4.4 **Equalisation of assets of husband and wife**

Provided the recipient is UK domiciled (or deemed domiciled) no inheritance tax is payable on transfers which you make to your wife or she makes to you, either during your lives or on death (22.17.1). But do not keep all of your assets until you die and then leave them to your wife because this may ultimately result in high inheritance tax on her death which is more than the combined tax if your estates were equal and you each left your assets to your children.

Thus, suppose you have £550,000 and your wife has nothing. If you die first, leaving it all to her, no tax is then payable. But if she still has £550,000 when she dies and has made no previous chargeable transfers, the inheritance tax at the present rate will be £110,000 (22.5.1). If you had given or bequeathed your wife £275,000, however, and left your remaining £275,000 to your children, on your death no inheritance tax would be paid. Similarly, on your wife's death nothing would be paid so that altogether £110,000 of inheritance tax would be saved compared with the position where your wife inherits all of your wealth. (Of course the position can be further improved if you both make lifetime gifts to your children.)

If your wife otherwise has insufficient funds, giving her assets will also enable her to make gifts to your children. These will not attract inheritance tax unless she dies within seven years (22.3) and her estate is sufficiently high. This strategy is particularly desirable if your wife is younger and in better health than you are. Note, however, the *associated operations rules* (22.29.3).

As mentioned earlier (26.1.2) equalising your assets is likely to produce income tax and capital gains tax savings.

From 5 December 2005, similar planning is appropriate for CPA couples (6.9). Of course, these tax planning considerations must be tempered by practical points, such as making sure your wife has sufficient to maintain her, should you die first. Also, a certain mutual trust is necessary. Your planning should also take account of your respective ages and states of health by arranging for a larger share to be in the hands of the one likely to live longer.

If you are buying a new home, you should ensure that this is put into the joint names of your wife and yourself. Since the matrimonial home often comprises the major part of the assets of a married couple, this is a very useful step towards equalising their respective estates.

26.4.5 **Wills**

You should think carefully about the preparation of your Will and, of course, obtain good legal advice. Substantial inheritance tax savings can result from a well drawn Will. For example, you should ensure that both your wife and yourself by your separate Wills leave at least £275,000 to other people so that you each get the benefit of the £275,000 nil rate band. (This presupposes the free band has not been exhausted by lifetime gifts and also that the survivor will have adequate funds for his or her old age.)

To take full advantage of indexation and the announced future increases (22.5), instead of £275,000 you could stipulate the amount of your unused nil rate band at death. Also, avoid leaving too much directly to your children if they are already wealthy; it is more beneficial for tax planning purposes to leave money in trust for your grandchildren. Such Will Trusts, however, should probably not be discretionary, but rather of the accumulation and maintenance variety (22.30.1).

26.4.6 **Annuities**

If you need to increase your income, annuities provide a means of doing this which at the same time immediately reduces the value of your estate. For example, if you buy an annuity for £10,000 which produces, say, £900 yearly until your death, no part of your original capital outlay is charged to inheritance tax on your death. You have thus saved potential tax on your death. Do not overlook the effects of inflation, however; an unindexed annuity which is sufficient for your present needs soon may be worth too little to maintain you.

26.4.7 **Using business and agricultural relief**

If you have a business, farm or shareholding in an Unlisted Securities Market (USM) company, the further improved relief rates (22.18) offer great potential inheritance tax savings. Subject to the rules, 100 per cent or 50 per cent relief will normally be obtained. You should therefore take advantage of the opportunity to create settlements and make gifts with less, or no, inheritance tax, even if you die within seven years. If any capital gains arise, it will normally be possible to obtain holdover relief. However, in cases where death is imminent, it may be better to hold the assets so as to obtain the tax free uplift in base value for capital gains tax purposes.

26.4.8 **Protecting family companies**

The *'related property' valuation rules* (22.12) may apply if you transfer valuable holdings in your family company to your children, etc. Thus, if you die within seven years, inheritance tax might be payable on the transfers. However, up to 100 per cent *business property relief* (22.18) may be available. The charge (if any) on the shares on your death could be even higher, however, particularly if the rules change and so you should plan to transfer shares to your children before they become too valuable, and your wife should do the same. The best time would be on the formation of a new company or early in its development.

If you are planning a new business venture, then do not put it into your main family company. Form a new company whose shares are owned by your children (or others whom you wish to succeed to your business). The new company should be encouraged to expand as much as possible and you may even let your old company run down. In this way the next generation of your family eventually will be left controlling the major company.

In the case of a partnership, the interest of each partner is valued on the appropriate share of the underlying assets. If, however, the partnership is incorporated into a company, the value of each partner's interest is normally reduced appreciably.

26.4.9 **Deeds of family arrangement**

Variations or disclaimers made within two years of any death not only effectively change the destination of property left by will (22.29.6), they are effective in changing the inheritance tax position. Property might be diverted from the surviving spouse to other beneficiaries, so as to use fully the nil rate band. Alternatively, substantial legacies may go to others than the surviving spouse, resulting in high inheritance tax. Assets can then be diverted to the surviving spouse, who might in turn pass the assets to others at a later stage, with a good chance of saving tax.

However, if you disclaim your legacy, it will revert to the estate and be re-allocated according to the will (or rules on intestacy if there is no will). Thus whether or not inheritance tax can be saved will depend on the facts in each case. Deeds of variation are effective in changing wills after death, provided that those involved take the necessary steps. However, it is better to ensure that your will is effectively drawn up so as to minimise inheritance tax. In this way, you will be more certain that your estate is passed on in accordance with your wishes. Then regular review is essential.

26.4.10 Providing the funds to pay inheritance tax on death

You may not be able, or indeed wish, to avoid leaving a large estate when you die. In this case you should ensure that sufficient funds are available for paying the inheritance tax. This avoids forced realisations of assets and, for example, the sale of shares in a family company which it might be desirable to keep.

Life assurance provides one of the best means of providing money to pay inheritance tax arising on your death, as well as being a very suitable vehicle for exempt gifts. Ensure, however, that the policy proceeds themselves are not subject to the tax, which could happen if the policy were taken out (with no trust provisions) by you on your own life. Consider taking out policies in trust for your children where you leave assets to them; this will put cash into their hands to pay the tax. They should be 'whole of life' policies, under which capital sums, with or without profits, or unit-linked to combat inflation, are payable when you die.

If both you and your wife have large estates then you should each insure your respective lives in trust for your children, assuming that you each leave your estates to them. If, however, you each leave your estate to the other by your will, then a joint life last survivor policy could be useful, under which a payment is made only on the second death. If the policy is correctly drawn (in trust for the eventual heirs on the second death) it will not attract inheritance tax. Further, the premium rate for such a policy is usually substantially lower than for two individual policies.

The policy can be written in trust for your heirs, under the Married Women's Property Acts or otherwise. Take care that there is at least one trustee other than you so that the proceeds may be claimed without delay on your death.

Temporary life assurance may be used to cover the five-year period following a gift or settlement on which you have paid tax at the lifetime rate. The amount covered should be the additional tax payable on that transfer should you die within five years (22.6). Temporary life assurance written in trust is also most useful for covering any inheritance tax payable on a gift (potentially exempt transfer (PET)) if you die within seven years.

26.5 Change of residence and domicile

Reference to the table at the beginning of Chapter 17 will illustrate the importance of residence and domicile in ascertaining whether or not an individual is liable to income tax, capital gains tax and inheritance tax. If you are able to become non-resident for tax purposes you will avoid liability to UK income tax on many classes of income and if you are also not ordinarily resident here you may not be liable for any UK capital gains tax on sales of assets here or abroad (see over). However, make sure that there are no vital rule changes arising from the current government review.

If you become neither domiciled (17.2) nor *deemed domiciled* (22.4) in this country you will only be liable for UK inheritance tax on assets situated here.

A very effective way of avoiding liability from UK taxes is to emigrate and take all of your assets out of this country. Once you have ceased to be resident and are no longer domiciled nor deemed domiciled here you will be outside the UK tax net regarding all income arising and assets situated abroad. (You should note that if you have shares in a UK company with its registered office here, the shares are treated for inheritance tax purposes as located in this country unless they are bearer securities kept abroad.)

If you have a large potential capital gain you should generally defer taking this until the tax year after you have ceased to be resident and ordinarily resident here and you should remain abroad for at least five complete tax years; in this way you will avoid capital gains tax. (If you wish you may then return to this country in a future tax year.)

As a pure tax-saving exercise, you should only consider emigrating if you are a very wealthy person; and even then you should only go to a country where you feel that you will be happy. If, however, you wish to retire to a 'place in the sun', then in choosing to which country you should go, you should take into account the tax which you would have to pay there. Once you have established your foreign residence and domicile, in order to preserve this situation, you must avoid paying regular substantial visits to the UK (19.4).

26.6 Year-end planning

Towards the end of the tax year (5 April), you should consider various tax-saving opportunities.

The following is a list of reliefs to use up and other things to be done on or before 5 April. Further details are given elsewhere in this book.

(1) Capital gains tax annual exemption (20.6).
(2) Realise losses to offset against gains in excess of your annual exemption (26.3.2).
(3) Inheritance tax annual exemption (22.17.2).
(4) Inheritance tax relief of £250 per gift to any one person (22.17.2).
(5) Normal expenditure gifts for inheritance tax (22.17.2).
(6) Nil rate band for inheritance tax (22.5.1).
(7) Take extra dividends and salary for yourself and your spouse from your family company to maximise the benefits of independent taxation (6.1) having regard to the new rules about tax on distributed income from small companies (13.7.1).
(8) Effect single 'gift aid' donations of any amount (15.2.1), thus getting relief for the current tax year.
(9) Pay personal pension contributions (14.6).

(10) Pay personal pension by 31 January (and retirement annuity) premiums to carry back to the previous tax year (14.6.2).
(11) Make investments qualifying for relief under the Enterprise Investment Scheme (11.26).
(12) Buy plant and machinery to obtain 25 per cent writing down allowance or 40/50 per cent first year allowance where applicable (11.9.1).
(13) Buy industrial and commercial buildings in enterprise zones obtaining 100 per cent initial allowance on the building content (11.12).
(14) Increase your contributions to your company pension scheme (10.11). (Your employer's contributions are geared to the company accounting date.)
(15) Ensure you make any necessary tax elections to do with your business and private affairs within the required time limits. A particular instance is trading loss relief (11.22).
(16) Make ISA investments by 5 April each year (8.12).

26.7 The seven ages of tax planning

Although tax planning is important at all stages of one's life, different features may be relevant at particular times. There follows a summary of particular tax planning points to remember at seven selected 'ages':

(1) Childhood.
(2) Student days.
(3) Early working life.
(4) Newly married.
(5) Parenthood.
(6) Middle age.
(7) Retirement.

Much of the advice given earlier in this chapter applies at most times in your life and thus is not highlighted in what follows; for example, tax planning for businesses (26.2.2), employments (26.2.5), companies (13.1) and capital gains tax (26.3). The points now classified under different 'ages' have particular relevance to certain times in your life. References are given to earlier paragraphs in this chapter, which will in turn refer you to further detail in the text.

26.7.1 Childhood

Tax planning for children normally involves other people such as their parents and grandparents. A chief objective is to provide for education and maintenance in the most tax-efficient way. Educational schemes may have become less attractive in view of, for example, the withdrawal of life assurance relief. However, lump sum school fee payments in advance by grandparents may prove of value in saving higher rate income tax and inheritance tax.

Older children may work in the family business at weekends and during the holidays, in which case a reasonable salary should be paid. This will be tax free to the extent of the unused personal allowance (£4,745). To avoid any National Insurance contributions the salary should be kept below £91 per week. Also, older children might occasionally buy and sell shares and thus make use of their annual capital gains exemption (£8,200).

Other tax planning points to note include:

(1) Changing wills to include new children (26.4.5).
(2) Settlements by grandparents (26.4.2).
(3) Repayment claims for children (26.2.7).
(4) Gifts to children to save inheritance tax (26.4.1).
(5) Accumulation and maintenance settlements (26.4.2).
(6) Discretionary settlements (26.4.2).
(7) Paying income from settlements for maintenance and education with possible tax repayments (26.2.7).

26.7.2 **Student days**

If you are a student (post-school), you will normally have attained your majority and this facilitates tax planning. In particular, none of your income will be assessed on your parents even though it arises from gifts which they make to you.

Your single personal allowance (£4,895) will normally cover income from jobs, investments, etc. before you pay any tax. Also, income distributions from certain settlements are likely to entitle you to reclaim at least part of if not the entire 40 per cent tax already suffered.

Your parents and grandparents might save inheritance tax by making gifts to you or in trust (26.4.2). If you invest the money given to you directly in stocks and shares you will have the annual exemption (£8,500) to cover any capital gains (26.3.1).

26.7.3 **Early working life**

In your early working days you may well be able to benefit from some of the tax planning points regarding employments (26.2.5) and businesses (26.2.2), noting particularly new businesses (26.2.8). If you work overseas in a business or employment, some tax benefits may result (26.2.23).

Make sure that you claim all the expenses to which you may be entitled in your employment (26.2.5) or business (26.2.2) including a proportion of your home expenses if relevant.

Whether you are employed or self-employed, you should consider pensions (26.2.19) or personal pension arrangements (26.2.18) as soon as practicable. These provide a very tax-effective way of providing for your security.

26.7.4 **Newly married**

When you marry, the opportunity arises for the parents and grandparents on both sides to make gifts and settlements (26.4.1 and 26.4.2), using the special inheritance tax marriage exemptions or otherwise. Also they should re-examine their wills.

Particular tax planning matters for you both to consider include:

(1) Wife's salary (26.2.10).
(2) Independent taxation of husband and wife (6.1) – separate rates and allowances for income and capital gains.
(3) House purchase (26.2.13).
(4) Life assurance (26.2.17).
(5) The making of new wills (26.4.5).

26.7.5 **Parenthood**

This is the time when you are likely to have a growing income but also to incur the largest expenses. Gifts (26.4.1) and accumulation and maintenance settlements (26.4.2) made in favour of your children by their grandparents are tax-efficient ways in which the gap can be bridged.

As you progress in your employment (26.2.5), business (26.2.2) or profession, the relevant tax planning points become even more important. Particular matters to note include new businesses (26.2.8) and incorporation (26.2.4). Also, you will be well advised to improve your life assurance (26.2.17) and pension (26.2.19) or personal pension (26.2.18) cover as appropriate. You may work overseas (26.2.23) or even completely change your domicile and residence (26.5) if, for example, you become extremely well-to-do.

As you become more wealthy, *capital tax planning* will grow in importance, including capital gains tax (26.3). Inheritance tax planning should include an examination of gifts and settlements (26.4.2), charitable gifts (26.4.3) and equalisation (26.4.4); attention to your will (26.4.5); the protection of family companies (26.4.8) and the provision of funds to pay the tax (26.4.10). Furthermore, assets producing income and capital gains should be split between you, so as to maximise the benefits of independent taxation.

26.7.6 **Middle age**

You will still need to consider the relevant business (26.2.2) or employment (26.2.5) tax planning points as well as life assurance (26.2.17), pensions (26.2.19) and personal pensions (26.2.18). Even if your earlier pension cover was inadequate, there is scope for compensating for this in later life.

As your children come of age, consider passing them income producing assets. When they marry, make use of the appropriate inheritance tax exemptions (26.4.1), thus guarding against tax payable if you die within seven years. Cover larger gifts by life assurance (26.2.17). When they in turn have children, consider accumulation and maintenance settlements in favour of your grandchildren (26.2.21).

Capital tax planning is vital during this period and if you can afford it, you should make gifts and settlements (26.3.3) to pass on your wealth during your lifetime. Also, provide for the payment of any inheritance tax (26.4). If you have a family company try to guard against future heavy inheritance tax on its shares and help succession by passing on shares to the next generation (26.4.8). Should your house be larger than you need, consider selling and re-investing or gifting the proceeds.

26.7.7 **Retirement**

Take advantage of the tax planning opportunities arising when your pension (26.2.18) becomes due, such as taking your full tax-free lump sum entitlement or deferring your benefits.

If you have a family company or business, maximise your capital gains tax retirement relief (26.3.5) on sale or gift. At the same time, use the limited capital gains tax gifts election (20.28) if appropriate. Also, do not overlook the valuable inheritance tax business relief (22.18) and agricultural relief (22.21). These will eliminate or substantially reduce the inheritance tax payable if you die within seven years of a gift.

Since more of your income is likely to arise from investments, you may be able to claim repayment of the income tax deducted at source (26.2.7) (excluding dividends). If your respective incomes are sufficiently small, you may both be entitled to age relief (3.2.10), together with a higher married couple's allowance.

With the sale of your business and perhaps house (26.2.13), you will have the chance of reviewing your will (26.4.5) and making gifts (26.4.1), including settlements (26.4.2). If you have surplus funds, then gifts to charity should be considered, being free of inheritance tax and capital gains tax; whilst the purchase of an annuity will increase your income but reduce your estate.

26.8 Tax planning after the General Election

This edition has been completed soon after the General Election, which was held on 5 May 2005. At first glance, the continuation in power of a Labour government, albeit with a much smaller overall majority, means that the general drift of tax policy and resultant tax saving strategy will not change.

However, it is not so simple. The economic situation is uncertain, as is who will lead the government. Thus tax changes and probably increases are to be expected.

We have a clear indication as to at least some of the measures which are likely to be enacted in 2005. These are covered by those parts of the original Finance Bill, which were left out so that the remainder could be enacted before Parliament was dissolved prior to the election, as Finance Act 2005.

A number of the measures relate to anti-avoidance and some are technical. Particular fields include arbitrage, schemes involving financial products and the location of assets and temporary absence from the UK for capital gains tax purposes. It seems that any of the relevant provisions could be introduced with effect from the date originally intended.

We can certainly expect more anti-avoidance provisions and wider use of the avoidance scheme disclosure rules. Thus, as ever, expert professional advice is important in all of these areas. At the same time, basic planning is most important and, with a view to combating possible tax rises, you should make full use of current opportunities, in case these are closed. An example is the domicile and residence rules. Also, use existing lower tax rates and reliefs in case these become less beneficial.

One area so far broadly left by the government is *inheritance tax*. However, in case of future changes, planning in this area is to be recommended, the more so because it is better carried out well before death and thus as early as possible. But watch out for recent anti-avoidance provisions which may affect your inheritance tax planning (there are likely to be more). Particular examples are *pre-owned assets* (22.29.7), *trust tax rate* increases (21.2.1) and the interaction of *private residence* and *gifts relief* (20.23). Maximise the benefits of the £275,000 nil rate band, business property and agricultural reliefs. These could be reduced in the future in spite of the nil rate band being enacted as £285,000 for 2006–07 and £300,000 for 2007–08. So act now, making gifts and settlements, if appropriate.

However, most gifts are potentially exempt transfers, which are taxed if you die within 7 years. The rates applying are those at death. So even if you were within the £275,000 nil rate band when you made the gifts, this band could be reduced by the time you die. Also, a higher rate than the present 40 per cent could apply.

So far as your will is concerned, it is advantageous to leave up to the full £275,000 to others than your spouse, so that the nil rate band is not wasted. Should the nil rate band be varied, it will be a simple matter for you to vary your will if it is not drafted to match the relief available.

Make good use of your annual and other exemptions. These include the £3,000 annual exemption, small gifts up to £250 per person, relief for normal expenditure out of income and certain marriage gifts. These reliefs normally take effect at once and so should be safe from future changes.

A more elaborate way of safeguarding your £275,000 nil rate band is by means of a *discretionary trust*. Funds settled on such trusts are immediately liable to inheritance tax at 20 per cent (22.30.2) unless you are within the nil rate band, when none is due. However, should the inheritance tax regime become harsher, extra tax may become due within the trust. So make sure that it can be quickly wound up, if necessary. Also, watch the increased income tax and capital gains tax which may arise (21.2).

Chapter 27

TAX TABLES

27.1 Income tax table for 2005–06

Income £	£	Income £	£
4,000	–	16,000	2,192
5,000	11	18,000	2,632
6,000	111	20,000	3,072
7,000	212	25,000	4,172
8,000	432	30,000	5,272
9,000	652	40,000	7,959
10,000	872	50,000	11,959
12,000	1,312	70,000	19,959
14,000	1,752	100,000	31,959

Notes:

(1) Personal relief has been taken into account.

(2) Other reliefs have been ignored.

(3) The above table applies provided you do not qualify for age relief (3.2.10) and normally applies whether you are married or single.

(4) All income is assumed to be earned (until the higher rate threshold has been passed).

27.2 Tax rates and allowances for 1992–93 to 2004–05

	92–93, 93–94 & 94–95	95–96	96–97	97–98	98–99	99–00	00–01	01–02	02–03	03–04	04–05
Income tax basic rate	25%	25%	24%	23%	23%	23%	22%	22%	22%	22%	22%
Single personal allowance	3,445ø	3,525ø	3,765ø	4,045ø	4,195ø	4,335ø	4,385ø	4,535ø	4,615ø	4,615ø	4,745ø
Married couple's allowance											
Age under 66	1,720§	1,720§	1,790§	1,830§	1,900§	1,970§	Nil	Nil	Nil	Nil	Nil
Widow's bereavement	1,720	1,720	1,790	1,830	1,900	1,970	2,000	Nil	Nil	Nil	Nil
Age allowance											
Age 65–74	4,200	4,630	4,910	5,220	5,410	5,720	5,790	5,990	6,100	6,610	6,830
Age 75	4,370	4,800	5,090	5,400	5,600	5,980	6,050	6,260	6,370	6,720	6,950
Life assurance relief – normal percentage of premiums (deducted from premiums)	12½%*	12½%*	12½%*	12½%*	12½%*	12½%*	12½%*	12½%*	12½%*	12½%*	12½%*

§ Limited to 20 per cent for 1994–95, 15 per cent from 1995–96 and 10 per cent for 1999–2000.

ø Available separately for husband and wife from 1990–91.

* Only on pre-14 March 1984 policies.

Note: Allowances for 2005–06 are detailed in Chapter 3 (3.0); income tax rates for 2005–06 are given in Chapter 5 (5.0).

27.3 Income tax rates: for 1988–89 and subsequent years

Slice of income £	Rate %	Total income (after allowances) £	Total tax £
for 1988–89			
19,300 (0–19,300)	25	19,300	4,825
Remainder	40		
for 1989–90 and 1990–91			
20,700 (0–20,700)	25	20,700	5,175
Remainder	40		
for 1991–92			
23,700 (0–23,700)	25	23,700	5,925
Remainder	40		
for 1992–93			
2,000 (0–2,000)	20	2,000	400
21,700 (2,000–23,700)	25	23,700	5,825
Remainder	40		
for 1993–94			
2,500 (0–2,500)	20	2,500	500
21,200 (2,500–23,700)	25	23,700	5,800
Remainder	40		
for 1994–95			
3,000 (0–3,000)	20	3,000	600
20,700 (3,000–23,700)	25	23,700	5,775
Remainder	40		
for 1995–96			
3,200 (0–3,200)	20	3,200	640
21,100 (3,200–24,300)	25	24,300	5,915
Remainder	40		
for 1996–97			
3,900 (0–3,900)	20	3,900	780
21,600 (3,900–25,500)	24	25,500	5,964
Remainder	40		
for 1997–98			
4,100 (0–4,100)	20	4,100	820
22,000 (4,100–26,100)	23	26,100	5,880
Remainder	40		
for 1998–99			
4,300 (0–4,300)	20	4,300	860
22,800 (4,300–27,100)	23	27,100	6,104
Remainder	40		

Slice of income £	Rate %	Total income (after allowances) £	Total tax £
for 1999–2000			
1,500 (0–1,500)	10	1,500	150
26,500 (1,500–28,000)	23	28,000	6,245
Remainder	40		
for 2000–01			
1,520 (0–1,520)	10	1,520	152
26,880 (1,520–28,400)	22	28,400	6,065.60
Remainder	40		
for 2001–02			
1,880 (0–1,880)	10	1,880	188
27,520 (1,880–29,400)	22	29,400	6,242.40
Remainder	40		
for 2002–03			
1,920 (0–1,920)	10	1,920	192
27,980 (1,920–29,900)	22	29,900	6,347.60
Remainder	40		
for 2003–04			
1,960 (0–1,960)	10	1,960	196
28,540 (1,960–30,500)	22	30,500	6,474.80
Remainder	40		
for 2004–05			
2,020 (0–2,020)	10	2,020	202
29,380 (2,020–31,400)	22	31,400	6,665.60
Remainder	40		

Note: The 10 per cent rate only applies to earned income, pensions and savings income. For 2004–05 savings income excluding dividends (5.2(4)) in your £2,020–£31,400 band is taxed at 20 per cent. Dividends within that band carry a 10 per cent tax credit (non-reclaimable) and attract no further tax (5.6.1).

27.4 Inheritance tax rates: from 15 March 1988 onwards

Slice of cumulative chargeable transfers £	Cumulative total £	% on slice
from 15 March 1988 to 5 April 1989		
The first		
110,000	110,000	Nil
Remainder		40

Slice of cumulative chargeable transfers £	Cumulative total £	% on slice
from 6 April 1989 to 5 April 1990		
The first		
118,000	118,000	Nil
Remainder		40
from 6 April 1990 to 5 April 1991		
The first128,000	128,000	Nil
Remainder		40
from 6 April 1991 to 9 March 1992		
The first		
140,000	140,000	Nil
Remainder		40
from 9 March 1992 to 5 April 1995		
The first		
150,000	150,000	Nil
Remainder		40
after 5 April 1995		
The first		
154,000	154,000	Nil
Remainder		40
after 5 April 1996		
The first		
200,000	200,000	Nil
Remainder		40
after 5 April 1997		
The first		
215,000	215,000	Nil
Remainder		40
after 5 April 1998		
The first		
223,000	223,000	Nil
Remainder		40
after 5 April 1999		
The first		
231,000	231,000	Nil
Remainder		40
after 5 April 2000		
The first		
234,000	234,000	Nil
Remainder		40

Slice of cumulative chargeable transfers £	Cumulative total £	% on slice
after 5 April 2001		
The first		
242,000	242,000	Nil
Remainder		40
after 5 April 2002		
The first		
250,000	250,000	Nil
Remainder		40
after 5 April 2003		
The first		
255,000	255,000	Nil
Remainder		40
after 5 April 2004		
The first		
263,000	263,000	Nil
Remainder		40
after 5 April 2005		
The first		
275,000	275,000	Nil
Remainder		40

GLOSSARY

The following is a selection of terms which are explained in more detail in the sections indicated.

***Ad valorem* duties** Duties which are charged as a percentage of the subject matter – particularly stamp duty (24.5)

Advance corporation tax Tax payable by companies on dividend payments, etc, which is offset against the full (mainstream) corporation tax liability (13.6)

All employee share ownership plan A new scheme to provide tax-free shares for employees (10.9.7)

Back duty Under-assessed tax for previous years, normally due to evasion (16.9)

Basic rate tax Income tax at 22 per cent (2.2)

Business Expansion Scheme (BES) Government scheme for encouraging investment in smaller companies by giving tax relief on money subscribed (11.25)

Child tax credit (CTC) New tax credit operating from 2001–02 (3.4)

Claw-back The loss of relief previously obtained, for example, life assurance relief (9.4)

Close companies Companies closely controlled by generally no more than five shareholders and their associates (13.17)

Close Investment Holding Company (CIC) A close company which is neither a trading company nor a property investment company, nor a member of a trading group (13.18)

Current use value The value of property on the basis that its use is limited to existing planning consents

Current year basis The uniform basis for assessing income tax liabilities from 1997–98 and sometimes earlier (11.7.4)

Domicile The country which you regard as your natural home (17.2)

Earned income Income derived from an individual's personal, mental or physical labour and some pensions (3.1)

Enterprise investment scheme (EIS) Government scheme which took over from the Business Expansion Scheme providing revised tax incentives (11.26)

Enterprise management incentives New share option schemes providing options for up to £100,000 worth of shares for each of no more than 15 key employees (10.9.8)

General Commissioners Lay people appointed to hear tax appeals (16.5)

Higher rate tax Income tax at the higher rates, currently 40 per cent (5.0)

HM Revenue and Customs The new integrated Inland Revenue and Customs and Excise department

Indexation allowance Capital gains tax relief for inflation (20.12)

Individual savings account (ISA) A new savings scheme which started on 6 April 1999 under which individuals are able to invest free of tax up to £7,000 each year (8.12)

Interest in possession Entitlement to receive the income of a settlement (22.30)

Lower rate tax Income tax at a lower rate, at present 20 per cent (5.1)

Mainstream corporation tax A company's main corporation tax liability based on its accounts (13.6.5)

Non-corporate distribution rate (NCDR) Newly introduced corporation tax charge of 19 per cent on distributed income otherwise taxed at the nil (starting) rate (13.7.1)

Partnership The relationship existing between two or more persons in business together with the object of making profits (12.1)

Personal allowance Certain deductions from your total income for tax purposes (3.2)

Personal equity plan (PEP) Share purchase scheme under which up to £9,000 *could* be invested each year with income tax and capital gains tax advantages (8.10)

Potentially exempt transfers (PETs) Gifts between individuals or to certain trusts which are only considered for inheritance tax if the donor dies within seven years (22.3)

Profit related pay (PRP) Incentive payments to employees which attract limited income tax relief, subject to the rules (10.15)

Rate applicable to trusts The tax rate applying to income and capital gains of discretionary trusts etc. currently 40 per cent (21.2.1)

Relevant base value Main deduction in computing realised development value on which development land tax was chargeable

Residence Where you are treated as living for tax purposes (17.3)

Self-assessment A system operating from 1996–97 under which taxpayers play a larger part in working out their tax liabilities (16.1)

Special Commissioners Full-time professionally qualified civil servants appointed to hear tax appeals (16.5)

Starting rate Income tax at the lowest rate, at present 10 per cent (5.1)

Taper relief Capital gains tax relief depending on period of ownership (20.12)

Tax avoidance Legally arranging your affairs to reduce your tax liability (15.10)

Tax evasion Illegal tax saving (15.10)

Tax exempt special savings account (TESSA) Savings account with bank or building society which offered tax-free interest (8.11)

Trust Otherwise known as a settlement – assets held by one or more trustees for the benefit of others (21.1)

Unearned income Income from investments as opposed to earned income such as salaries and pensions (3.1)

Venture Capital Trusts (VCTs) Quoted investment vehicles concentrating on smaller non-quoted companies and offering good tax benefits to shareholders investing for at least five years (8.13)

Vulnerable beneficiaries Certain beneficiaries affording trusts tax reductions (21.2.2)

Working families tax credit (WFTC) New tax credit operating from October 1999 (3.4), now called Working Tax Credit

Year of assessment Year ending 5 April, for which tax is payable (2.8)

INDEX

C

D

E

U

V